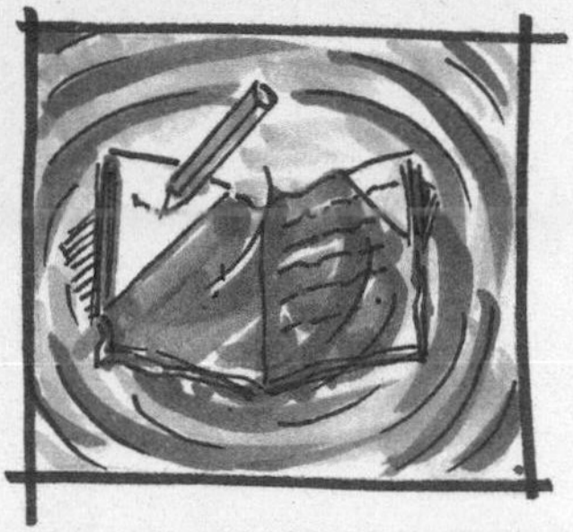

岸本斉史

For quite some time now, there have been occasions when I think of ideas while in the tub. It's because the blood flow to my head improves and makes it easier for ideas to spring forth. However, I cannot take notes in the tub... And after I get out of the tub, before I realize it, I've ended up forgetting what those ideas inside my head were. Both my mind and body have been washed clean.

—Masashi Kishimoto, 2012

Author/artist Masashi Kishimoto was born in 1974 in rural Okayama Prefecture, Japan. After spending time in art college, he won the Hop Step Award for new manga artists with his manga **Karakuri** (Mechanism). Kishimoto decided to base his next story on traditional Japanese culture. His first version of **Naruto**, drawn in 1997, was a one-shot story about fox spirits; his final version, which debuted in **Weekly Shonen Jump** in 1999, quickly became the most popular ninja manga in Japan.

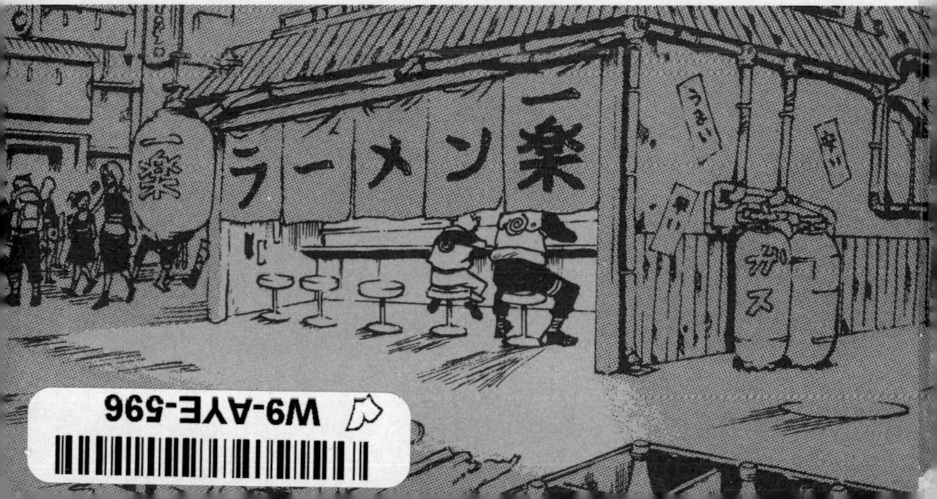
一楽
ラーメン一楽

NARUTO VOL. 60
SHONEN JUMP Manga Edition

STORY AND ART BY MASASHI KISHIMOTO

Translation/Mari Morimoto
English Adaptation/Joel Enos
Touch-up Art & Lettering/John Hunt
Design/Sam Elzway
Editor/Joel Enos

Printed in the U.S.A.

Published by VIZ Media, LLC
P.O. Box 77010
San Francisco, CA 94107

10 9 8 7 6 5 4 3 2
First printing, February 2013
Second printing, January 2015

www.viz.com

SHONEN JUMP MANGA EDITION

NARUTO

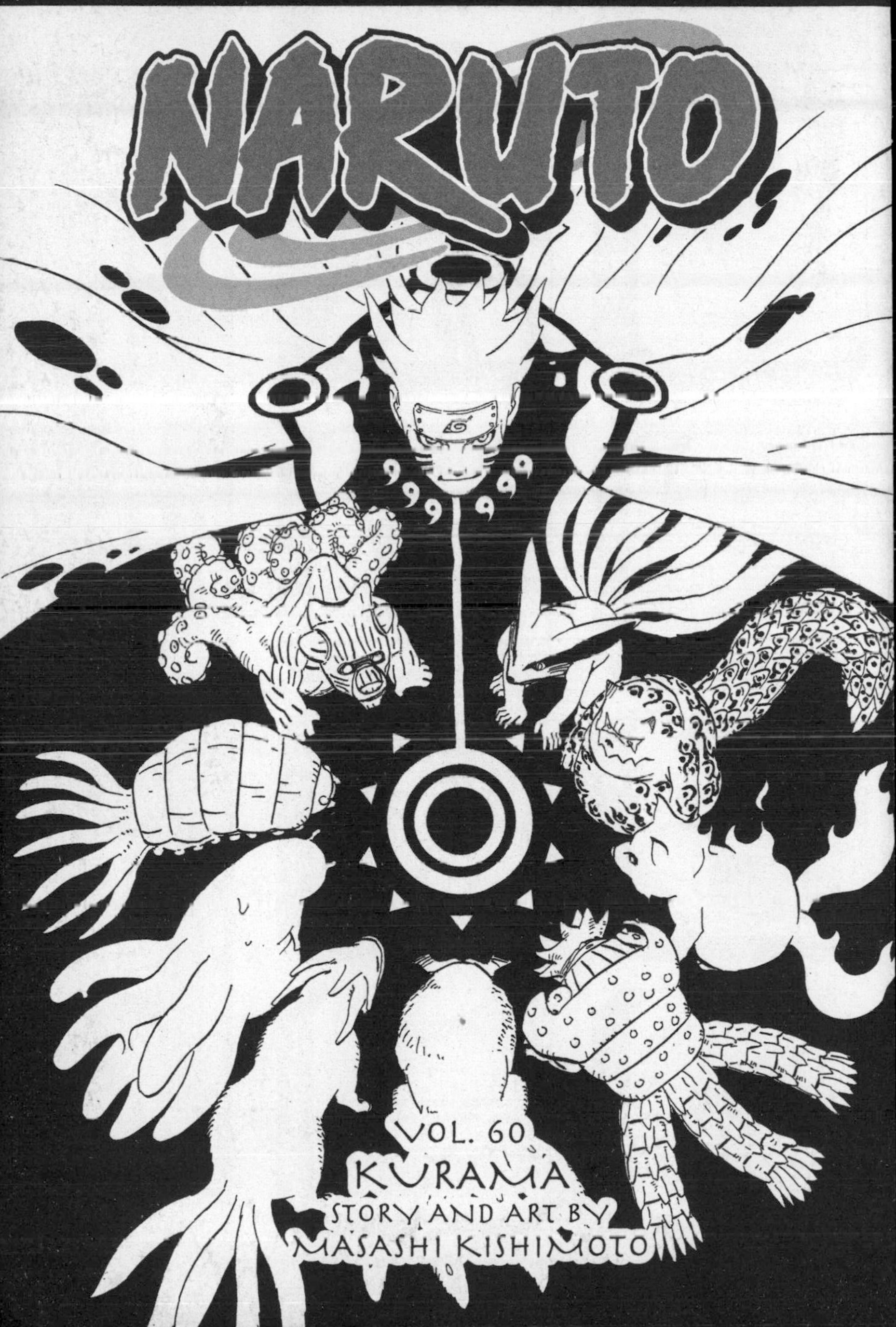

VOL. 60

KURAMA

STORY AND ART BY

MASASHI KISHIMOTO

CHARACTERS

Naruto ナルト
Sasuke サスケ
Kakashi カカシ
Sakura サクラ
Sai サイ
Yamato ヤマト
Tsunade 綱手
Gaara 我愛羅

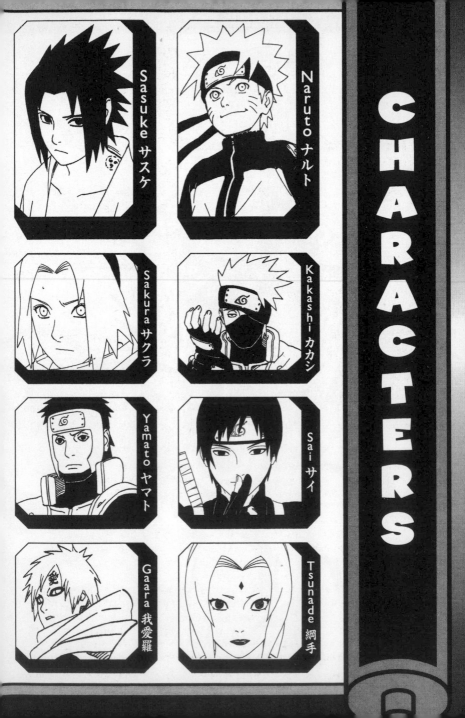

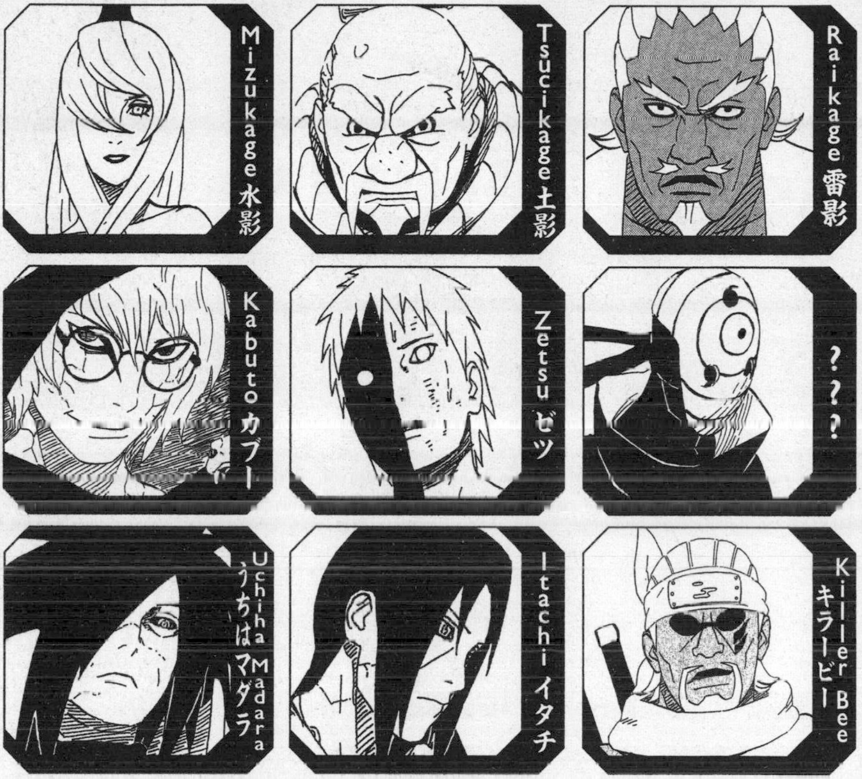
Raikage 雷影
Tsucikage 土影
Mizukage 水影
???
Zetsu ゼツ
Kabuto カブト
Killer Bee キラービー
Itachi イタチ
Uchiha Madara うちはマダラ

THE STORY SO FAR...

Naruto, the biggest troublemaker at the Ninja Academy in the Village of Konohagakure, finally becomes a ninja along with his classmates Sasuke and Sakura. They grow and mature through countless trials and battles. However, Sasuke, unable to give up his quest for vengeance, leaves Konohagakure to seek Orochimaru and his power.

Two years pass. Naruto grows up and engages in fierce battles against the Tailed Beast-targeting Akatsuki. Elsewhere, after winning the heroic battle against Itachi and learning his older brother's true intentions, Sasuke allies with the Akatsuki and sets out to destroy Konoha.

The Fourth Great Ninja War against the Akatsuki begins. After a series of unfavorable battles early on, the Allied Shinobi Forces begin to rally and make a comeback. However, the war situation deteriorates once again thanks to Uchiha Madara, who has been summoned back to life by Kabuto, and the Five Shadows finally assemble upon the battlefield! Meanwhile, Naruto and Bee violently clash with six jinchûriki manipulated by the masked Madara!!

NARUTO

VOL. 60
KURAMA

CONTENTS

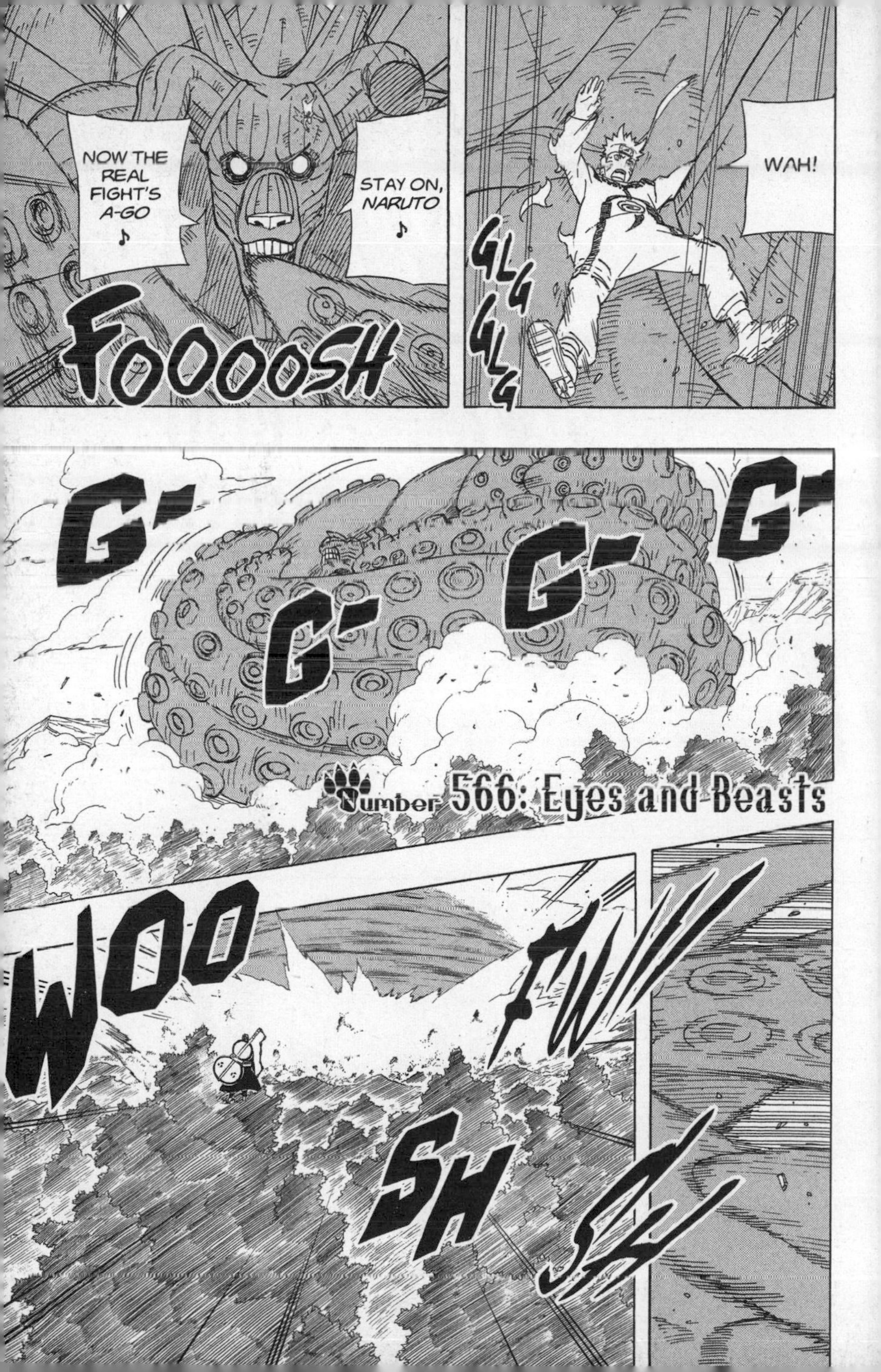
WAH!
GLG GLG
STAY ON, NARUTO ♪
NOW THE REAL FIGHT'S A-GO ♪
FOOOOSH
G-
G-
G-
G-
Number 566: Eyes and Beasts
FW
SH
WOO
SH

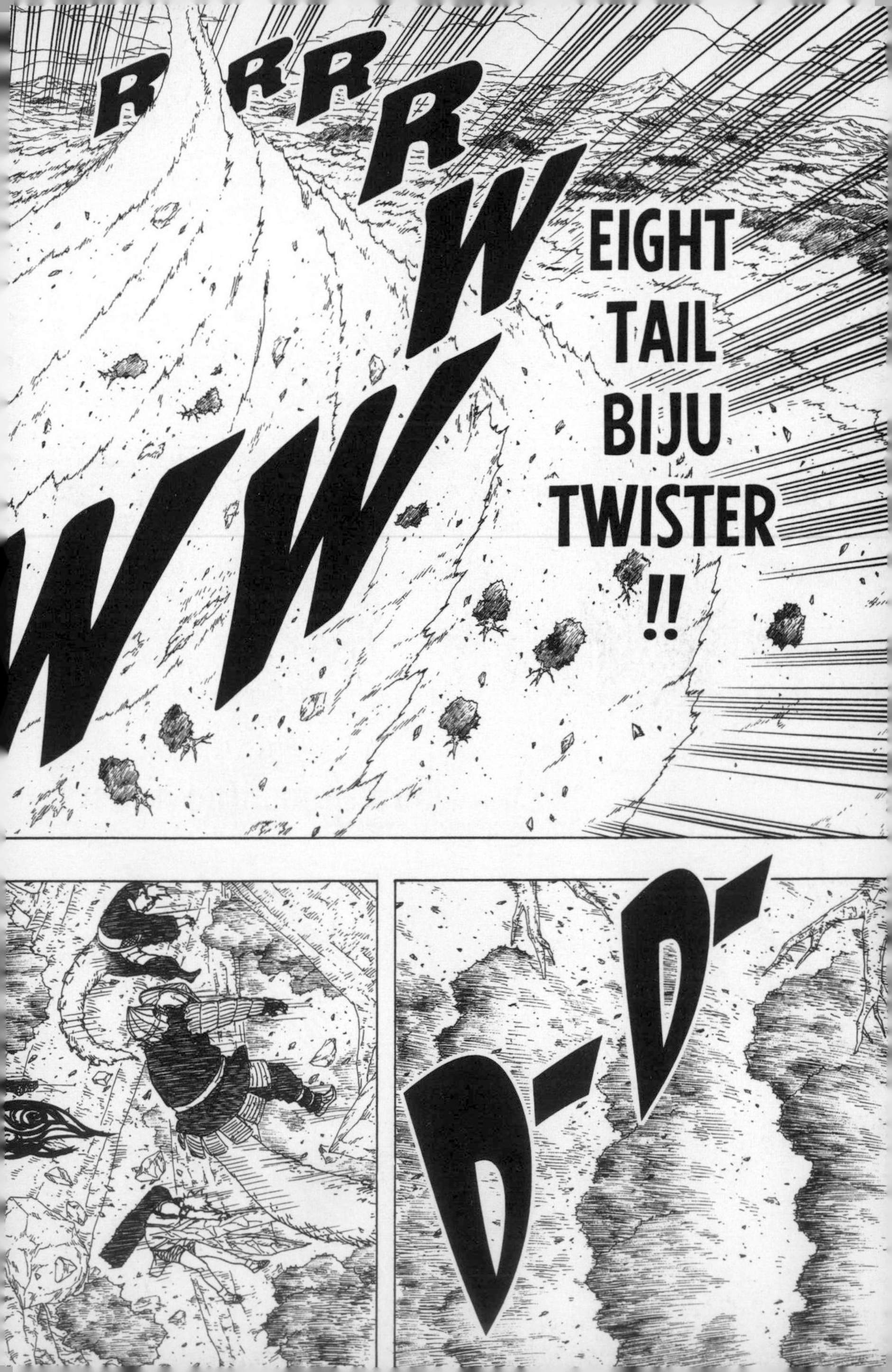
RRRRRWWWW
EIGHT TAIL BIJU TWISTER!!
D-D-

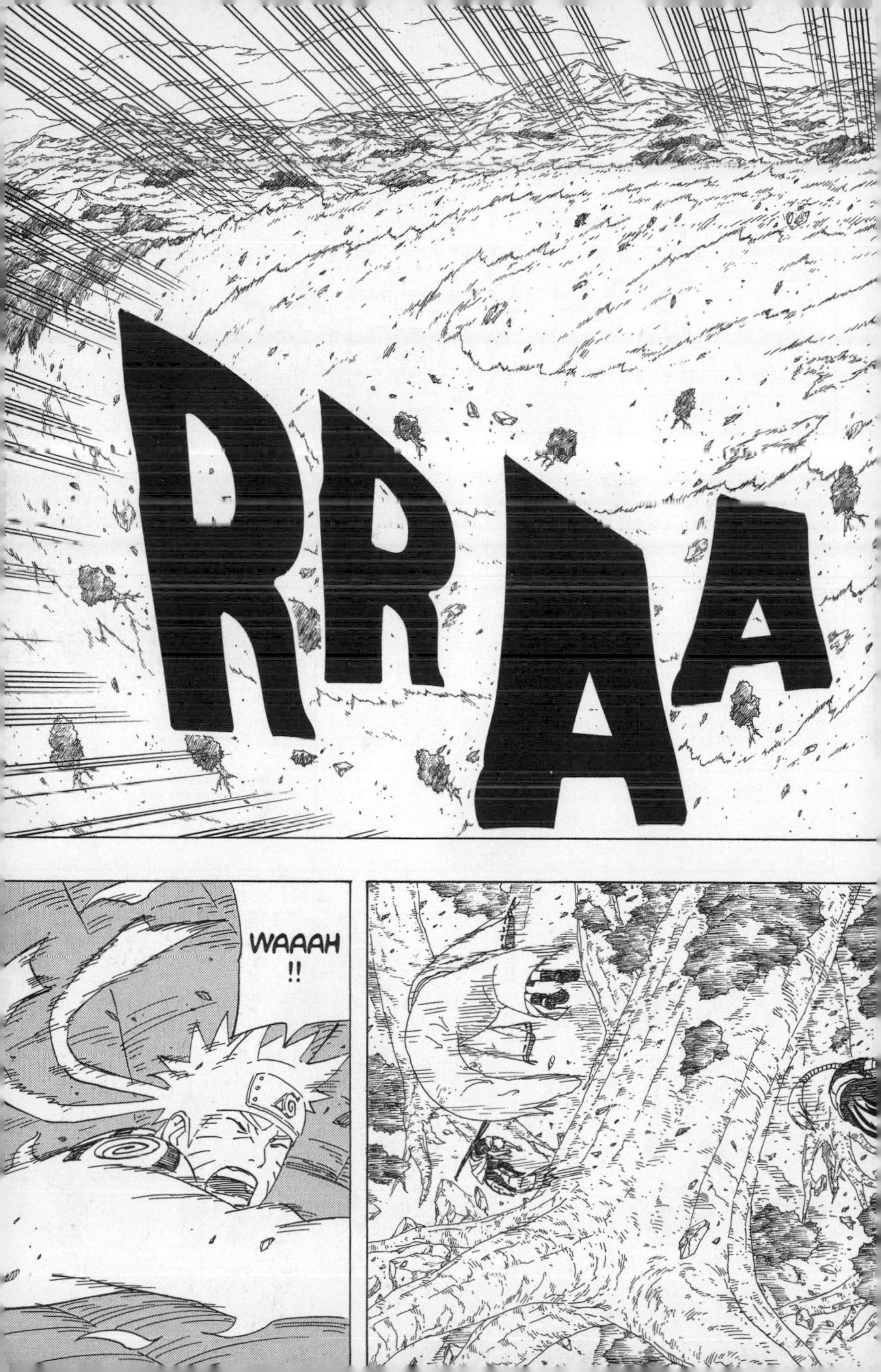
RRAA
WAAAH
!!

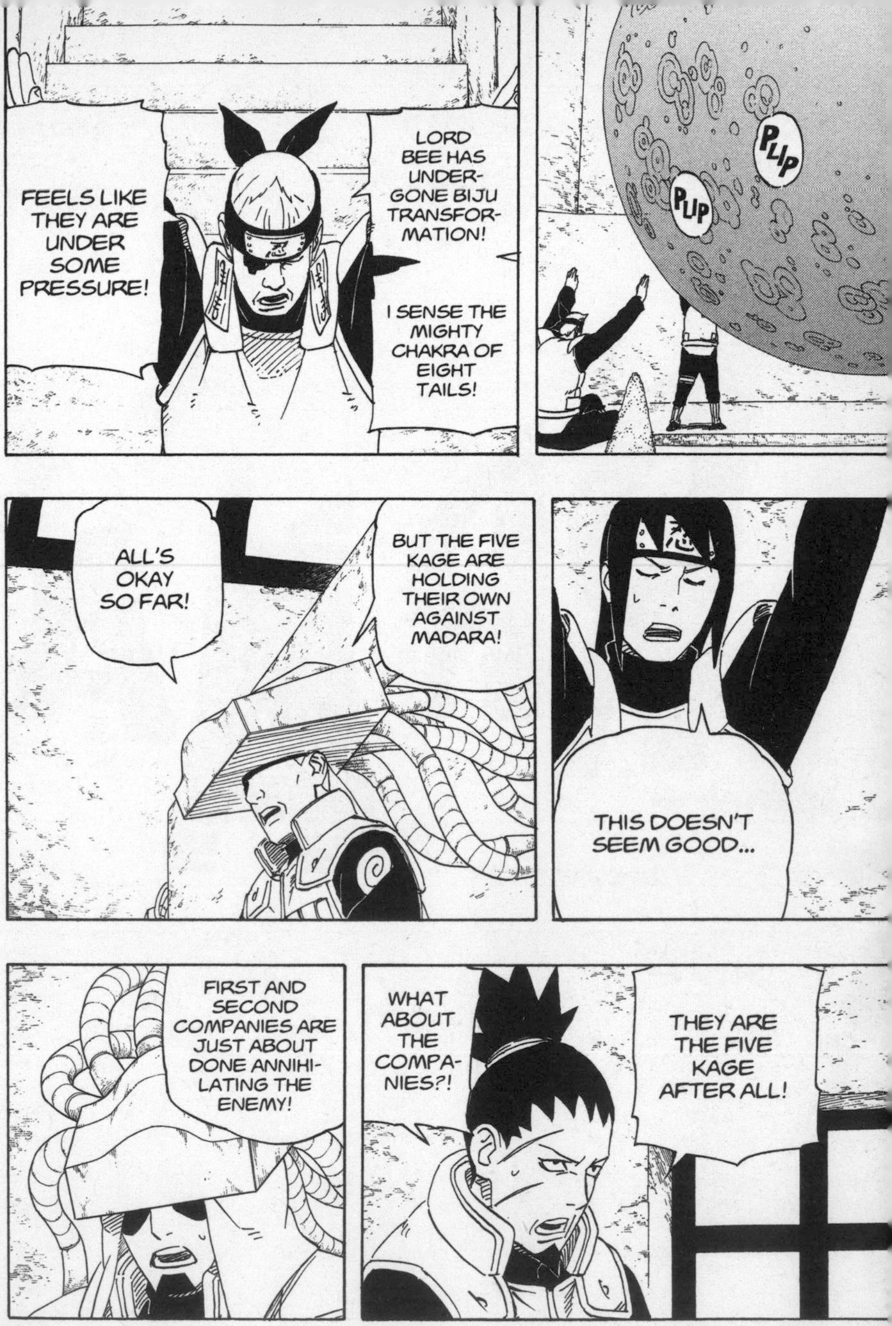
PLIP
PLIP
LORD BEE HAS UNDERGONE BIJU TRANSFORMATION!
I SENSE THE MIGHTY CHAKRA OF EIGHT TAILS!
FEELS LIKE THEY ARE UNDER SOME PRESSURE!
THIS DOESN'T SEEM GOOD...
BUT THE FIVE KAGE ARE HOLDING THEIR OWN AGAINST MADARA!
ALL'S OKAY SO FAR!
THEY ARE THE FIVE KAGE AFTER ALL!
WHAT ABOUT THE COMPANIES?!
FIRST AND SECOND COMPANIES ARE JUST ABOUT DONE ANNIHILATING THE ENEMY!

READ THIS WAY

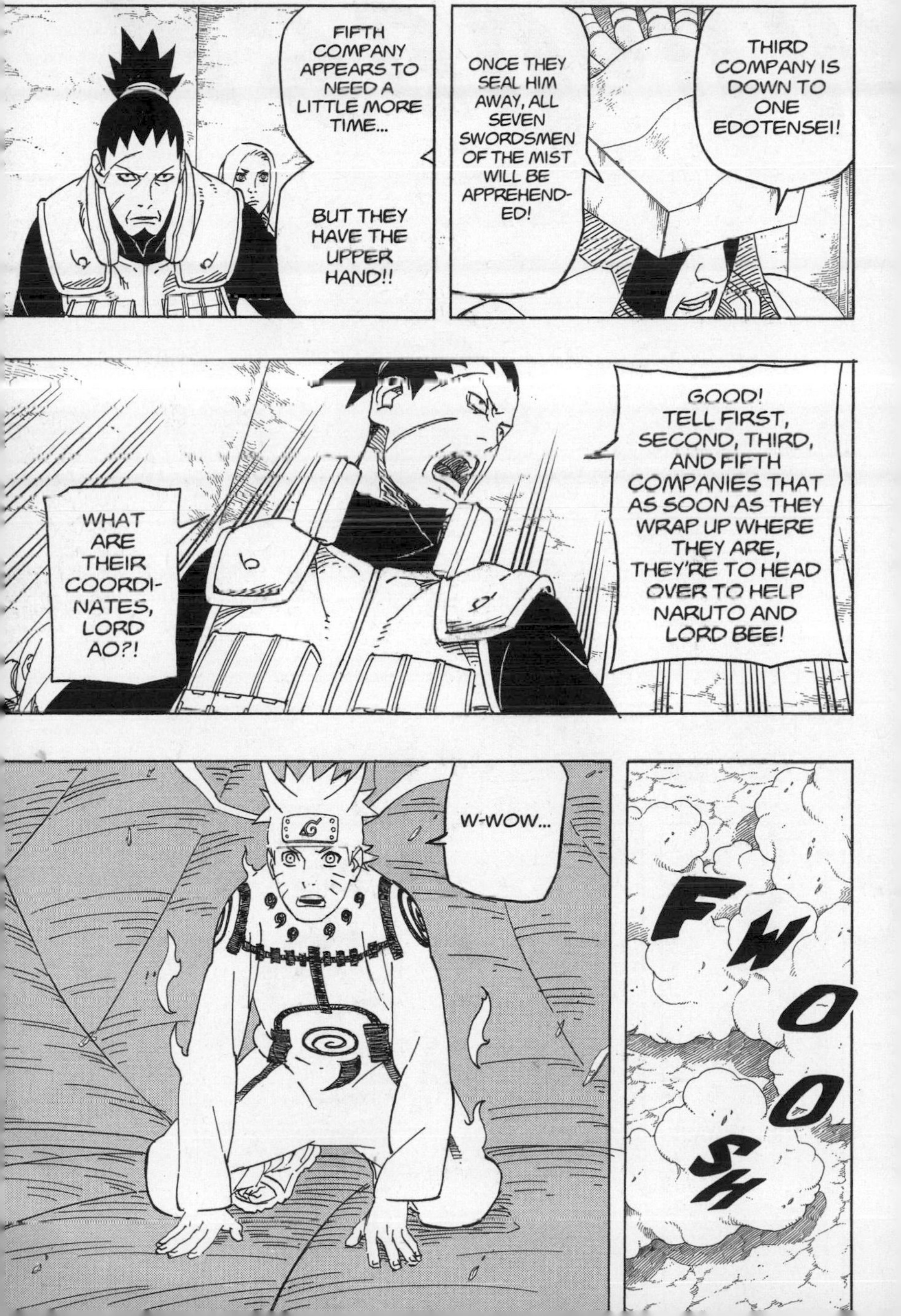
THIRD COMPANY IS DOWN TO ONE EDOTENSEI!
ONCE THEY SEAL HIM AWAY, ALL SEVEN SWORDSMEN OF THE MIST WILL BE APPREHENDED!
FIFTH COMPANY APPEARS TO NEED A LITTLE MORE TIME...
BUT THEY HAVE THE UPPER HAND!!
GOOD! TELL FIRST, SECOND, THIRD, AND FIFTH COMPANIES THAT AS SOON AS THEY WRAP UP WHERE THEY ARE, THEY'RE TO HEAD OVER TO HELP NARUTO AND LORD BEE!
WHAT ARE THEIR COORDINATES, LORD AO?!
FWOOSH
W-WOW...

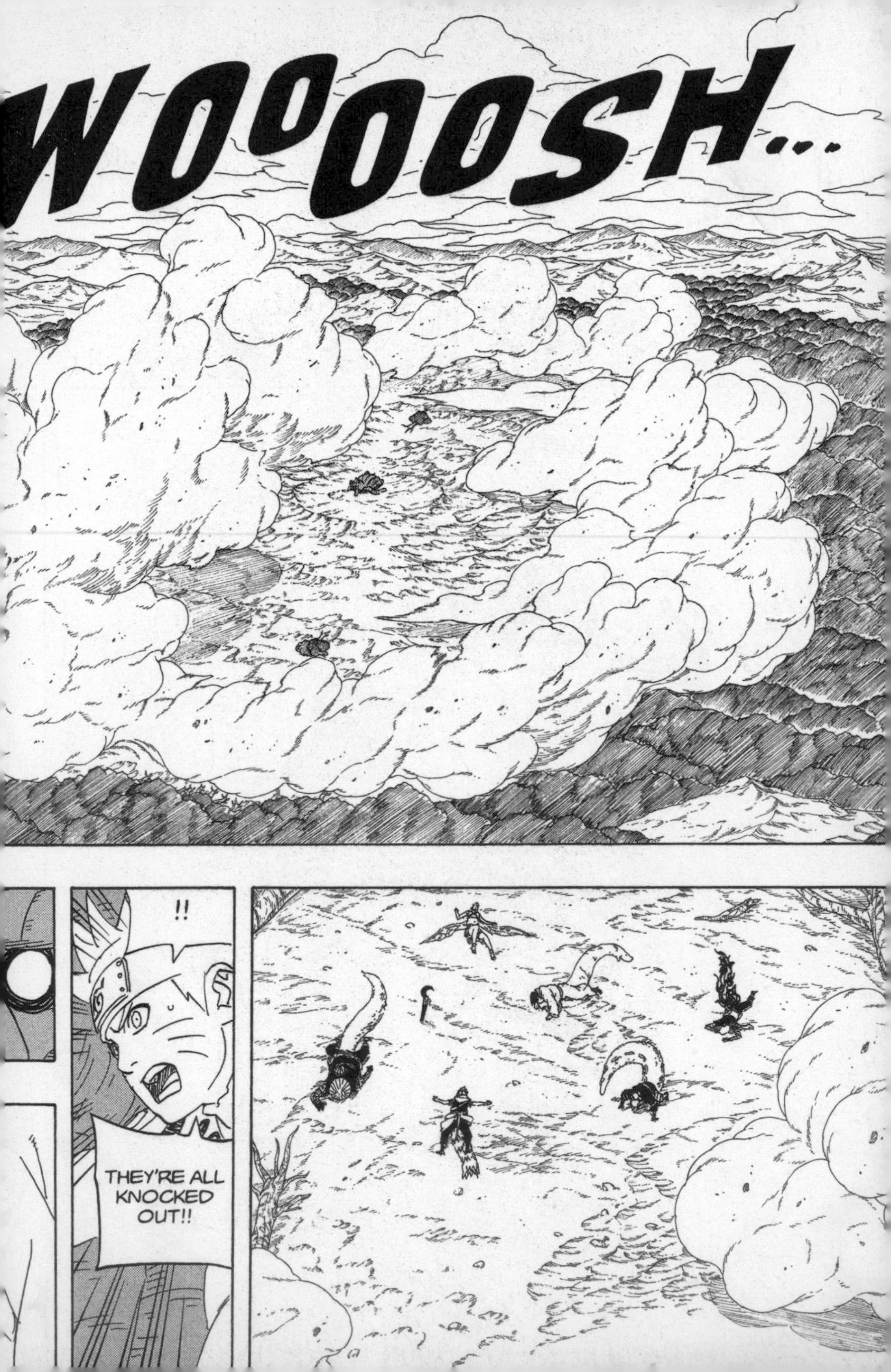
WOOOOSH...
!!
THEY'RE ALL KNOCKED OUT!!

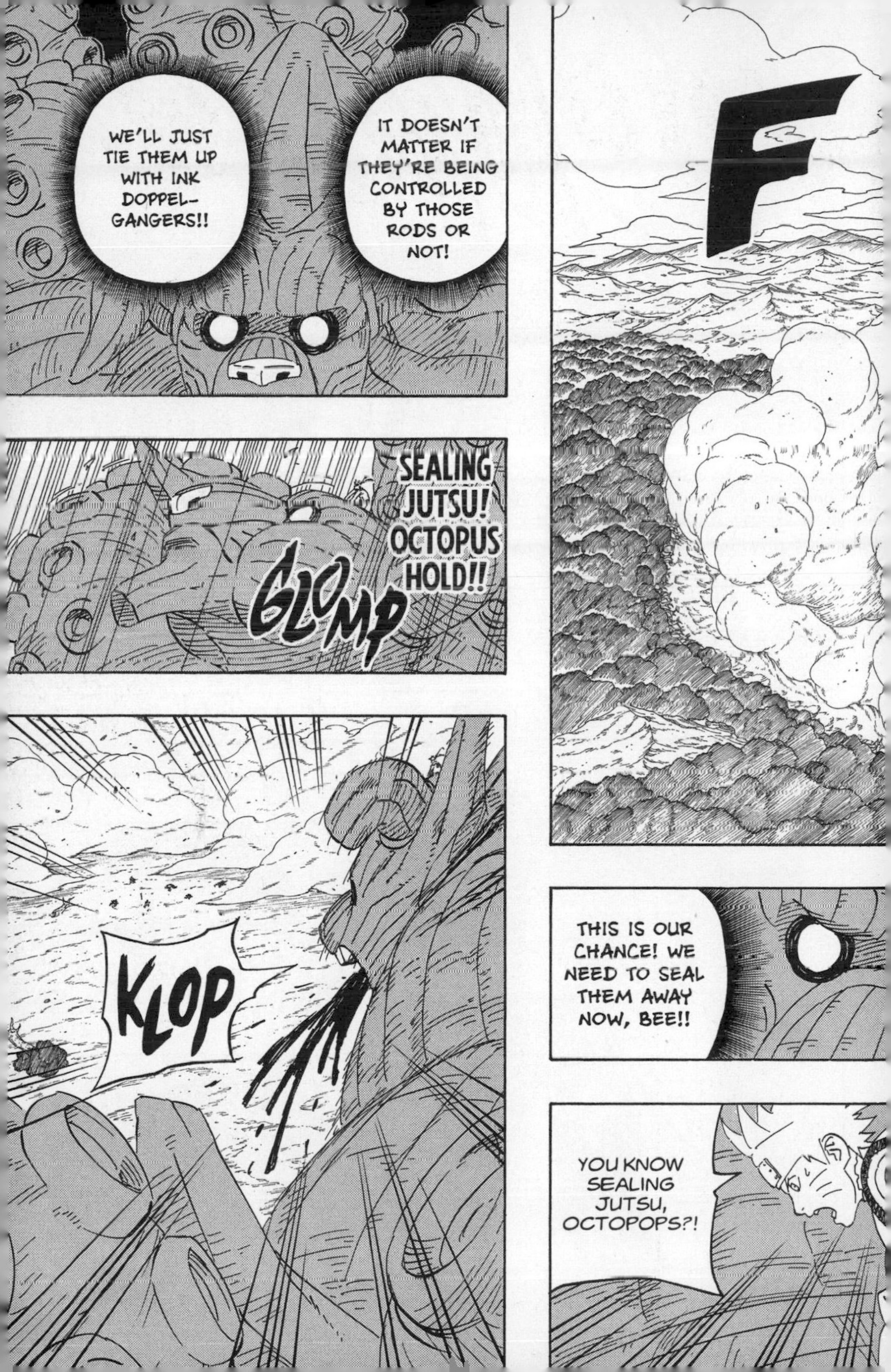
F
THIS IS OUR CHANCE! WE NEED TO SEAL THEM AWAY NOW, BEE!!
YOU KNOW SEALING JUTSU, OCTOPOPS?!
IT DOESN'T MATTER IF THEY'RE BEING CONTROLLED BY THOSE RODS OR NOT!
WE'LL JUST TIE THEM UP WITH INK DOPPEL-GANGERS!!
SEALING JUTSU! OCTOPUS HOLD!!
GLOMP
KLOP

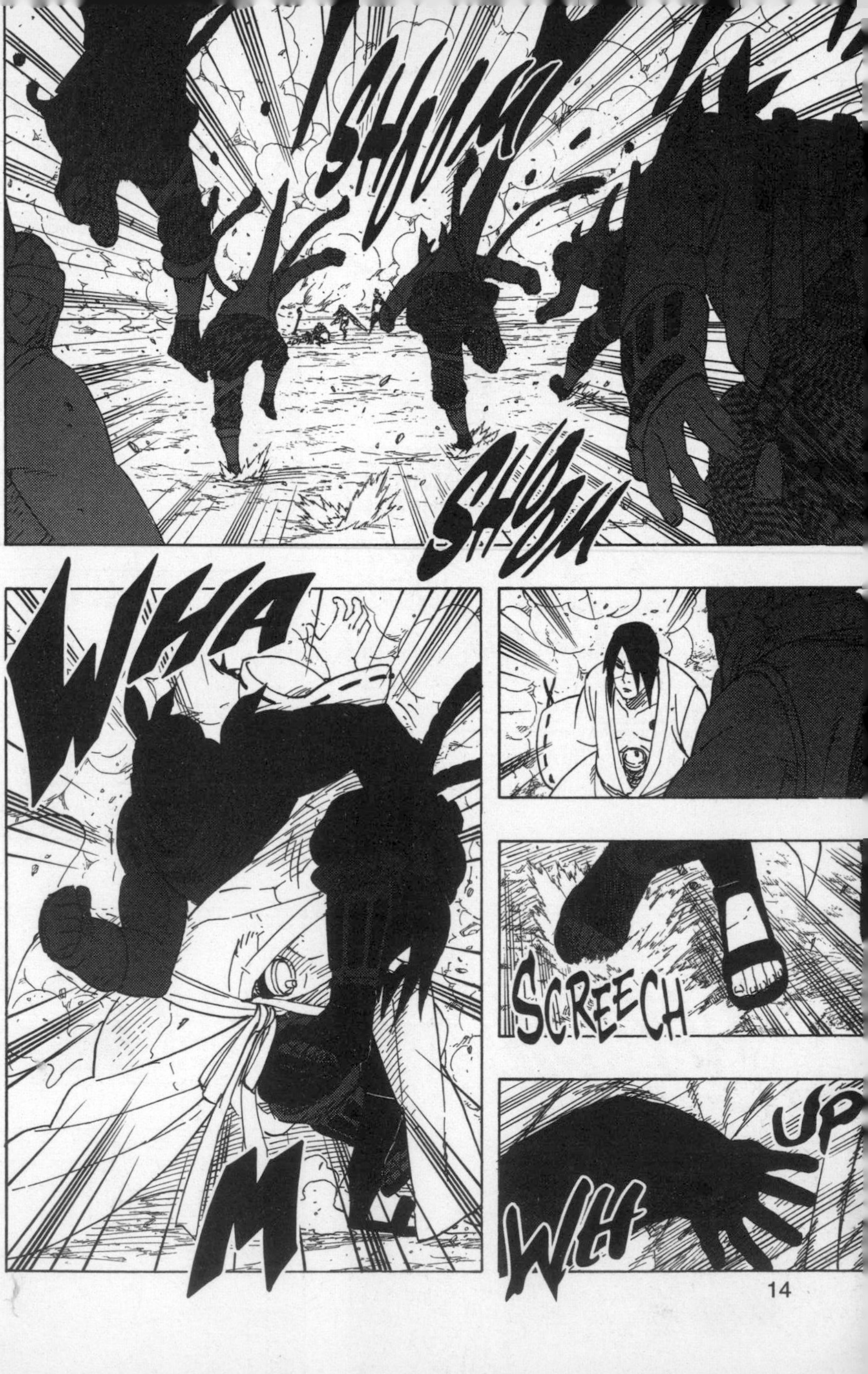
WHAM
SCREECH
WHUP

READ THIS WAY

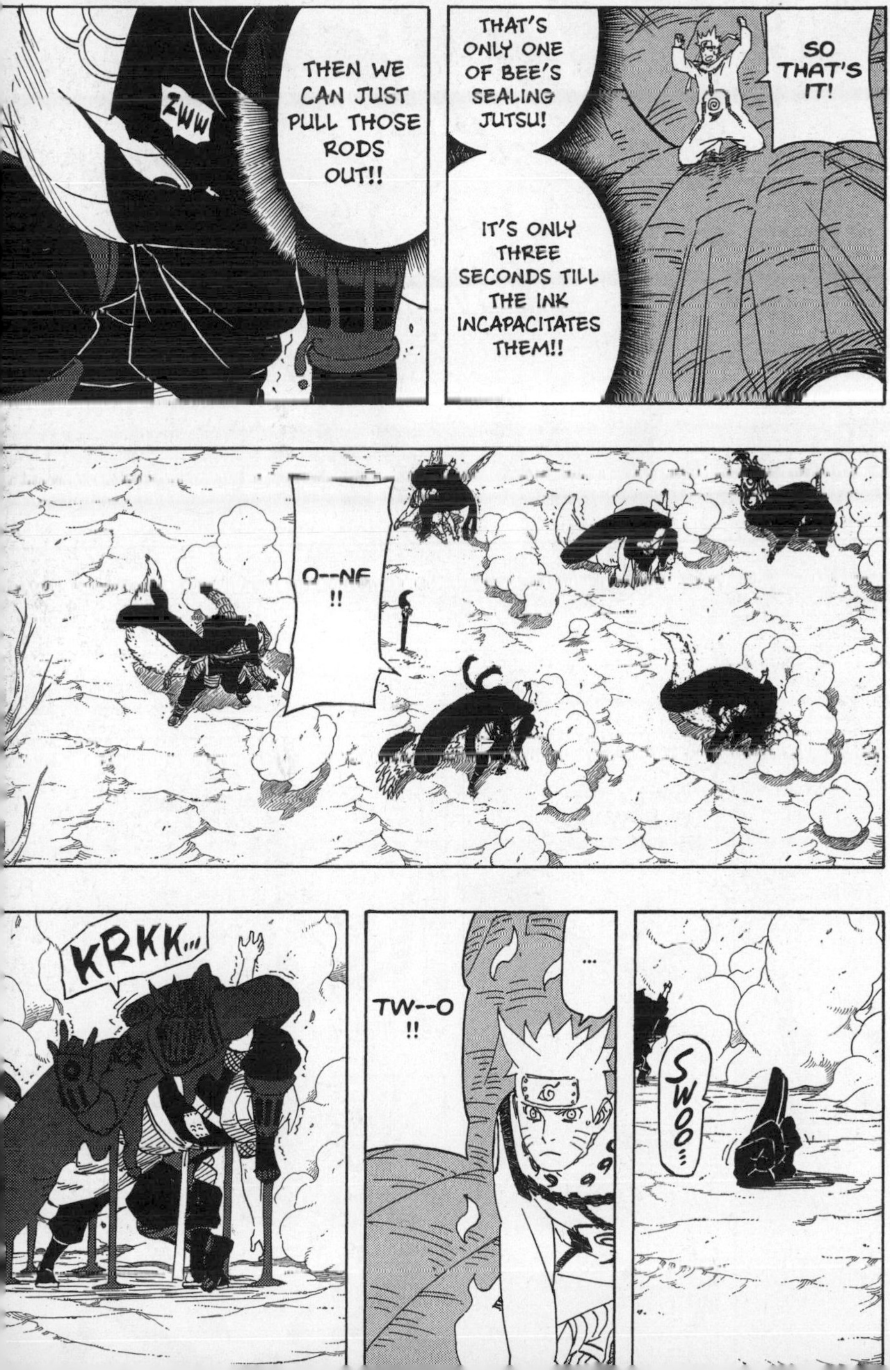
SO THAT'S IT!
THAT'S ONLY ONE OF BEE'S SEALING JUTSU!
IT'S ONLY THREE SECONDS TILL THE INK INCAPACITATES THEM!!
ZWW
THEN WE CAN JUST PULL THOSE RODS OUT!!
O--NE !!
SWOO...
...
TW--O !!
KRKK...

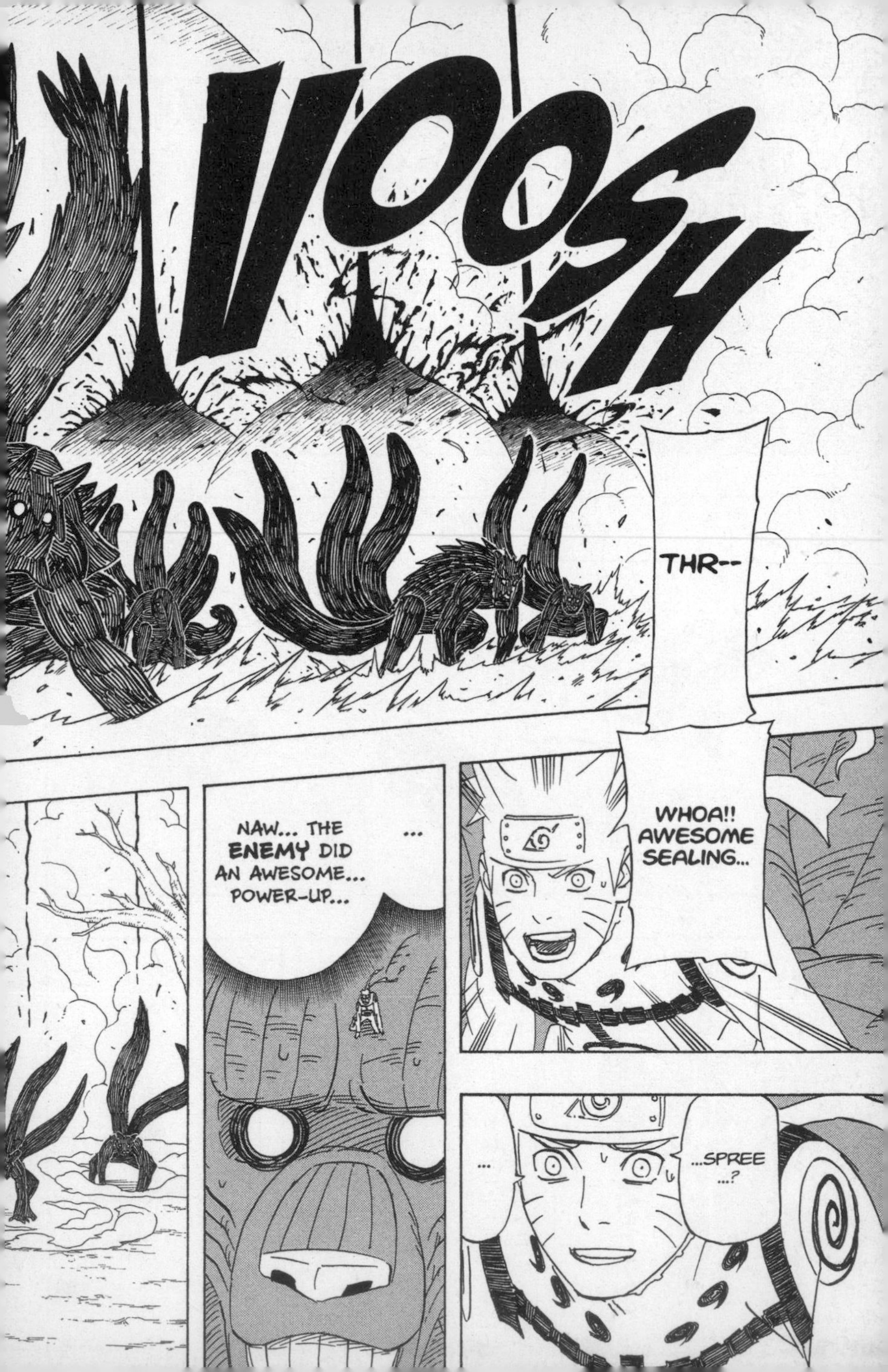
VOOSH
THR--
WHOA!! AWESOME SEALING...
...
NAW... THE ENEMY DID AN AWESOME... POWER-UP...
...SPREE ...?
...

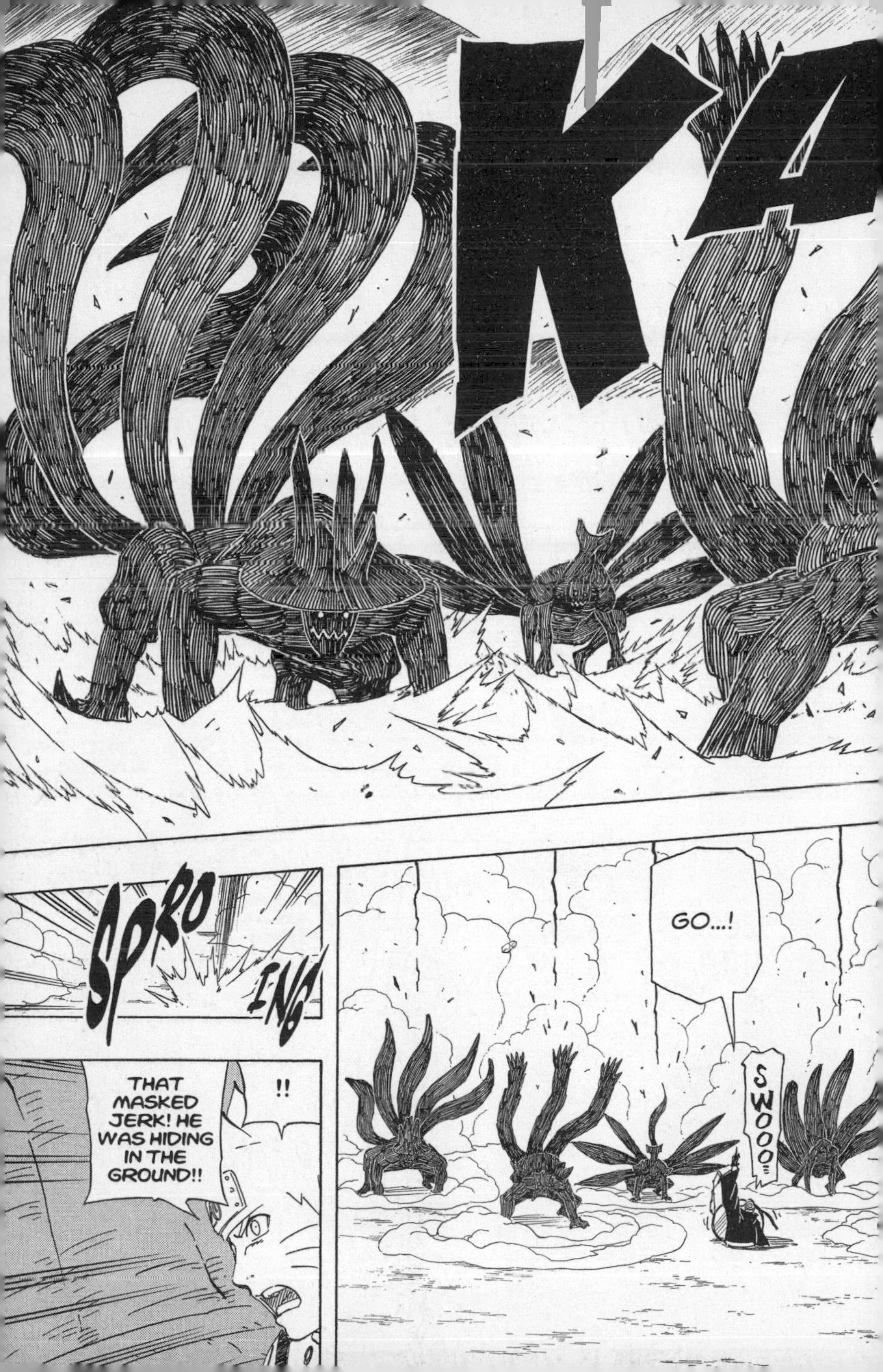
KA
GO...!
SWOOOO
SPROING
!!
THAT MASKED JERK! HE WAS HIDING IN THE GROUND!!

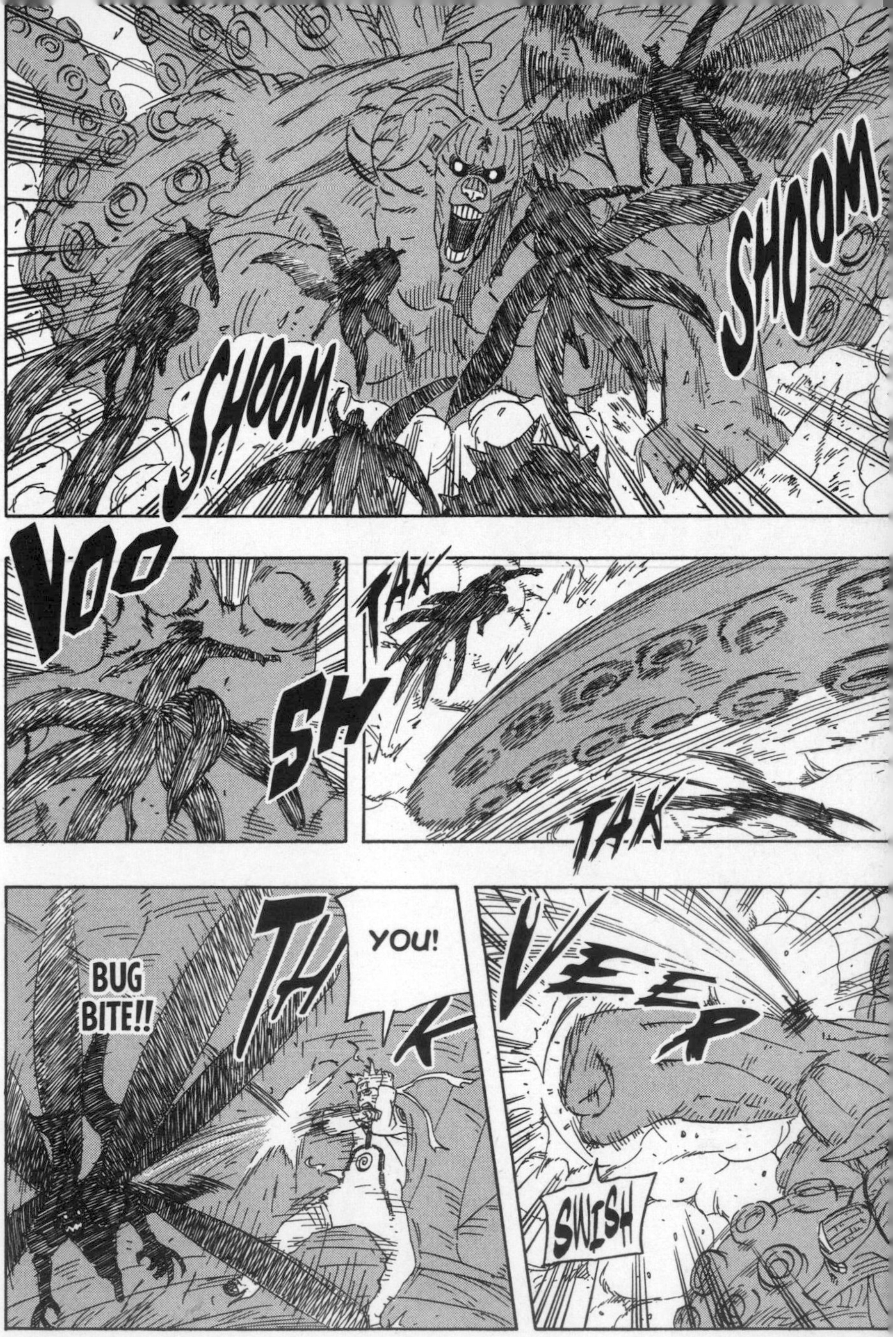
SHOOM
SHOOM
TAK
SH
TAK
VOO
VEEP
SWISH
YOU!
THK
BUG BITE!!

READ THIS WAY

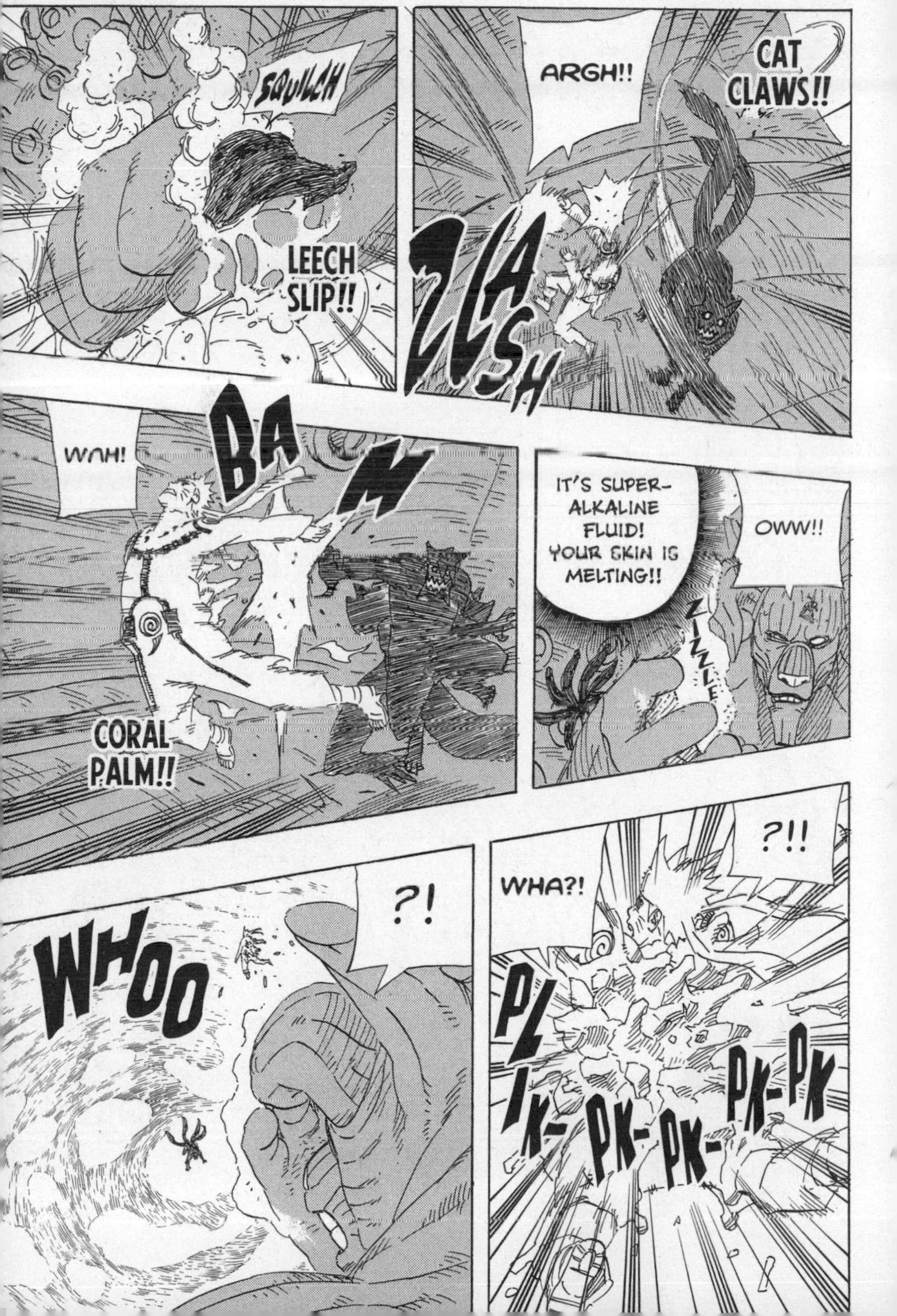
CAT CLAWS!!
ARGH!!
ZLASH
SQUILCH
LEECH SLIP!!
OWW!!
IT'S SUPER-ALKALINE FLUID! YOUR SKIN IS MELTING!!
ZIZZLE
WAH!
BAM
CORAL PALM!!
?!!
WHA?!
PLIK-PK-PK-PK-PK
?!
WHOO

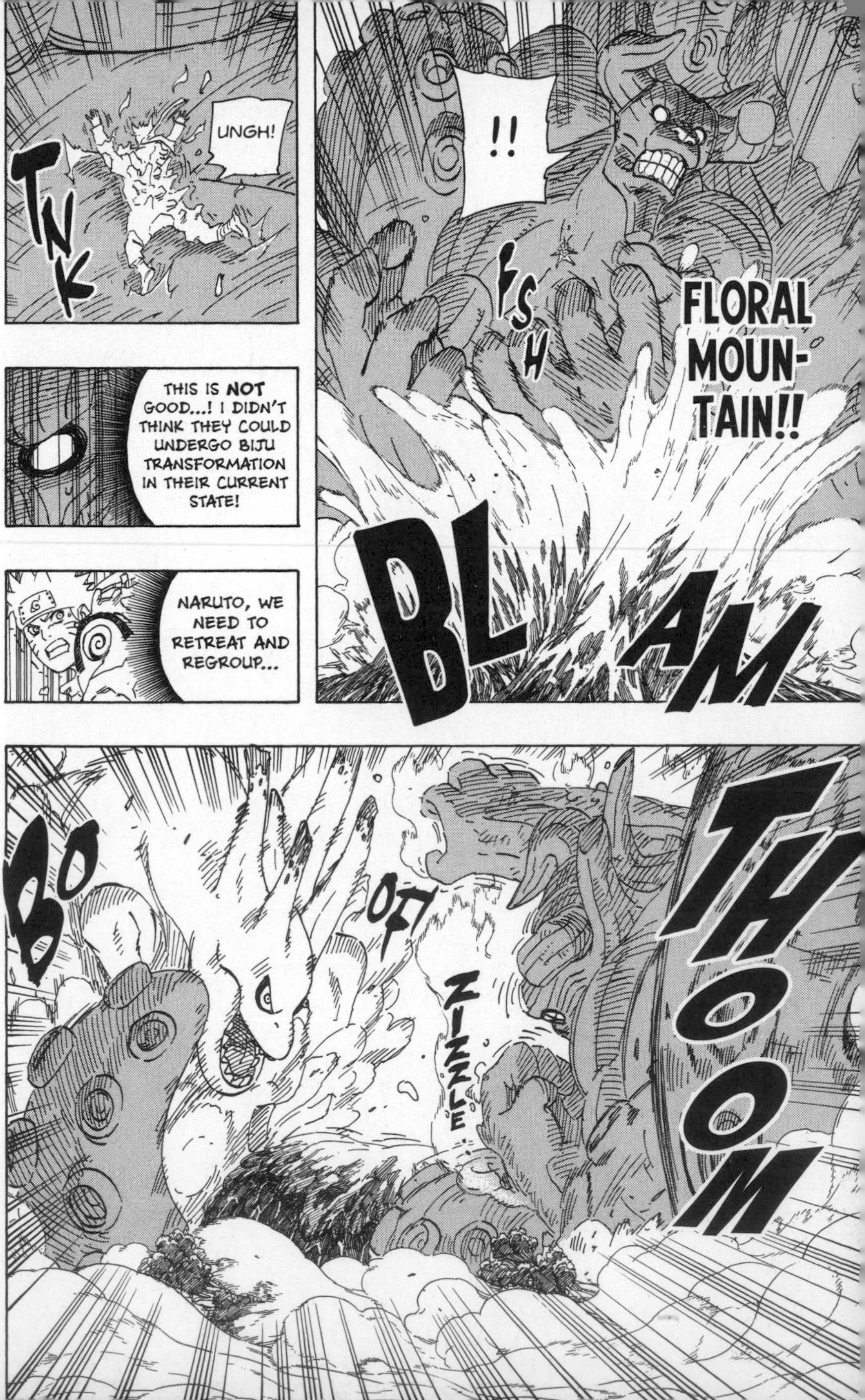
!!
FSH
FLORAL MOUNTAIN!!
BLAM
UNGH!
TNK
THIS IS NOT GOOD...! I DIDN'T THINK THEY COULD UNDERGO BIJU TRANSFORMATION IN THEIR CURRENT STATE!
NARUTO, WE NEED TO RETREAT AND REGROUP...
THOOM
ZIZZLE

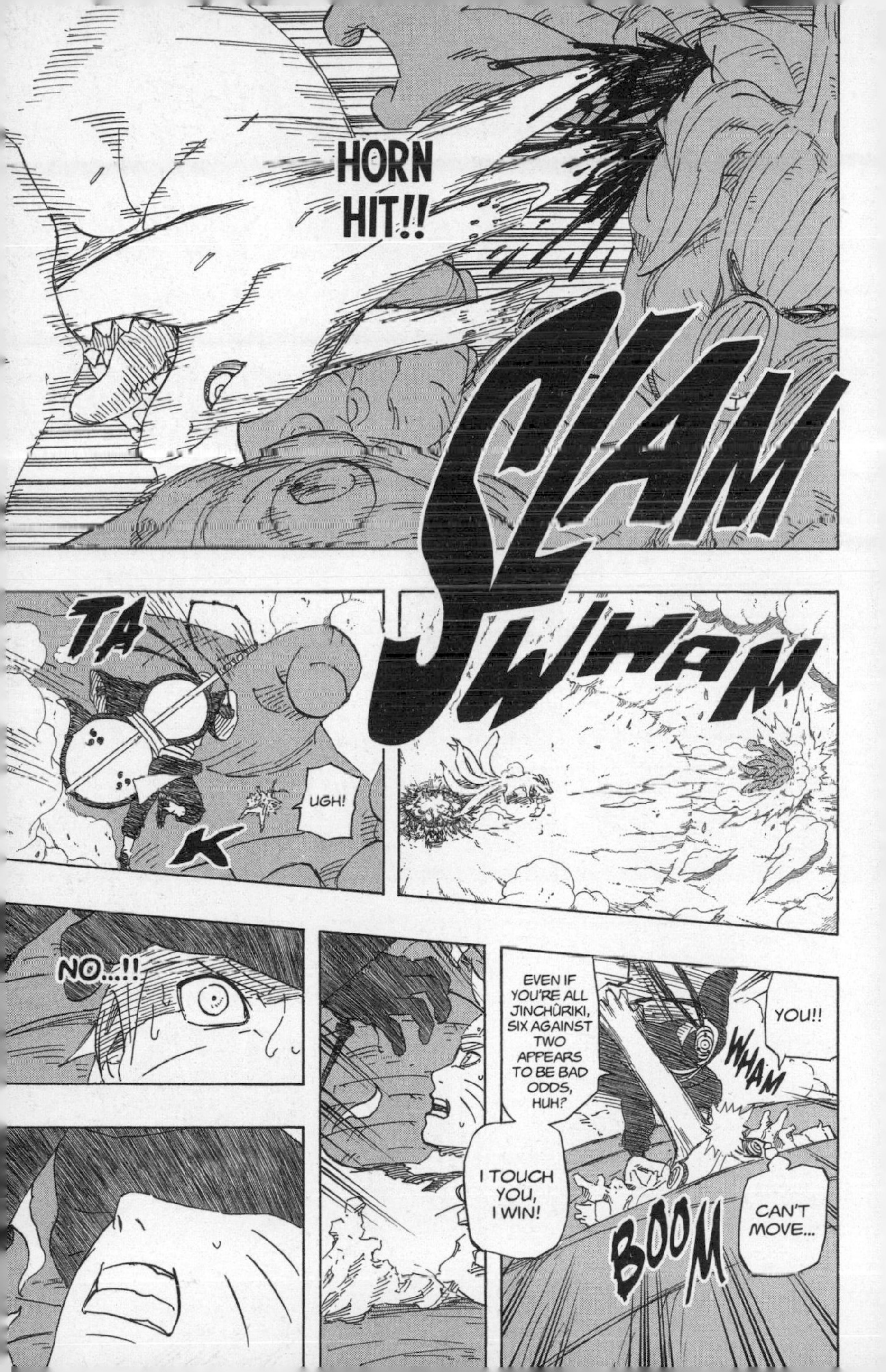

HORN HIT!!
SLAM
WHAM
TA
K
UGH!
YOU!!
EVEN IF YOU'RE ALL JINCHÛRIKI, SIX AGAINST TWO APPEARS TO BE BAD ODDS, HUH?
WHAM
CAN'T MOVE...
I TOUCH YOU, I WIN!
BOOM
NO...!!

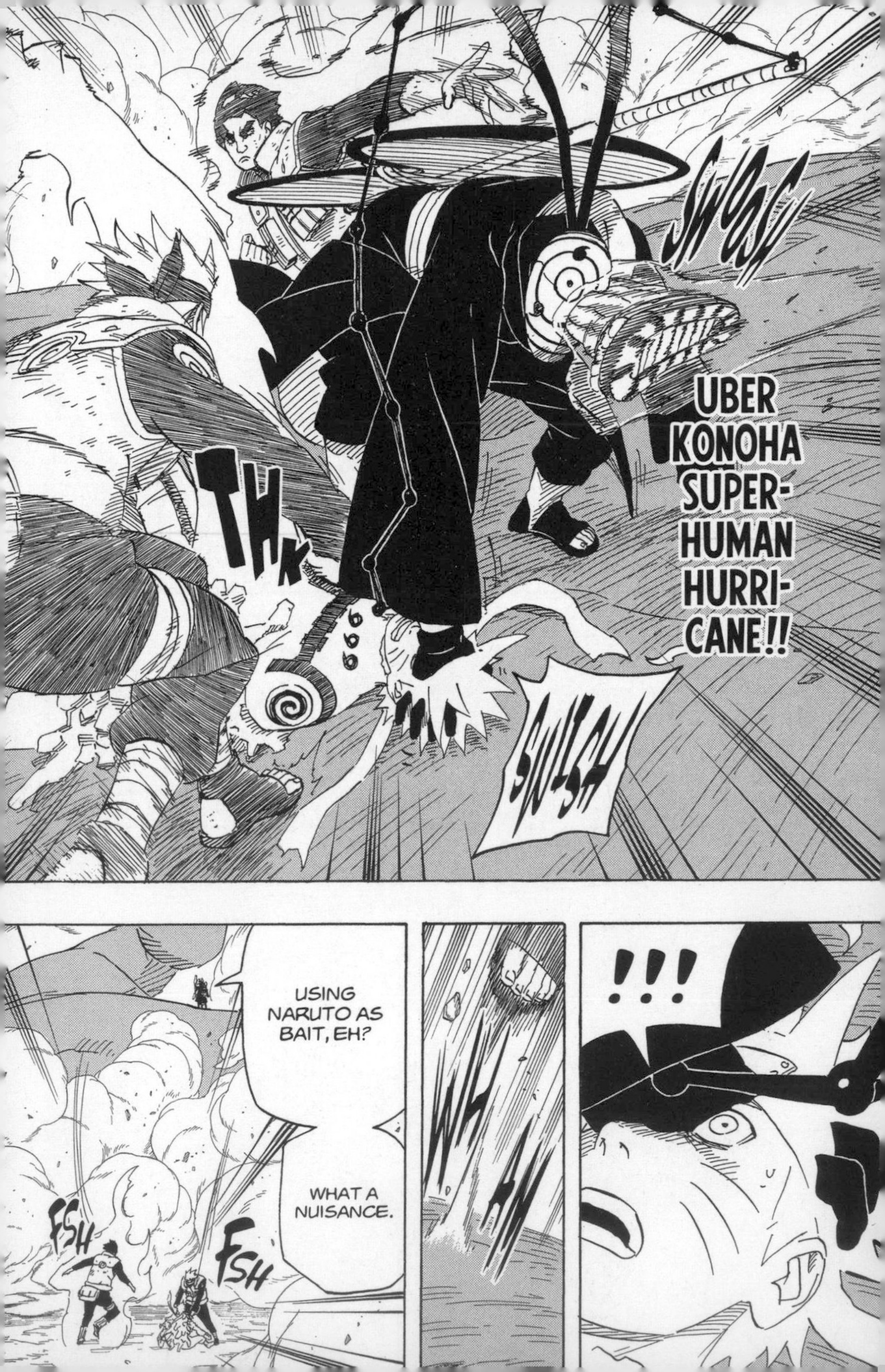
SWOSH
UBER KONOHA SUPER-HUMAN HURRI-CANE!!
THK
!!!
USING NARUTO AS BAIT, EH?
WHAT A NUISANCE.
FSH
FSH

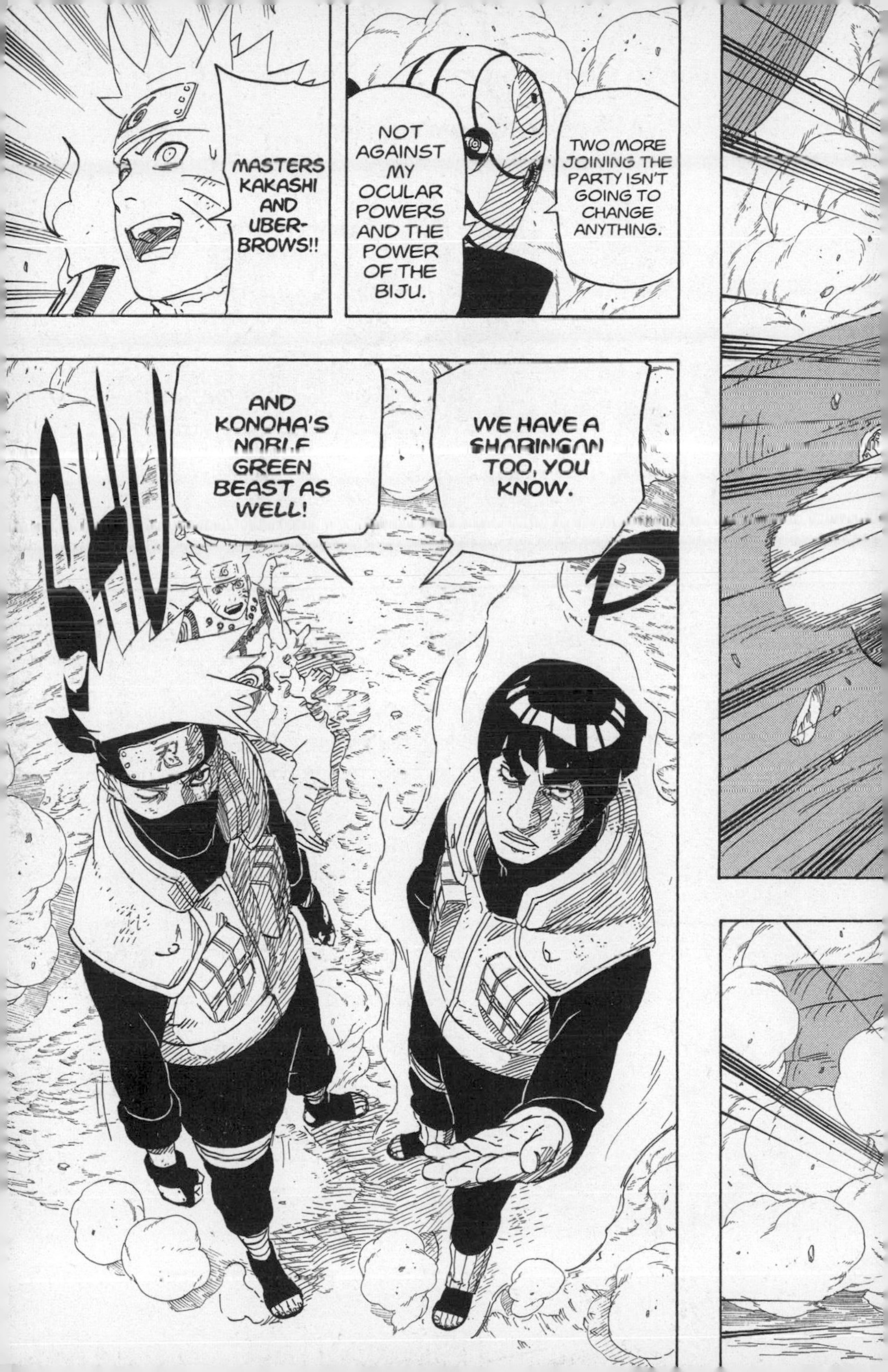
TWO MORE JOINING THE PARTY ISN'T GOING TO CHANGE ANYTHING.
NOT AGAINST MY OCULAR POWERS AND THE POWER OF THE BIJU.
MASTERS KAKASHI AND UBER-BROWS!!
WE HAVE A SHARINGAN TOO, YOU KNOW.
AND KONOHA'S NOBLE GREEN BEAST AS WELL!

Illustration to Commemorate Reaching Volume 60 [1]

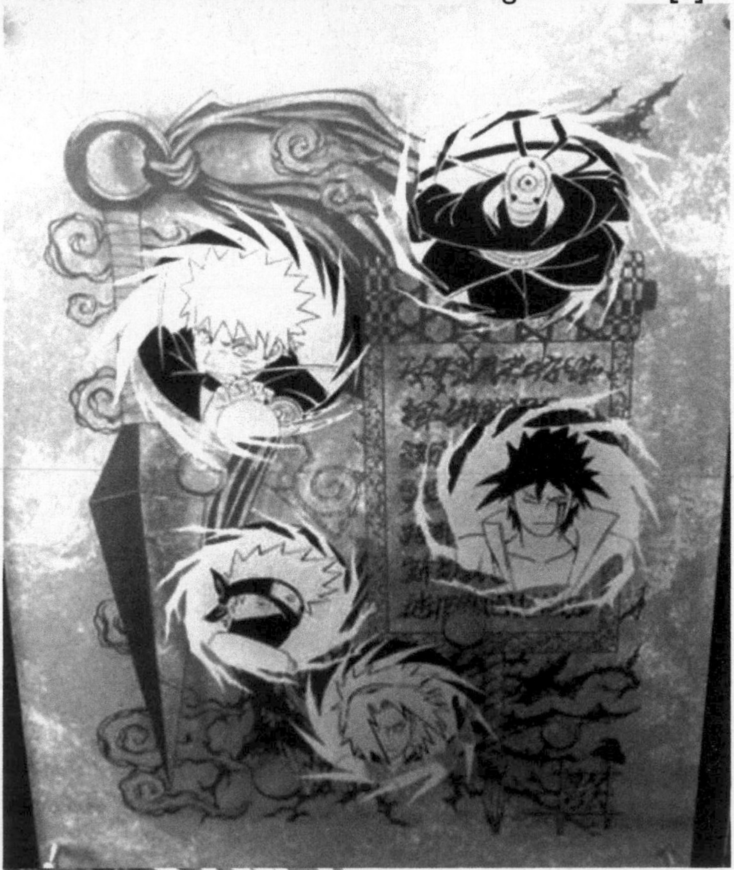

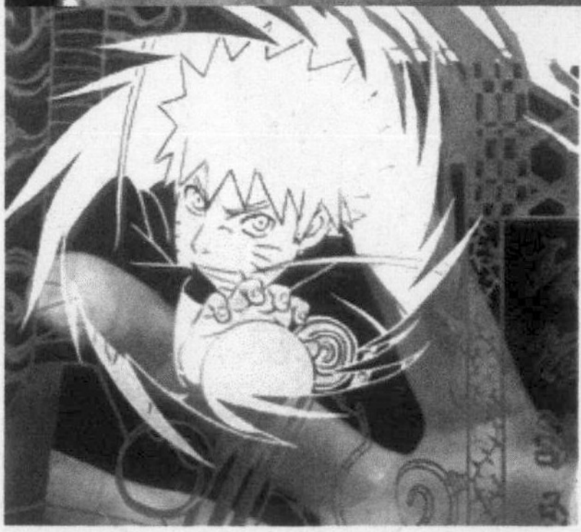

Naruto Kirie(Papercutting) Art

Created by Atsuhiro Sato

You can see how it's done at the artist's website:

http://Kirieatsu.blog.fc2.com/

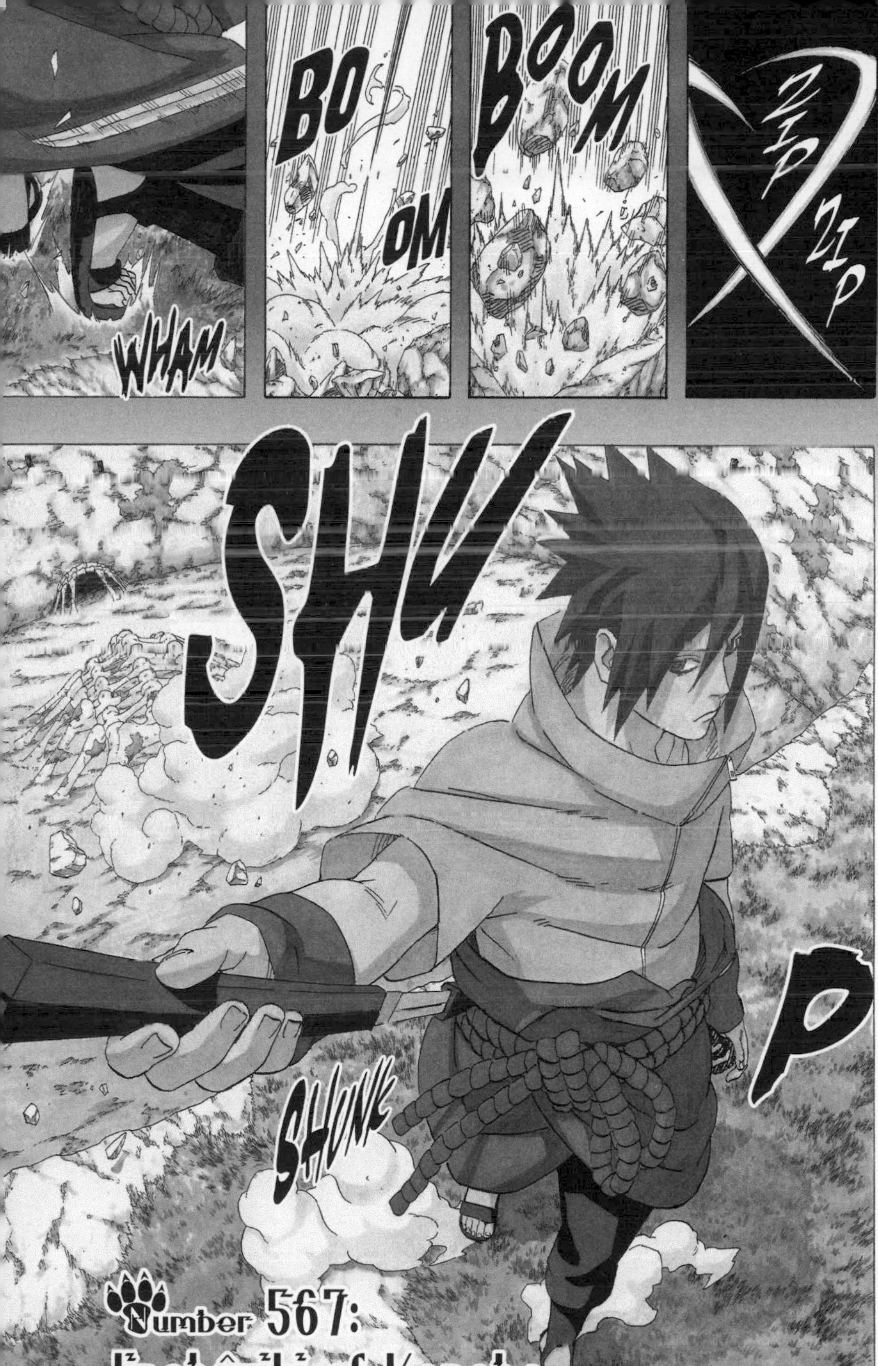
ZIP ZIP
BOOM
BO OM
WHAM
SHU
P
SHUNK
Number 567:
Jinchûriki of Konoha

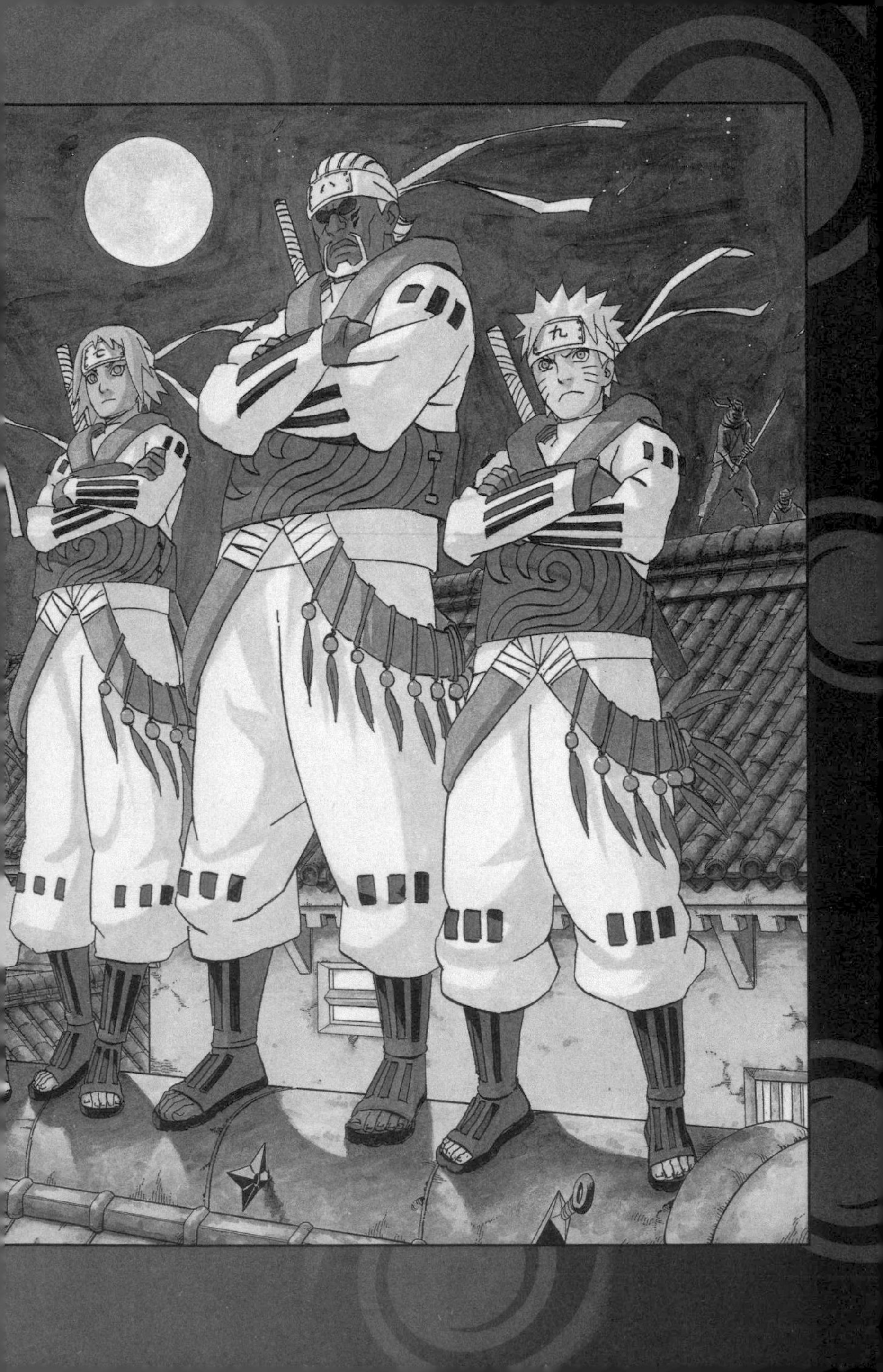

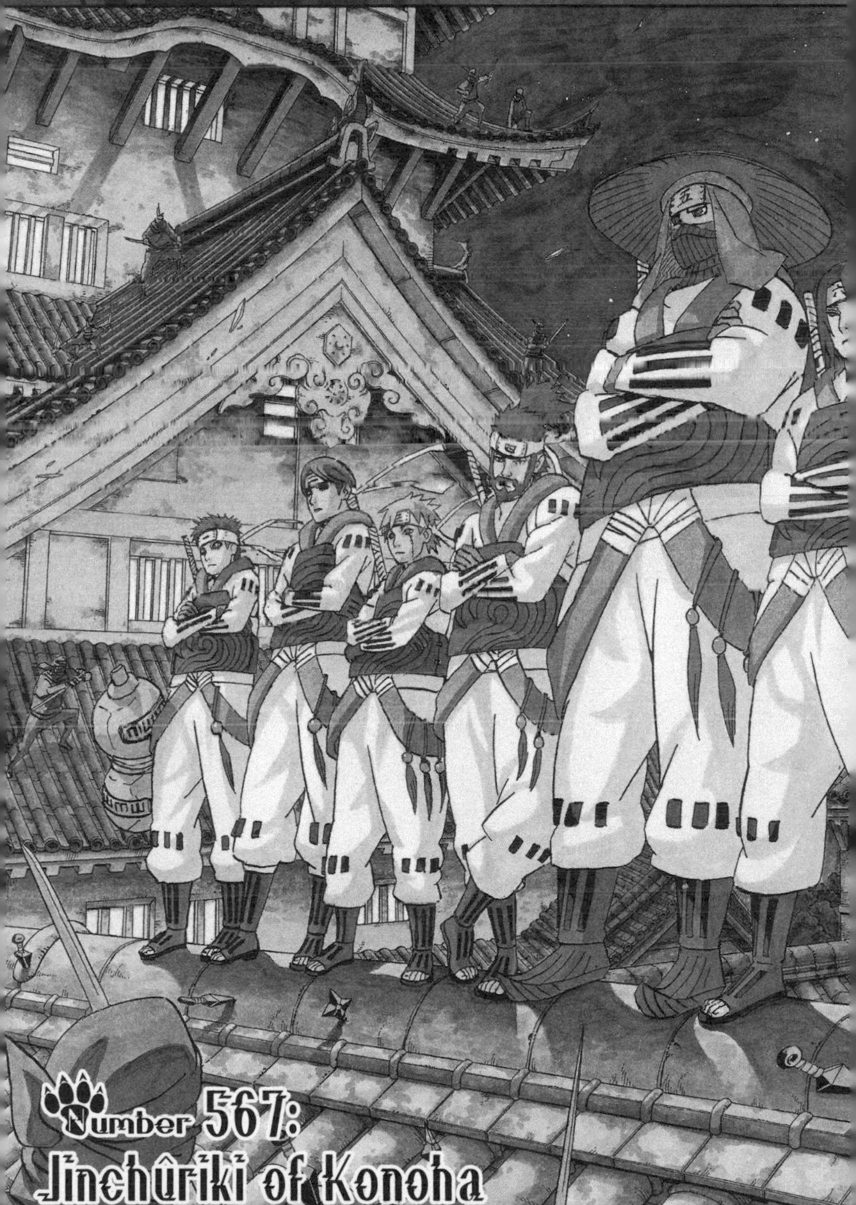
Number 567:
Jinchûriki of Konoha

Illustration to Commemorate Reaching Volume 60 [2]

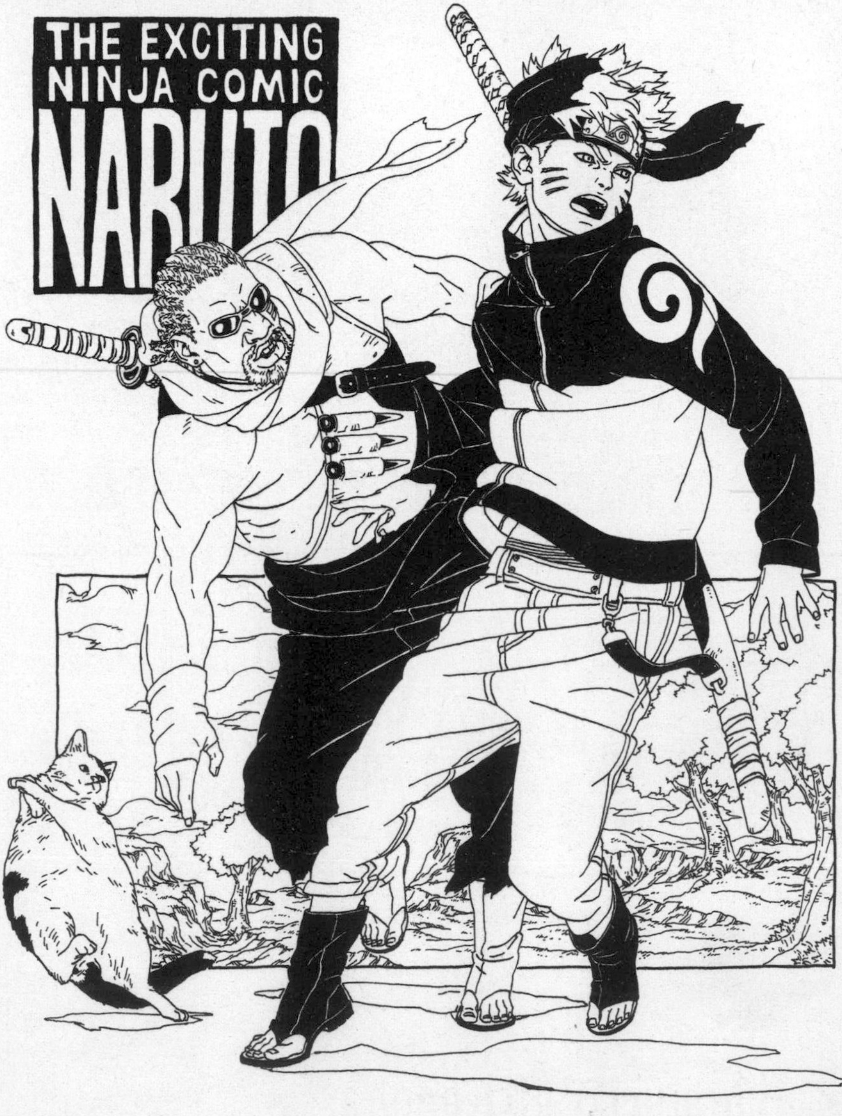
THE EXCITING
NINJA COMIC
NARUTO

Mikio Ikemoto

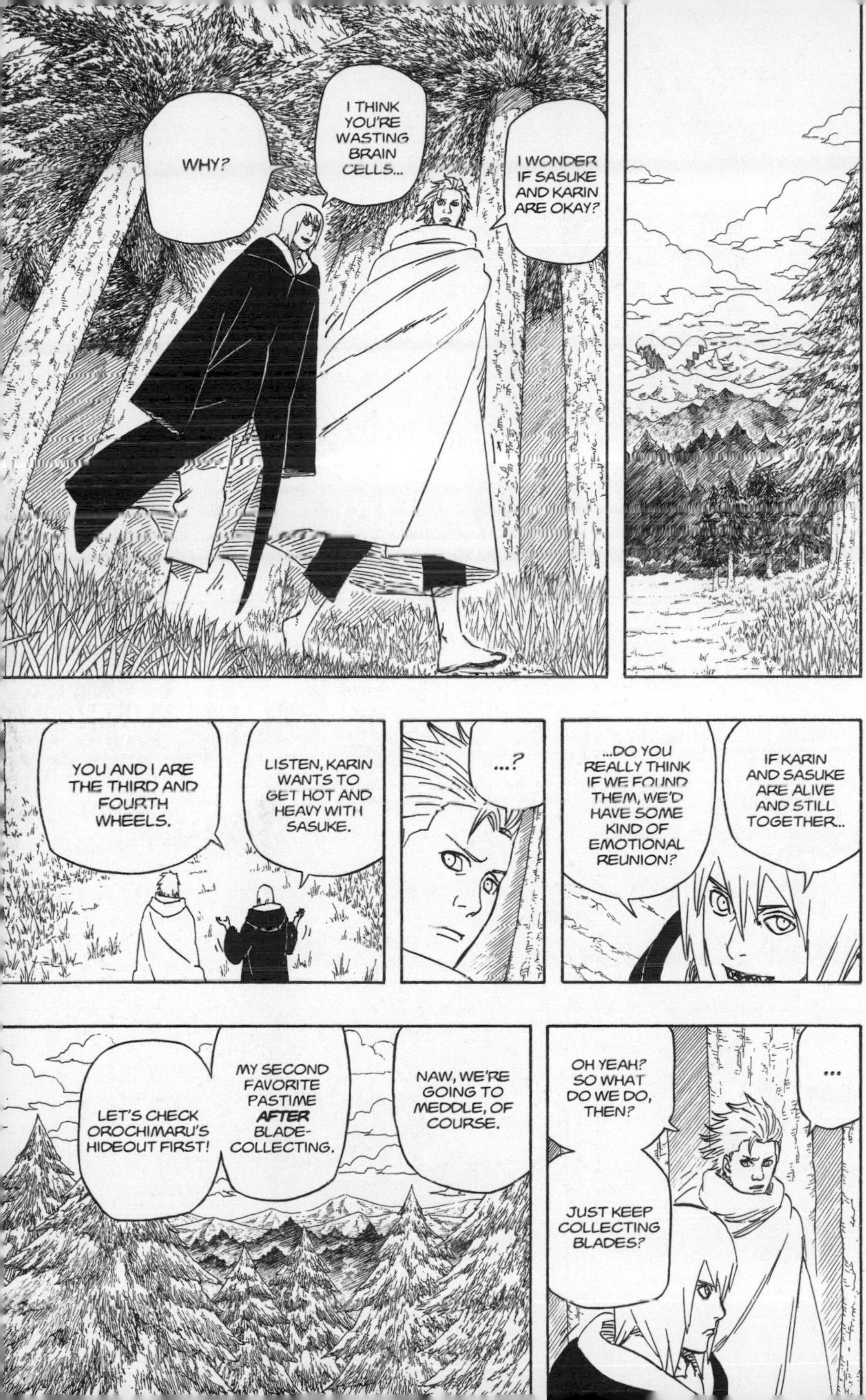
I WONDER IF SASUKE AND KARIN ARE OKAY?
I THINK YOU'RE WASTING BRAIN CELLS...
WHY?
IF KARIN AND SASUKE ARE ALIVE AND STILL TOGETHER..
...DO YOU REALLY THINK IF WE FOUND THEM, WE'D HAVE SOME KIND OF EMOTIONAL REUNION?
...?
LISTEN, KARIN WANTS TO GET HOT AND HEAVY WITH SASUKE.
YOU AND I ARE THE THIRD AND FOURTH WHEELS.
...
OH YEAH? SO WHAT DO WE DO, THEN?
JUST KEEP COLLECTING BLADES?
NAW, WE'RE GOING TO MEDDLE, OF COURSE.
MY SECOND FAVORITE PASTIME **AFTER** BLADE-COLLECTING.
LET'S CHECK OROCHIMARU'S HIDEOUT FIRST!

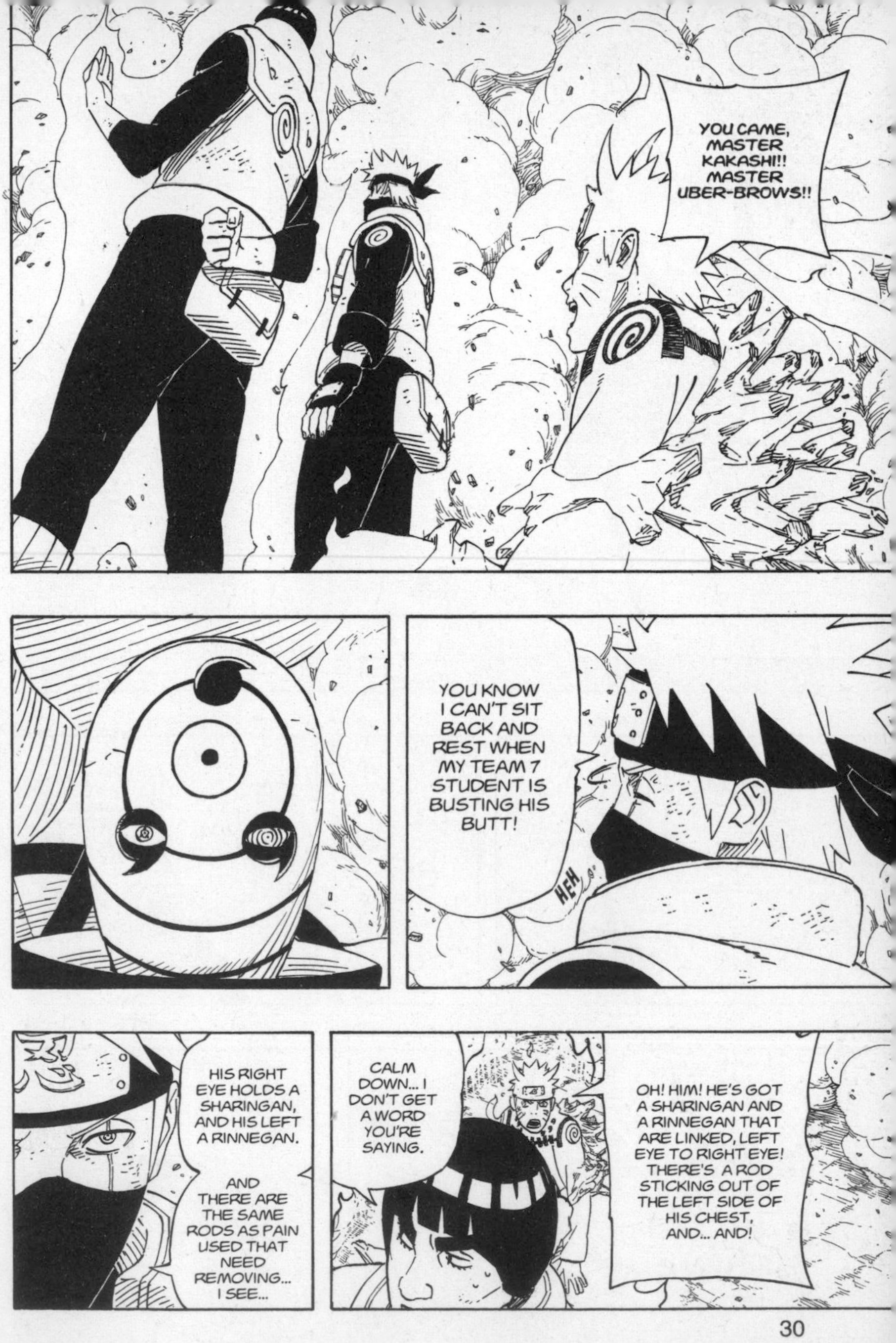
YOU CAME, MASTER KAKASHI!! MASTER UBER-BROWS!!
YOU KNOW I CAN'T SIT BACK AND REST WHEN MY TEAM 7 STUDENT IS BUSTING HIS BUTT!
HEH
OH! HIM! HE'S GOT A SHARINGAN AND A RINNEGAN THAT ARE LINKED, LEFT EYE TO RIGHT EYE! THERE'S A ROD STICKING OUT OF THE LEFT SIDE OF HIS CHEST, AND... AND!
CALM DOWN... I DON'T GET A WORD YOU'RE SAYING.
HIS RIGHT EYE HOLDS A SHARINGAN, AND HIS LEFT A RINNEGAN.
AND THERE ARE THE SAME RODS AS PAIN USED THAT NEED REMOVING... I SEE...

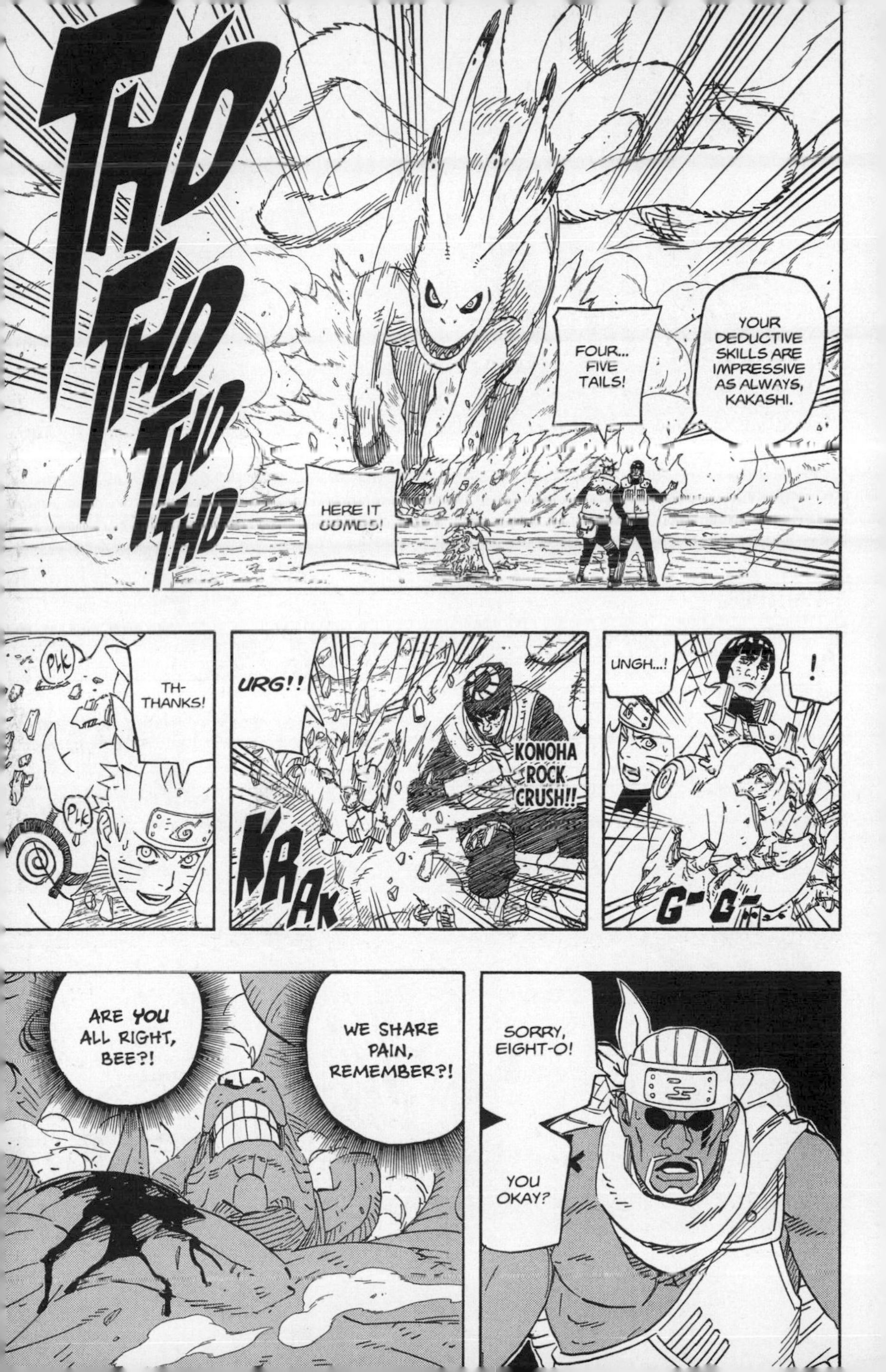
YOUR DEDUCTIVE SKILLS ARE IMPRESSIVE AS ALWAYS, KAKASHI.
FOUR... FIVE TAILS!
HERE IT COMES!
THD THD THD THD
!
UNGH...!
G-G-
URG!!
KONOHA ROCK CRUSH!!
KRAK
TH-THANKS!
PLK
PLK
SORRY, EIGHT-O!
YOU OKAY?
WE SHARE PAIN, REMEMBER?!
ARE YOU ALL RIGHT, BEE?!

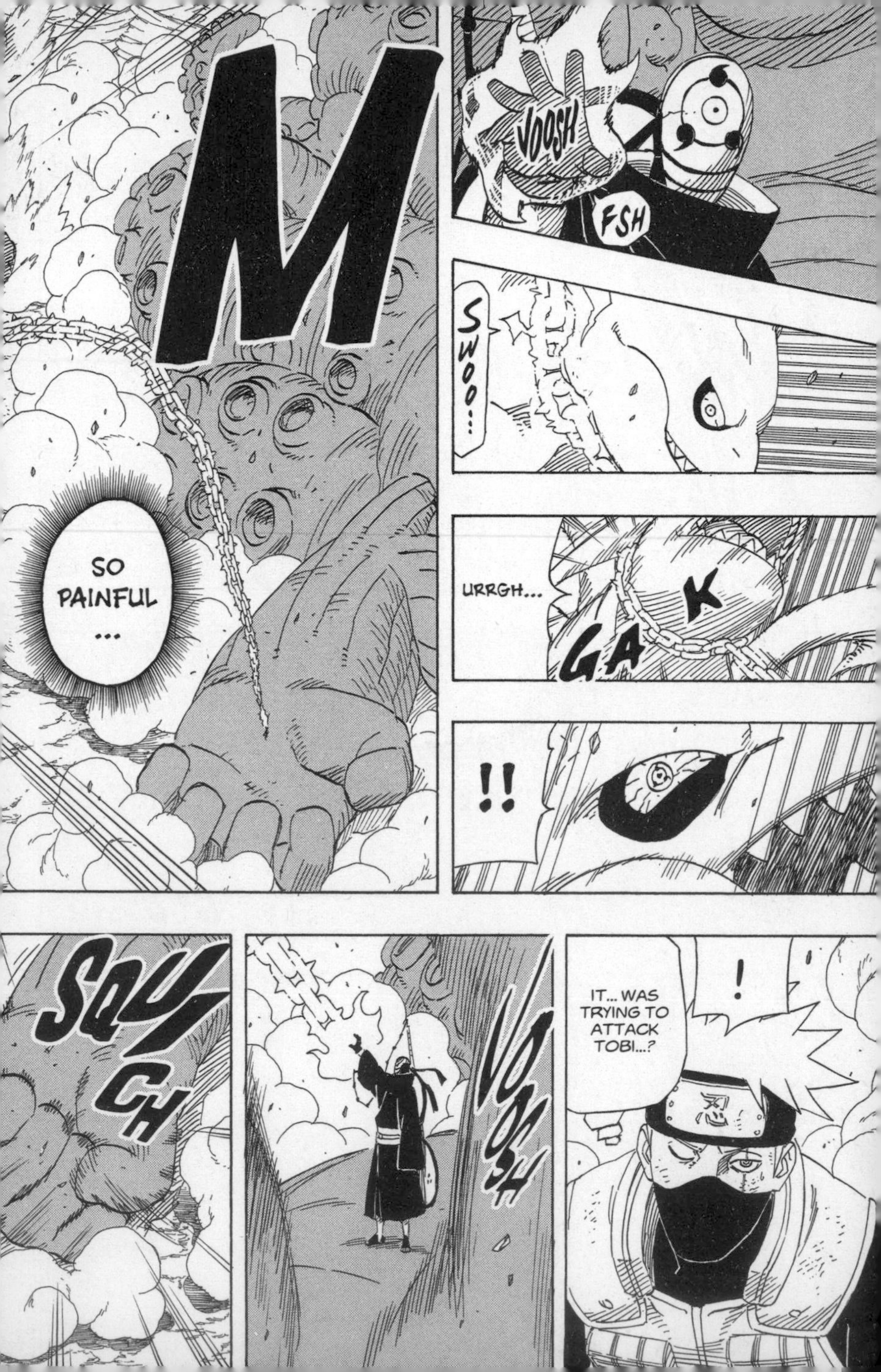
VOOSH
FSH
SWOOO...
URRGH...
GAK
!!
M
SO PAINFUL ...
!
IT... WAS TRYING TO ATTACK TOBI...?
VOOSH
SQUCH

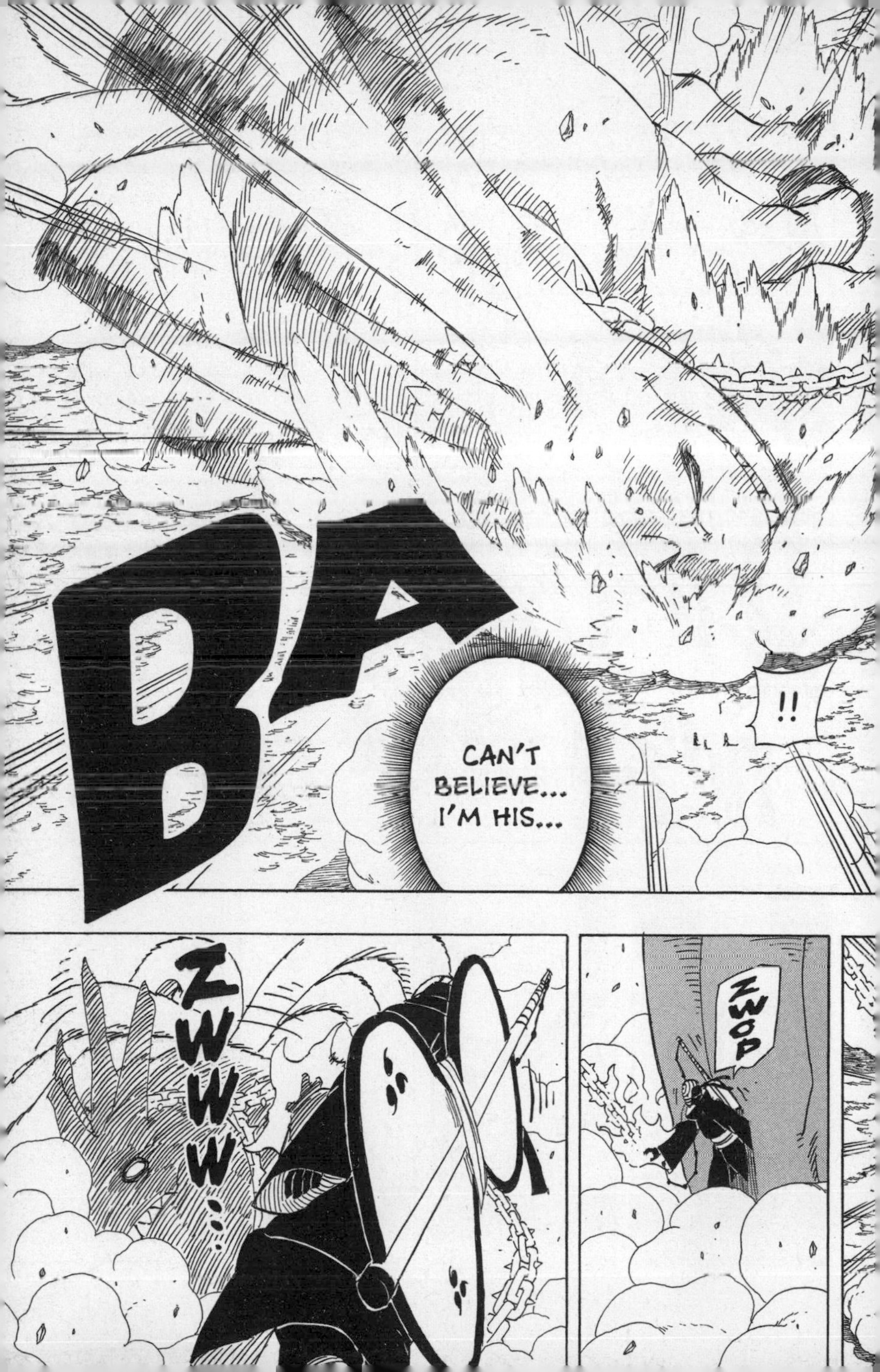
!!
CAN'T BELIEVE... I'M HIS...
BA
ZWOP
ZWWWW..

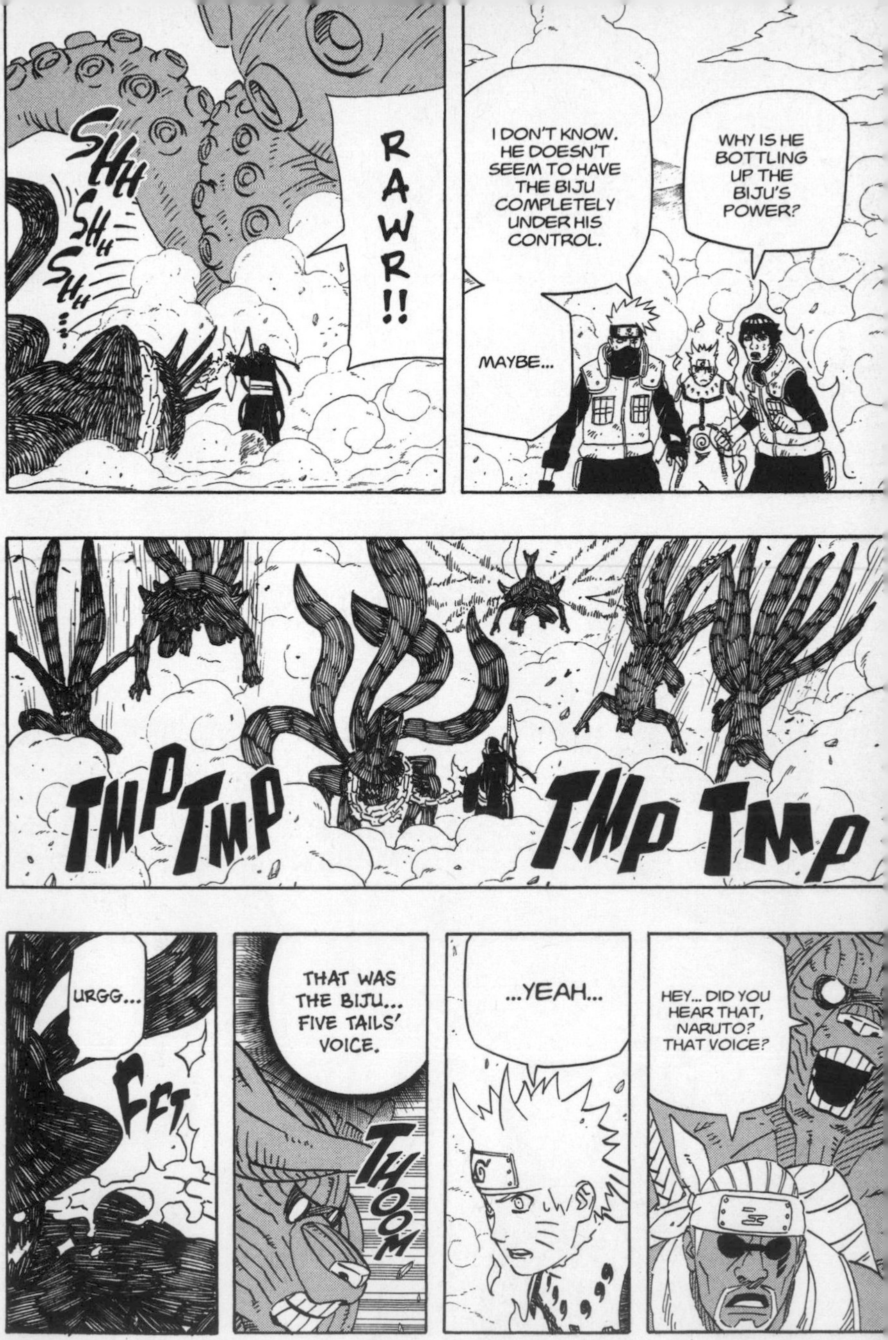
WHY IS HE BOTTLING UP THE BIJU'S POWER?
I DON'T KNOW. HE DOESN'T SEEM TO HAVE THE BIJU COMPLETELY UNDER HIS CONTROL.
MAYBE...
RAWR!!
SHH SHH SHH
TMP TMP
TMP TMP
HEY... DID YOU HEAR THAT, NARUTO? THAT VOICE?
...YEAH...
THAT WAS THE BIJU... FIVE TAILS' VOICE.
THOOM
URGG...
FFT

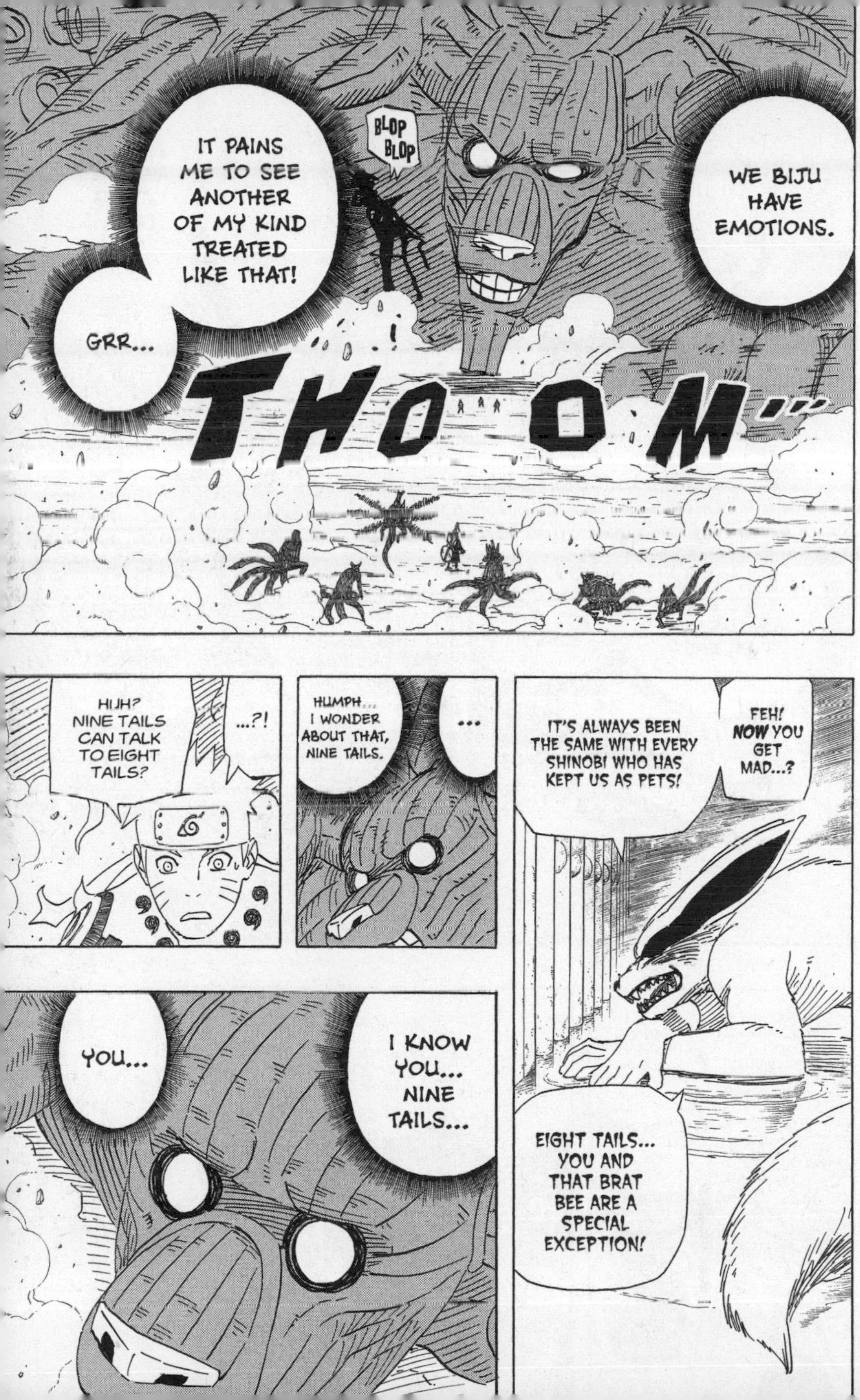
WE BIJU HAVE EMOTIONS.
BLOP BLOP
IT PAINS ME TO SEE ANOTHER OF MY KIND TREATED LIKE THAT!
GRR...
THOOM
FEH! **NOW** YOU GET MAD...?
IT'S ALWAYS BEEN THE SAME WITH EVERY SHINOBI WHO HAS KEPT US AS PETS!
EIGHT TAILS... YOU AND THAT BRAT BEE ARE A SPECIAL EXCEPTION!
...
HUMPH... I WONDER ABOUT THAT, NINE TAILS.
...?!
HUH? NINE TAILS CAN TALK TO EIGHT TAILS?
I KNOW YOU... NINE TAILS...
YOU...

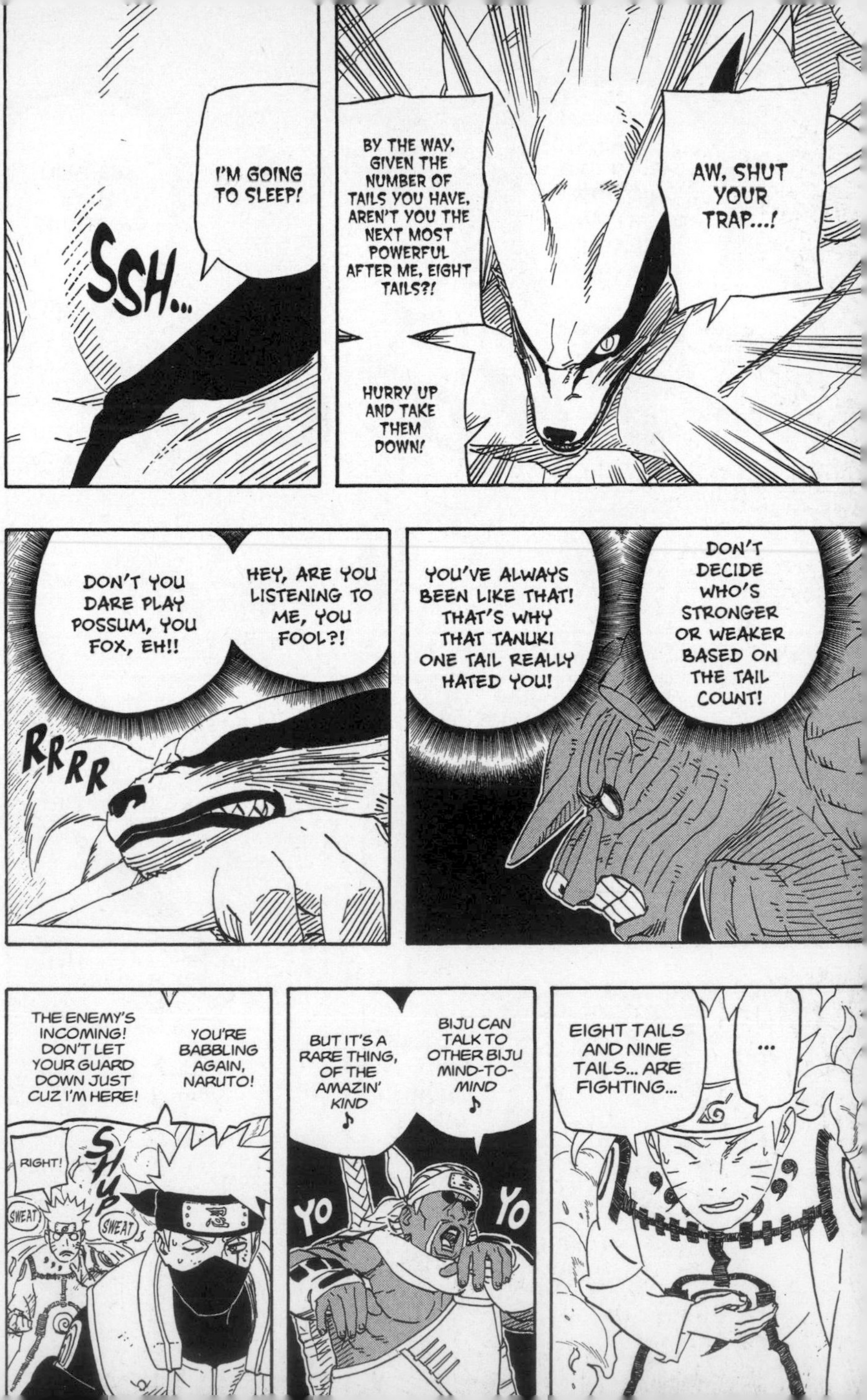
AW, SHUT YOUR TRAP...!
BY THE WAY, GIVEN THE NUMBER OF TAILS YOU HAVE, AREN'T YOU THE NEXT MOST POWERFUL AFTER ME, EIGHT TAILS?!
HURRY UP AND TAKE THEM DOWN!
I'M GOING TO SLEEP!
SSH...
DON'T DECIDE WHO'S STRONGER OR WEAKER BASED ON THE TAIL COUNT!
YOU'VE ALWAYS BEEN LIKE THAT! THAT'S WHY THAT TANUKI ONE TAIL REALLY HATED YOU!
HEY, ARE YOU LISTENING TO ME, YOU FOOL?!
DON'T YOU DARE PLAY POSSUM, YOU FOX, EH!!
RRRR
...
EIGHT TAILS AND NINE TAILS... ARE FIGHTING...
BIJU CAN TALK TO OTHER BIJU MIND-TO-MIND ♪
BUT IT'S A RARE THING, OF THE AMAZIN' KIND ♪
YO
YO
YOU'RE BABBLING AGAIN, NARUTO!
THE ENEMY'S INCOMING! DON'T LET YOUR GUARD DOWN JUST CUZ I'M HERE!
SHUP
RIGHT!
SWEAT
SWEAT

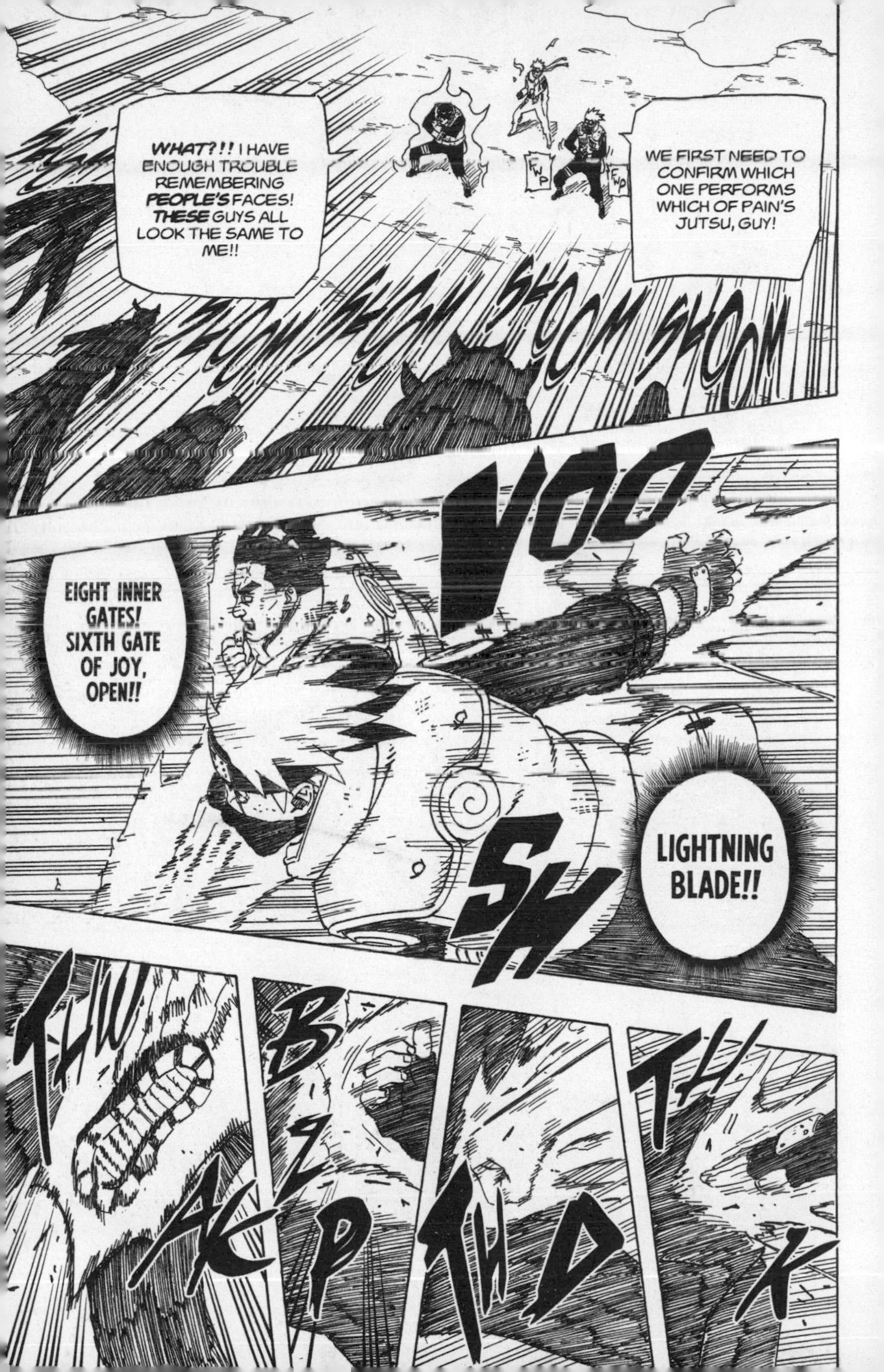
WE FIRST NEED TO CONFIRM WHICH ONE PERFORMS WHICH OF PAIN'S JUTSU, GUY!
FWP
FWP
WHAT?!! I HAVE ENOUGH TROUBLE REMEMBERING PEOPLE'S FACES! THESE GUYS ALL LOOK THE SAME TO ME!!
SHOOM SHOOM
VOO
EIGHT INNER GATES! SIXTH GATE OF JOY, OPEN!!
SH
LIGHTNING BLADE!!
THWAK

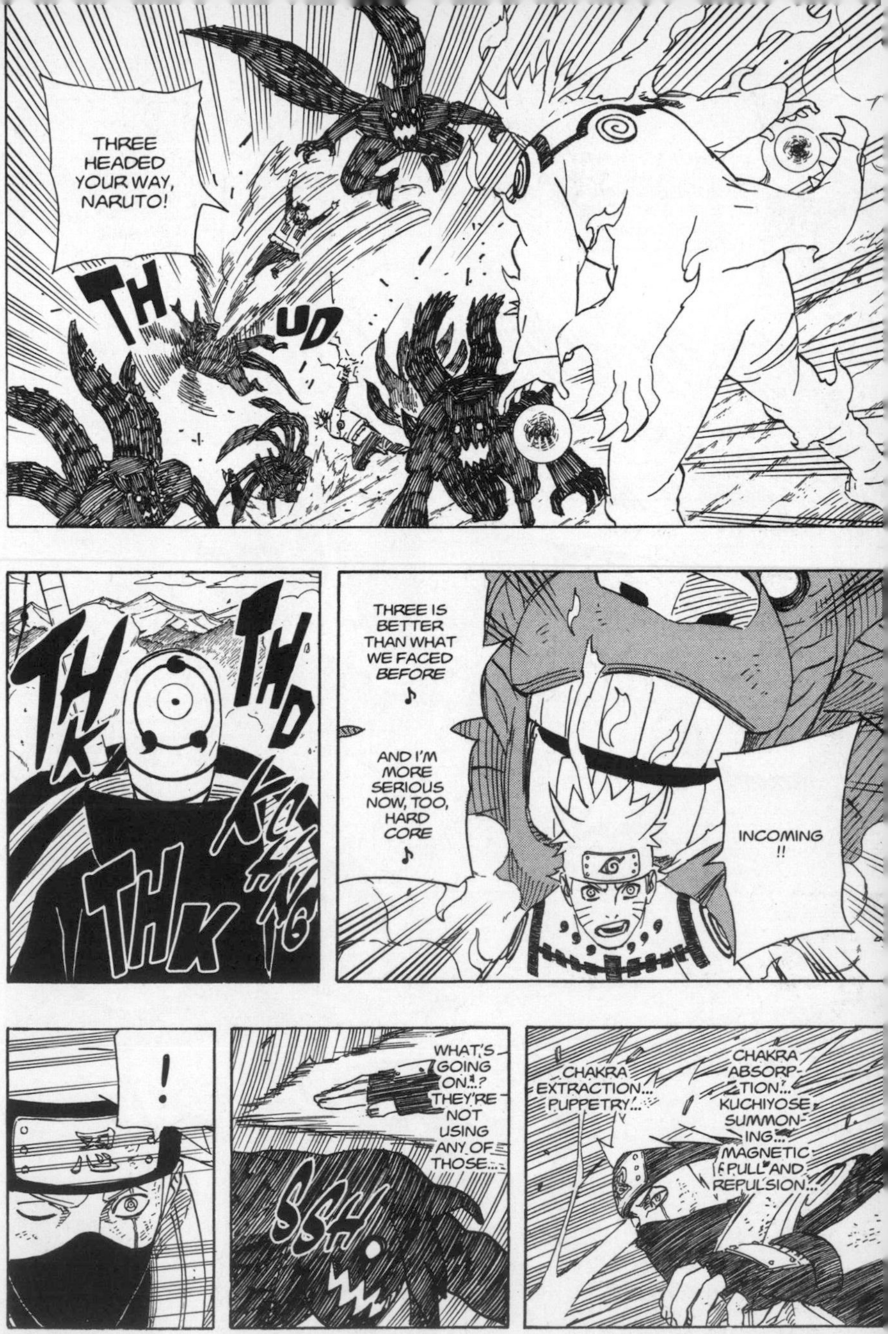
THREE HEADED YOUR WAY, NARUTO!
THUD
THREE IS BETTER THAN WHAT WE FACED BEFORE ♪
AND I'M MORE SERIOUS NOW, TOO, HARD CORE ♪
INCOMING !!
THK
THD
KCHNG
THK
CHAKRA ABSORPTION... KUCHIYOSE SUMMONING... MAGNETIC PULL AND REPULSION...
CHAKRA EXTRACTION... PUPPETRY...
WHAT'S GOING ON...? THEY'RE NOT USING ANY OF THOSE...
SSH
!

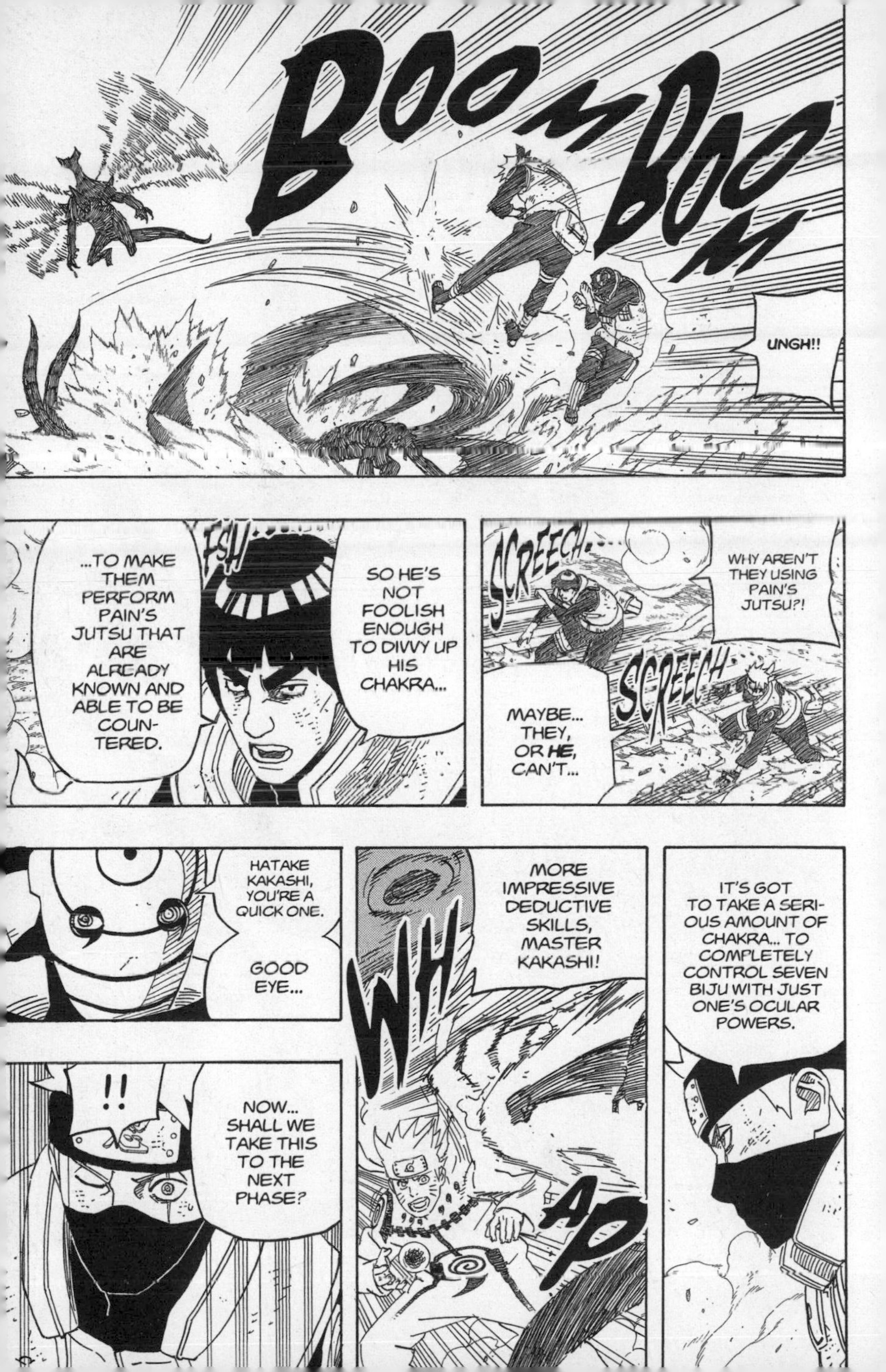
BOOM BOOM
UNGH!!
WHY AREN'T THEY USING PAIN'S JUTSU?!
SCREECH
SCREECH
MAYBE... THEY, OR **HE**, CAN'T...
FSH
SO HE'S NOT FOOLISH ENOUGH TO DIVVY UP HIS CHAKRA...
...TO MAKE THEM PERFORM PAIN'S JUTSU THAT ARE ALREADY KNOWN AND ABLE TO BE COUN-TERED.
IT'S GOT TO TAKE A SERI-OUS AMOUNT OF CHAKRA... TO COMPLETELY CONTROL SEVEN BIJU WITH JUST ONE'S OCULAR POWERS.
MORE IMPRESSIVE DEDUCTIVE SKILLS, MASTER KAKASHI!
WHAP
HATAKE KAKASHI, YOU'RE A QUICK ONE.
GOOD EYE...
!!
NOW... SHALL WE TAKE THIS TO THE NEXT PHASE?

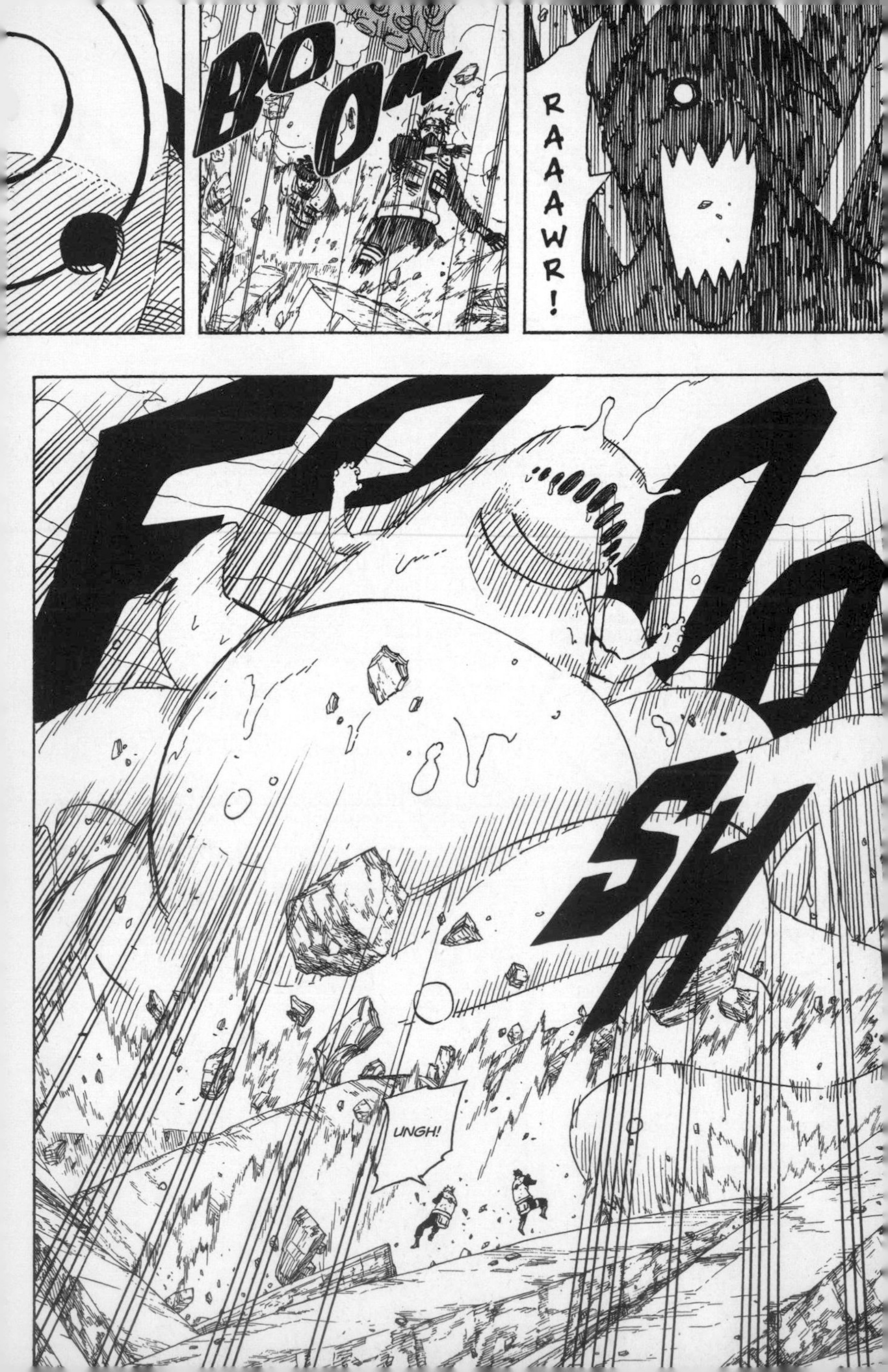
RAAAAWR!
BOOM
FOOOSH
UNGH!

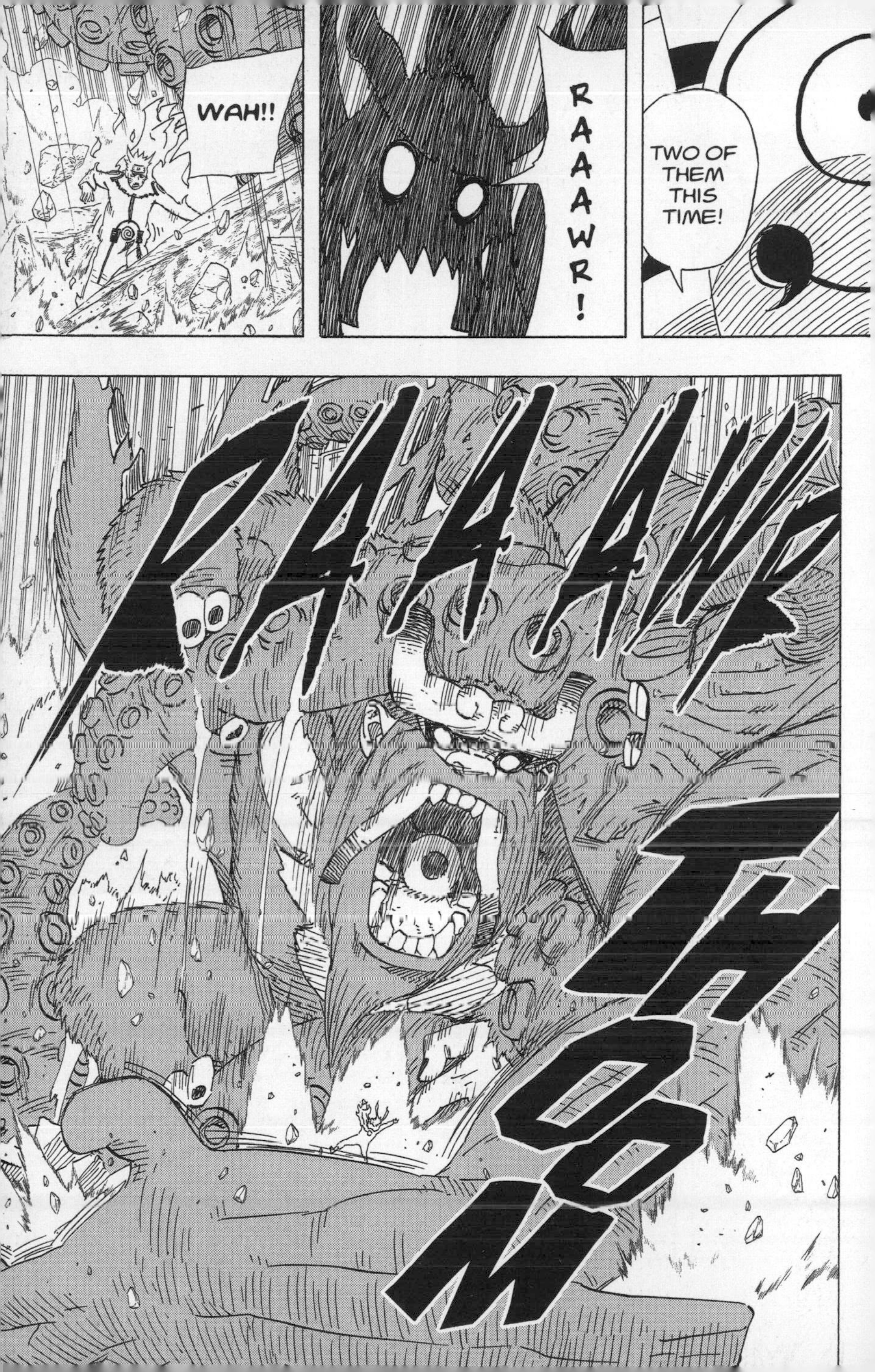
TWO OF THEM THIS TIME!
RAAAAWR!
WAH!!
RAAAAW
THOOM

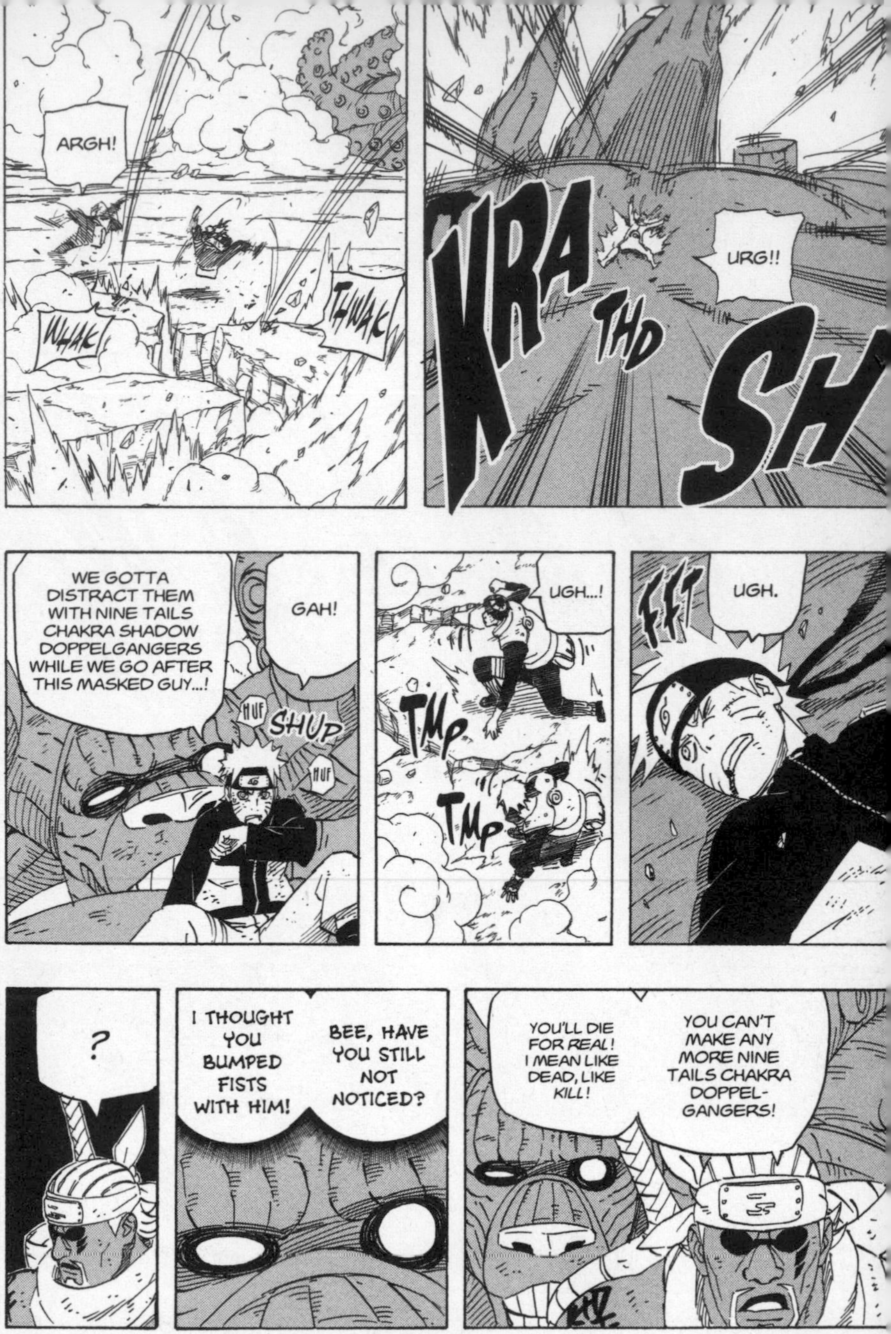
URG!!
KRA
THD
SH
ARGH!
THWAK
WHAK
UGH.
FFT
UGH...!
TMP
TMP
GAH!
WE GOTTA DISTRACT THEM WITH NINE TAILS CHAKRA SHADOW DOPPELGANGERS WHILE WE GO AFTER THIS MASKED GUY...!
HUF
SHUP
HUF
YOU CAN'T MAKE ANY MORE NINE TAILS CHAKRA DOPPEL-GANGERS!
YOU'LL DIE FOR REAL! I MEAN LIKE DEAD, LIKE KILL!
BEE, HAVE YOU STILL NOT NOTICED?
I THOUGHT YOU BUMPED FISTS WITH HIM!
?

READ THIS WAY

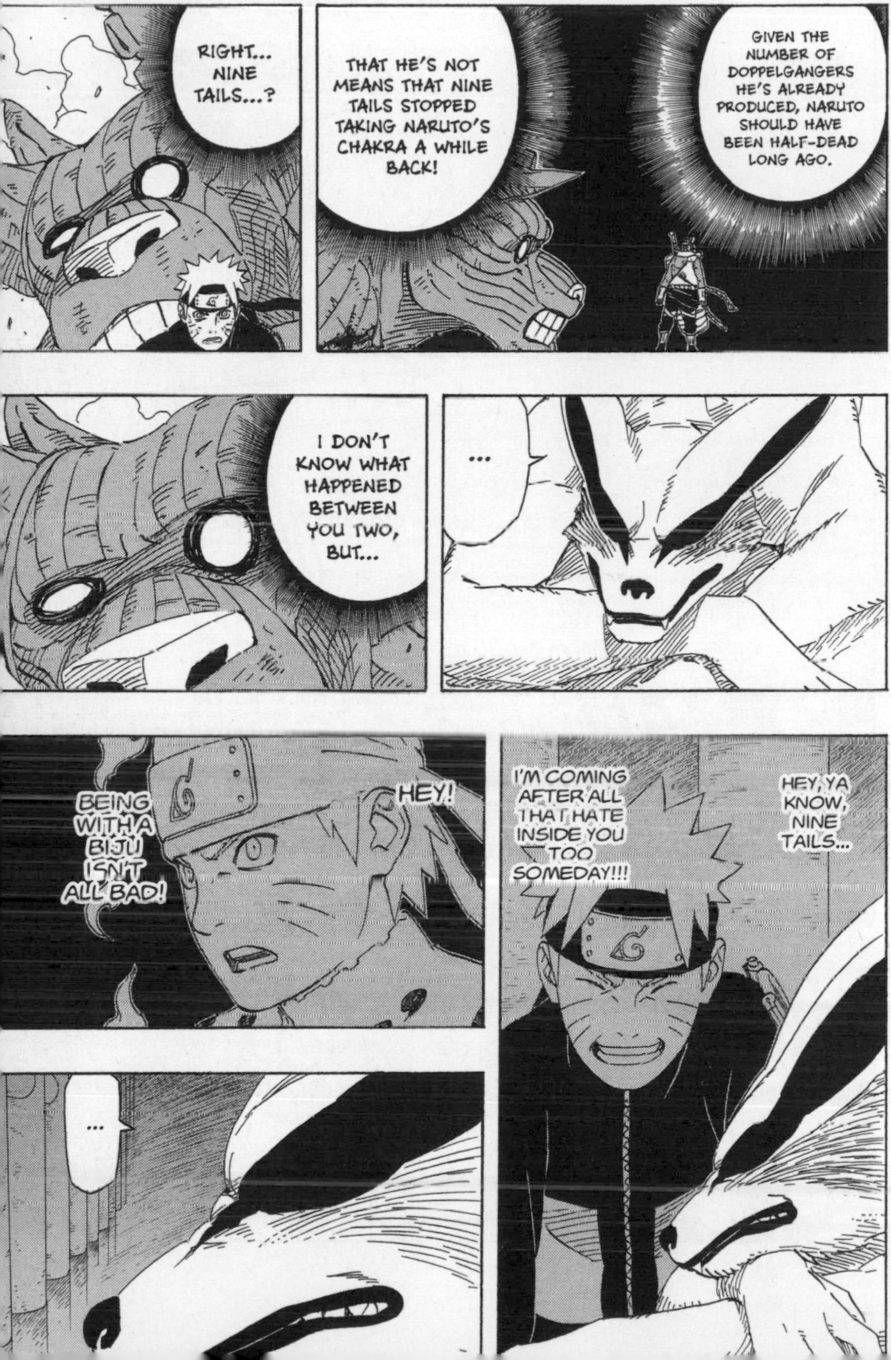
GIVEN THE NUMBER OF DOPPELGANGERS HE'S ALREADY PRODUCED, NARUTO SHOULD HAVE BEEN HALF-DEAD LONG AGO.
THAT HE'S NOT MEANS THAT NINE TAILS STOPPED TAKING NARUTO'S CHAKRA A WHILE BACK!
RIGHT... NINE TAILS...?
...
I DON'T KNOW WHAT HAPPENED BETWEEN YOU TWO, BUT...
HEY, YA KNOW, NINE TAILS...
I'M COMING AFTER ALL THAT HATE INSIDE YOU TOO SOMEDAY!!!
HEY!
BEING WITH A BIJU ISN'T ALL BAD!
...

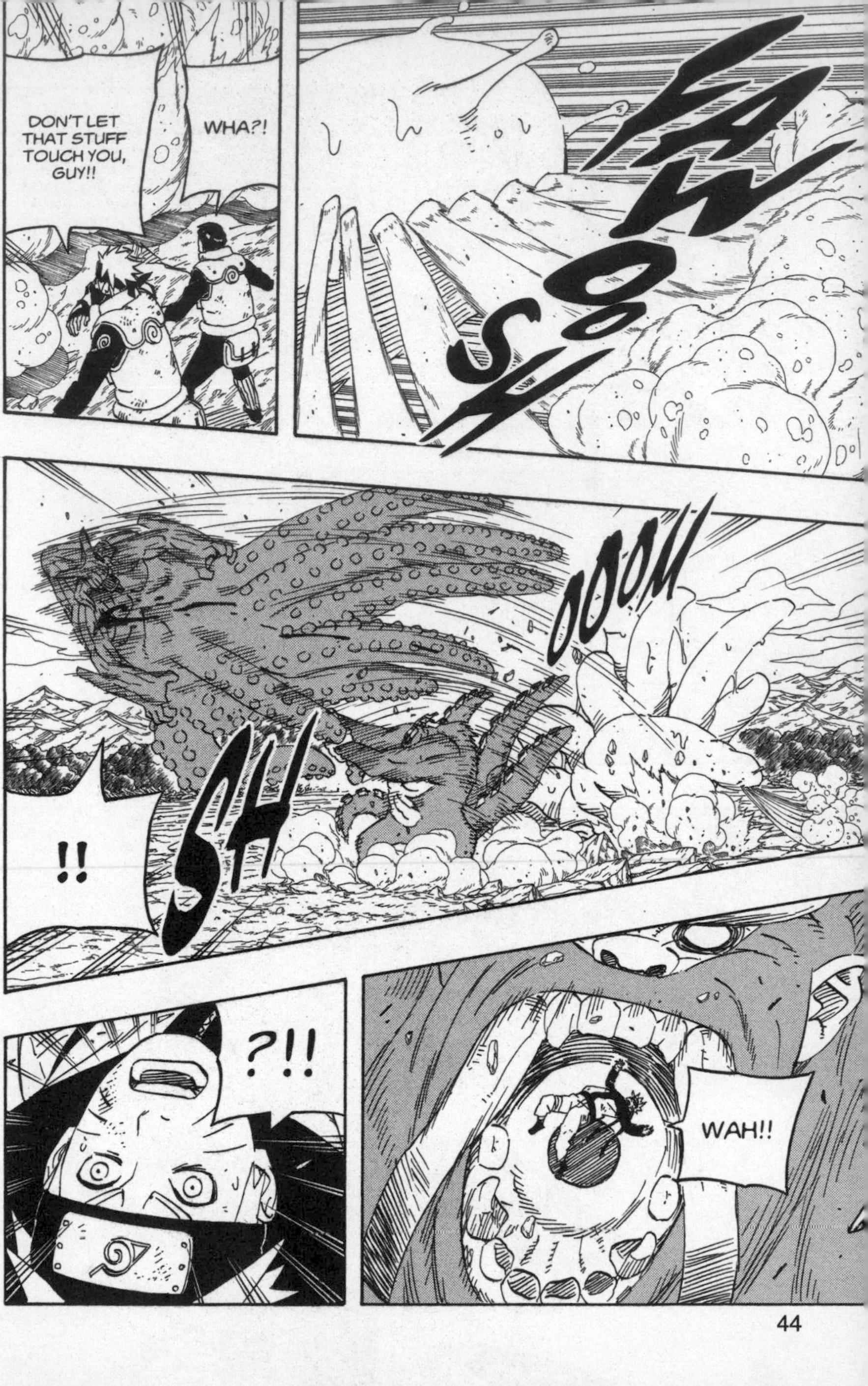
FWOOSH
WHA?!
DON'T LET THAT STUFF TOUCH YOU, GUY!!
OOOM
SH
!!
WAH!!
?!!

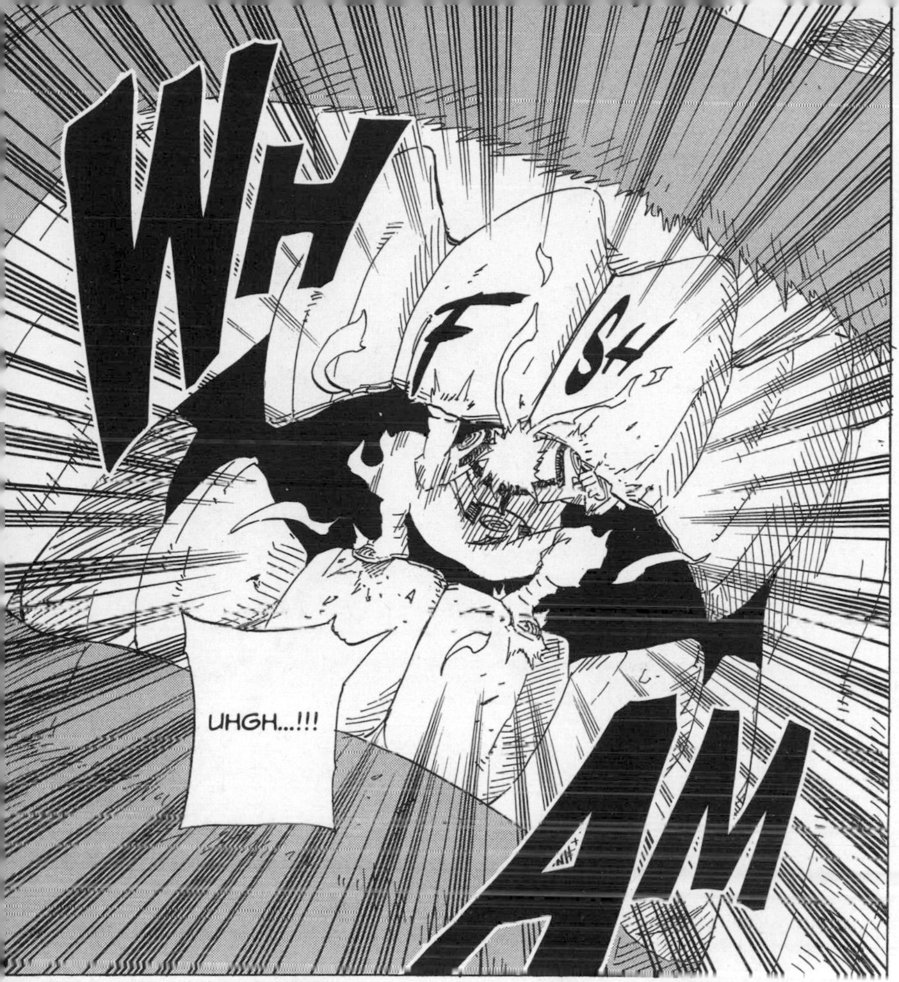
WHAM
FSH
UHGH...!!!

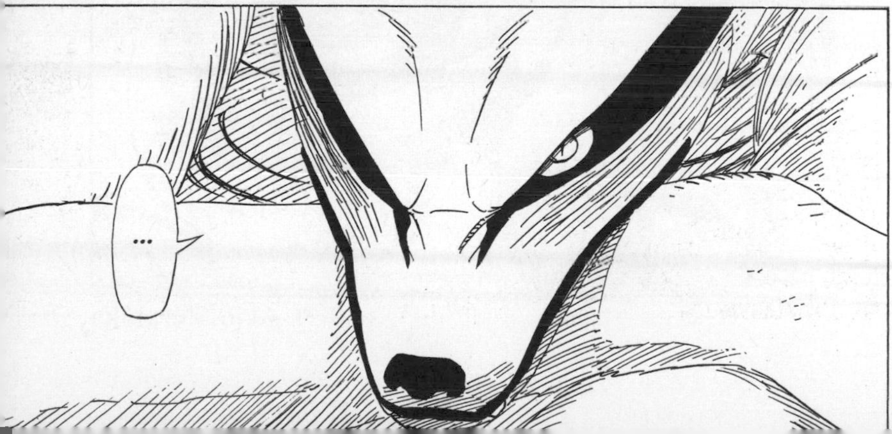
...

Illustration to Commemorate Reaching Volume 60 [3]

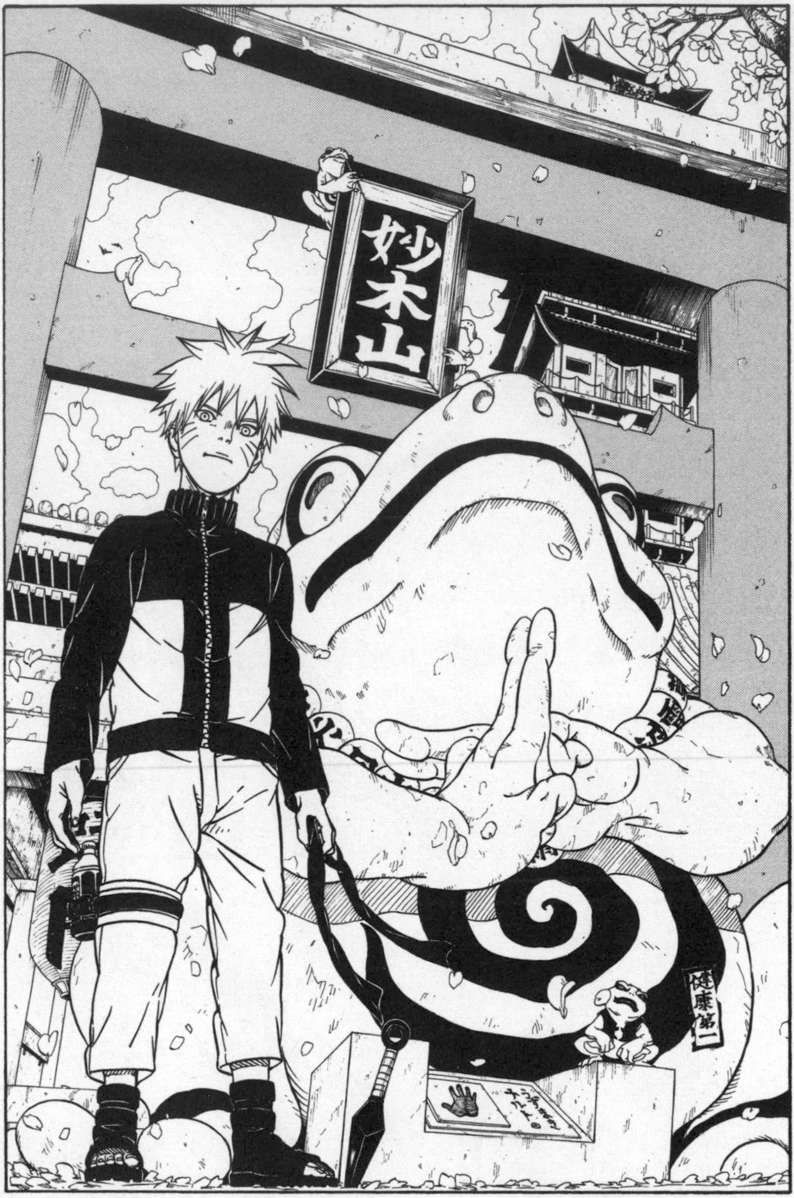
妙木山
健康第一

Akio Shirasaka

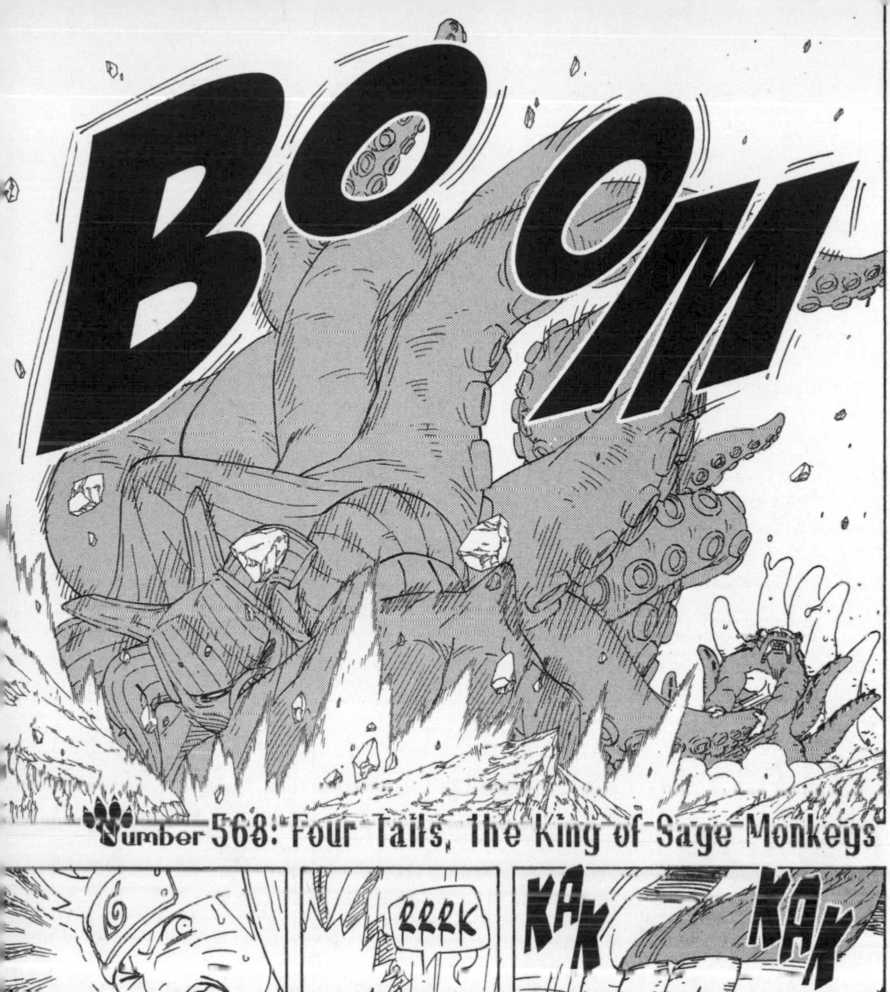
BOOM

Number 568: Four Tails, the King of Sage Monkeys

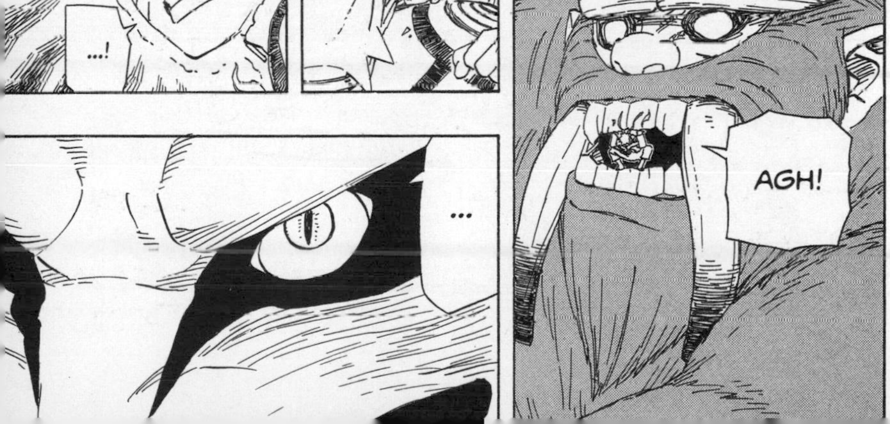
KAK KAK
AGH!
RRRK
...!
...

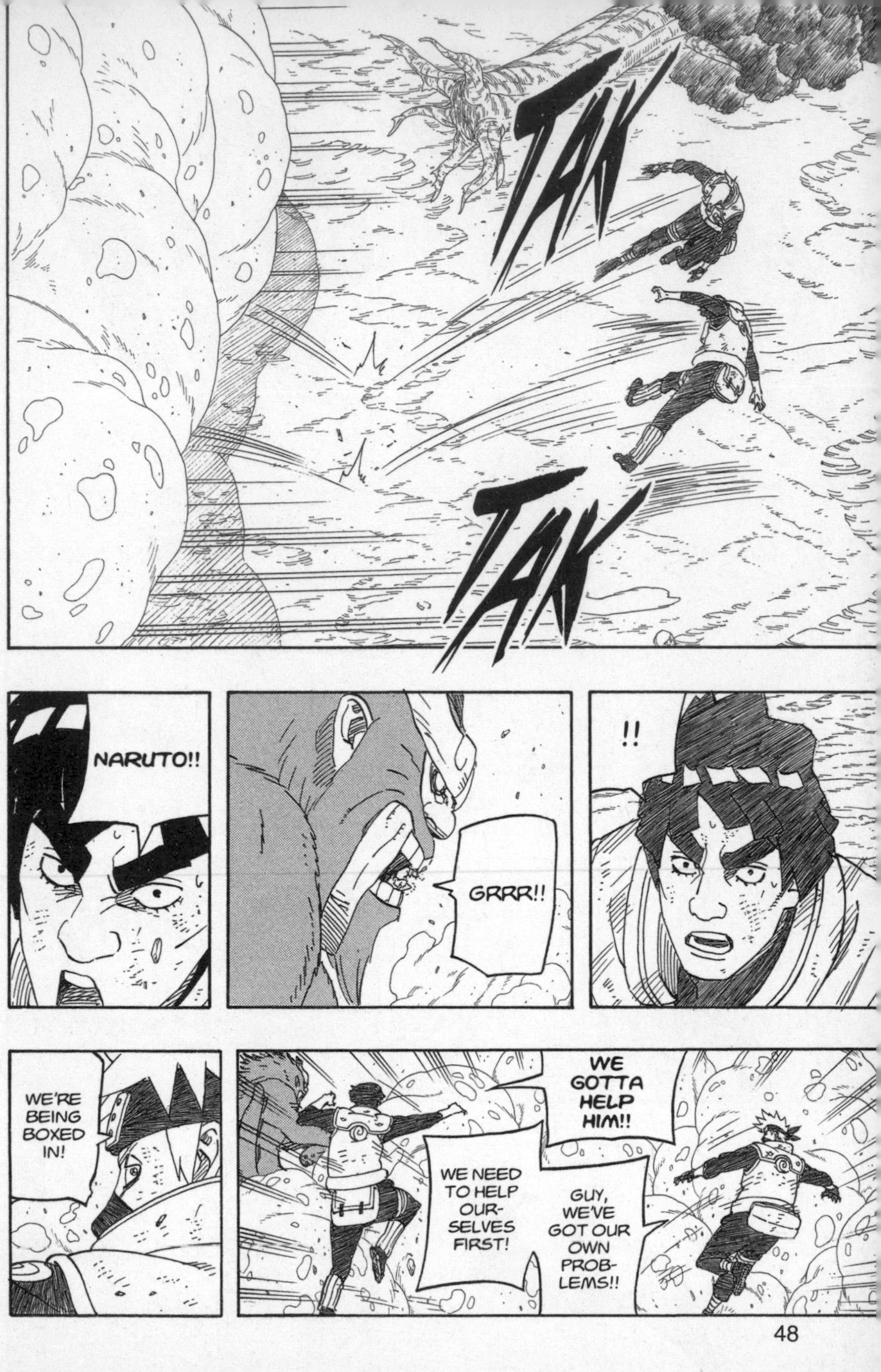
TAK
TAK
!!
GRRR!!
NARUTO!!
WE GOTTA HELP HIM!!
GUY, WE'VE GOT OUR OWN PROB-LEMS!!
WE NEED TO HELP OUR-SELVES FIRST!
WE'RE BEING BOXED IN!

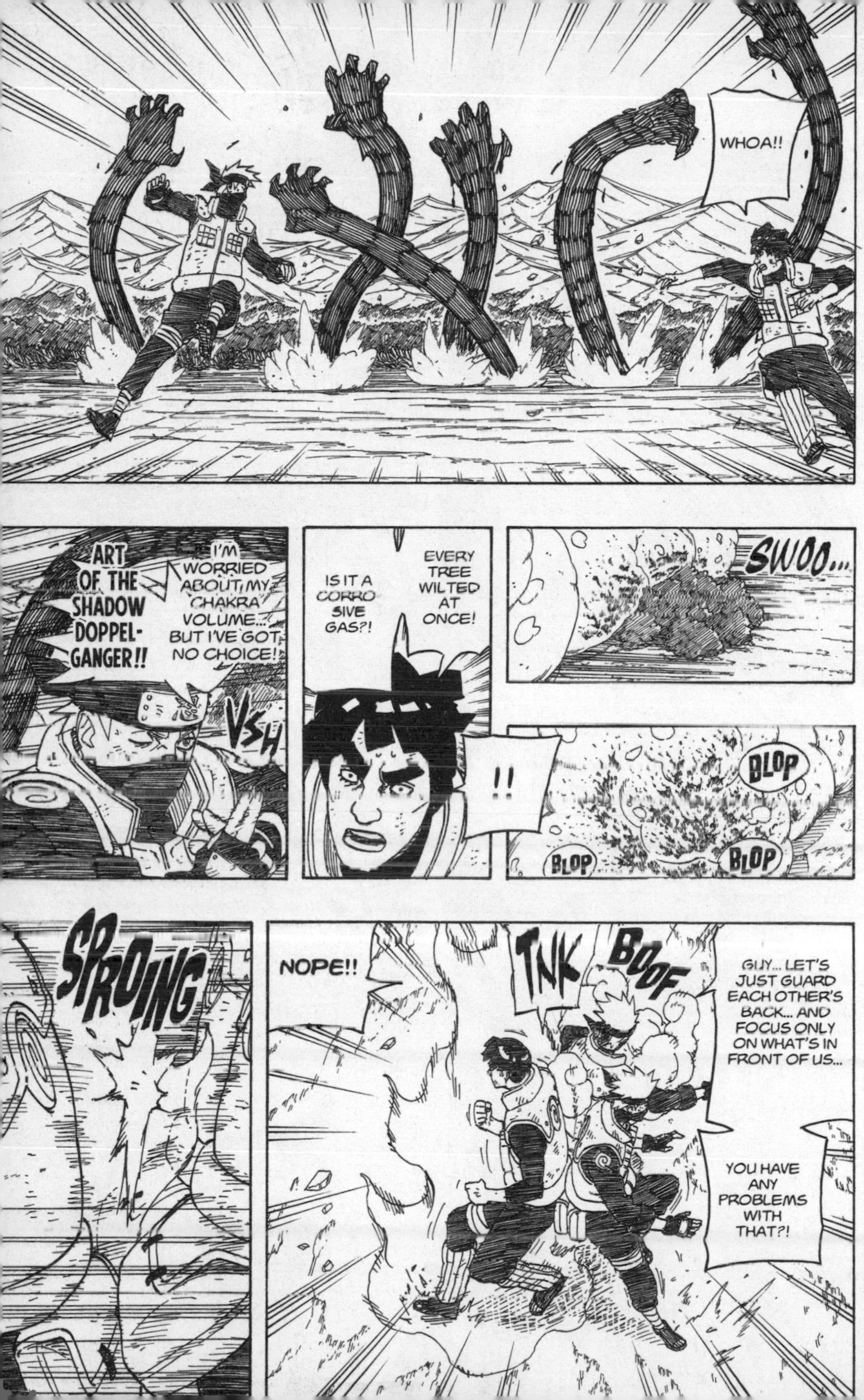
WHOA!!
SWOO...
BLOP
BLOP
BLOP
EVERY TREE WILTED AT ONCE!
IS IT A CORROSIVE GAS?!
!!
I'M WORRIED ABOUT MY CHAKRA VOLUME... BUT I'VE GOT NO CHOICE!
ART OF THE SHADOW DOPPELGANGER!!
VSH
GUY... LET'S JUST GUARD EACH OTHER'S BACK... AND FOCUS ONLY ON WHAT'S IN FRONT OF US...
BOOF
TNK
YOU HAVE ANY PROBLEMS WITH THAT?!
NOPE!!
SPROING

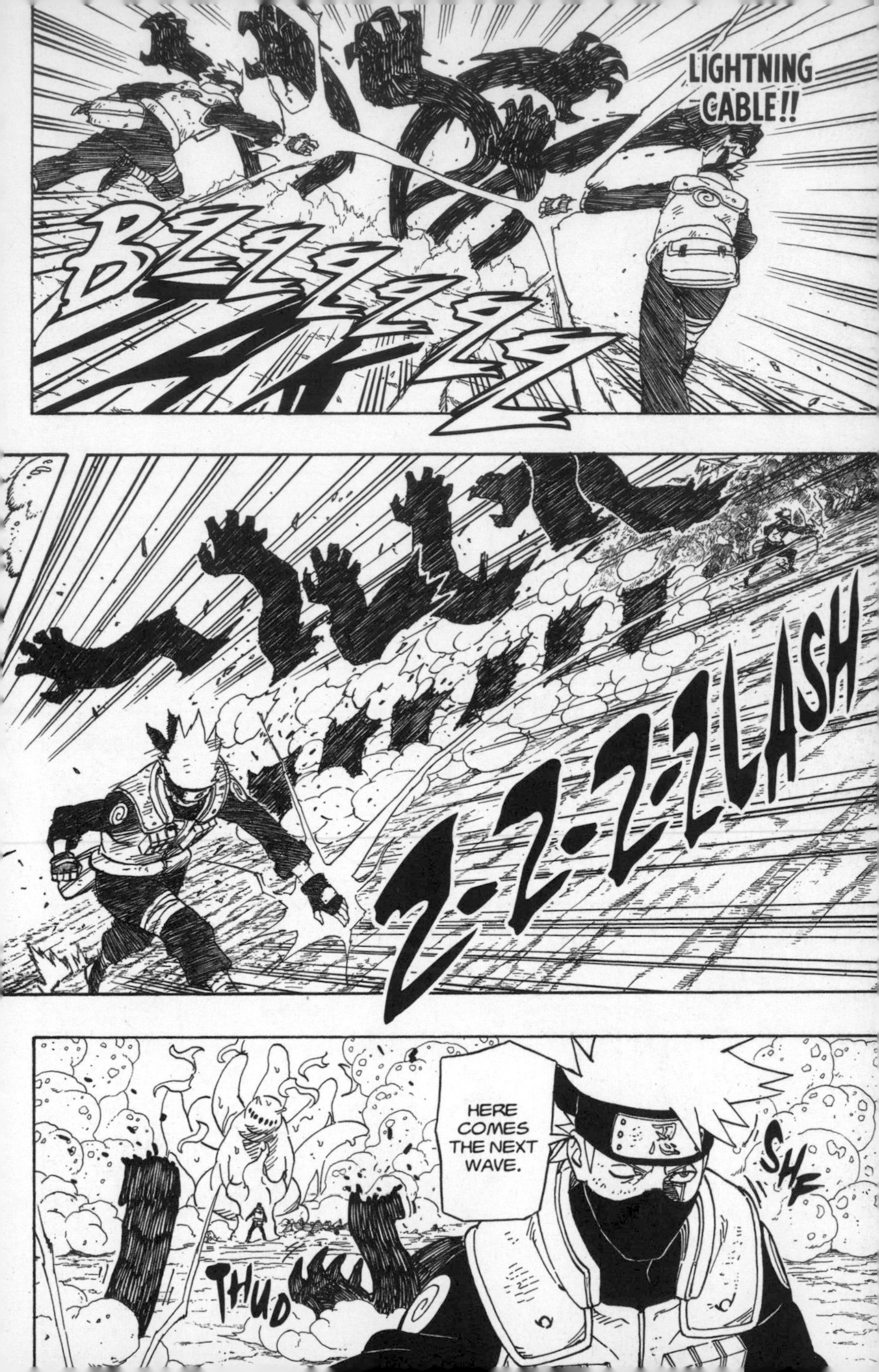
LIGHTNING CABLE!!
BZZZZZZZT
Z-Z-Z-ZZLASH
SHF
HERE COMES THE NEXT WAVE.
THUD

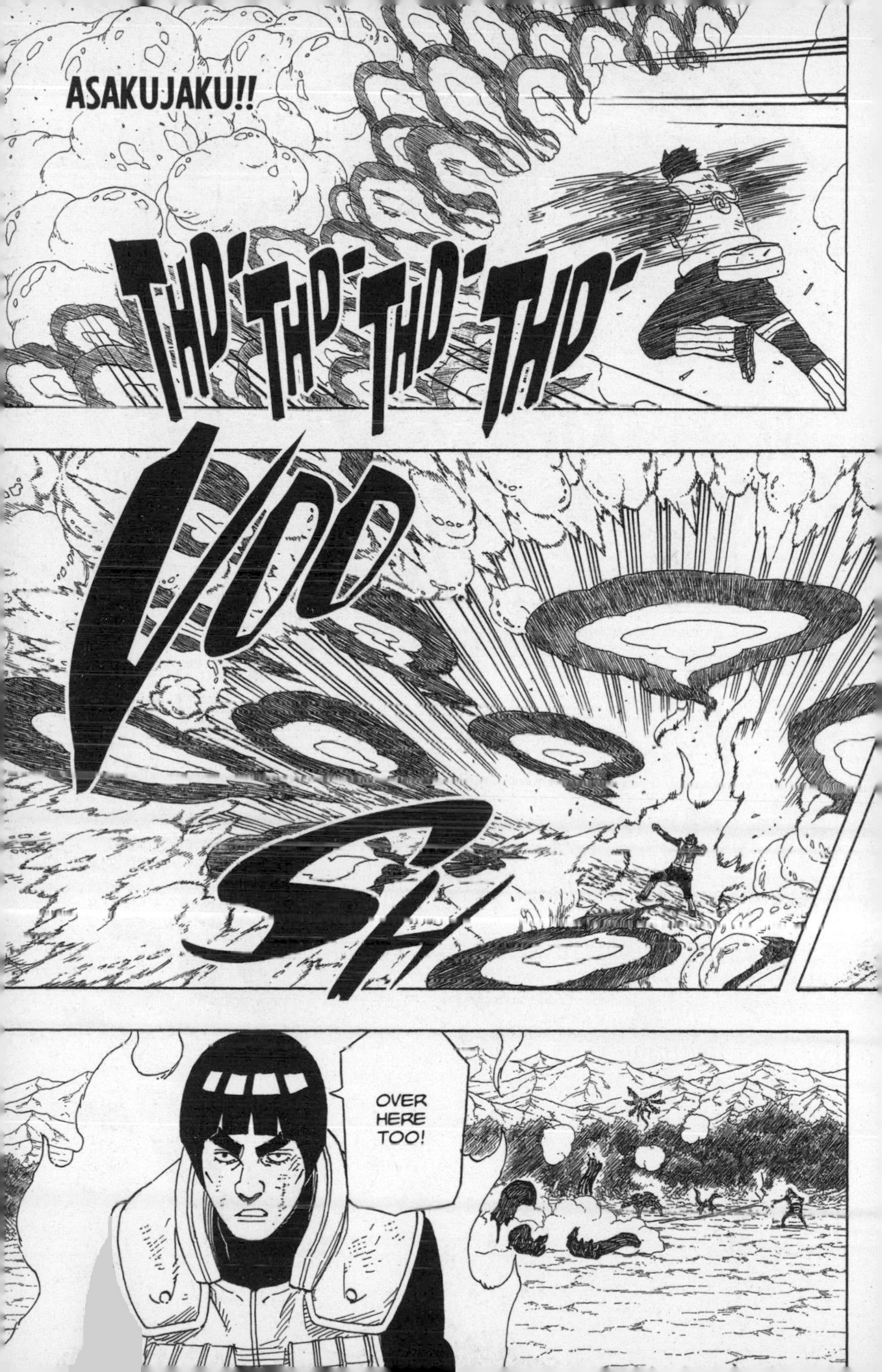
ASAKUJAKU!!
THD THD THD THD
VROOSH
OVER
HERE
TOO!

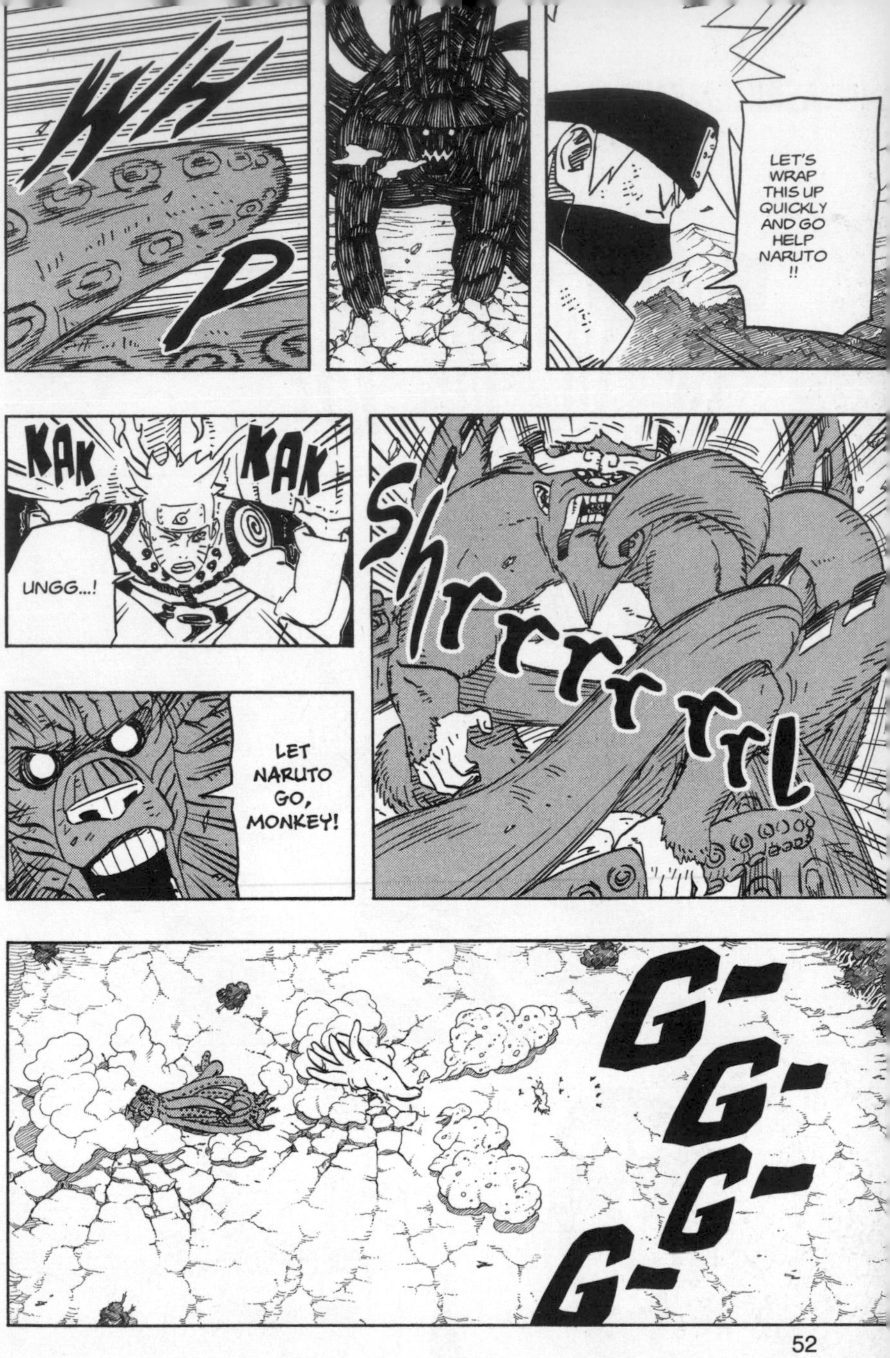
LET'S WRAP THIS UP QUICKLY AND GO HELP NARUTO !!
WHP
Shrrrrrrrl
KAK KAK
UNGG...!
LET NARUTO GO, MONKEY!
G-G-G-G-

READ THIS WAY

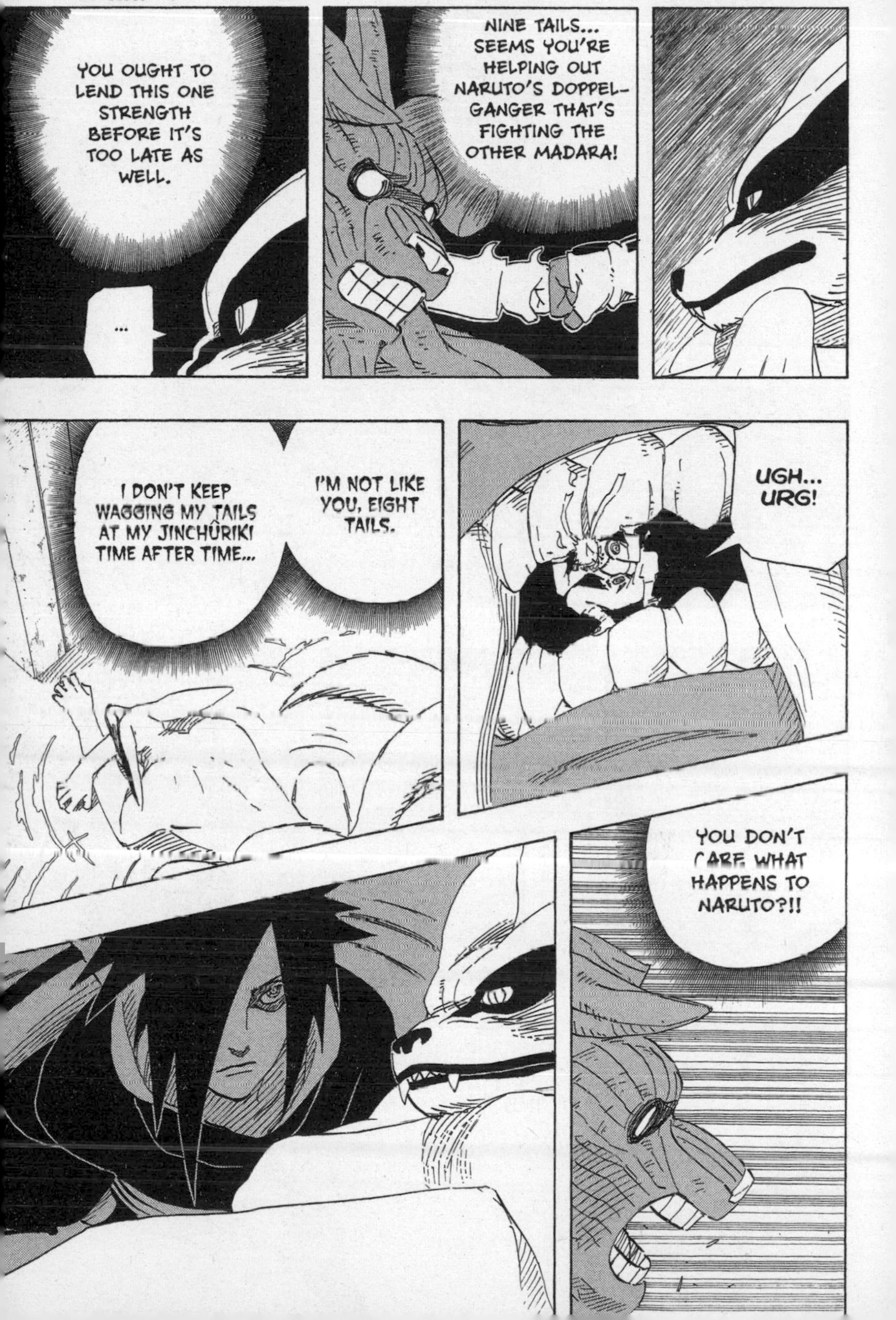
NINE TAILS... SEEMS YOU'RE HELPING OUT NARUTO'S DOPPEL-GANGER THAT'S FIGHTING THE OTHER MADARA!
YOU OUGHT TO LEND THIS ONE STRENGTH BEFORE IT'S TOO LATE AS WELL.
...
UGH... URG!
I'M NOT LIKE YOU, EIGHT TAILS.
I DON'T KEEP WAGGING MY TAILS AT MY JINCHÛRIKI TIME AFTER TIME...
YOU DON'T CARE WHAT HAPPENS TO NARUTO?!!

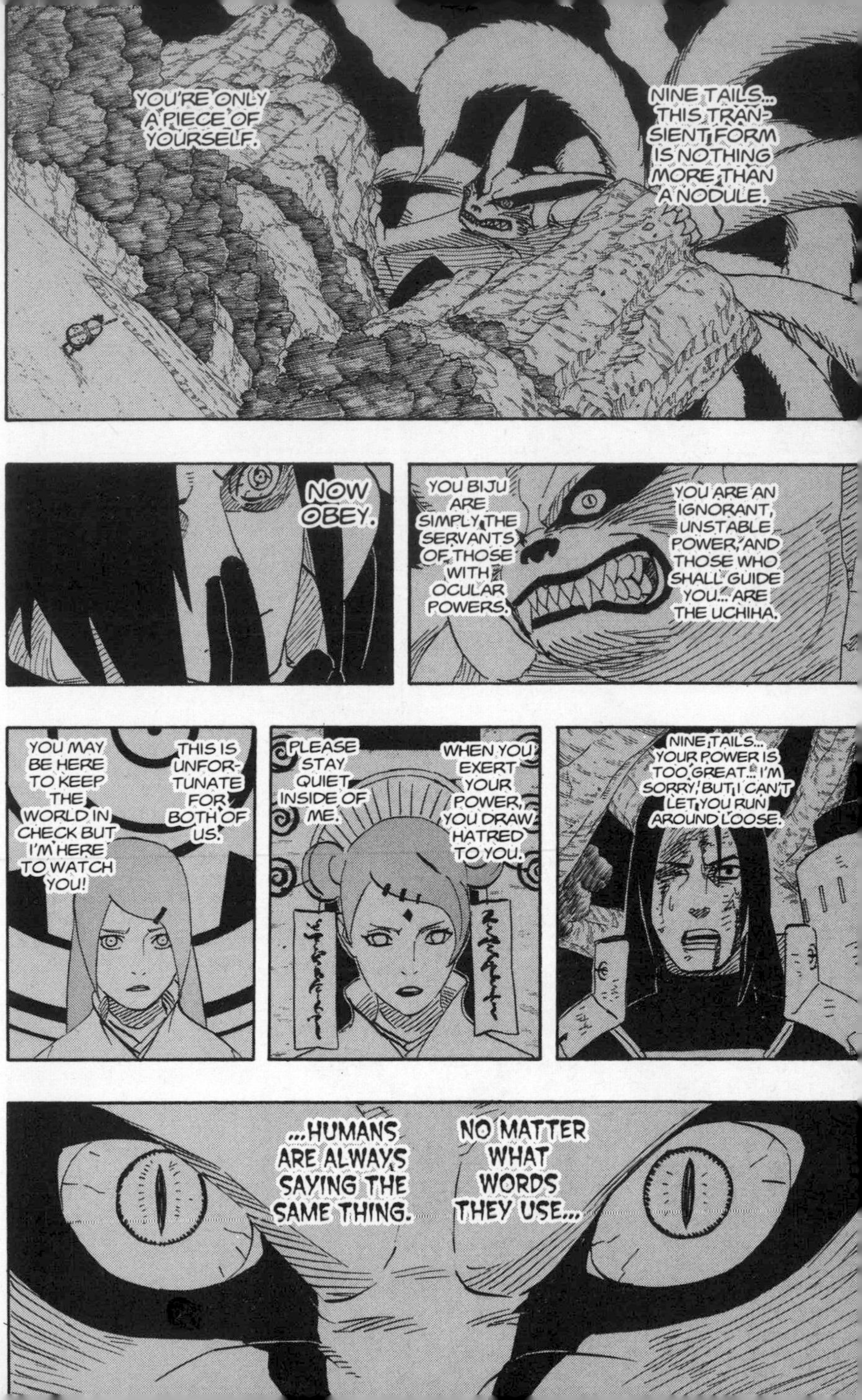
NINE TAILS... THIS TRANSIENT FORM IS NOTHING MORE THAN A NODULE.
YOU'RE ONLY A PIECE OF YOURSELF.
YOU ARE AN IGNORANT, UNSTABLE POWER, AND THOSE WHO SHALL GUIDE YOU... ARE THE UCHIHA.
YOU BIJU ARE SIMPLY THE SERVANTS OF THOSE WITH OCULAR POWERS.
NOW OBEY.
NINE TAILS... YOUR POWER IS TOO GREAT... I'M SORRY, BUT I CAN'T LET YOU RUN AROUND LOOSE.
WHEN YOU EXERT YOUR POWER, YOU DRAW HATRED TO YOU.
PLEASE STAY QUIET INSIDE OF ME.
THIS IS UNFORTUNATE FOR BOTH OF US.
YOU MAY BE HERE TO KEEP THE WORLD IN CHECK BUT I'M HERE TO WATCH YOU!
NO MATTER WHAT WORDS THEY USE...
...HUMANS ARE ALWAYS SAYING THE SAME THING.

READ THIS WAY

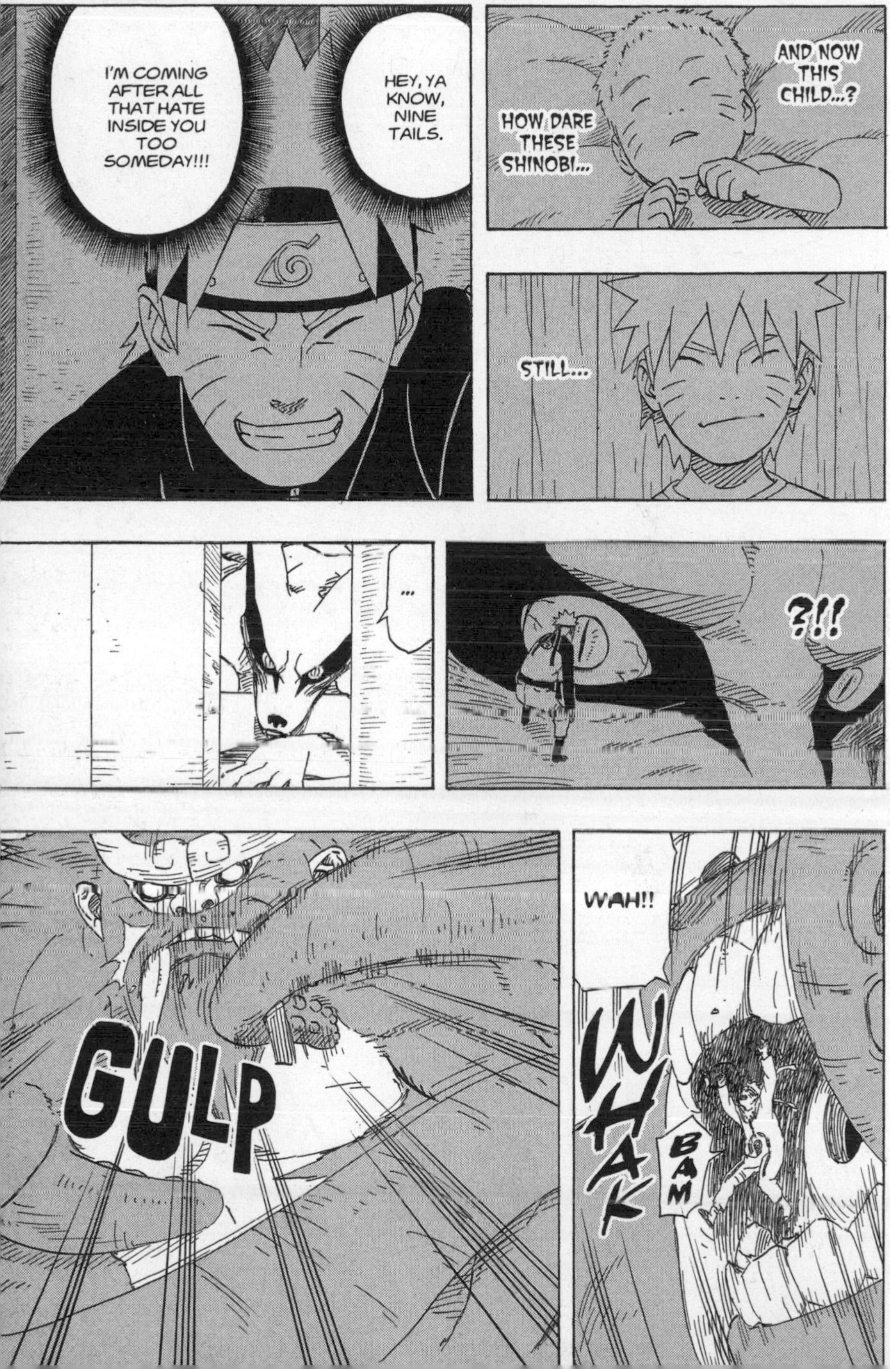

AND NOW THIS CHILD...?
HOW DARE THESE SHINOBI...
STILL...
HEY, YA KNOW, NINE TAILS.
I'M COMING AFTER ALL THAT HATE INSIDE YOU TOO SOMEDAY!!!
?!!
...
WAH!!
WHAK
BAM
GULP

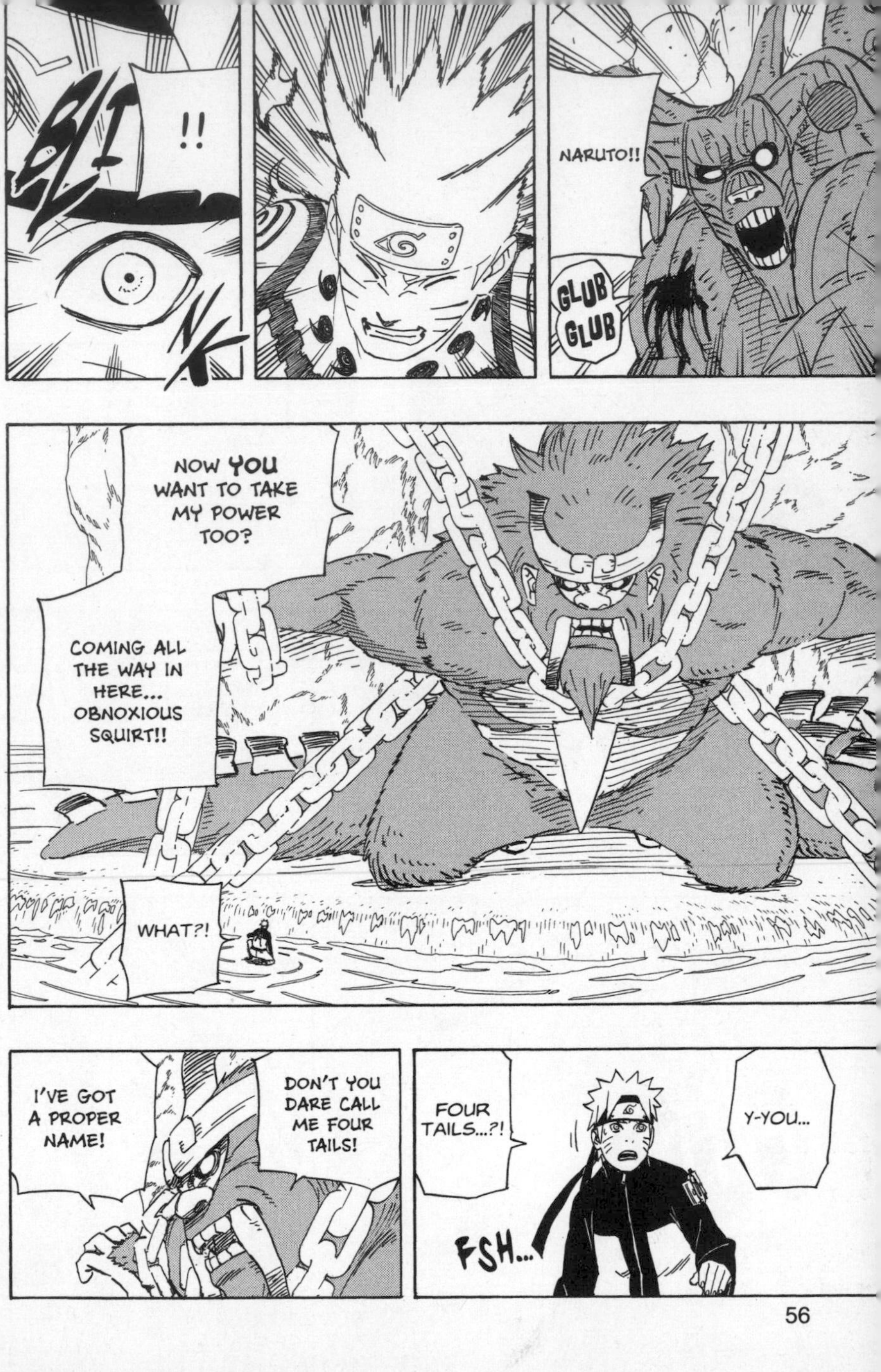
NARUTO!!
GLUB GLUB
!!
BLINK
NOW YOU WANT TO TAKE MY POWER TOO?
COMING ALL THE WAY IN HERE... OBNOXIOUS SQUIRT!!
WHAT?!
Y-YOU...
FOUR TAILS...?!
FSH...
DON'T YOU DARE CALL ME FOUR TAILS!
I'VE GOT A PROPER NAME!

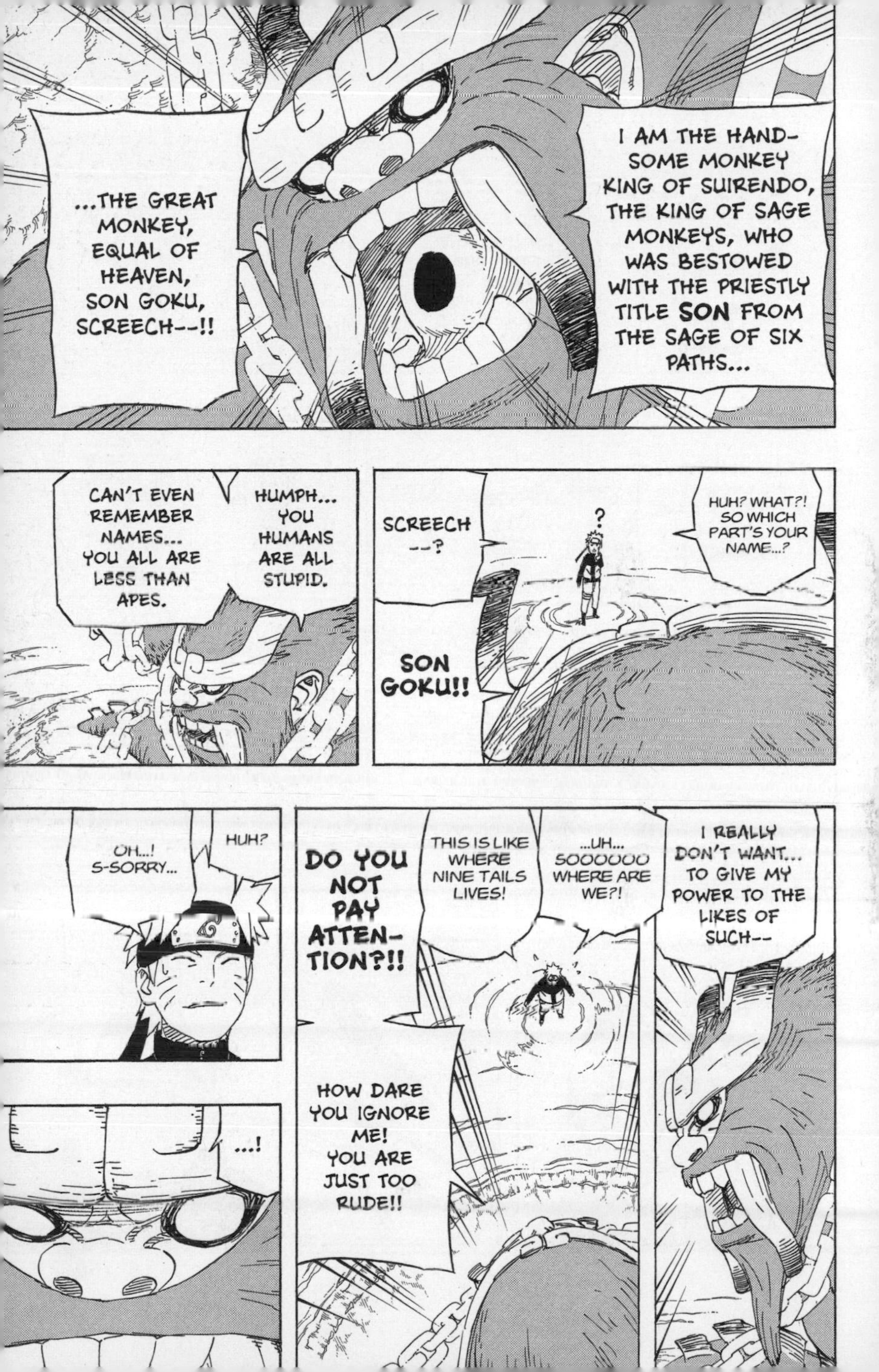
I AM THE HAND-SOME MONKEY KING OF SUIRENDO, THE KING OF SAGE MONKEYS, WHO WAS BESTOWED WITH THE PRIESTLY TITLE SON FROM THE SAGE OF SIX PATHS...
...THE GREAT MONKEY, EQUAL OF HEAVEN, SON GOKU, SCREECH--!!
HUH? WHAT?! SO WHICH PART'S YOUR NAME...?
SCREECH --?
SON GOKU!!
HUMPH... YOU HUMANS ARE ALL STUPID.
CAN'T EVEN REMEMBER NAMES... YOU ALL ARE LESS THAN APES.
I REALLY DON'T WANT... TO GIVE MY POWER TO THE LIKES OF SUCH--
...UH... SOOOOOO WHERE ARE WE?!
THIS IS LIKE WHERE NINE TAILS LIVES!
DO YOU NOT PAY ATTEN-TION?!!
HOW DARE YOU IGNORE ME! YOU ARE JUST TOO RUDE!!
HUH?
OH...! S-SORRY...
...!

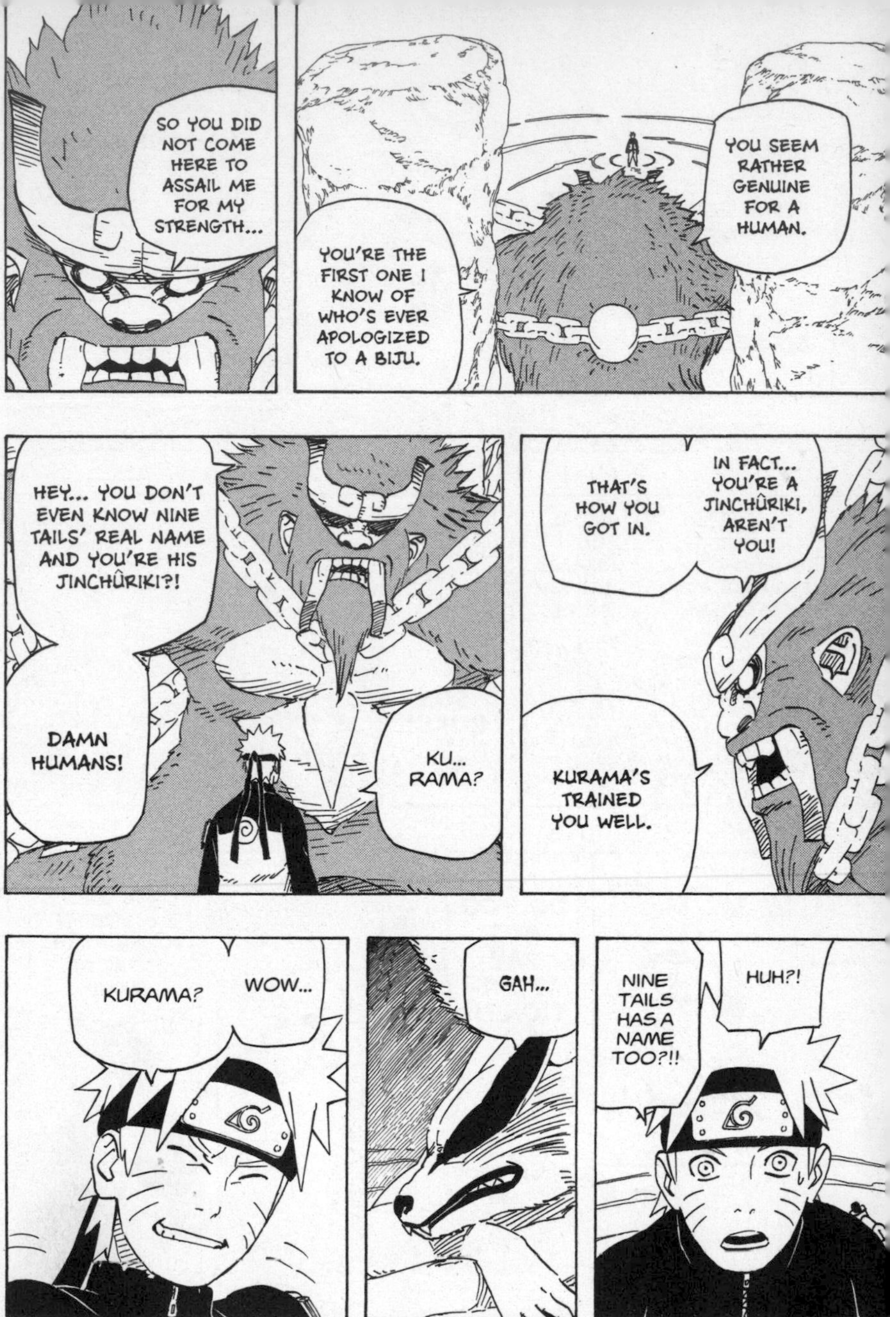
YOU SEEM RATHER GENUINE FOR A HUMAN.
YOU'RE THE FIRST ONE I KNOW OF WHO'S EVER APOLOGIZED TO A BIJU.
SO YOU DID NOT COME HERE TO ASSAIL ME FOR MY STRENGTH...
IN FACT... YOU'RE A JINCHÛRIKI, AREN'T YOU!
THAT'S HOW YOU GOT IN.
KURAMA'S TRAINED YOU WELL.
HEY... YOU DON'T EVEN KNOW NINE TAILS' REAL NAME AND YOU'RE HIS JINCHÛRIKI?!
KU... RAMA?
DAMN HUMANS!
HUH?!
NINE TAILS HAS A NAME TOO?!!
GAH...
WOW...
KURAMA?

READ THIS WAY

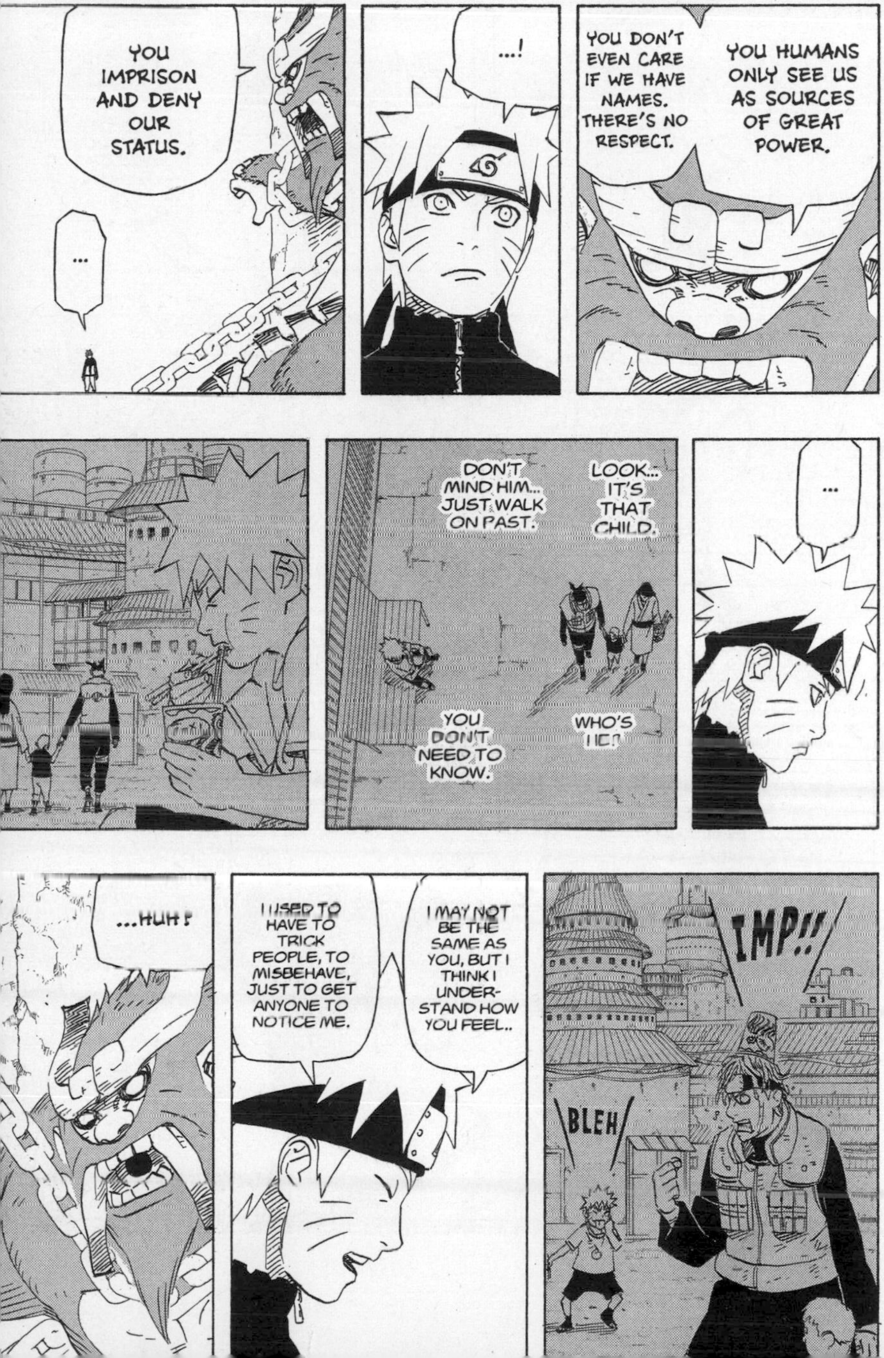
YOU HUMANS ONLY SEE US AS SOURCES OF GREAT POWER.
YOU DON'T EVEN CARE IF WE HAVE NAMES. THERE'S NO RESPECT.
...!
YOU IMPRISON AND DENY OUR STATUS.
...
...
LOOK... IT'S THAT CHILD.
DON'T MIND HIM... JUST WALK ON PAST.
WHO'S HE?
YOU DON'T NEED TO KNOW.
IMP!!
BLEH
I MAY NOT BE THE SAME AS YOU, BUT I THINK I UNDERSTAND HOW YOU FEEL..
I USED TO HAVE TO TRICK PEOPLE, TO MISBEHAVE, JUST TO GET ANYONE TO NOTICE ME.
...HUH?

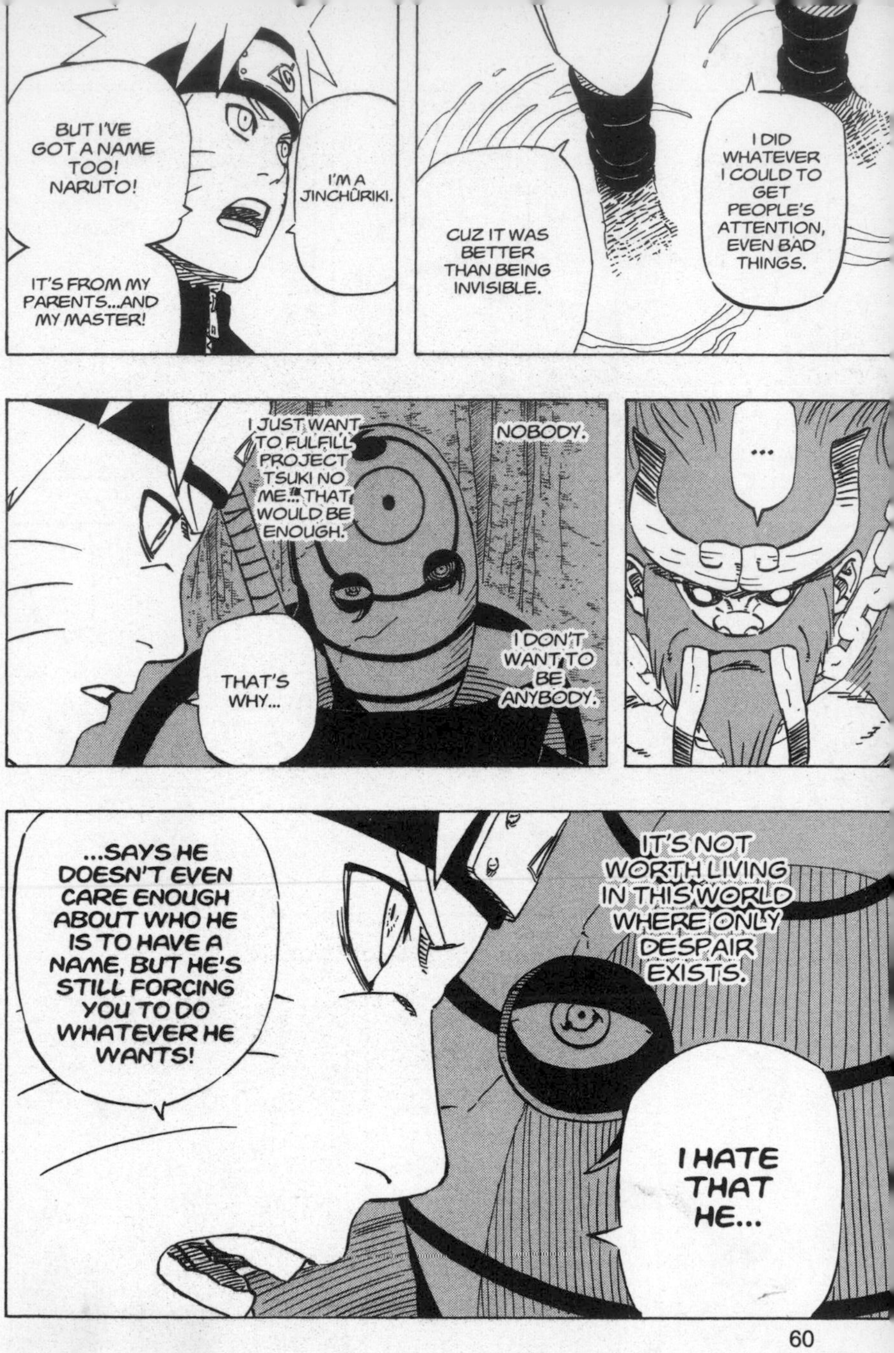
I DID WHATEVER I COULD TO GET PEOPLE'S ATTENTION, EVEN BAD THINGS.
CUZ IT WAS BETTER THAN BEING INVISIBLE.
I'M A JINCHŪRIKI.
BUT I'VE GOT A NAME TOO! NARUTO!
IT'S FROM MY PARENTS...AND MY MASTER!
...
NOBODY.
I DON'T WANT TO BE ANYBODY.
I JUST WANT TO FULFILL PROJECT TSUKI NO ME... THAT WOULD BE ENOUGH.
THAT'S WHY...
IT'S NOT WORTH LIVING IN THIS WORLD WHERE ONLY DESPAIR EXISTS.
I HATE THAT HE...
...SAYS HE DOESN'T EVEN CARE ENOUGH ABOUT WHO HE IS TO HAVE A NAME, BUT HE'S STILL FORCING YOU TO DO WHATEVER HE WANTS!

READ THIS WAY

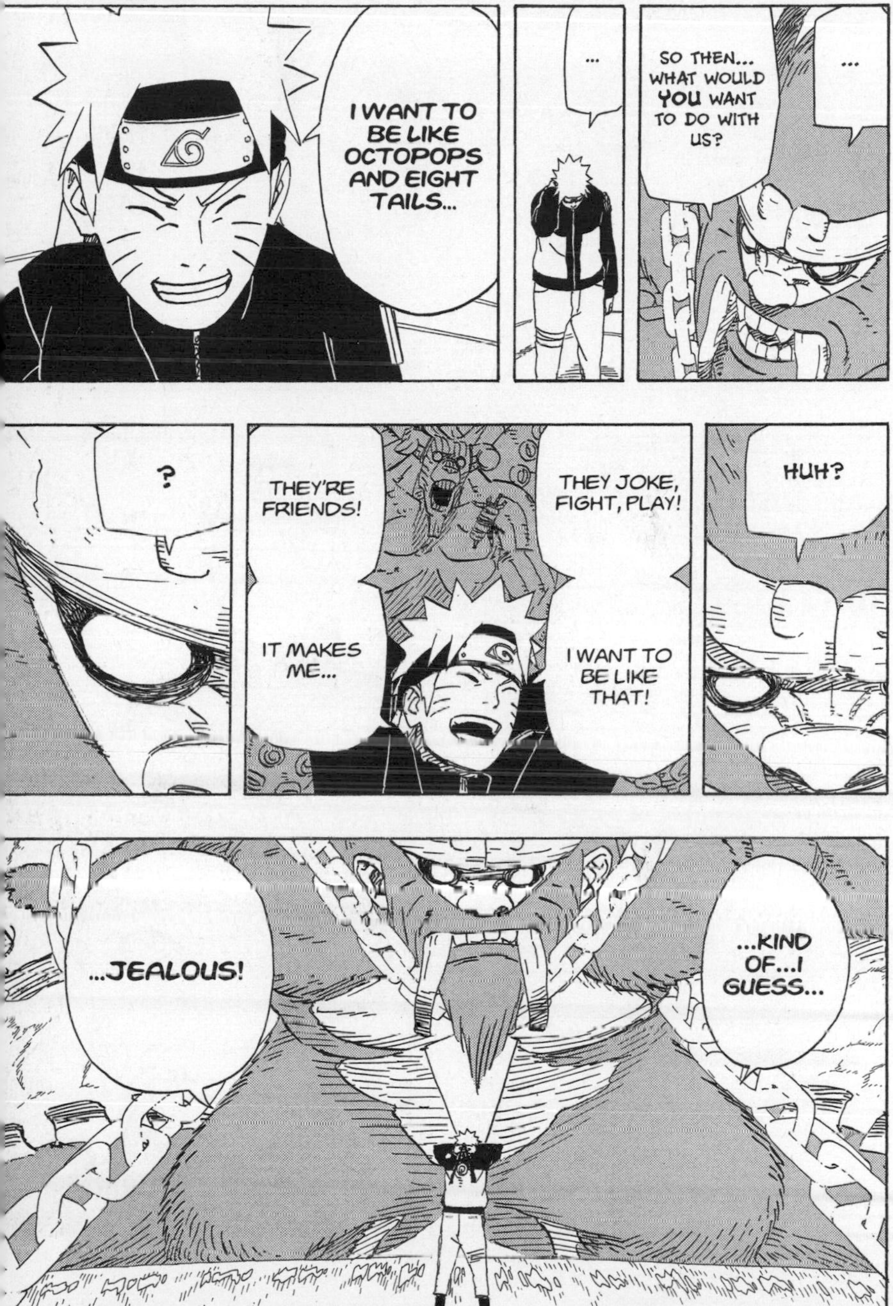
...
SO THEN... WHAT WOULD YOU WANT TO DO WITH US?
...
I WANT TO BE LIKE OCTOPOPS AND EIGHT TAILS...
HUH?
THEY JOKE, FIGHT, PLAY!
THEY'RE FRIENDS!
I WANT TO BE LIKE THAT!
IT MAKES ME...
?
...KIND OF...I GUESS...
...JEALOUS!

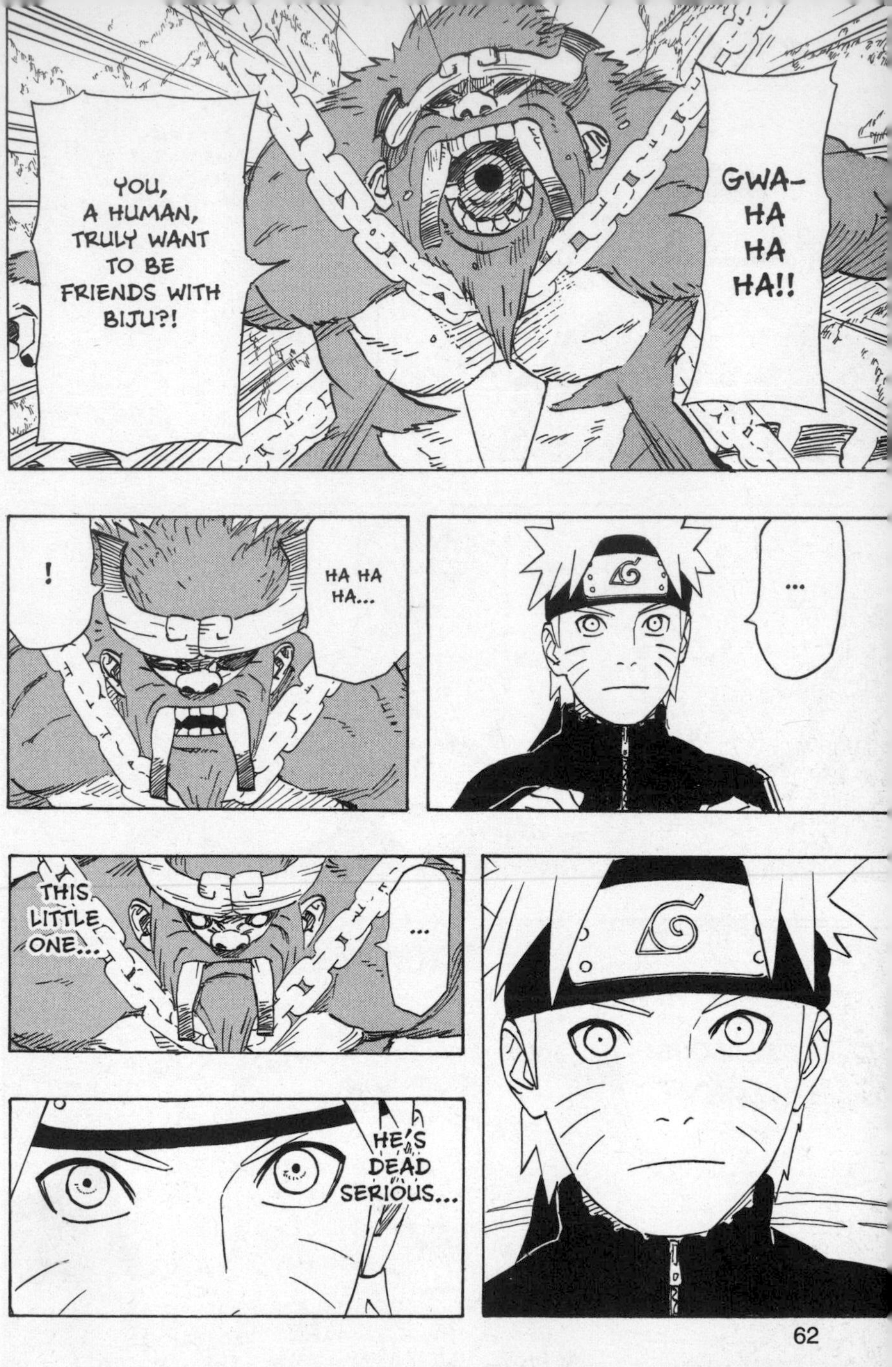

GWA-HA HA HA!!
YOU, A HUMAN, TRULY WANT TO BE FRIENDS WITH BIJU?!
...
HA HA HA...
!
...
THIS LITTLE ONE...
HE'S DEAD SERIOUS...

READ THIS WAY

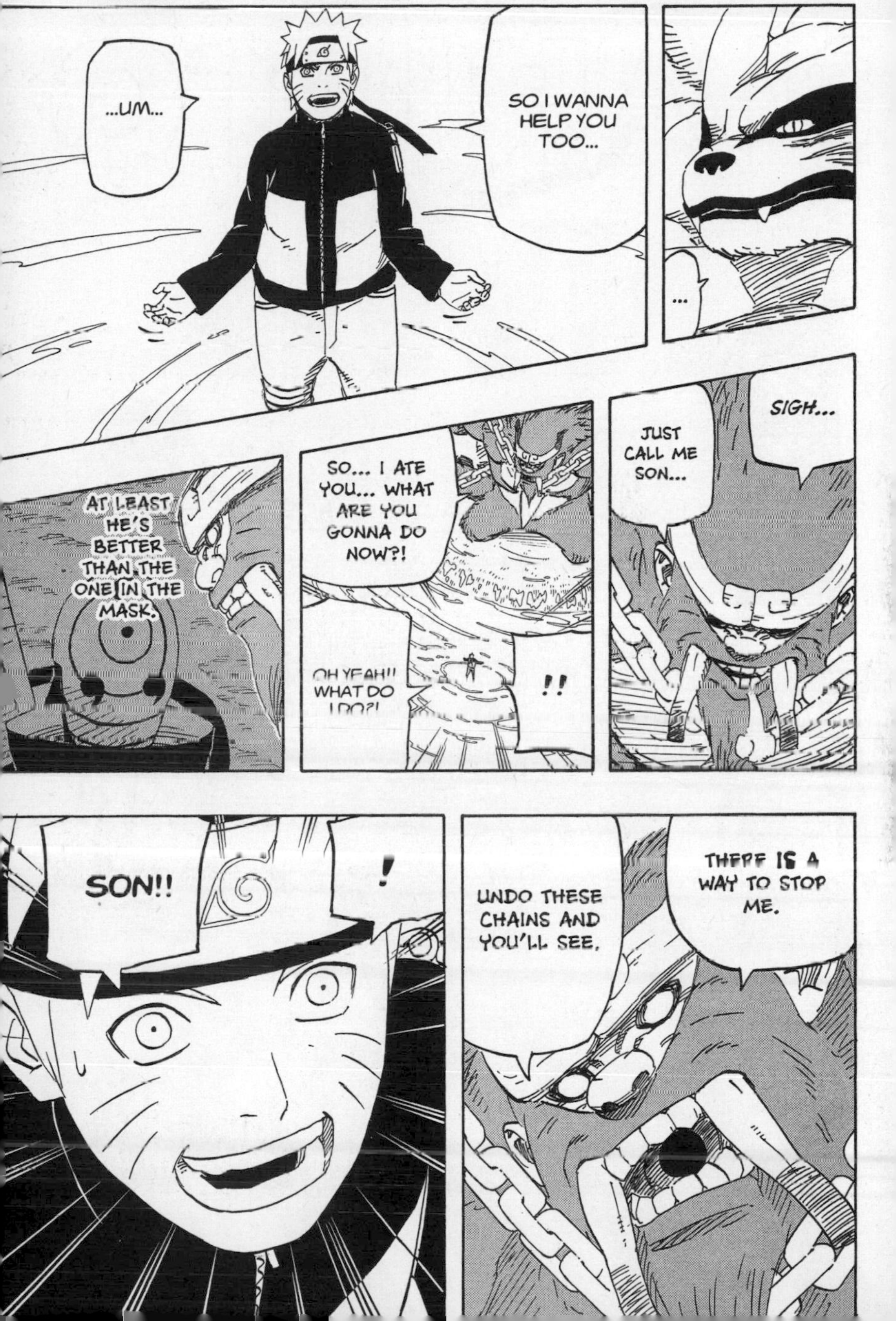
...
SO I WANNA HELP YOU TOO...
...UM...
SIGH...
JUST CALL ME SON...
SO... I ATE YOU... WHAT ARE YOU GONNA DO NOW?!
!!
OH YEAH!! WHAT DO I DO?!
AT LEAST HE'S BETTER THAN THE ONE IN THE MASK.
THERE IS A WAY TO STOP ME.
UNDO THESE CHAINS AND YOU'LL SEE.
!
SON!!

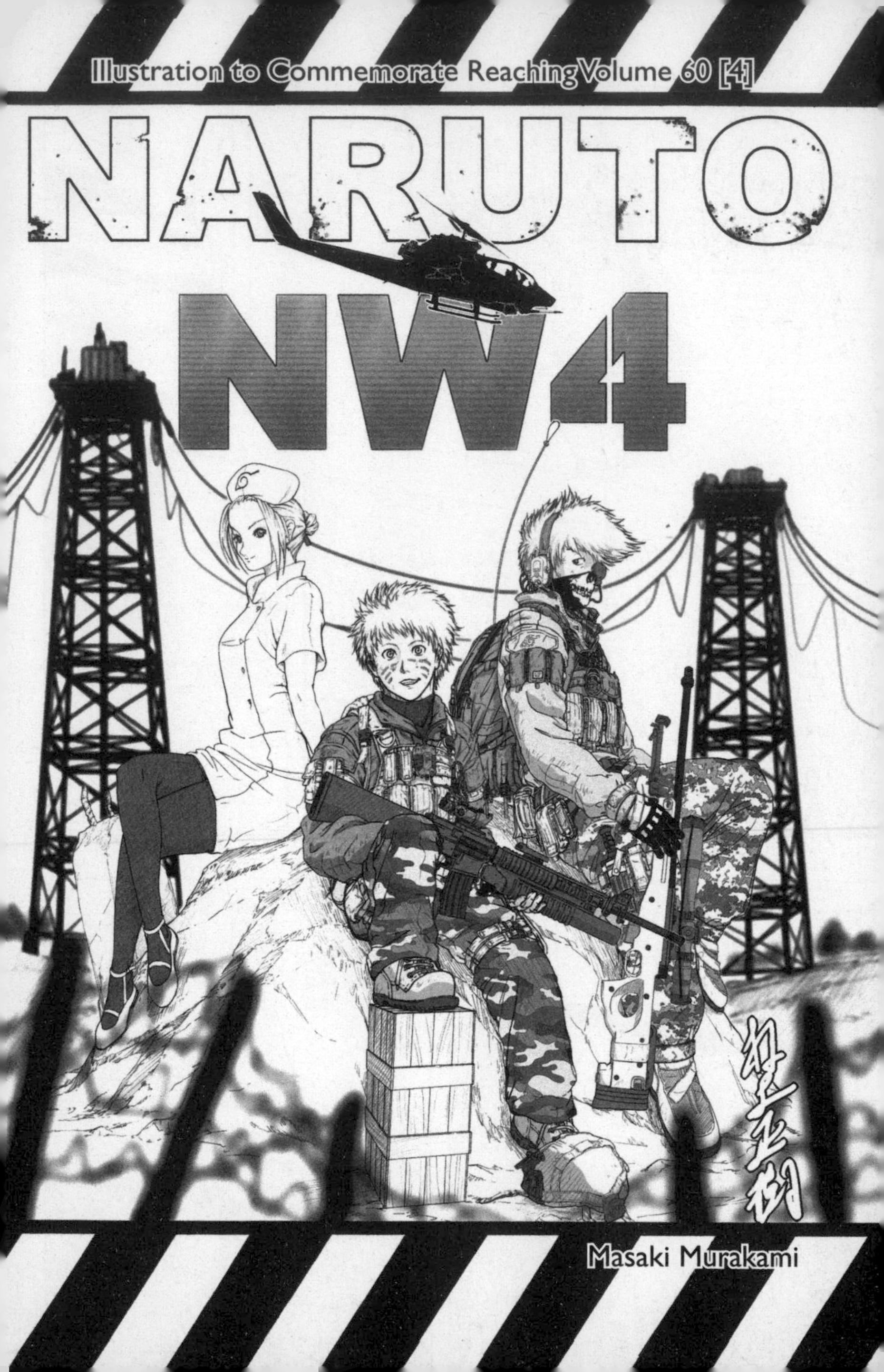
Illustration to Commemorate Reaching Volume 60 [4]
NARUTO
NW4
Masaki Murakami

Number 569: Proof of Will!

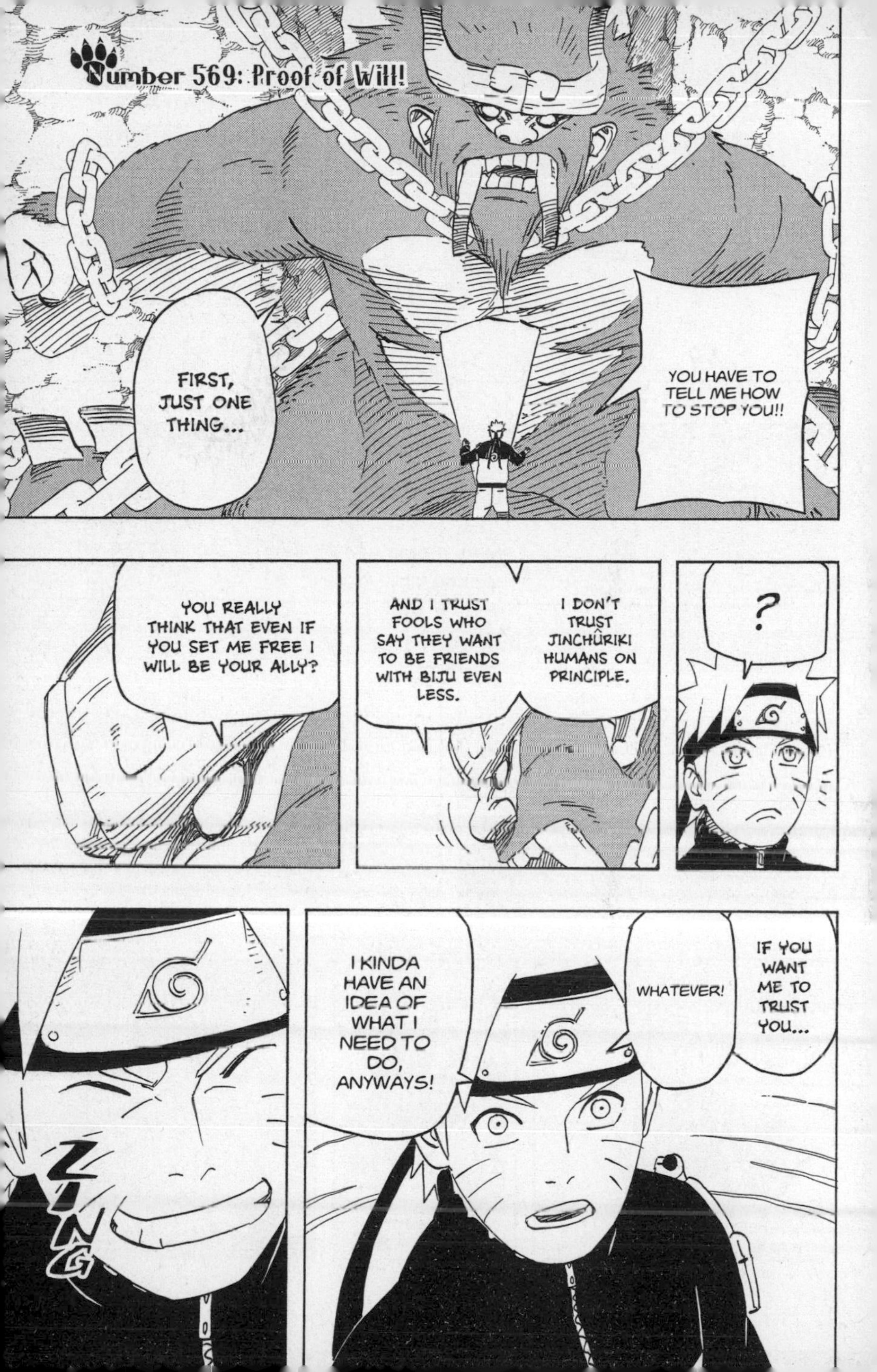
YOU HAVE TO TELL ME HOW TO STOP YOU!!
FIRST, JUST ONE THING...
?
I DON'T TRUST JINCHÛRIKI HUMANS ON PRINCIPLE.
AND I TRUST FOOLS WHO SAY THEY WANT TO BE FRIENDS WITH BIJU EVEN LESS.
YOU REALLY THINK THAT EVEN IF YOU SET ME FREE I WILL BE YOUR ALLY?
IF YOU WANT ME TO TRUST YOU...
WHATEVER!
I KINDA HAVE AN IDEA OF WHAT I NEED TO DO, ANYWAYS!
ZING

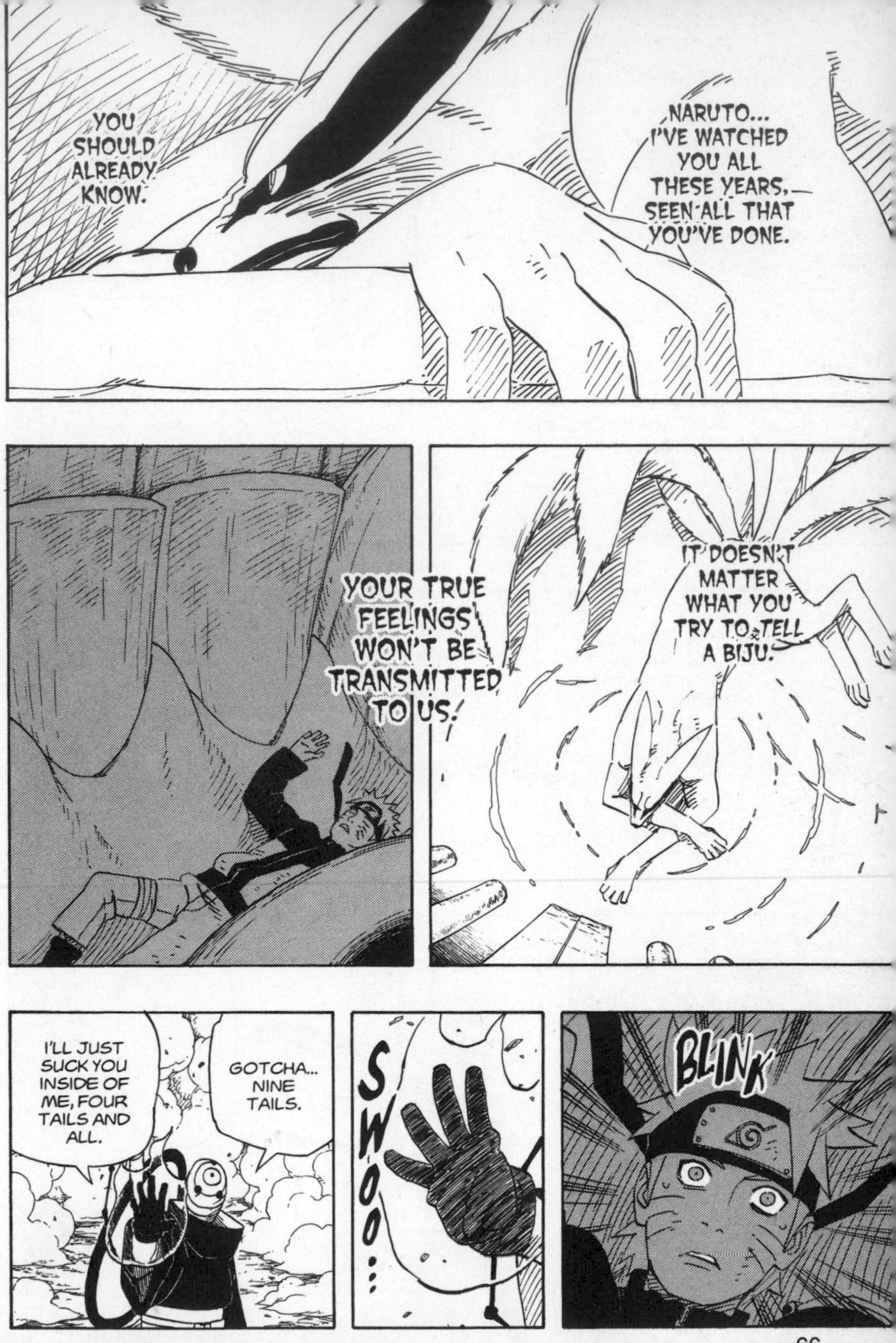

NARUTO... I'VE WATCHED YOU ALL THESE YEARS, SEEN ALL THAT YOU'VE DONE.
YOU SHOULD ALREADY KNOW.
IT DOESN'T MATTER WHAT YOU TRY TO TELL A BIJU.
YOUR TRUE FEELINGS WON'T BE TRANSMITTED TO US.
BLINK
SWOO...
GOTCHA... NINE TAILS.
I'LL JUST SUCK YOU INSIDE OF ME, FOUR TAILS AND ALL.

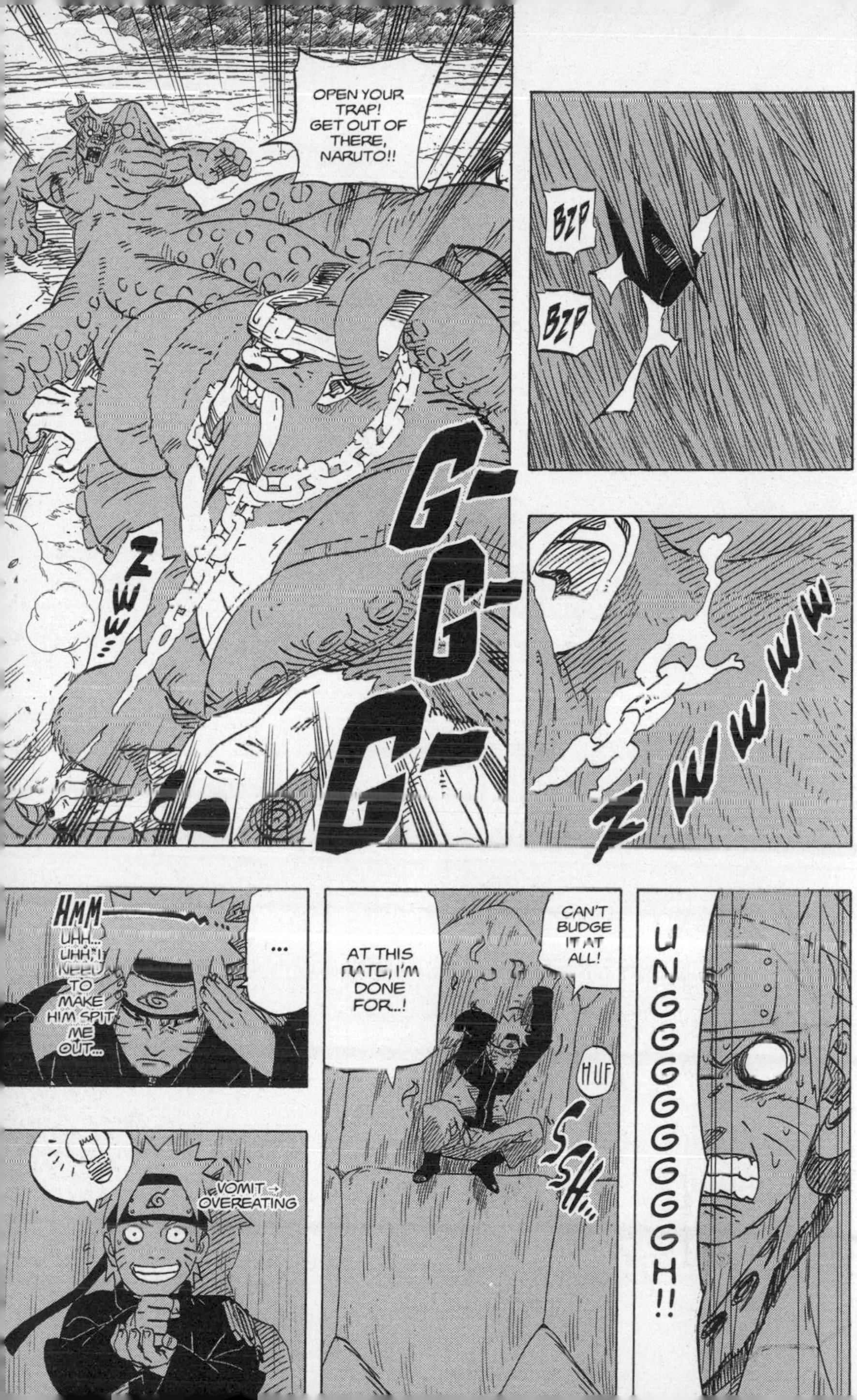
BZP
BZP
ZWWWWW
OPEN YOUR TRAP! GET OUT OF THERE, NARUTO!!
ZWW...
G-G-G-
UNGGGGGGGGGH!!
CAN'T BUDGE IT AT ALL!
AT THIS RATE, I'M DONE FOR...!
HUF
SSH...
...
HMM
UHH... UHH, I NEED TO MAKE HIM SPIT ME OUT...
VOMIT → OVEREATING

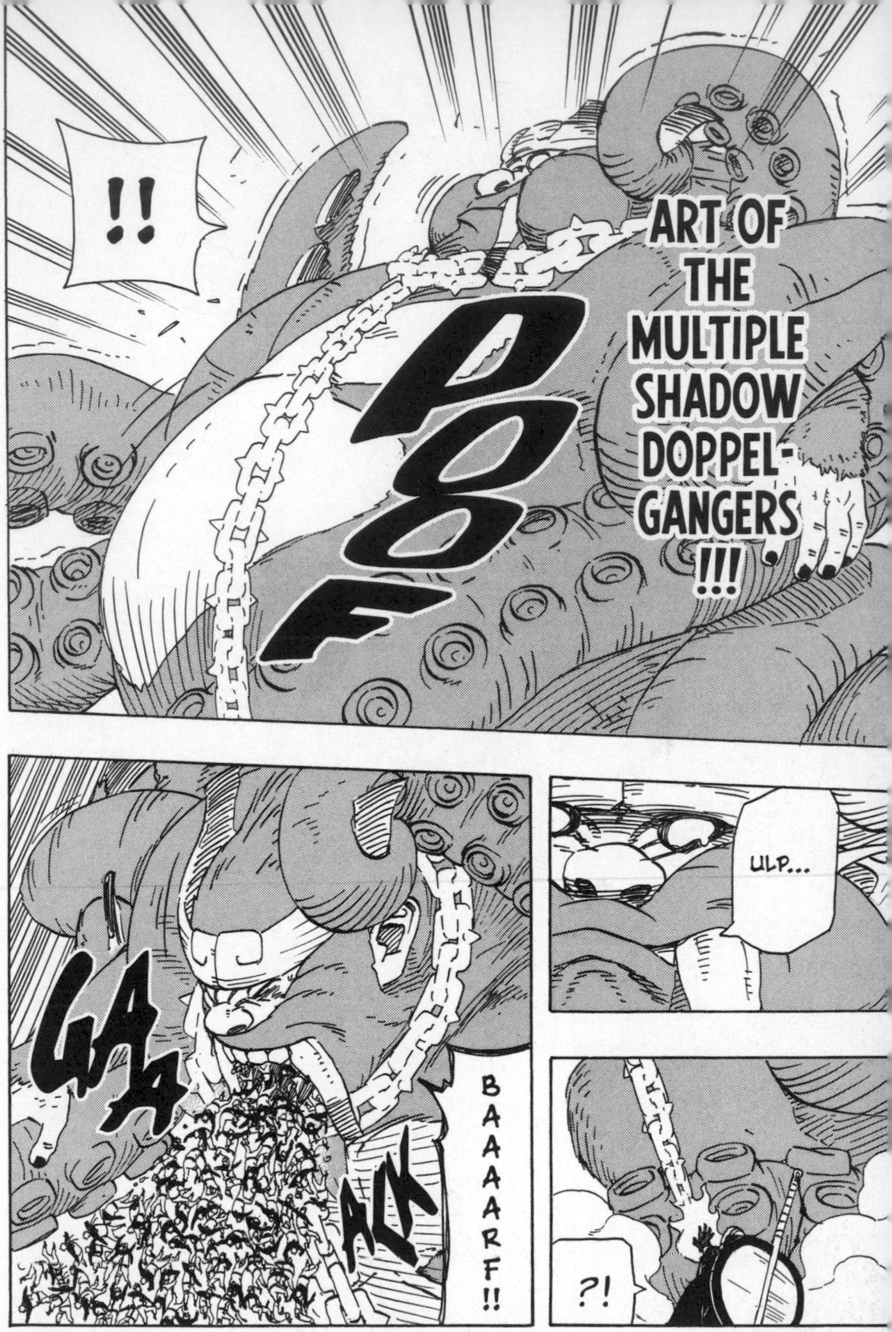
ART OF THE MULTIPLE SHADOW DOPPEL-GANGERS!!!
POOF
!!
ULP...
?!
BAAAARF!!
GAA
ACK

READ THIS WAY

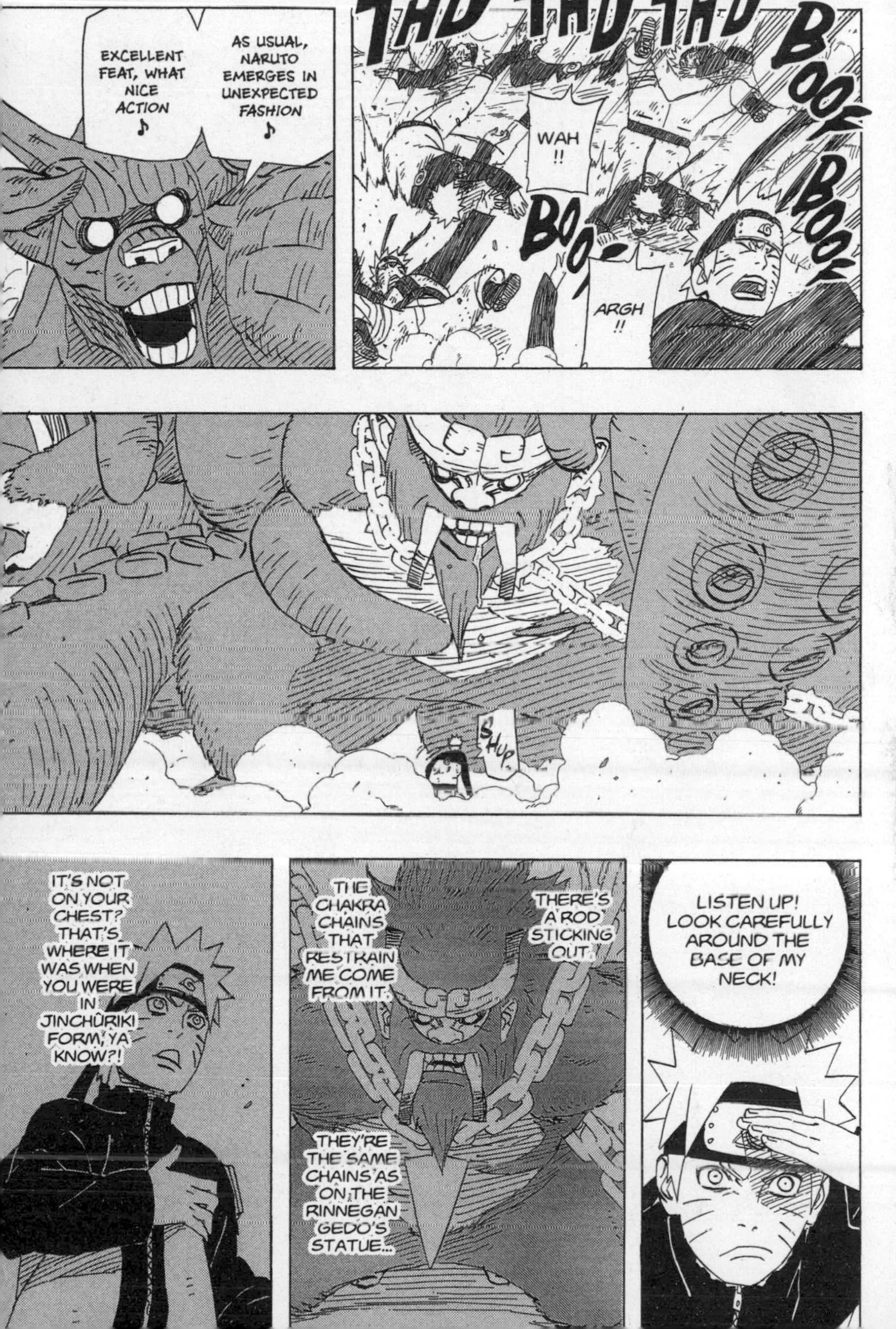
THD THD THD
BOOF
BOOF
WAH !!
BOO
ARGH !!
AS USUAL, NARUTO EMERGES IN UNEXPECTED FASHION ♪
EXCELLENT FEAT, WHAT NICE ACTION ♪
SHUP
LISTEN UP! LOOK CAREFULLY AROUND THE BASE OF MY NECK!
THERE'S A ROD STICKING OUT.
THE CHAKRA CHAINS THAT RESTRAIN ME COME FROM IT.
THEY'RE THE SAME CHAINS AS ON THE RINNEGAN GEDO'S STATUE...
IT'S NOT ON YOUR CHEST? THAT'S WHERE IT WAS WHEN YOU WERE IN JINCHÛRIKI FORM, YA KNOW?!

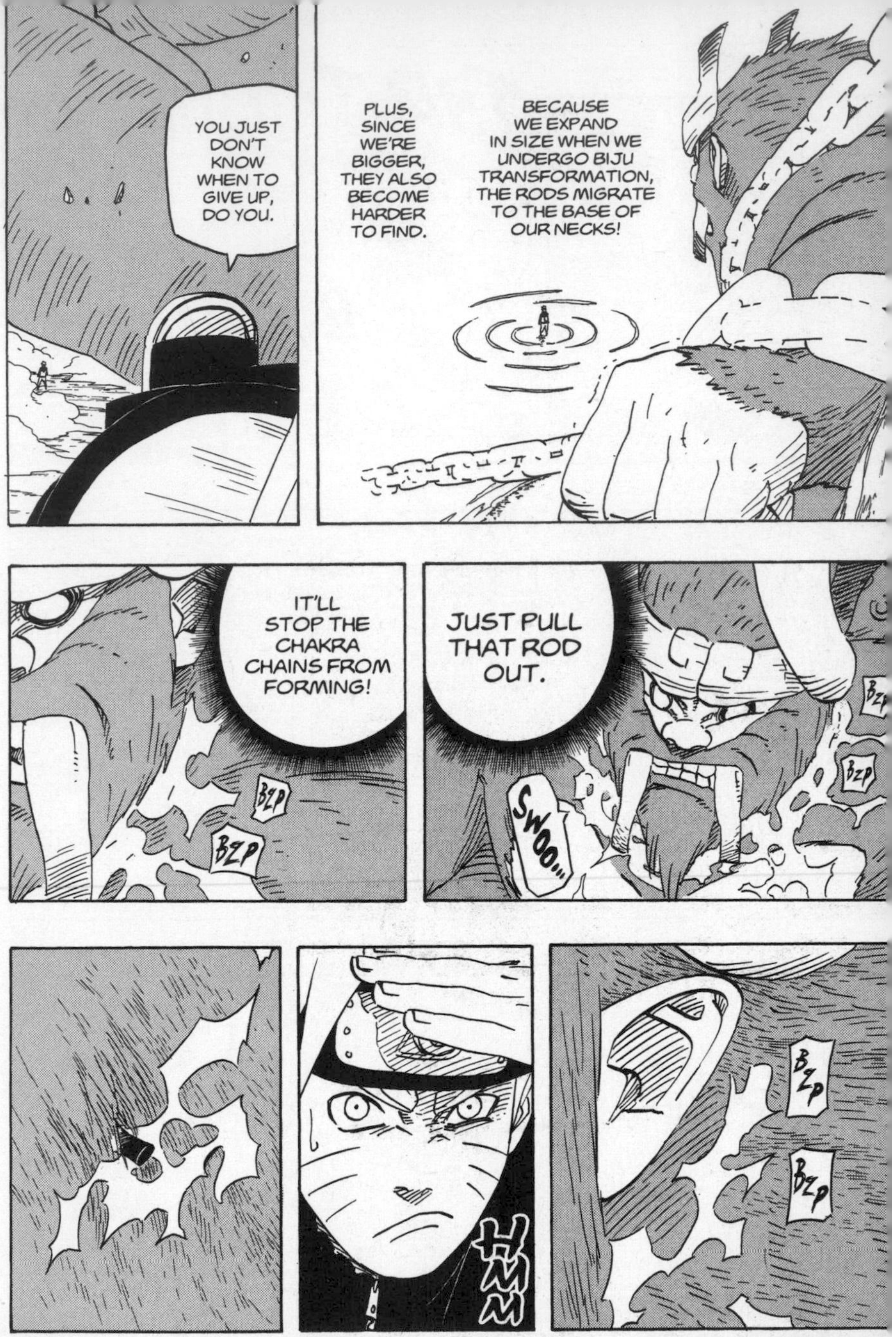
BECAUSE WE EXPAND IN SIZE WHEN WE UNDERGO BIJU TRANSFORMATION, THE RODS MIGRATE TO THE BASE OF OUR NECKS!
PLUS, SINCE WE'RE BIGGER, THEY ALSO BECOME HARDER TO FIND.
YOU JUST DON'T KNOW WHEN TO GIVE UP, DO YOU.
JUST PULL THAT ROD OUT.
BZP
BZP
SWOO...
IT'LL STOP THE CHAKRA CHAINS FROM FORMING!
BZP
BZP
BZP
BZP
HMM

READ THIS WAY

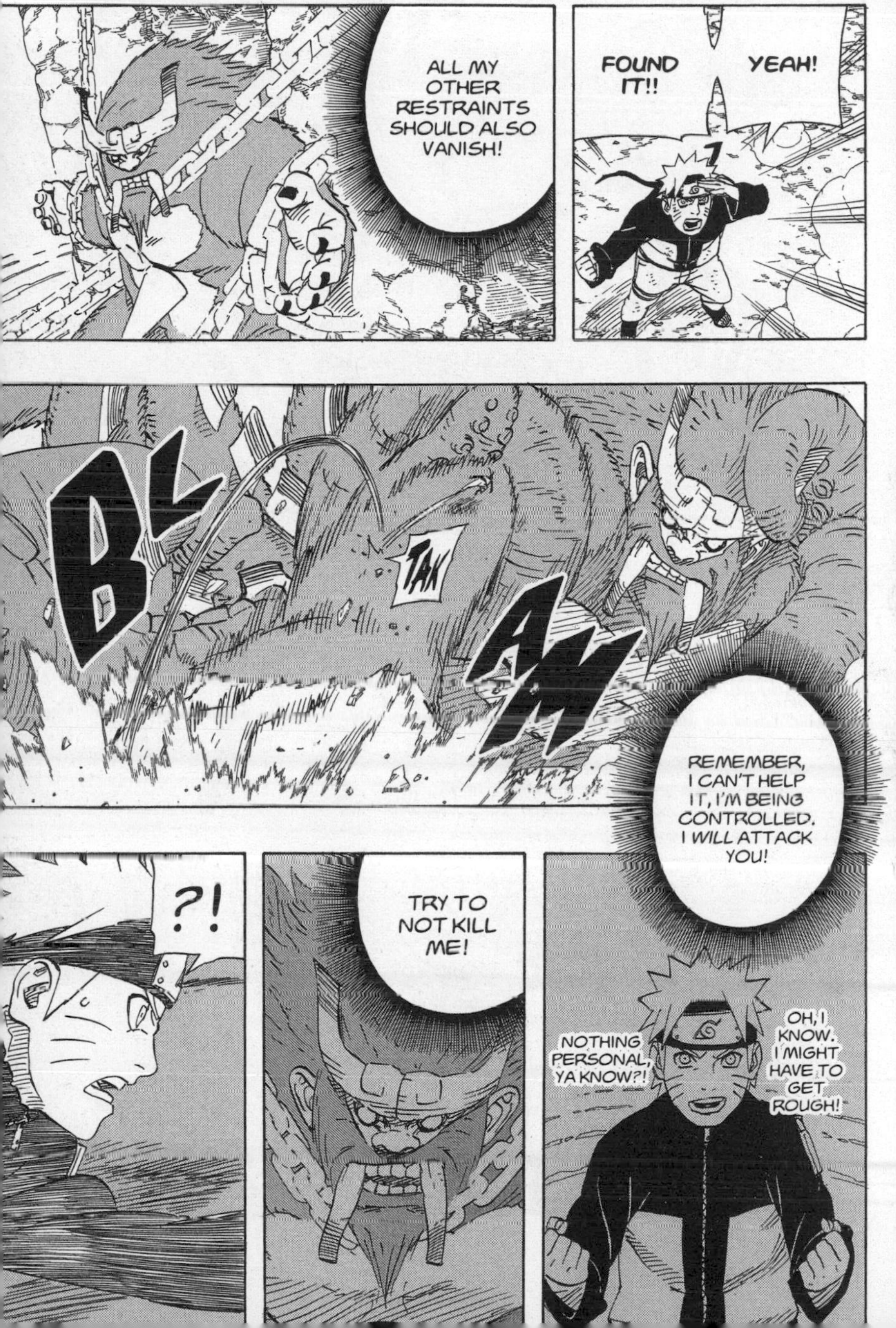
YEAH!
FOUND IT!!
ALL MY OTHER RESTRAINTS SHOULD ALSO VANISH!
BLAM
TAK
REMEMBER, I CAN'T HELP IT, I'M BEING CONTROLLED. I WILL ATTACK YOU!
OH, I KNOW. I MIGHT HAVE TO GET ROUGH!
NOTHING PERSONAL, YA KNOW?!
TRY TO NOT KILL ME!
?!

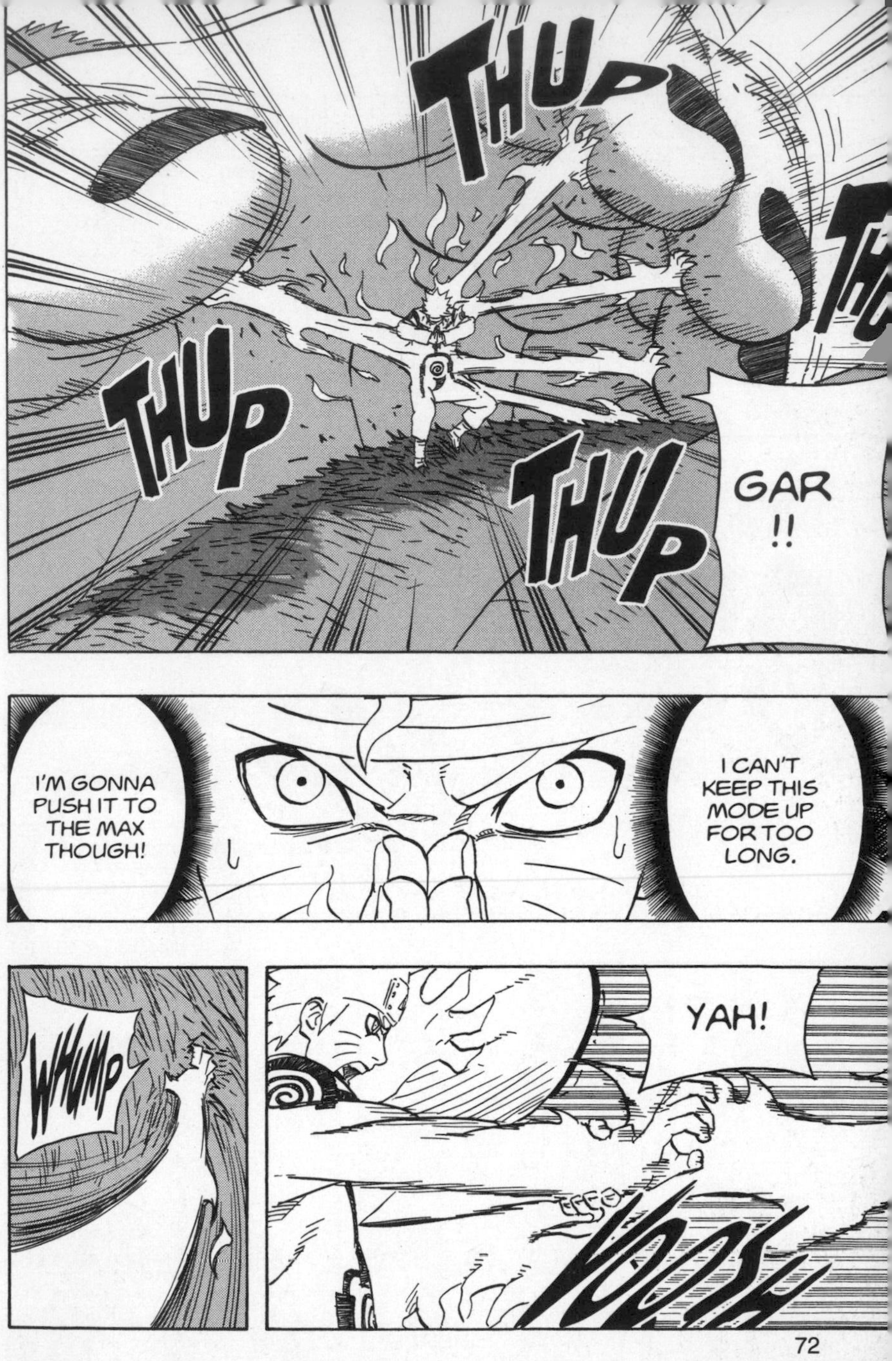
THUP
GAR !!
THUP
THUP
I CAN'T KEEP THIS MODE UP FOR TOO LONG.
I'M GONNA PUSH IT TO THE MAX THOUGH!
YAH!
WHUMP

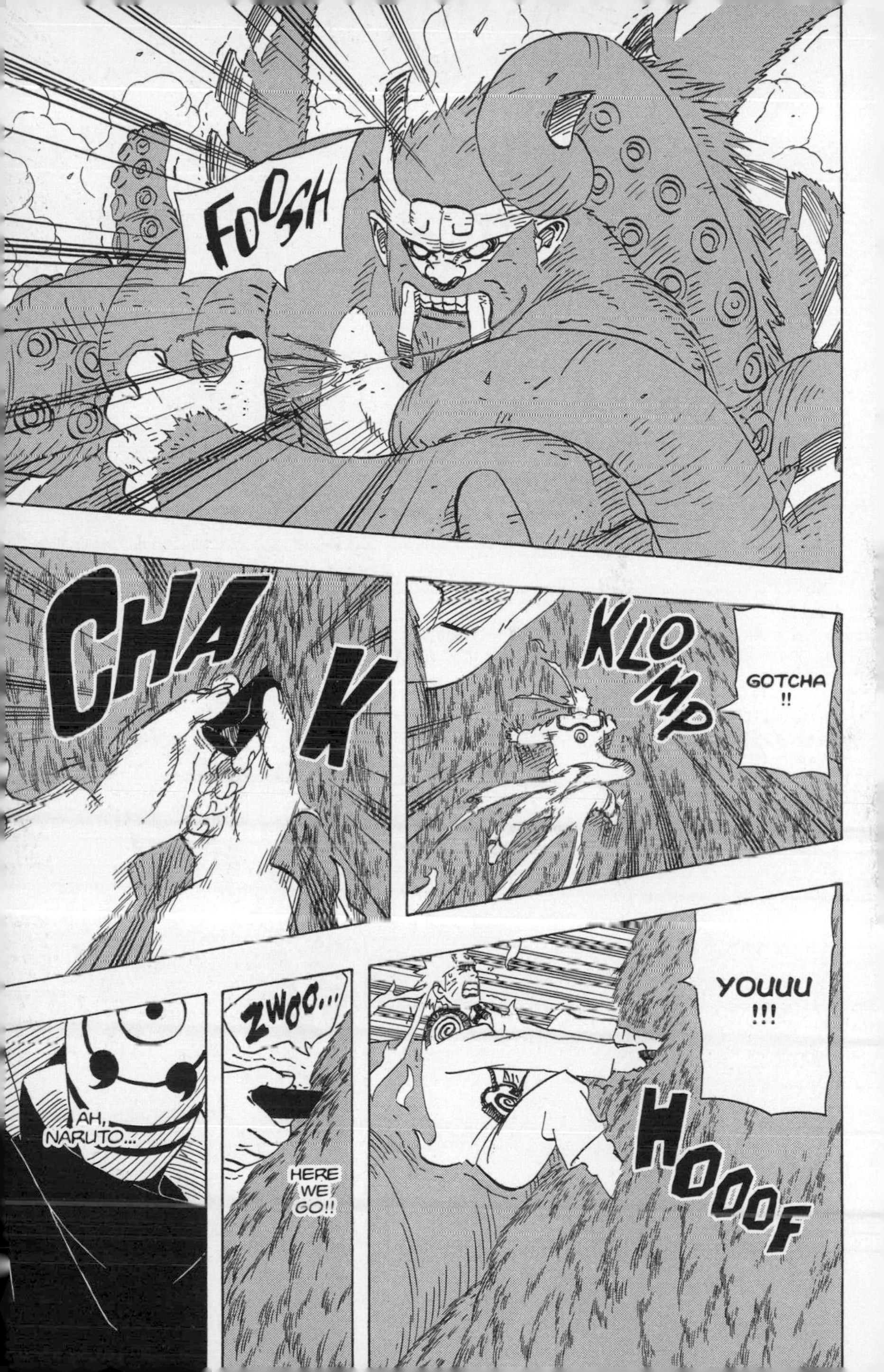
FOOSH
KLOMP
GOTCHA !!
CHAK
YOUUU !!!
HOOOF
ZWOO...
HERE WE GO!!
AH, NARUTO...

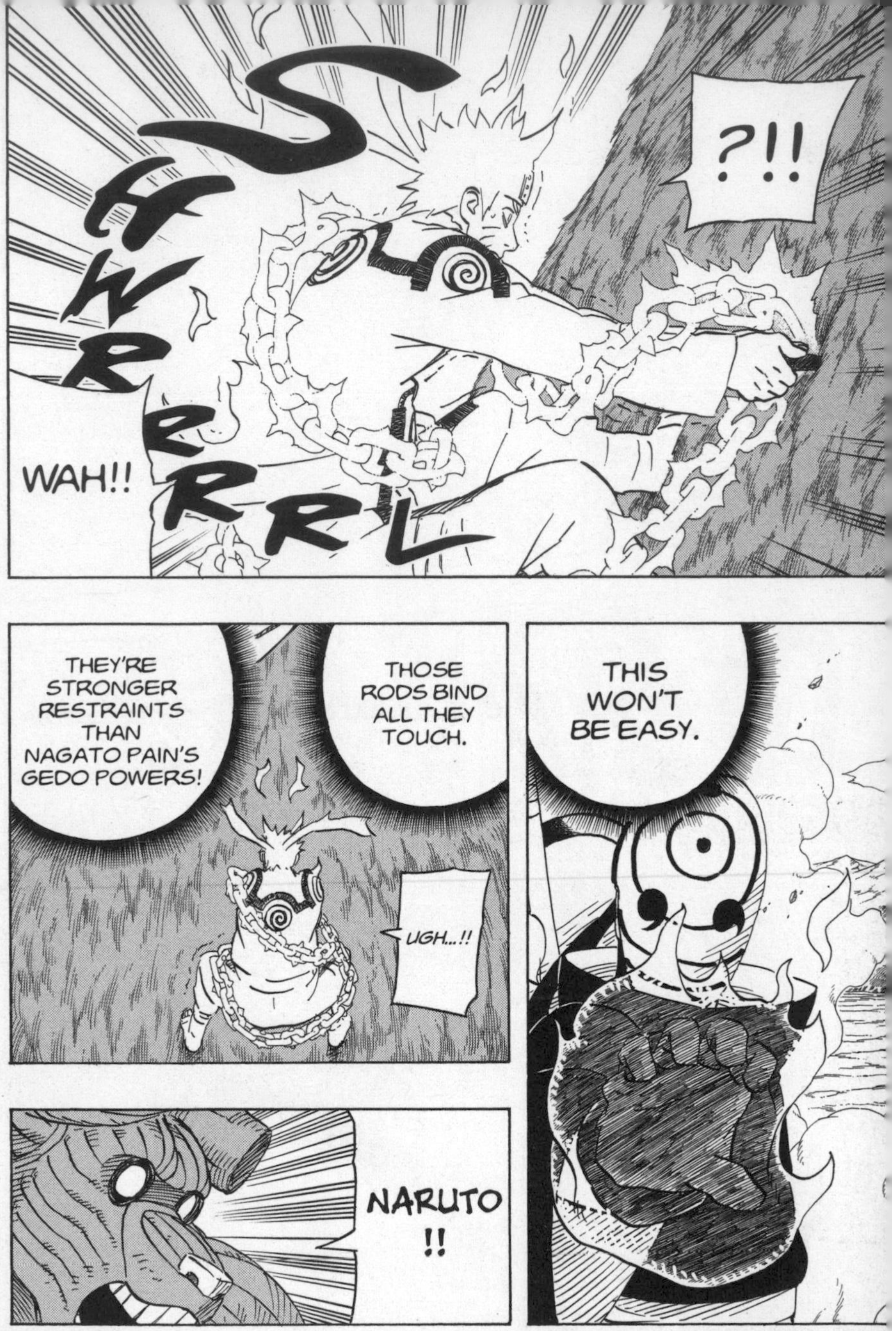
?!!
SHWRRRRL
WAH!!
THIS WON'T BE EASY.
THOSE RODS BIND ALL THEY TOUCH.
THEY'RE STRONGER RESTRAINTS THAN NAGATO PAIN'S GEDO POWERS!
UGH...!!
NARUTO !!

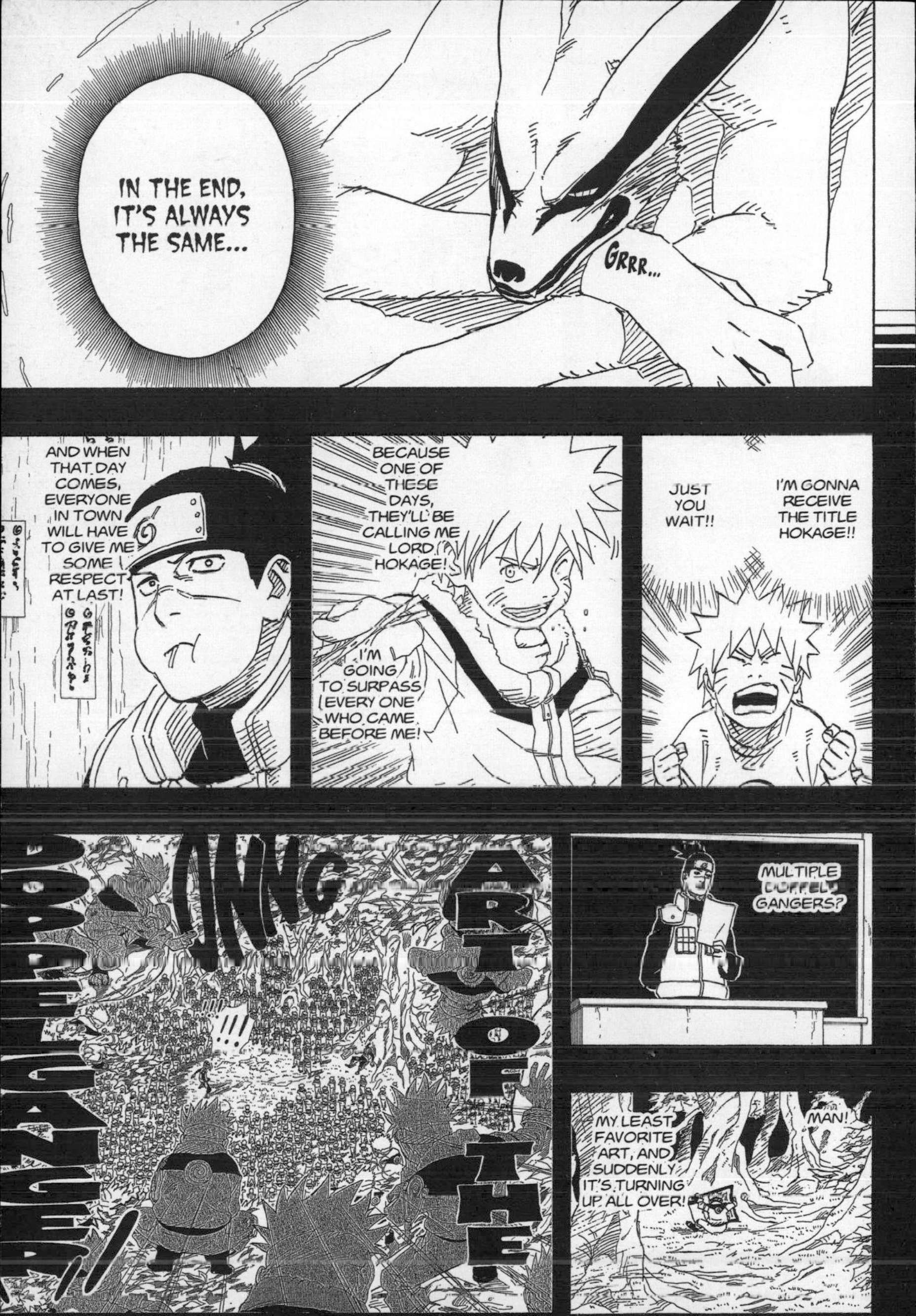
IN THE END, IT'S ALWAYS THE SAME...
GRRR...
I'M GONNA RECEIVE THE TITLE HOKAGE!!
JUST YOU WAIT!!
BECAUSE ONE OF THESE DAYS, THEY'LL BE CALLING ME LORD HOKAGE!
I'M GOING TO SURPASS EVERY ONE WHO CAME BEFORE ME!
AND WHEN THAT DAY COMES, EVERYONE IN TOWN WILL HAVE TO GIVE ME SOME RESPECT AT LAST!
MULTIPLE DOPPEL-GANGERS?
MAN!
MY LEAST FAVORITE ART, AND SUDDENLY IT'S TURNING UP ALL OVER!
ART OF THE
!!!

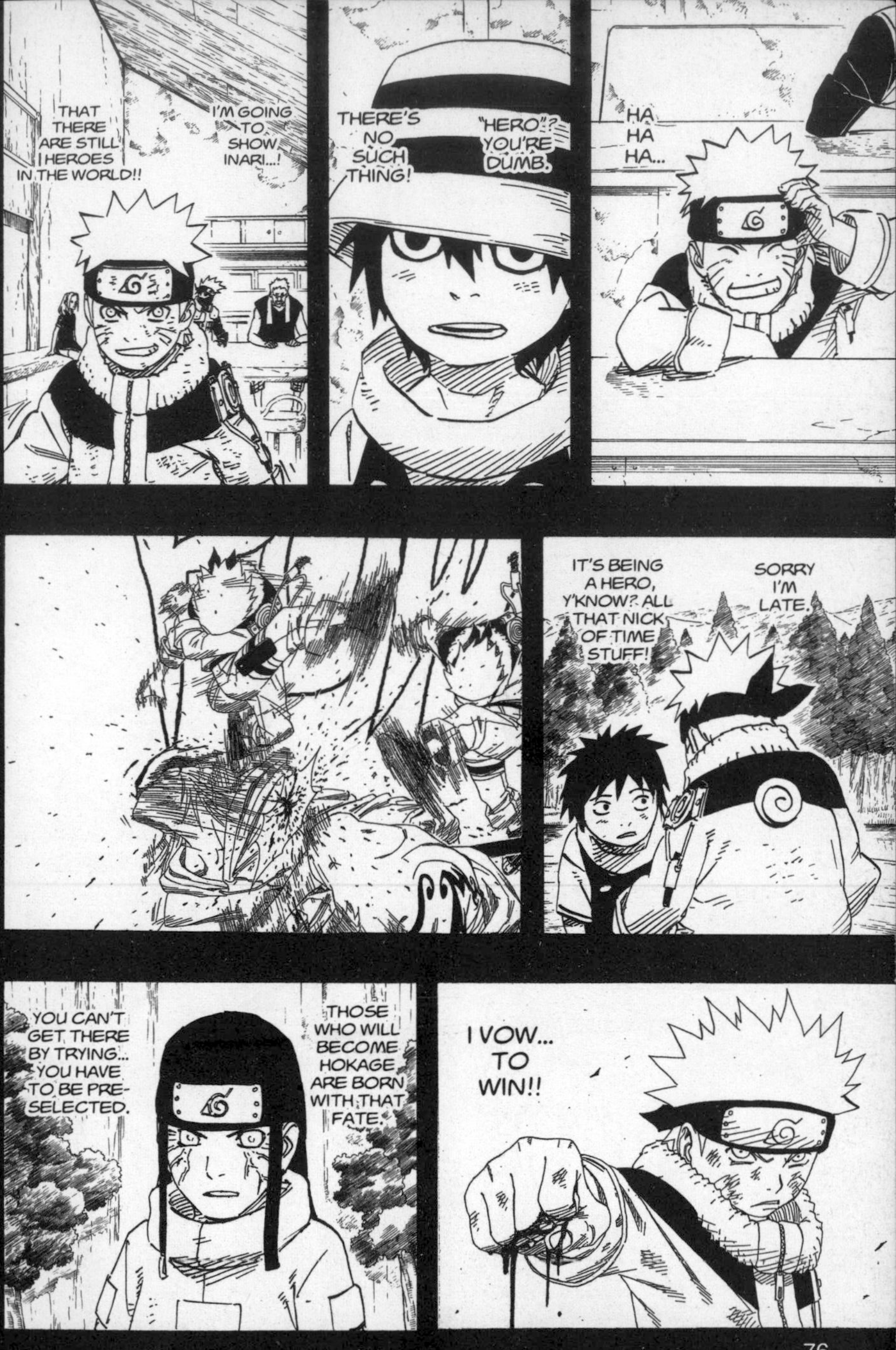
HA HA HA...
"HERO"? YOU'RE DUMB.
THERE'S NO SUCH THING!
I'M GOING TO SHOW INARI...!
THAT THERE ARE STILL HEROES IN THE WORLD!!
SORRY I'M LATE.
IT'S BEING A HERO, Y'KNOW? ALL THAT NICK OF TIME STUFF!
I VOW... TO WIN!!
THOSE WHO WILL BECOME HOKAGE ARE BORN WITH THAT FATE.
YOU CAN'T GET THERE BY TRYING... YOU HAVE TO BE PRE-SELECTED.

READ THIS WAY

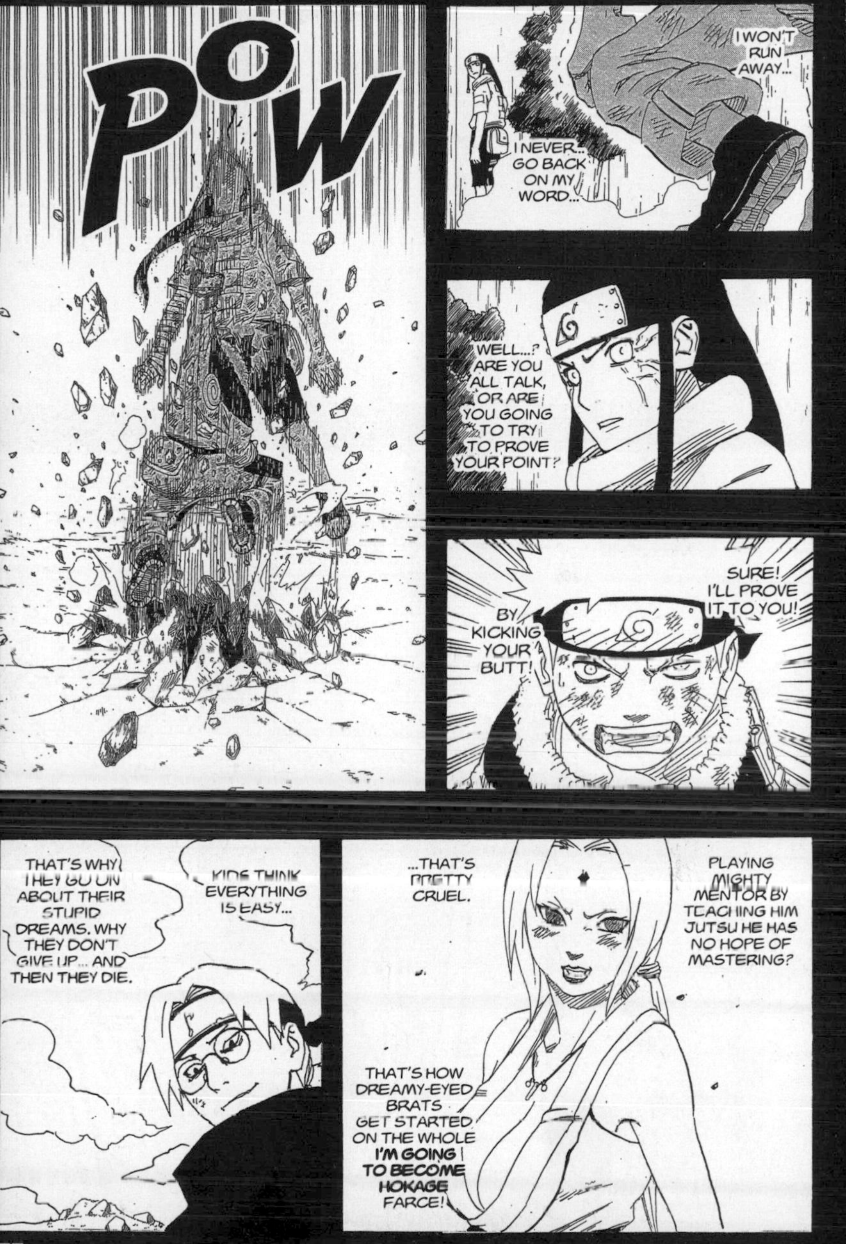
I WON'T RUN AWAY...
I NEVER... GO BACK ON MY WORD...
WELL...? ARE YOU ALL TALK, OR ARE YOU GOING TO TRY TO PROVE YOUR POINT?
SURE! I'LL PROVE IT TO YOU!
BY KICKING YOUR BUTT!
POW
PLAYING MIGHTY MENTOR BY TEACHING HIM JUTSU HE HAS NO HOPE OF MASTERING?
...THAT'S PRETTY CRUEL.
THAT'S HOW DREAMY-EYED BRATS GET STARTED ON THE WHOLE **I'M GOING TO BECOME HOKAGE** FARCE!
KIDS THINK EVERYTHING IS EASY...
THAT'S WHY THEY GO ON ABOUT THEIR STUPID DREAMS. WHY THEY DON'T GIVE UP... AND THEN THEY DIE.

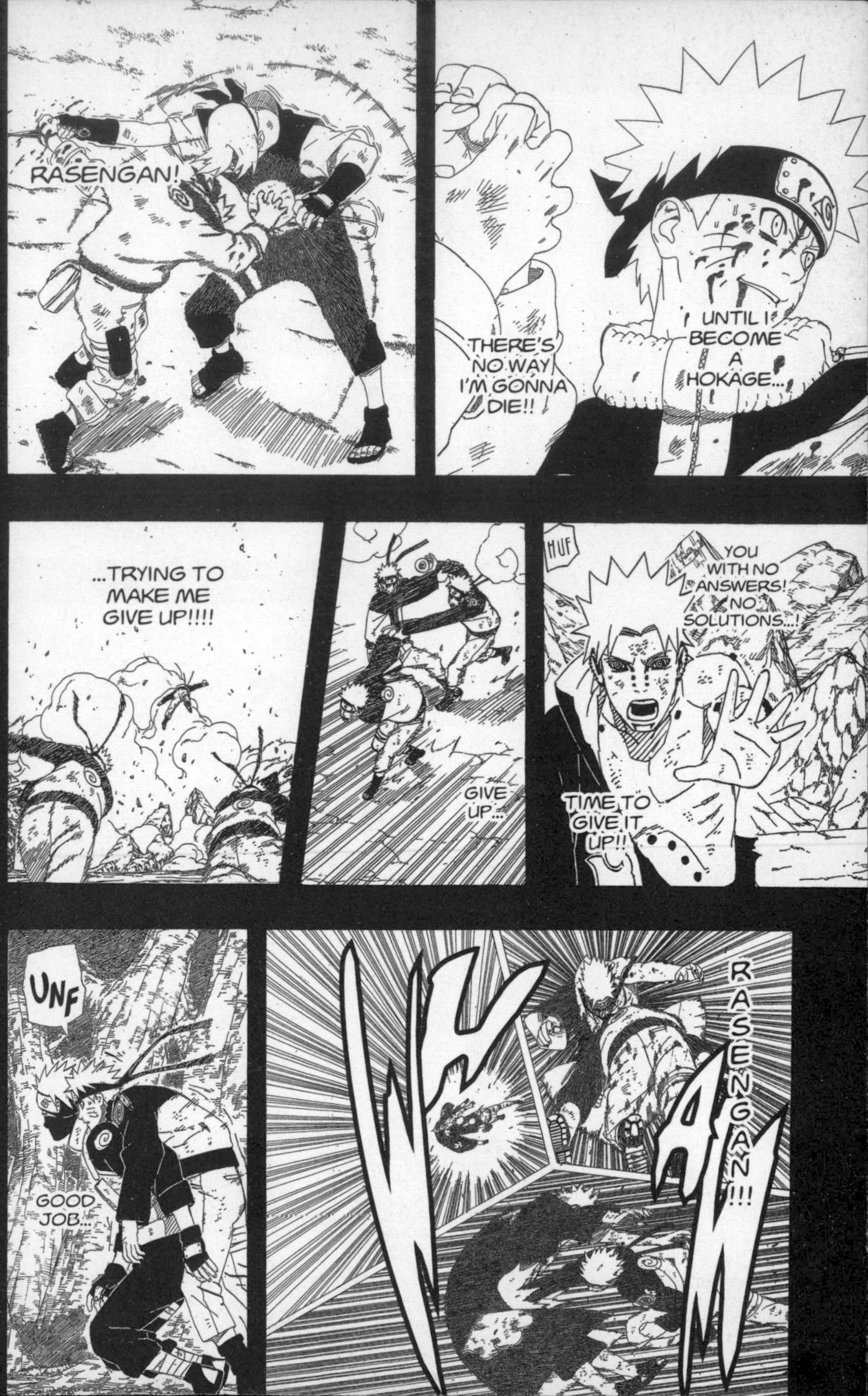
UNTIL I BECOME A HOKAGE...
THERE'S NO WAY I'M GONNA DIE!!
RASENGAN!
HUF
YOU WITH NO ANSWERS! NO SOLUTIONS...!
TIME TO GIVE IT UP!!
GIVE UP...
...TRYING TO MAKE ME GIVE UP!!!!
RASENGAN!!!
WHAM
UNF
GOOD JOB...

READ THIS WAY

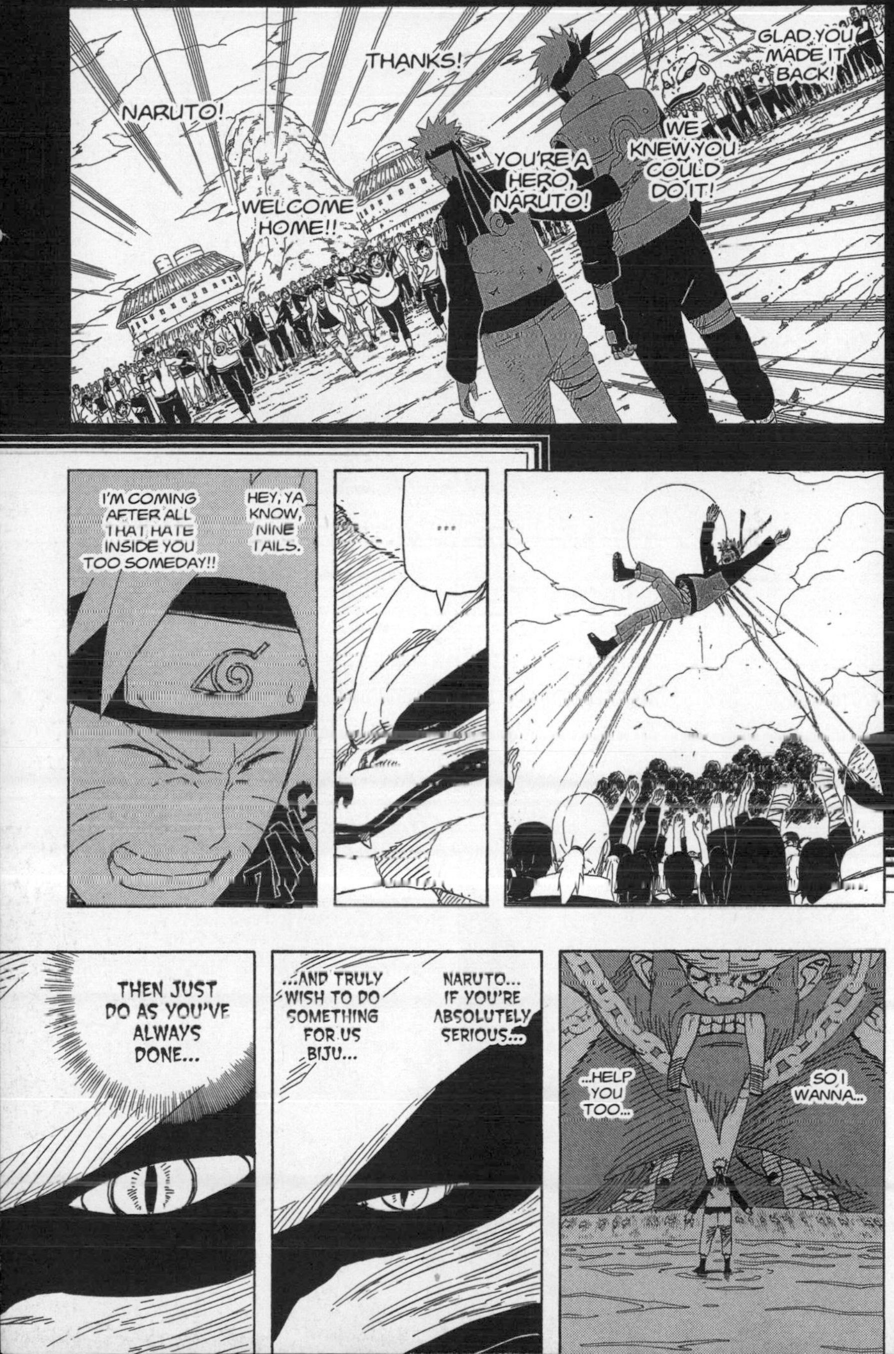

GLAD YOU MADE IT BACK!
WE KNEW YOU COULD DO IT!
THANKS!
YOU'RE A HERO, NARUTO!
NARUTO!
WELCOME HOME!!
...
HEY, YA KNOW, NINE TAILS.
I'M COMING AFTER ALL THAT HATE INSIDE YOU TOO SOMEDAY!!
SO I WANNA...
...HELP YOU TOO...
NARUTO... IF YOU'RE ABSOLUTELY SERIOUS...
...AND TRULY WISH TO DO SOMETHING FOR US BIJU...
THEN JUST DO AS YOU'VE ALWAYS DONE...

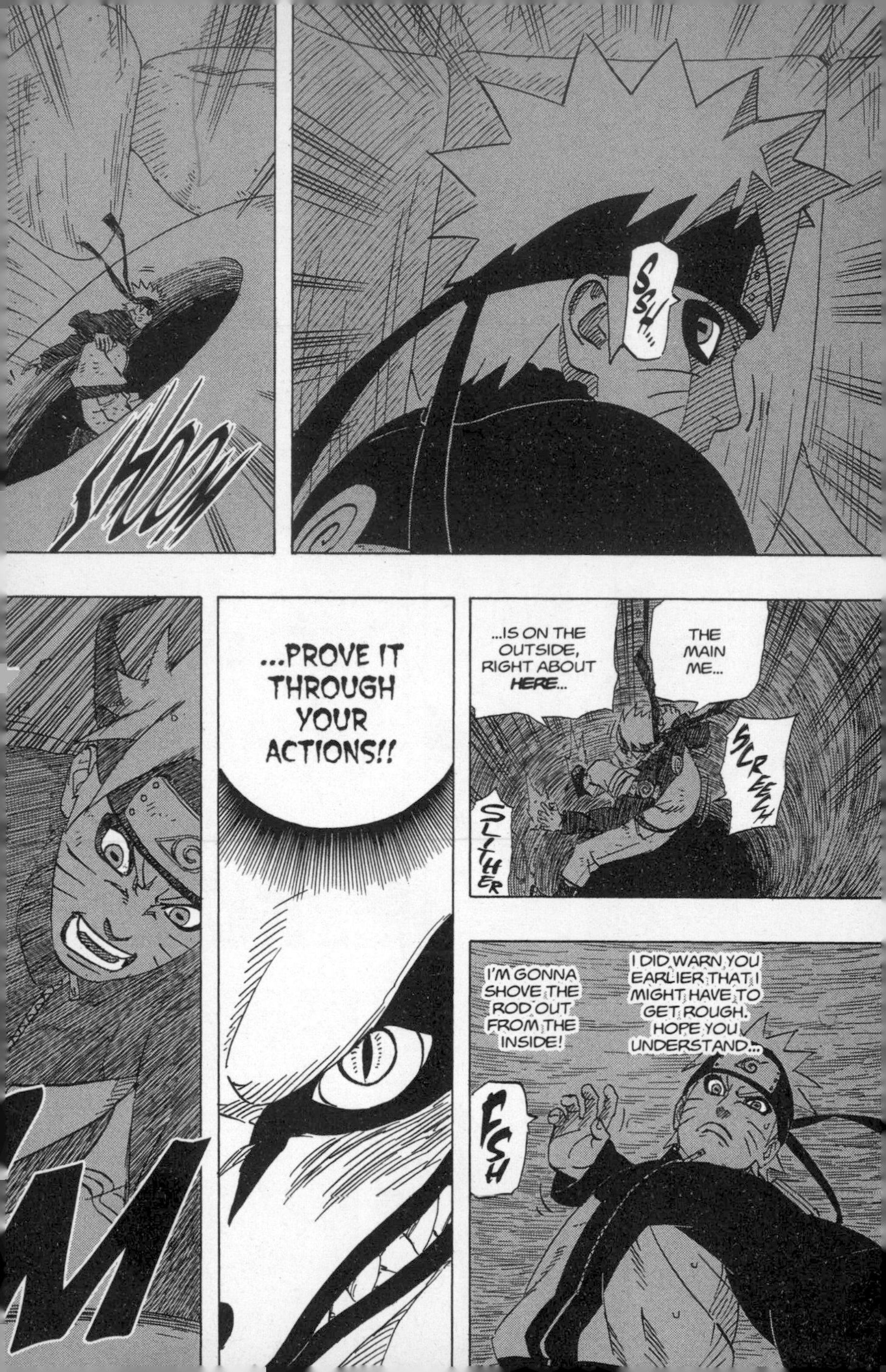
SSH
THE MAIN ME...
...IS ON THE OUTSIDE, RIGHT ABOUT HERE...
SCREECH
SLITHER
I DID WARN YOU EARLIER THAT I MIGHT HAVE TO GET ROUGH. HOPE YOU UNDERSTAND...
I'M GONNA SHOVE THE ROD OUT FROM THE INSIDE!
FSH
...PROVE IT THROUGH YOUR ACTIONS!!

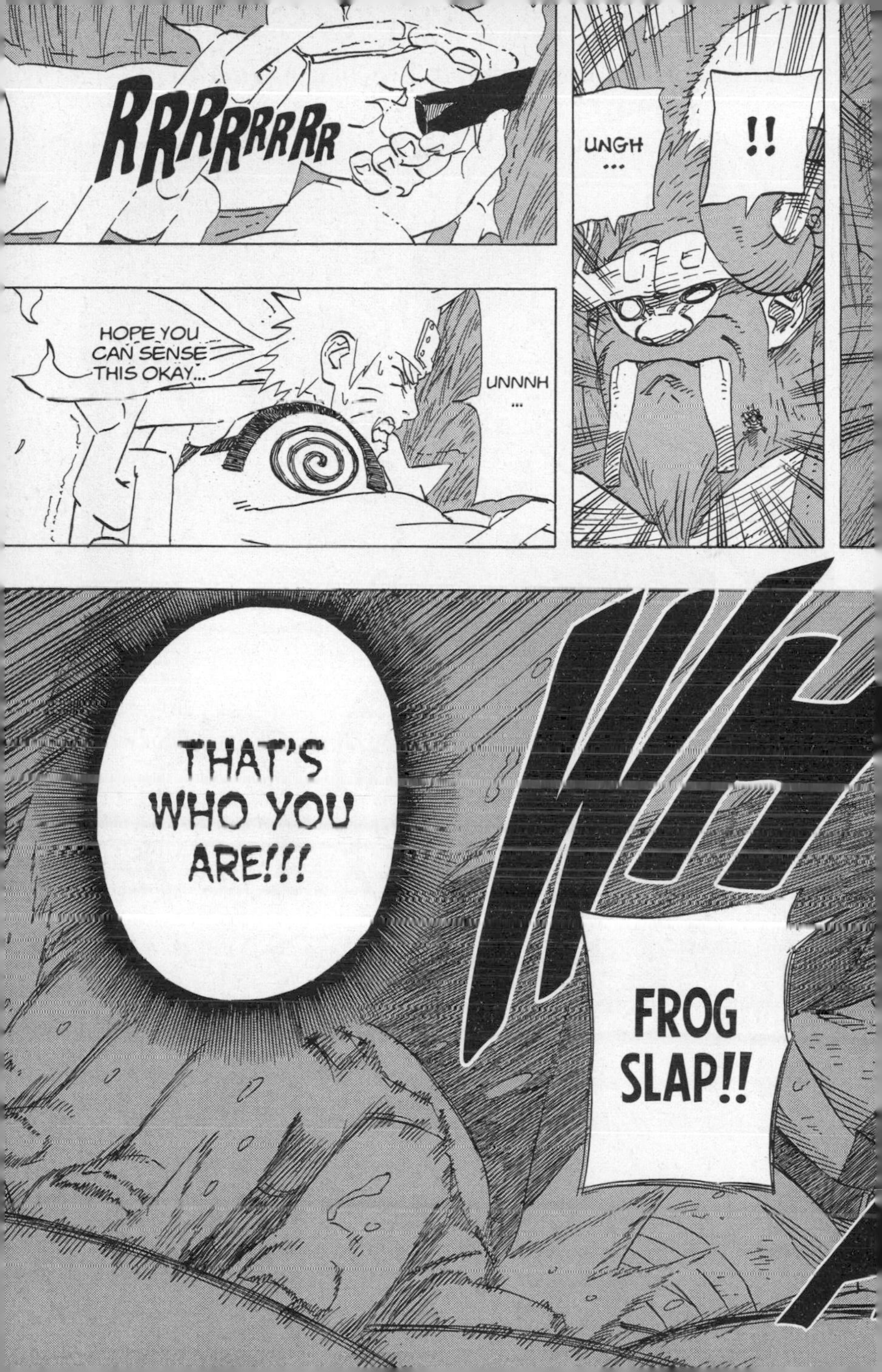
!!
UNGH ...
RRRRRRRR
UNNNH ...
HOPE YOU CAN SENSE THIS OKAY...
THAT'S WHO YOU ARE!!!
FROG SLAP!!

Illustration to Commemorate Reaching Volume 60 [5]

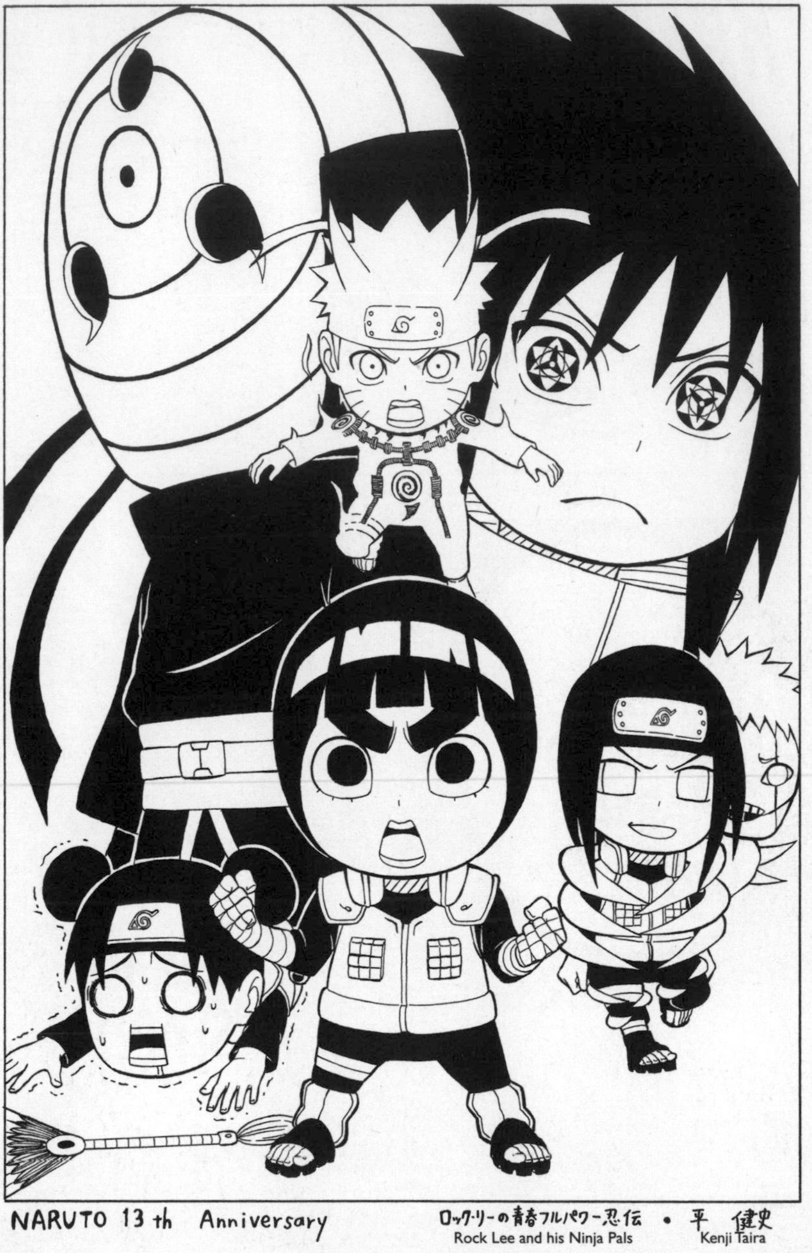

NARUTO 13 th Anniversary

ロック・リーの青春フルパワー忍伝 • 平 健史
Rock Lee and his Ninja Pals Kenji Taira

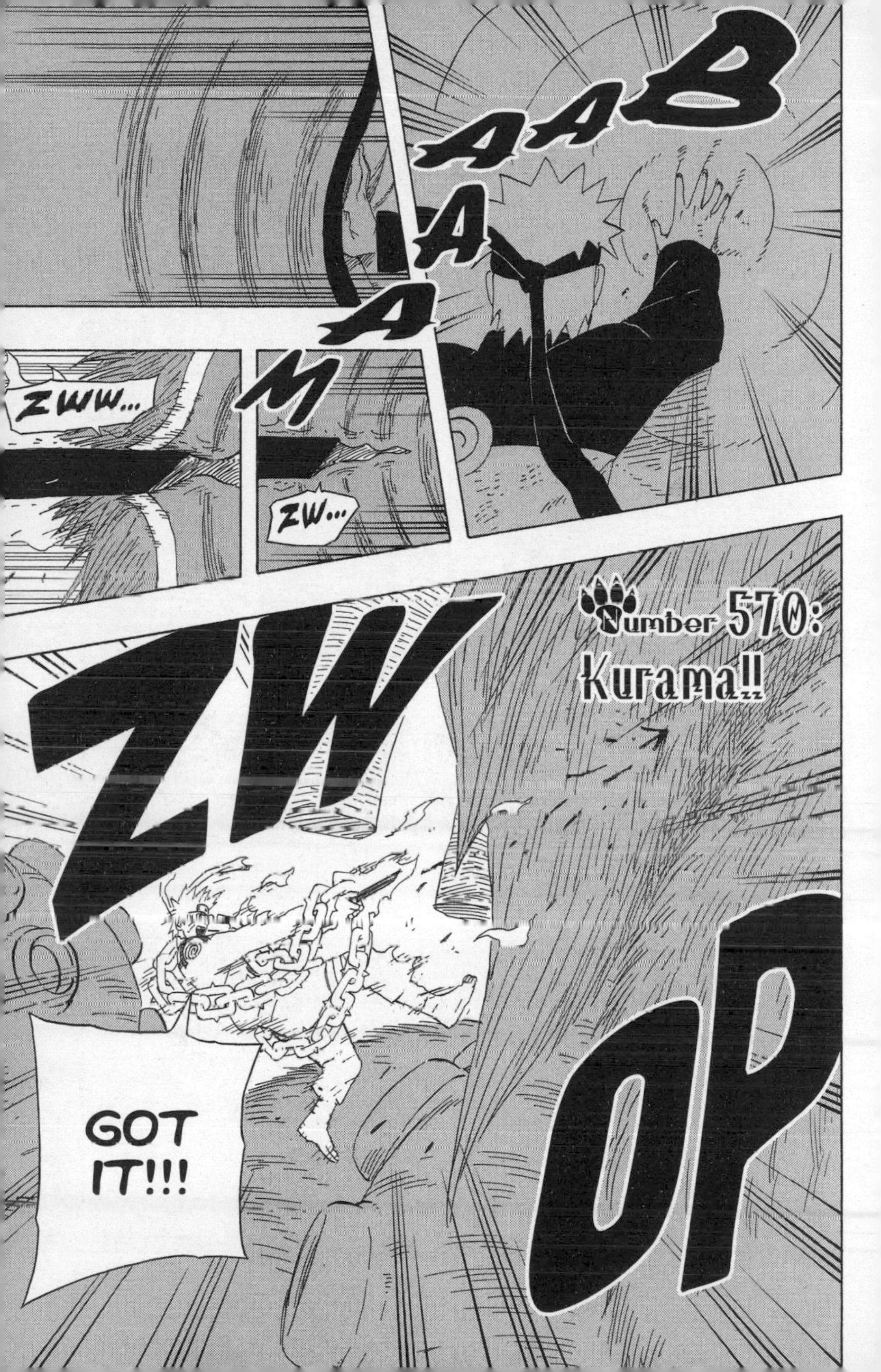
BAAAAAM
ZW...
ZWW...
Number 570: Kurama!!
ZWOP
GOT IT!!!

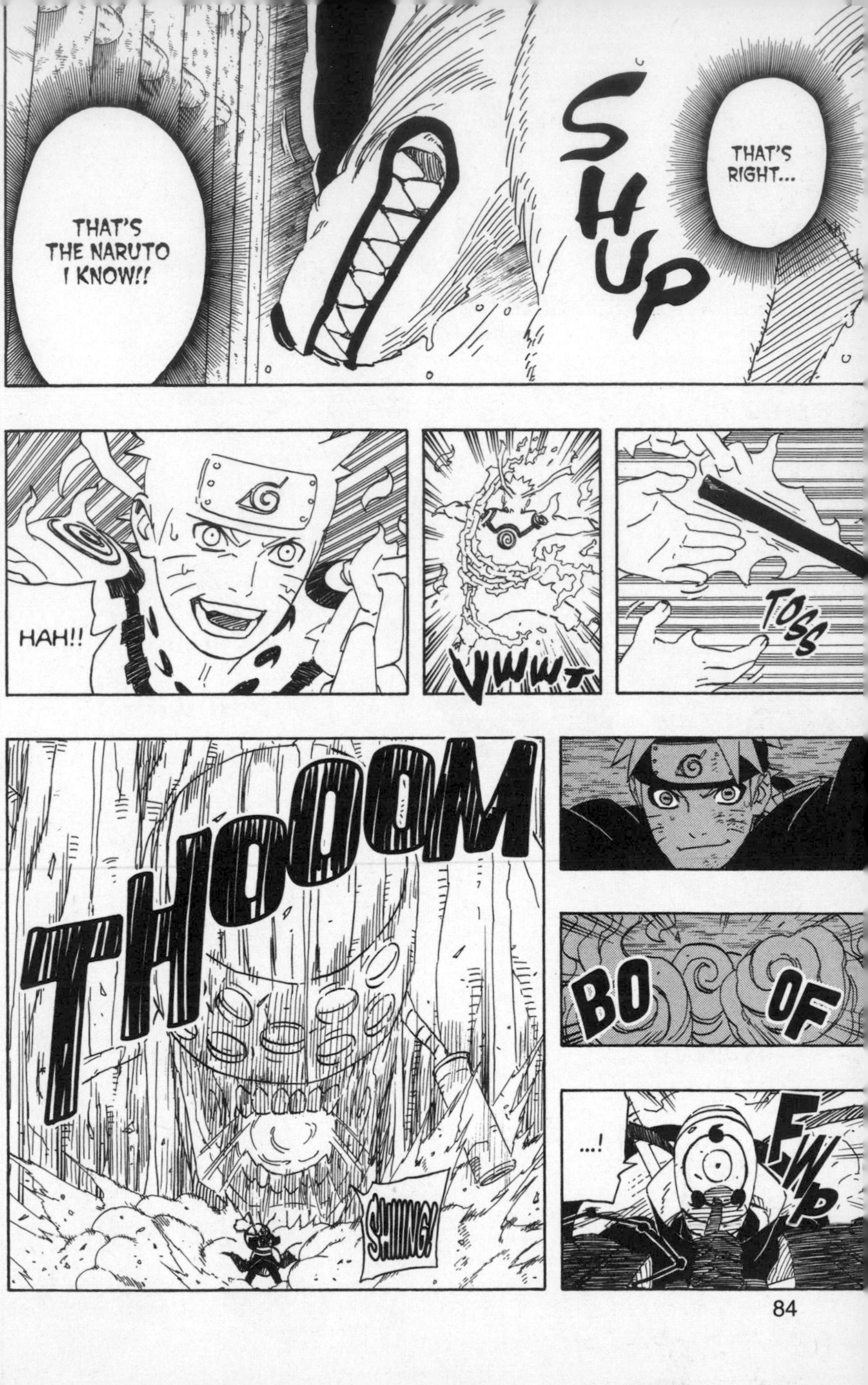
THAT'S RIGHT...
SHUP
THAT'S THE NARUTO I KNOW!!
TOSS
VWWT
HAH!!
BOOF
...!
FWP
THOOOM
SHIIING!

READ THIS WAY

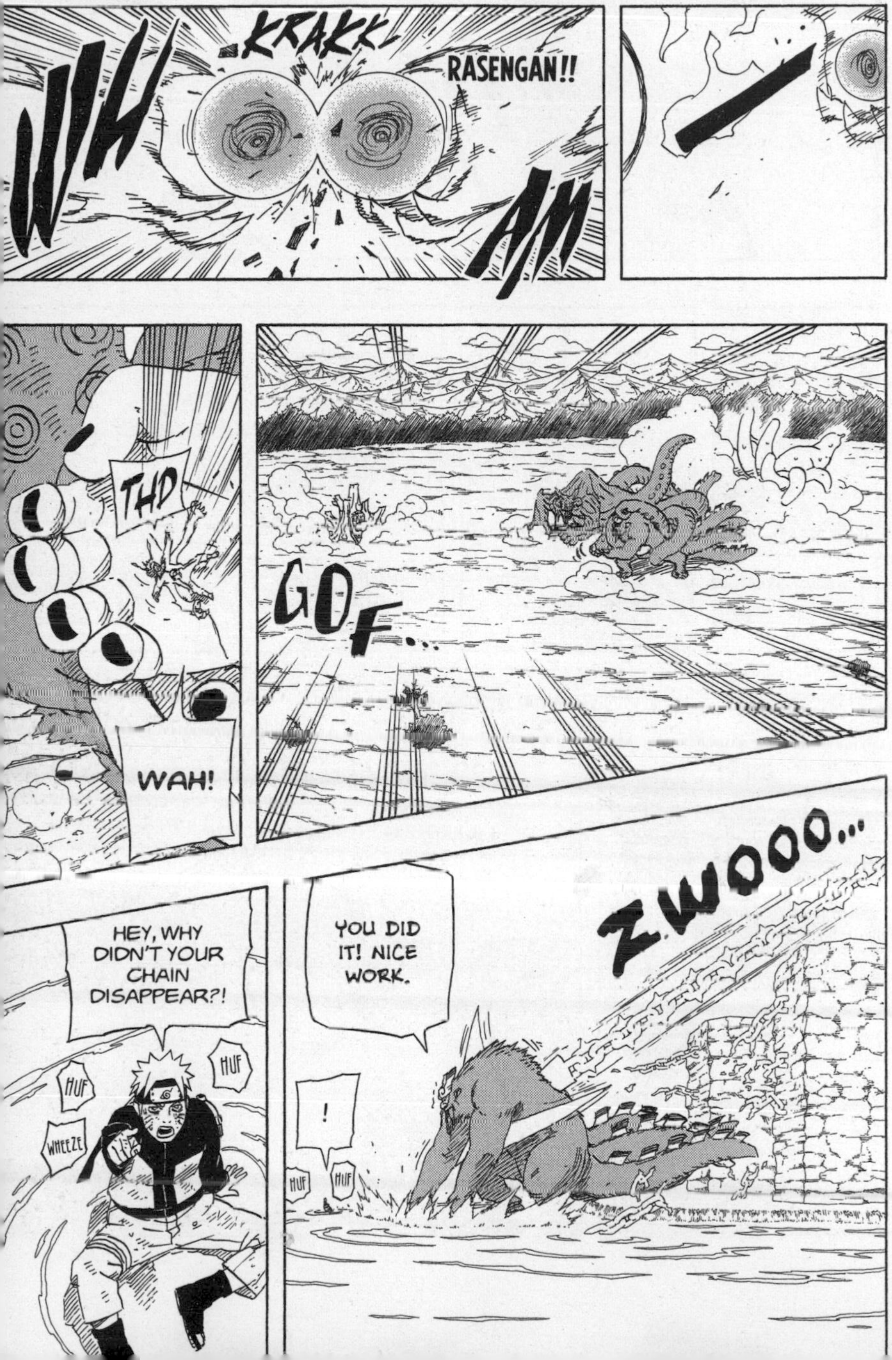
RASENGAN!!
KRAKK
WHAM
GOF...
THD
WAH!
ZWOOO...
YOU DID IT! NICE WORK.
HUF
HUF
!
HEY, WHY DIDN'T YOUR CHAIN DISAPPEAR?!
HUF
HUF
WHEEZE

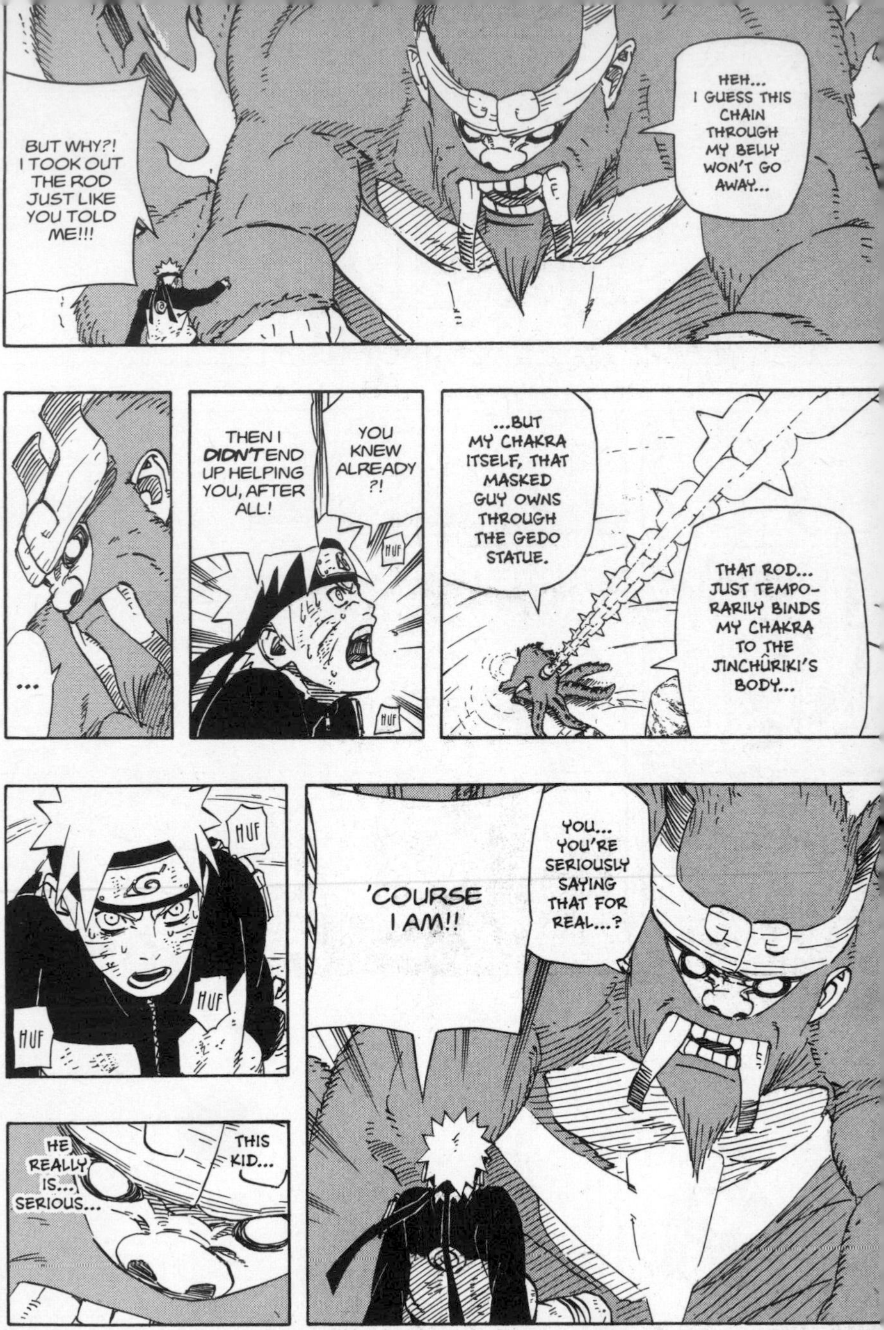
HEH... I GUESS THIS CHAIN THROUGH MY BELLY WON'T GO AWAY...
BUT WHY?! I TOOK OUT THE ROD JUST LIKE YOU TOLD ME!!!
THAT ROD... JUST TEMPORARILY BINDS MY CHAKRA TO THE JINCHŪRIKI'S BODY...
...BUT MY CHAKRA ITSELF, THAT MASKED GUY OWNS THROUGH THE GEDO STATUE.
YOU KNEW ALREADY?!
THEN I DIDN'T END UP HELPING YOU, AFTER ALL!
HUF
HUF
...
YOU... YOU'RE SERIOUSLY SAYING THAT FOR REAL...?
'COURSE I AM!!
HUF
HUF
HUF
THIS KID...
HE REALLY IS... SERIOUS...

READ THIS WAY

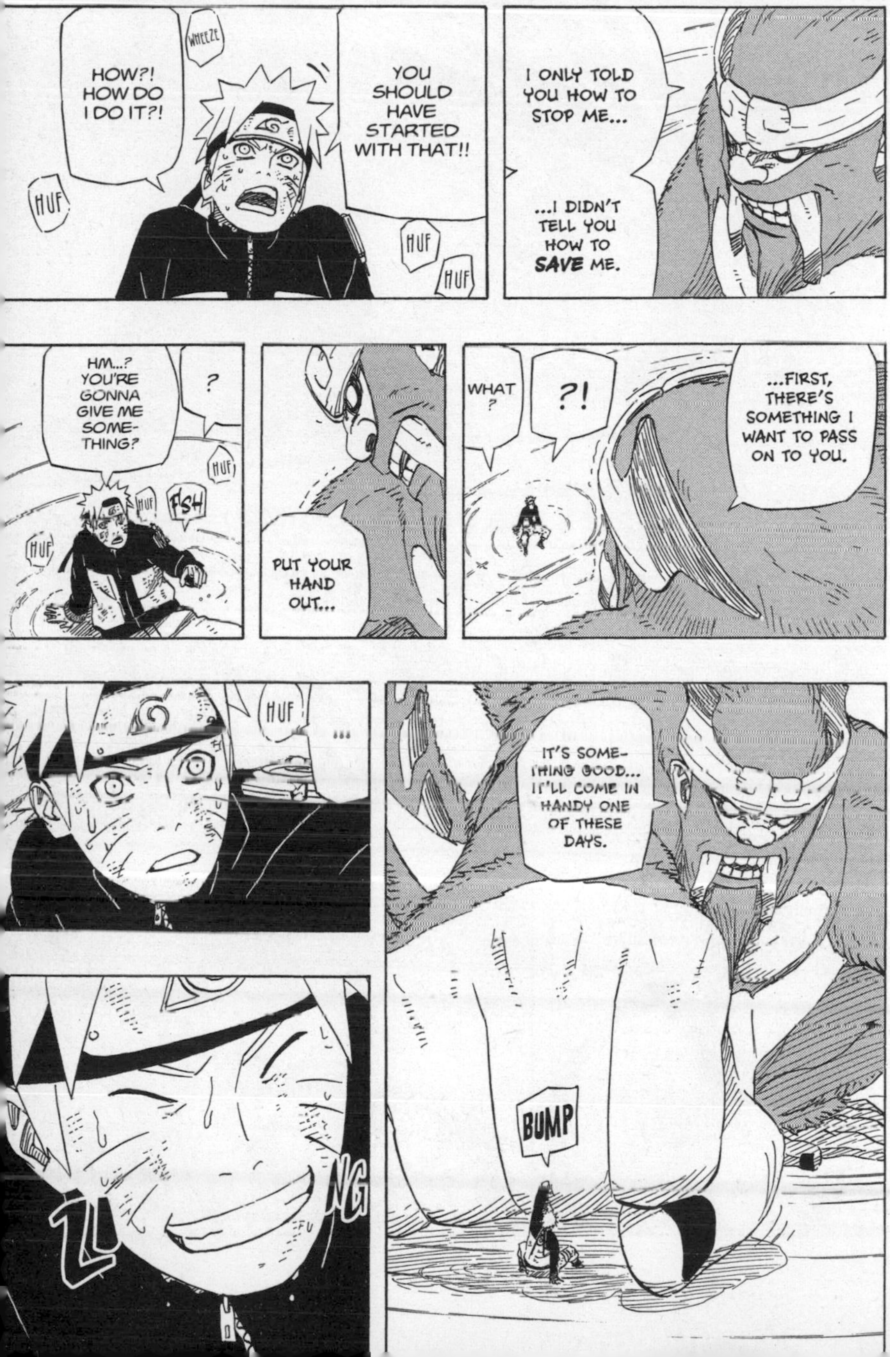
I ONLY TOLD YOU HOW TO STOP ME...
...I DIDN'T TELL YOU HOW TO SAVE ME.
WHEEZE
YOU SHOULD HAVE STARTED WITH THAT!!
HUF
HUF
HOW?! HOW DO I DO IT?!
HUF
...FIRST, THERE'S SOMETHING I WANT TO PASS ON TO YOU.
?!
WHAT?
PUT YOUR HAND OUT...
?
HM...? YOU'RE GONNA GIVE ME SOMETHING?
HUF
FSH
HUF
HUF
IT'S SOMETHING GOOD... IT'LL COME IN HANDY ONE OF THESE DAYS.
BUMP
HUF
...
FU

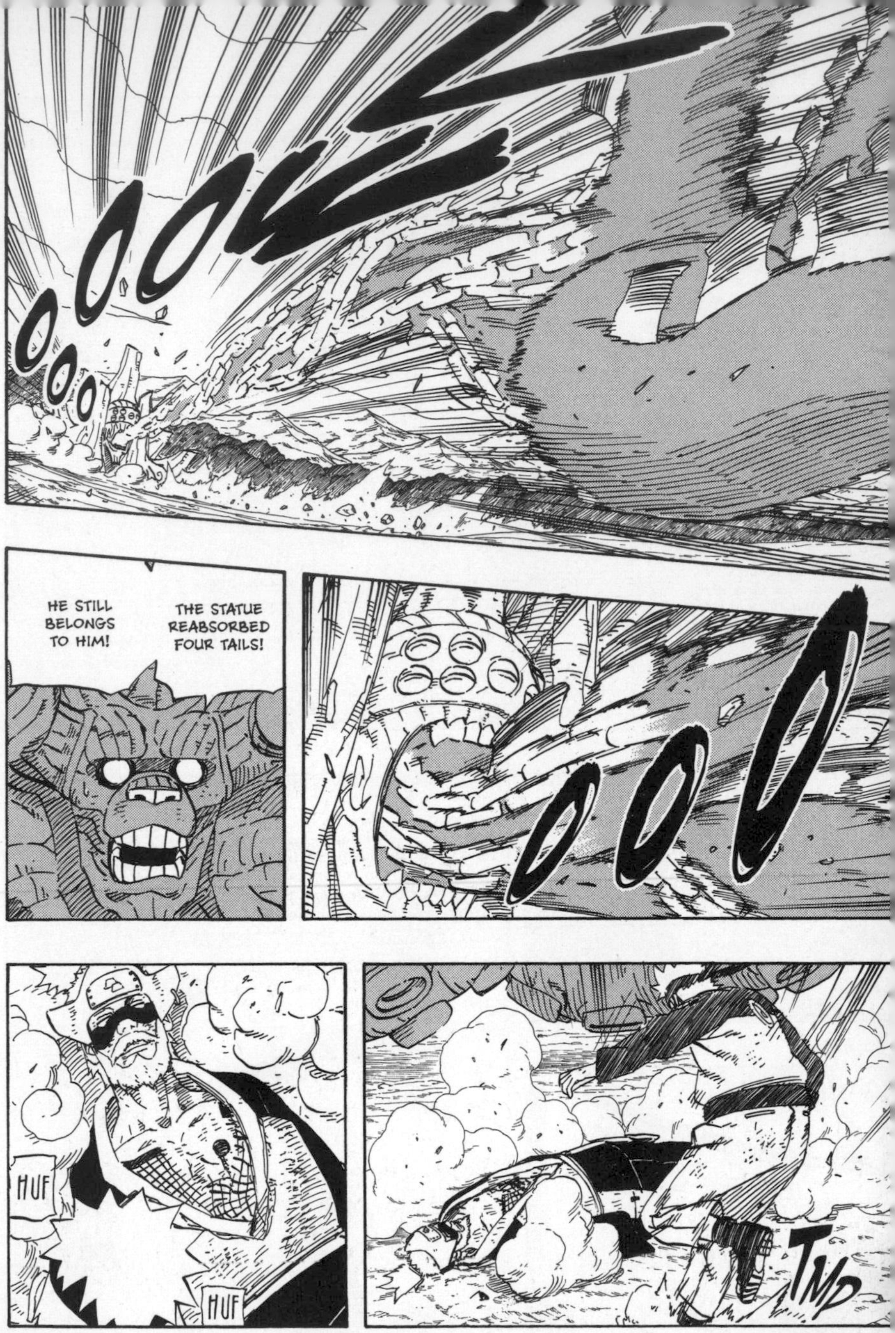
THE STATUE REABSORBED FOUR TAILS!
HE STILL BELONGS TO HIM!
TMP
HUF
HUF

READ THIS WAY

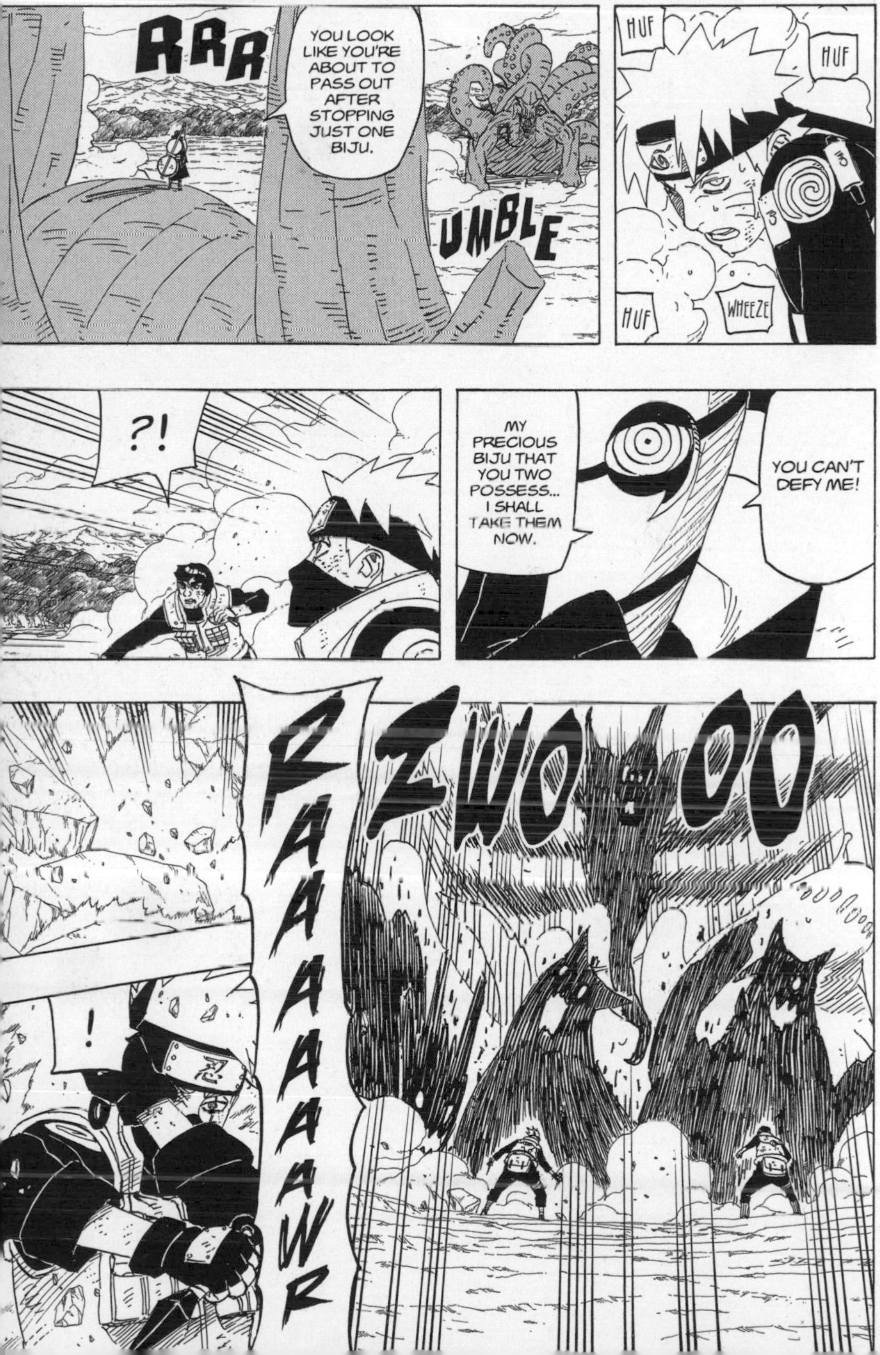
HUF
HUF
HUF
WHEEZE
RRRUMBLE
YOU LOOK LIKE YOU'RE ABOUT TO PASS OUT AFTER STOPPING JUST ONE BIJU.
MY PRECIOUS BIJU THAT YOU TWO POSSESS... I SHALL TAKE THEM NOW.
YOU CAN'T DEFY ME!
?!
ZWOOOO
RAAAAAAAAAWR
!

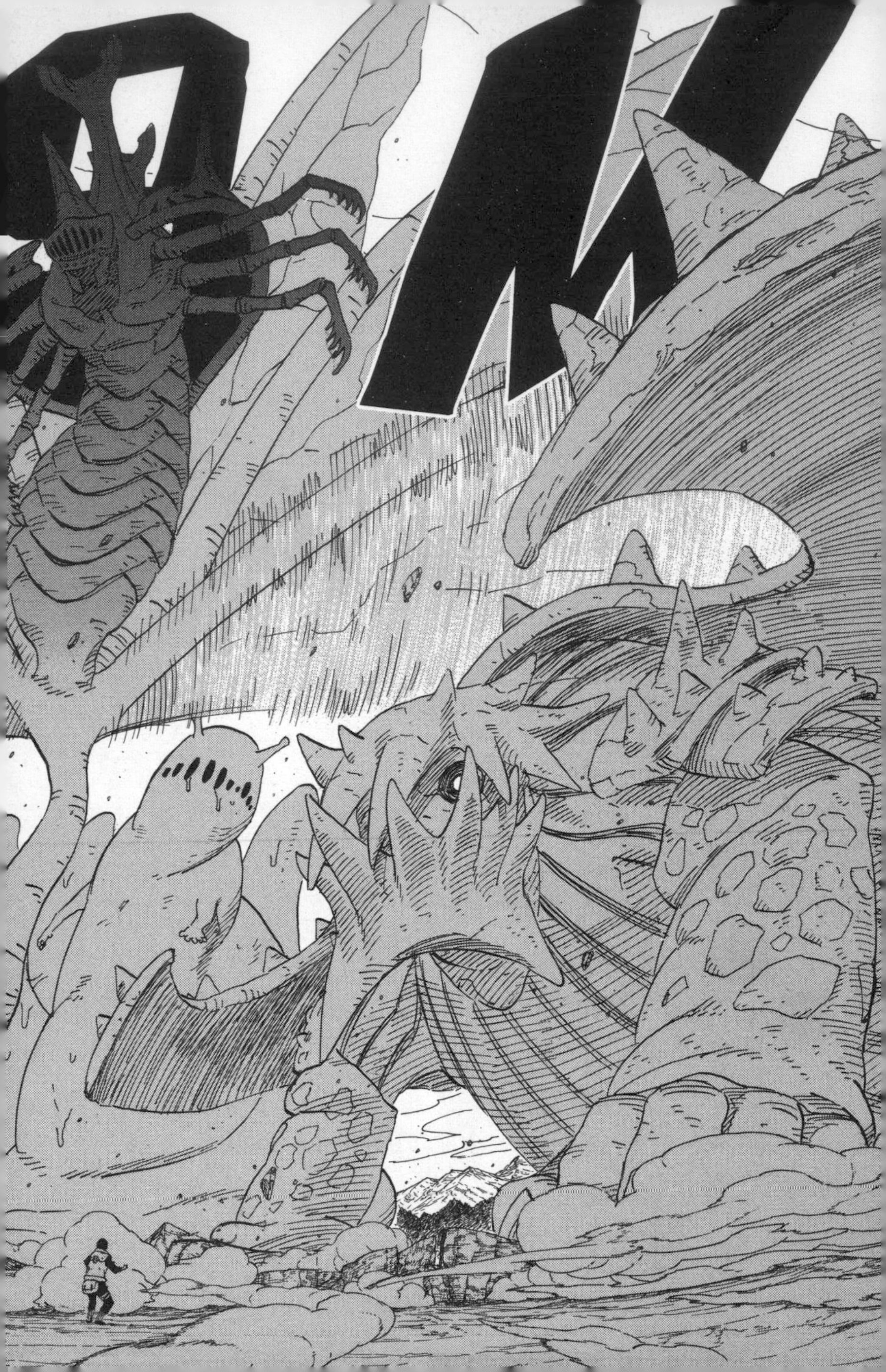

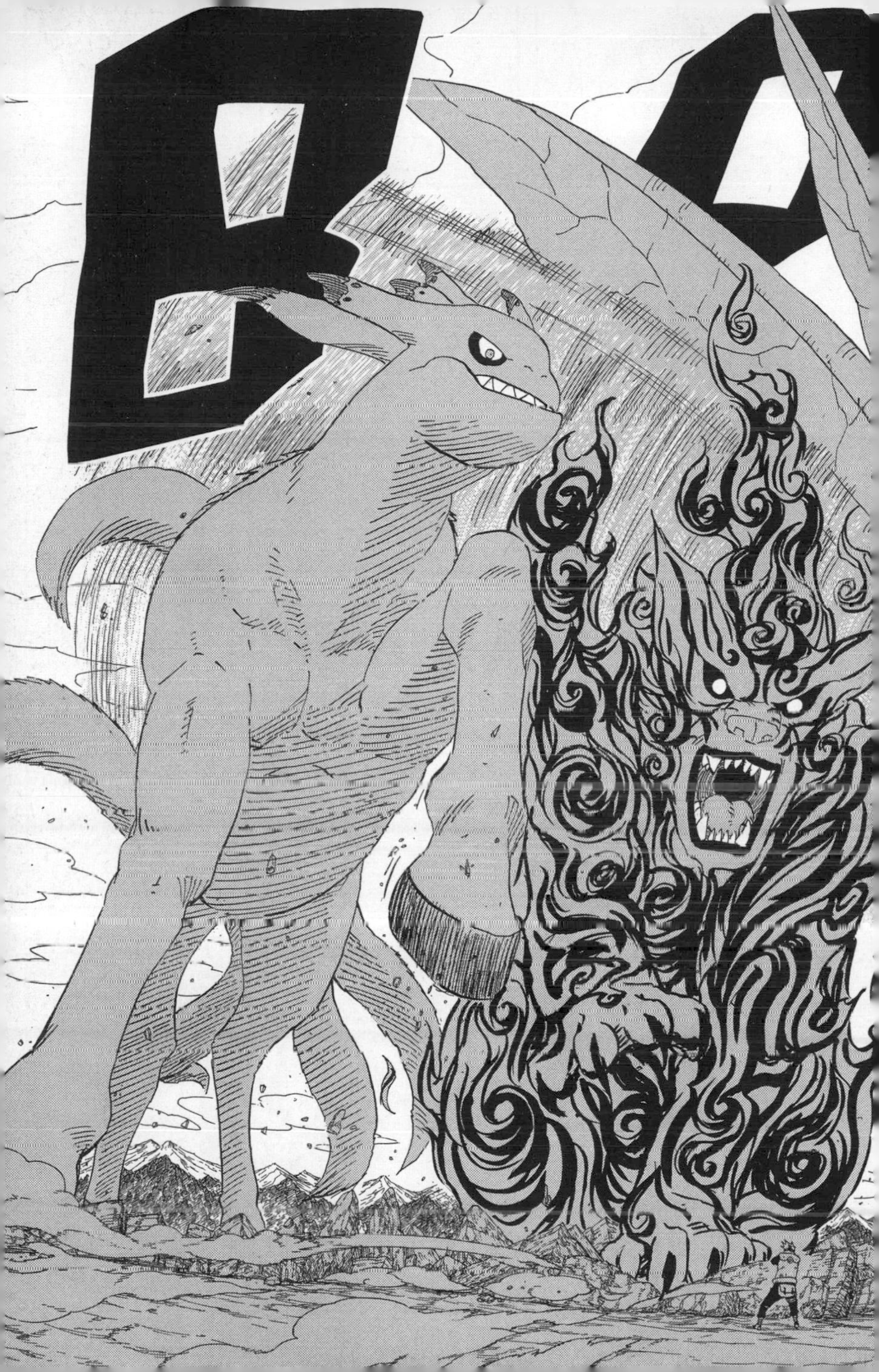
BA

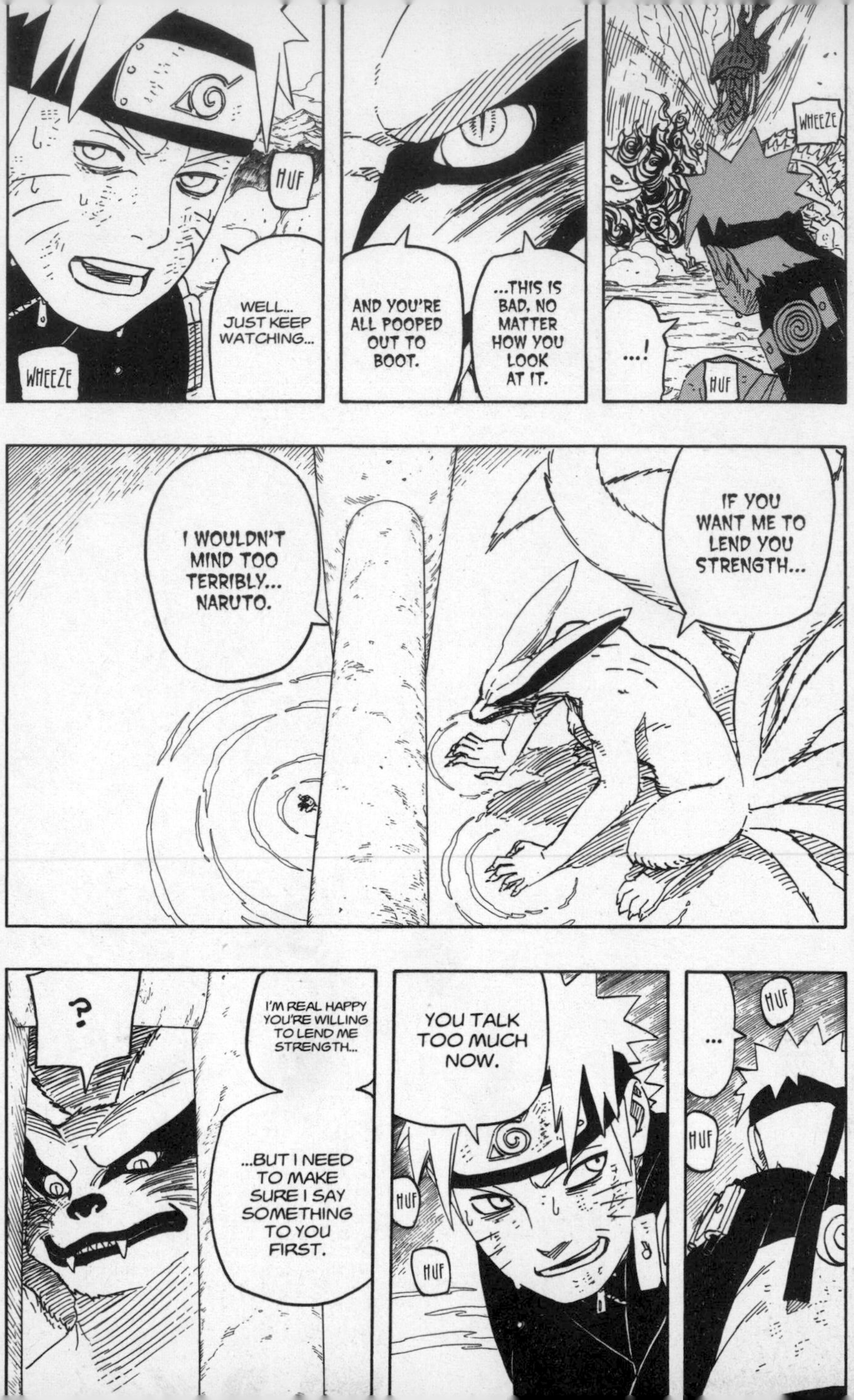
WHEEZE
...!
HUF
...THIS IS BAD, NO MATTER HOW YOU LOOK AT IT.
AND YOU'RE ALL POOPED OUT TO BOOT.
HUF
WELL... JUST KEEP WATCHING...
WHEEZE
IF YOU WANT ME TO LEND YOU STRENGTH...
I WOULDN'T MIND TOO TERRIBLY... NARUTO.
HUF
...
HUF
YOU TALK TOO MUCH NOW.
HUF
HUF
I'M REAL HAPPY YOU'RE WILLING TO LEND ME STRENGTH...
...BUT I NEED TO MAKE SURE I SAY SOMETHING TO YOU FIRST.
?

READ THIS WAY

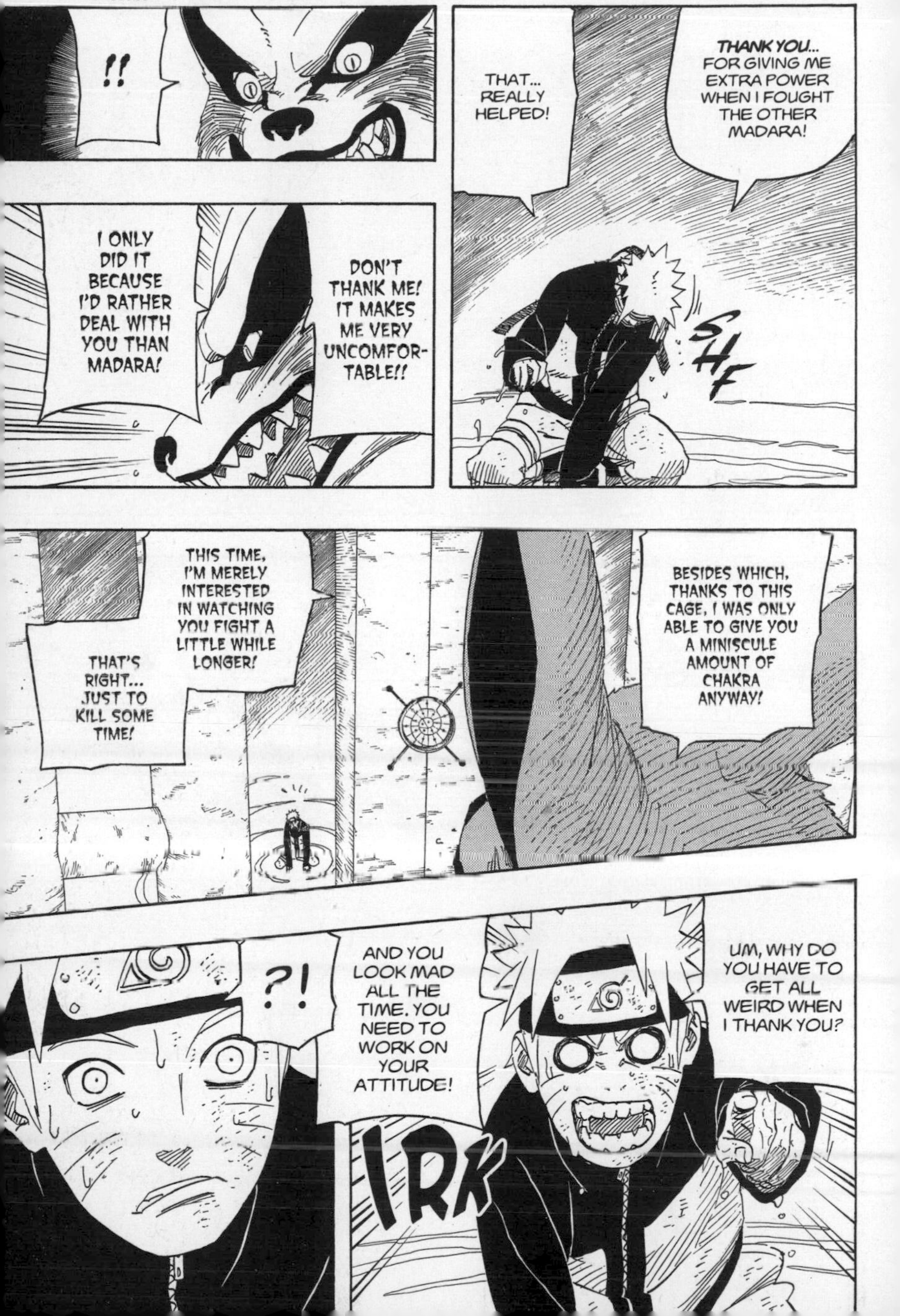
THANK YOU... FOR GIVING ME EXTRA POWER WHEN I FOUGHT THE OTHER MADARA!
THAT... REALLY HELPED!
SHF
!!
DON'T THANK ME! IT MAKES ME VERY UNCOMFORTABLE!!
I ONLY DID IT BECAUSE I'D RATHER DEAL WITH YOU THAN MADARA!
BESIDES WHICH, THANKS TO THIS CAGE, I WAS ONLY ABLE TO GIVE YOU A MINISCULE AMOUNT OF CHAKRA ANYWAY!
THIS TIME, I'M MERELY INTERESTED IN WATCHING YOU FIGHT A LITTLE WHILE LONGER!
THAT'S RIGHT... JUST TO KILL SOME TIME!
UM, WHY DO YOU HAVE TO GET ALL WEIRD WHEN I THANK YOU?
AND YOU LOOK MAD ALL THE TIME. YOU NEED TO WORK ON YOUR ATTITUDE!
IRK
?!

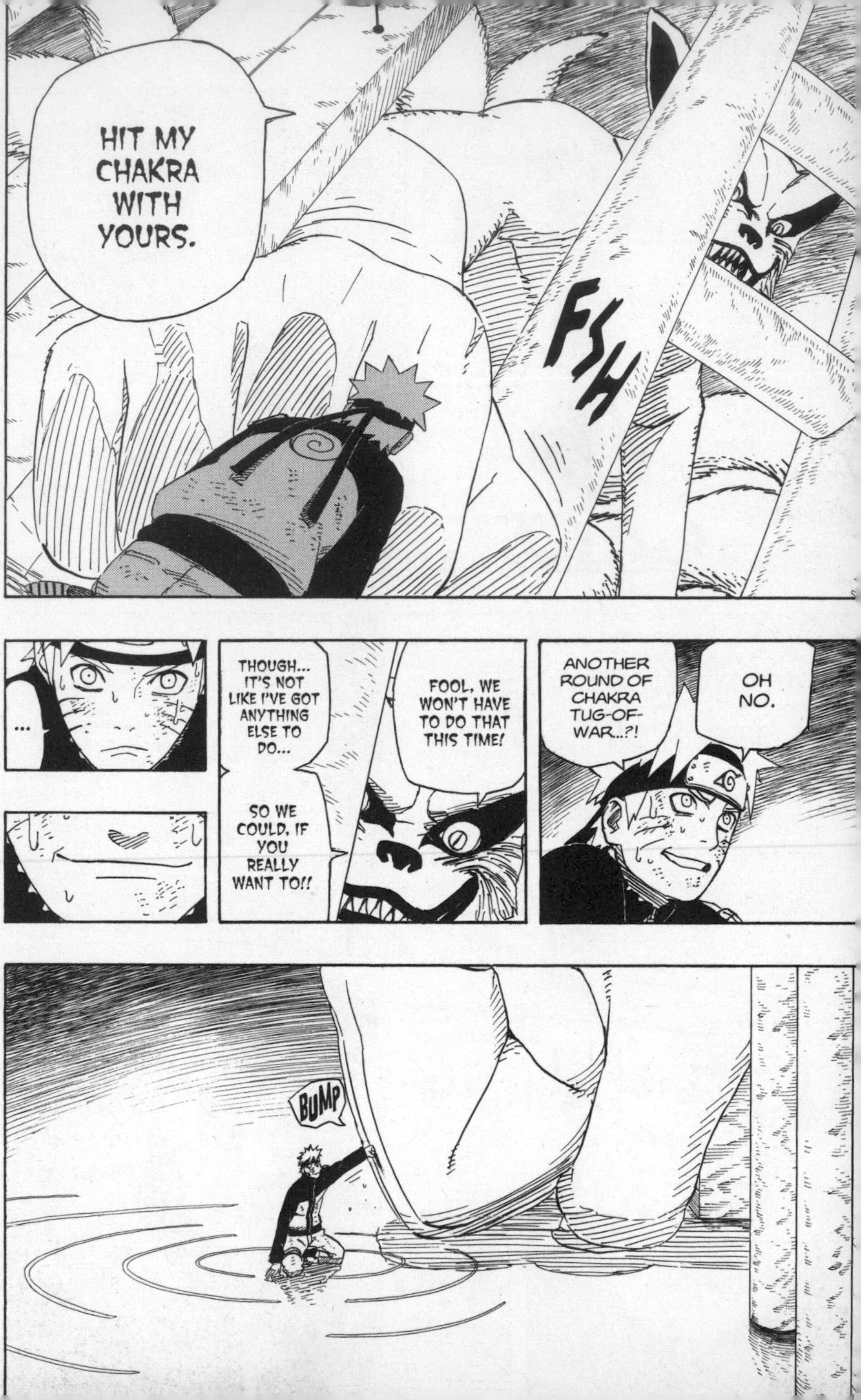
HIT MY CHAKRA WITH YOURS.
FSH
OH NO.
ANOTHER ROUND OF CHAKRA TUG-OF-WAR...?!
FOOL, WE WON'T HAVE TO DO THAT THIS TIME!
THOUGH... IT'S NOT LIKE I'VE GOT ANYTHING ELSE TO DO...
SO WE COULD, IF YOU REALLY WANT TO!!
...
BUMP

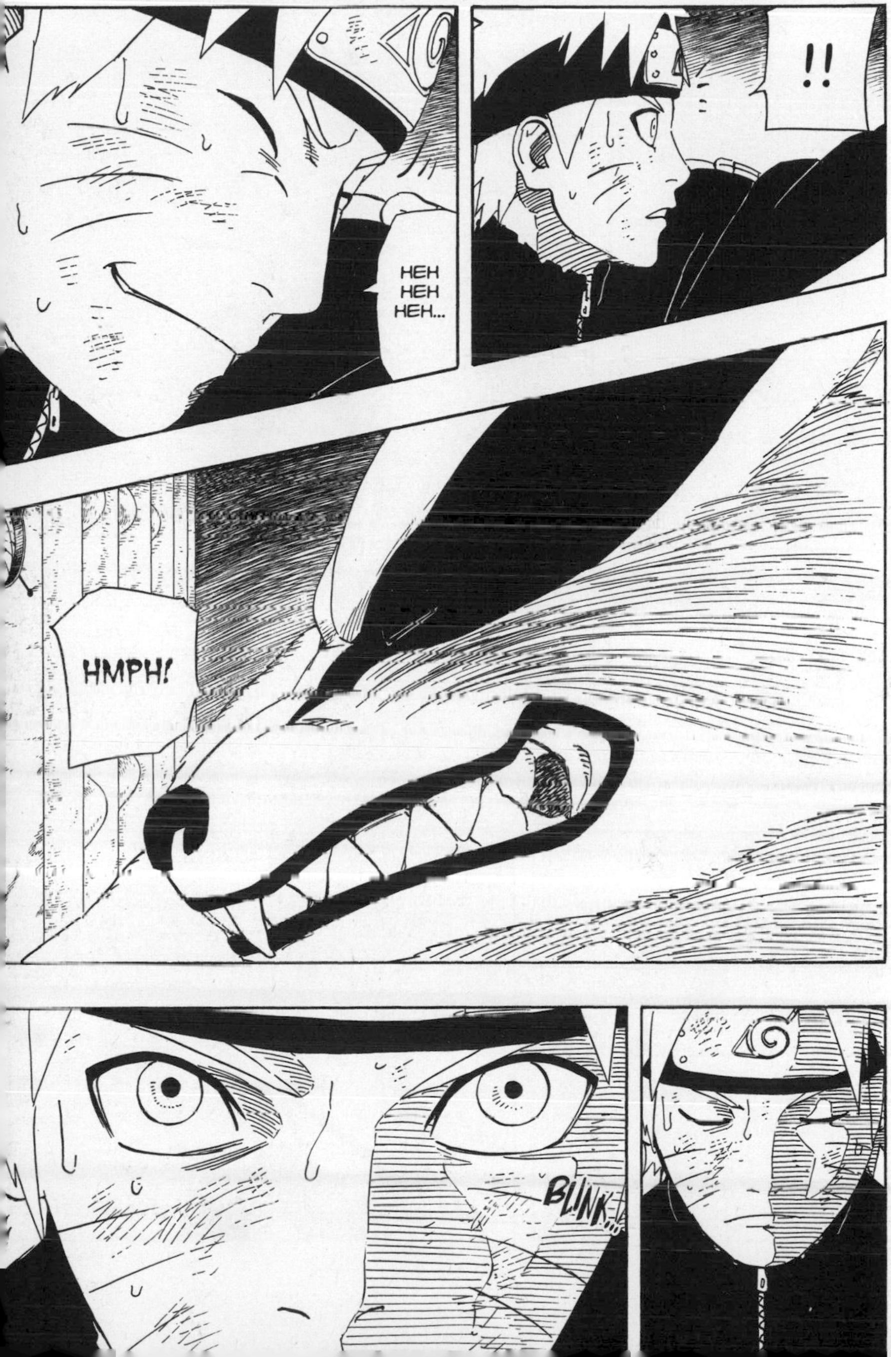
READ THIS WAY
!!
HEH HEH HEH...
HMPH!
BLINK...

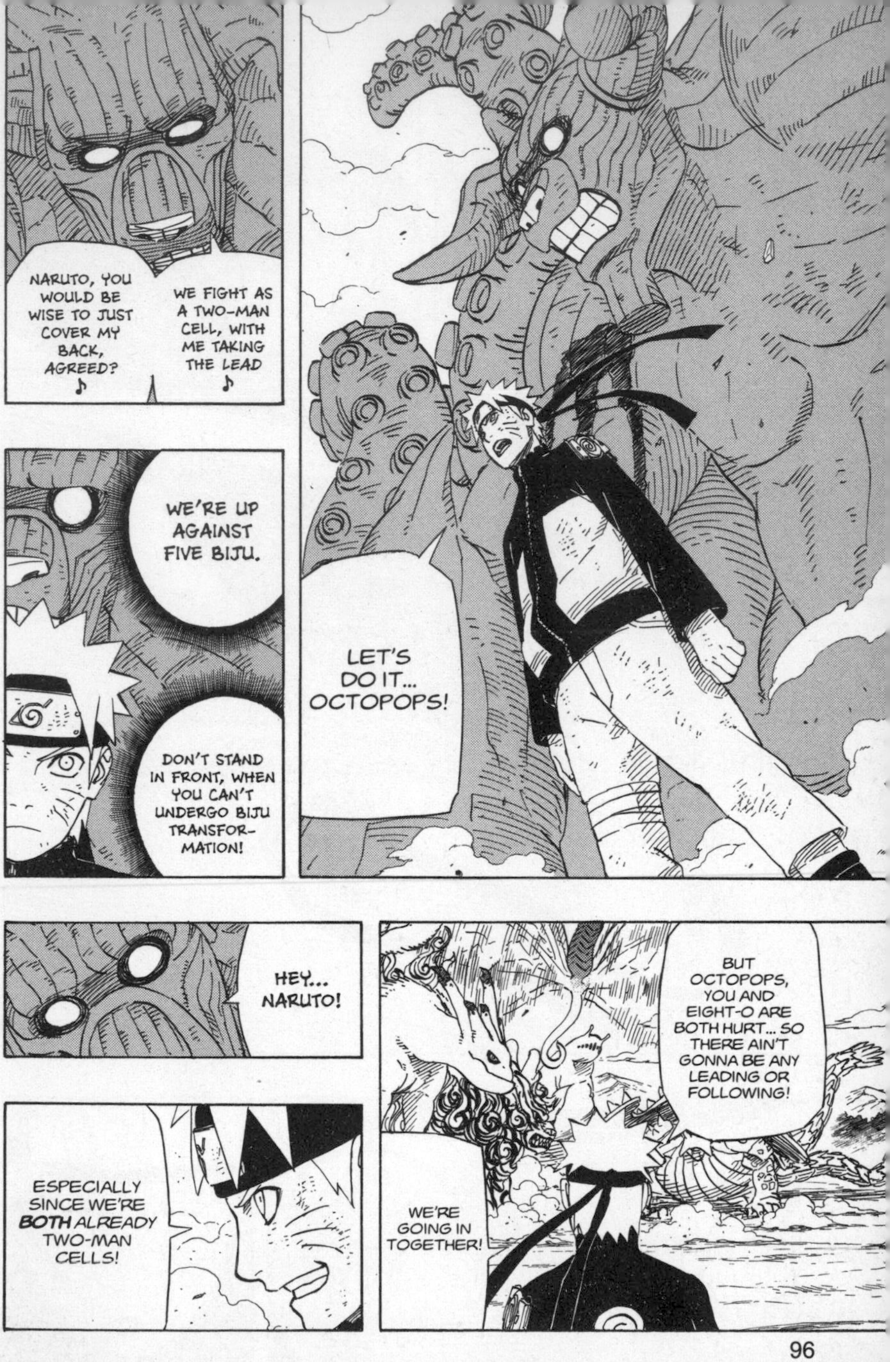
LET'S DO IT... OCTOPOPS!
WE FIGHT AS A TWO-MAN CELL, WITH ME TAKING THE LEAD ♪
NARUTO, YOU WOULD BE WISE TO JUST COVER MY BACK, AGREED? ♪
WE'RE UP AGAINST FIVE BIJU.
DON'T STAND IN FRONT, WHEN YOU CAN'T UNDERGO BIJU TRANSFOR-MATION!
BUT OCTOPOPS, YOU AND EIGHT-O ARE BOTH HURT... SO THERE AIN'T GONNA BE ANY LEADING OR FOLLOWING!
WE'RE GOING IN TOGETHER!
HEY... NARUTO!
ESPECIALLY SINCE WE'RE **BOTH** ALREADY TWO-MAN CELLS!

READ THIS WAY

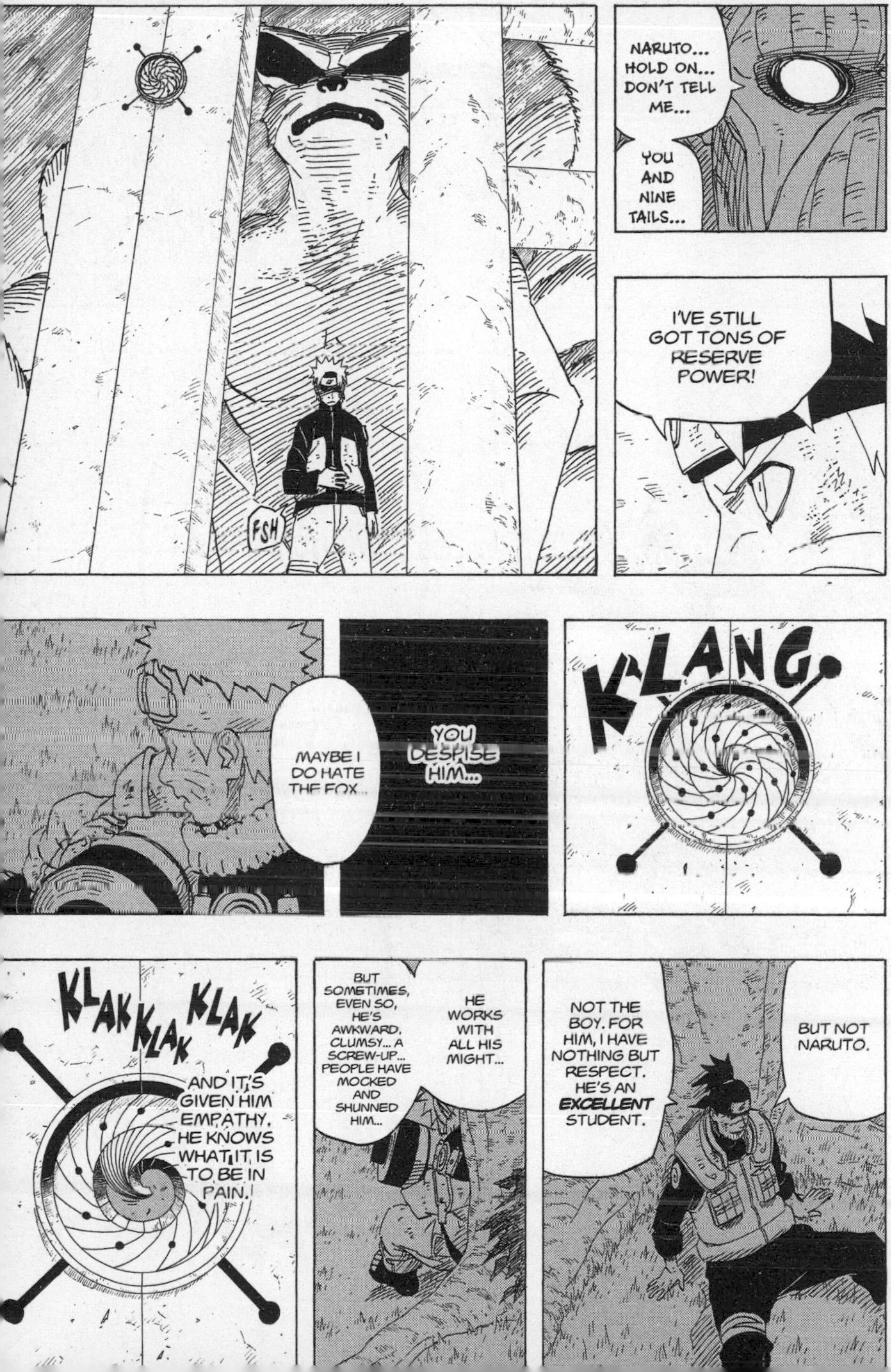

NARUTO... HOLD ON... DON'T TELL ME...
YOU AND NINE TAILS...
I'VE STILL GOT TONS OF RESERVE POWER!
FSH
KLANG
YOU DESPISE HIM...
MAYBE I DO HATE THE FOX...
BUT NOT NARUTO.
NOT THE BOY. FOR HIM, I HAVE NOTHING BUT RESPECT. HE'S AN EXCELLENT STUDENT.
HE WORKS WITH ALL HIS MIGHT...
BUT SOMETIMES, EVEN SO, HE'S AWKWARD, CLUMSY... A SCREW-UP... PEOPLE HAVE MOCKED AND SHUNNED HIM...
KLAK KLAK KLAK
AND IT'S GIVEN HIM EMPATHY. HE KNOWS WHAT IT IS TO BE IN PAIN.

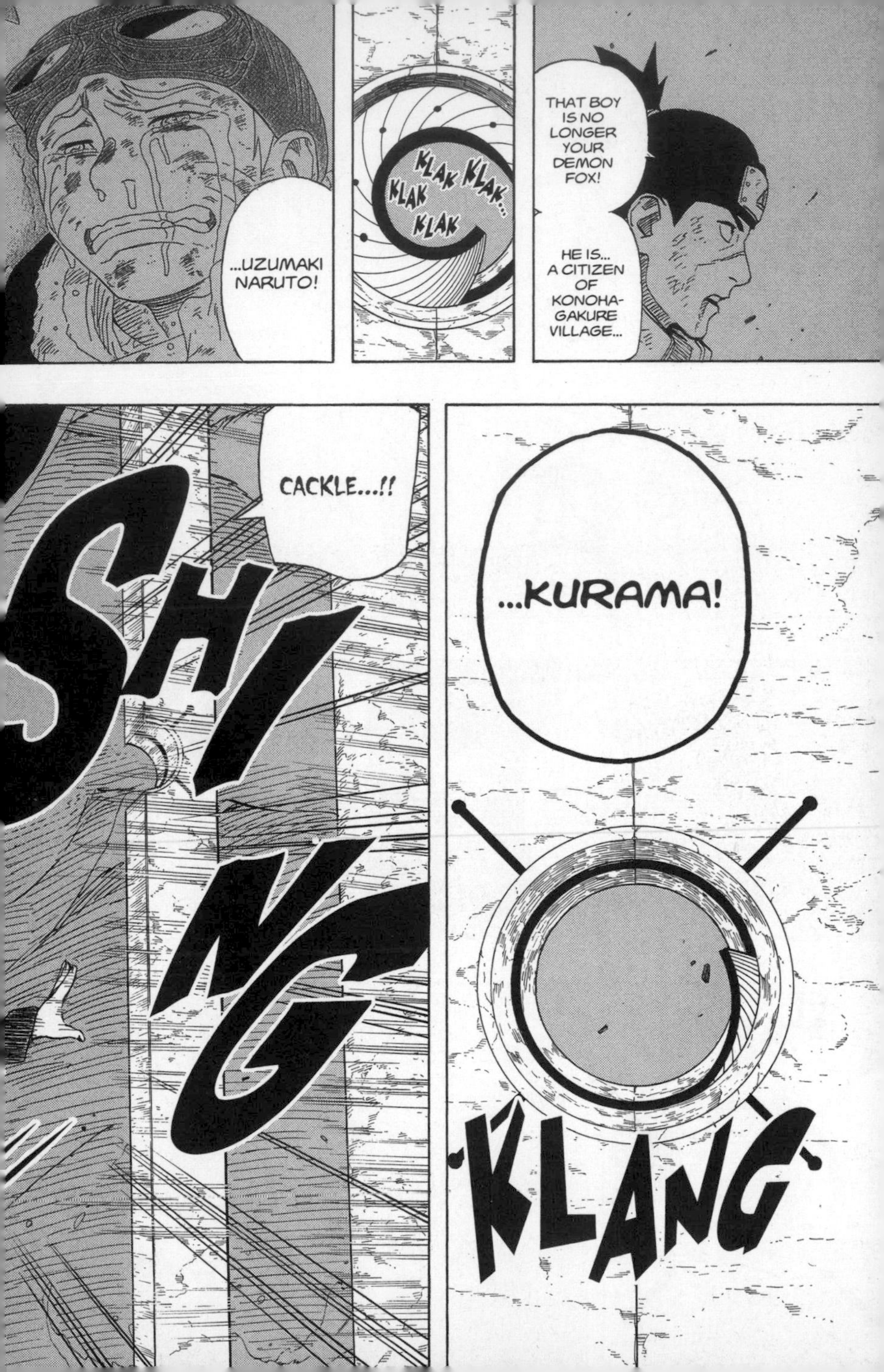
THAT BOY IS NO LONGER YOUR DEMON FOX!
HE IS... A CITIZEN OF KONOHA-GAKURE VILLAGE...
KLAK KLAK KLAK... KLAK
...UZUMAKI NARUTO!
...KURAMA!
KLANG
CACKLE...!!
SHING

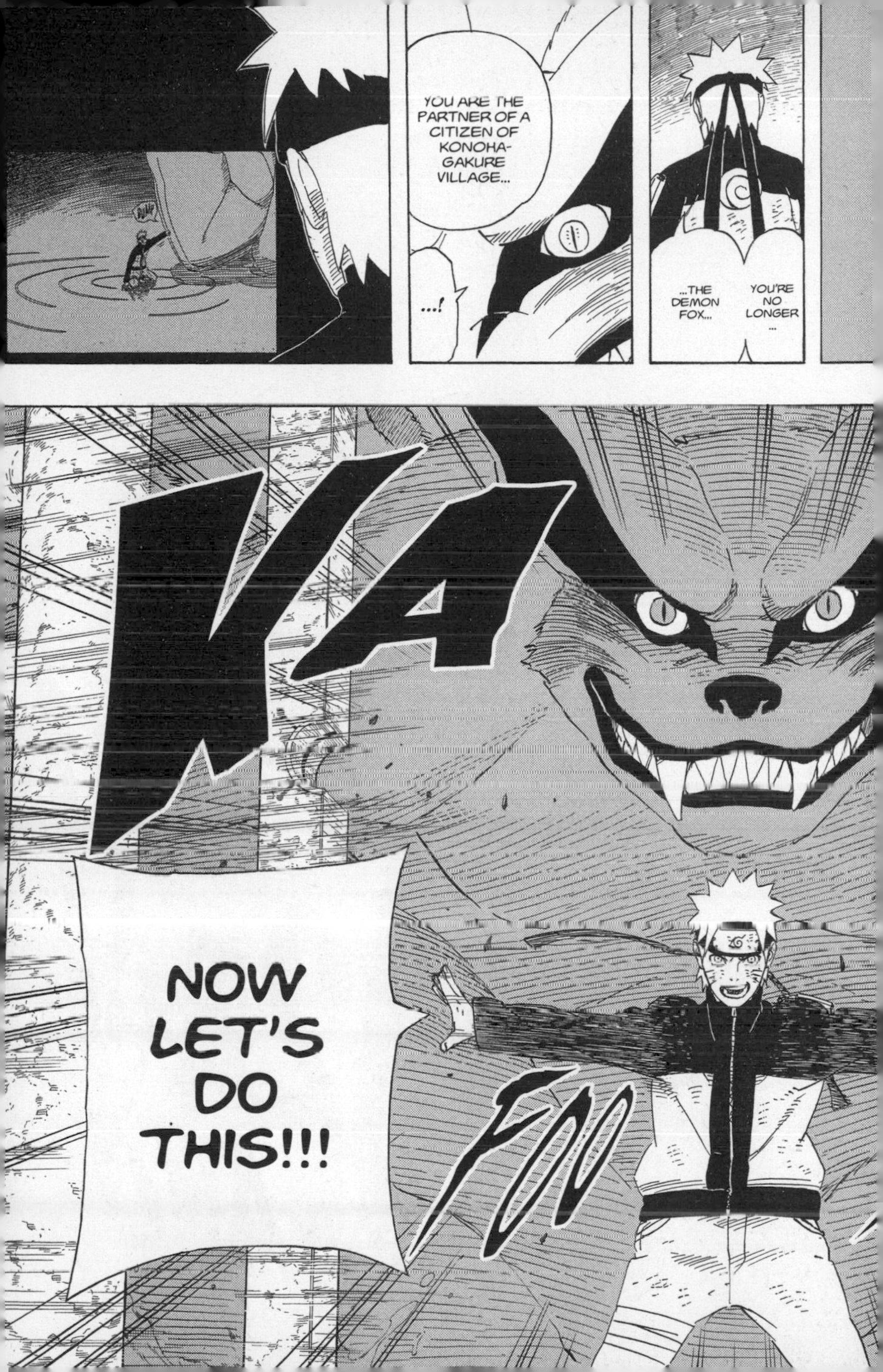
YOU'RE NO LONGER ...
...THE DEMON FOX...
YOU ARE THE PARTNER OF A CITIZEN OF KONOHA-GAKURE VILLAGE...
...!
KA
NOW LET'S DO THIS!!!

Illustration to Commemorate Reaching Volume 60 [6]

Yuichi Itakura

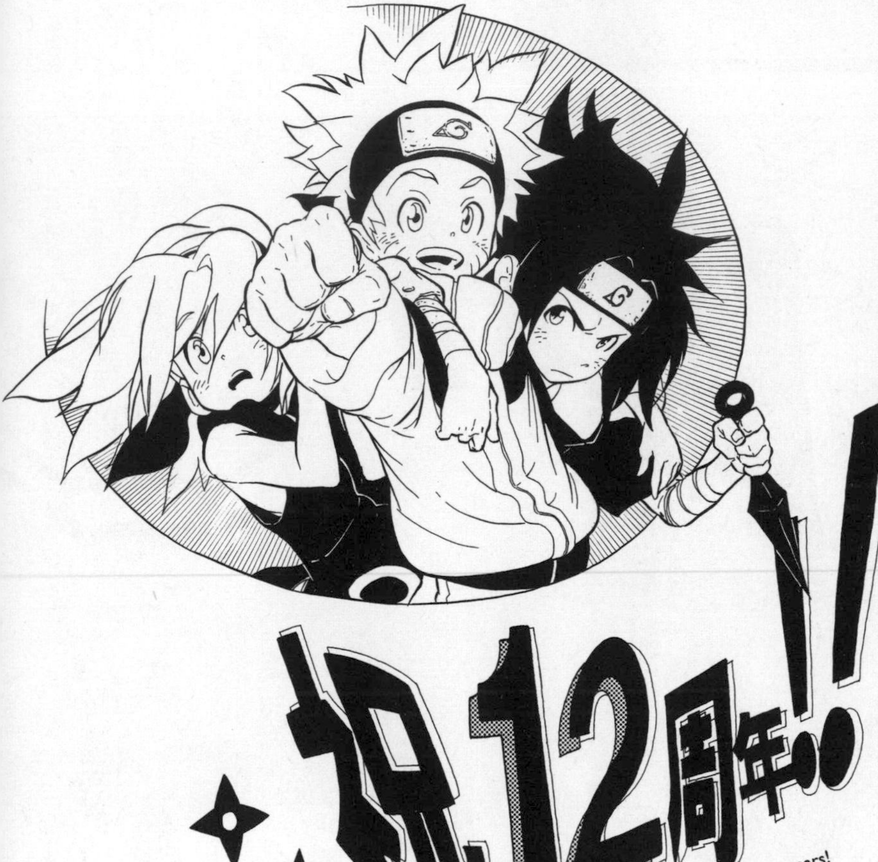
祝12周年!!
Congrats on 12 years!
体に気をつけて頑張って下さい！
Take care and keep up the great work!

Number 571: Biju Mode!!

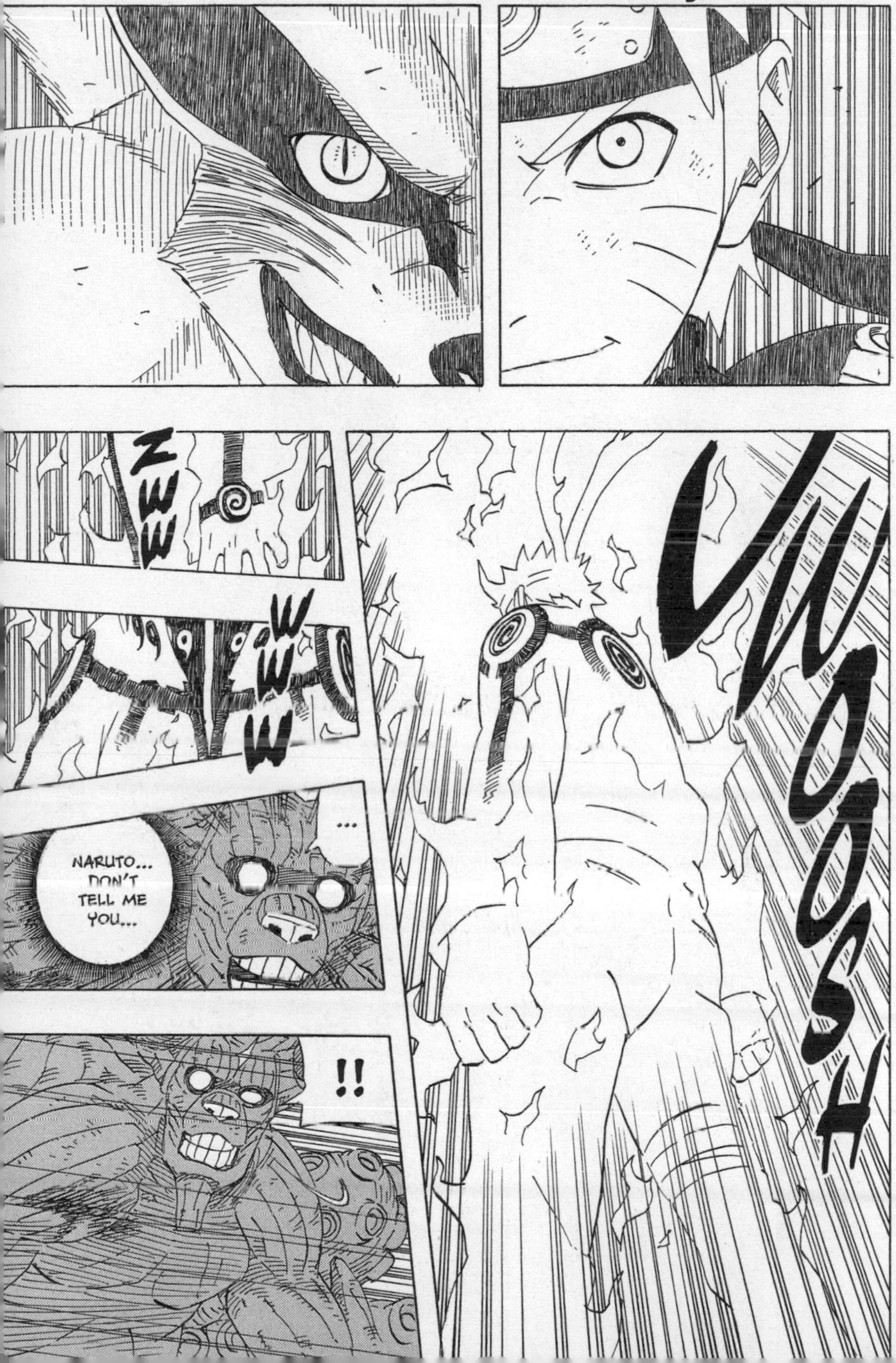
WHOOSH
ZWWW
WWWW
...
NARUTO... DON'T TELL ME YOU...
!!

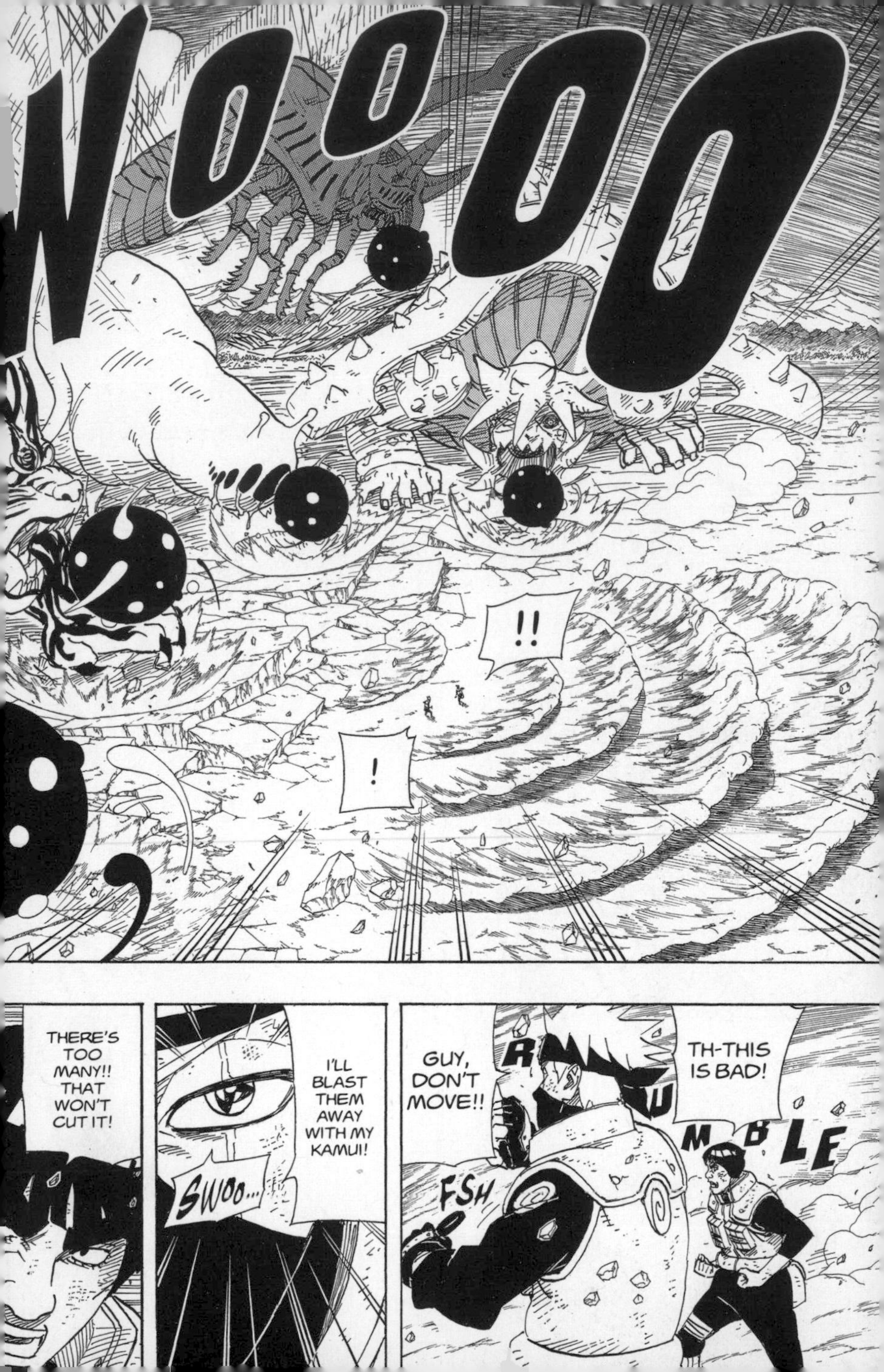
WOOOOO
!!
!
TH-THIS IS BAD!
RUMBLE
GUY, DON'T MOVE!!
FSH
I'LL BLAST THEM AWAY WITH MY KAMUI!
SWOO...
THERE'S TOO MANY!! THAT WON'T CUT IT!

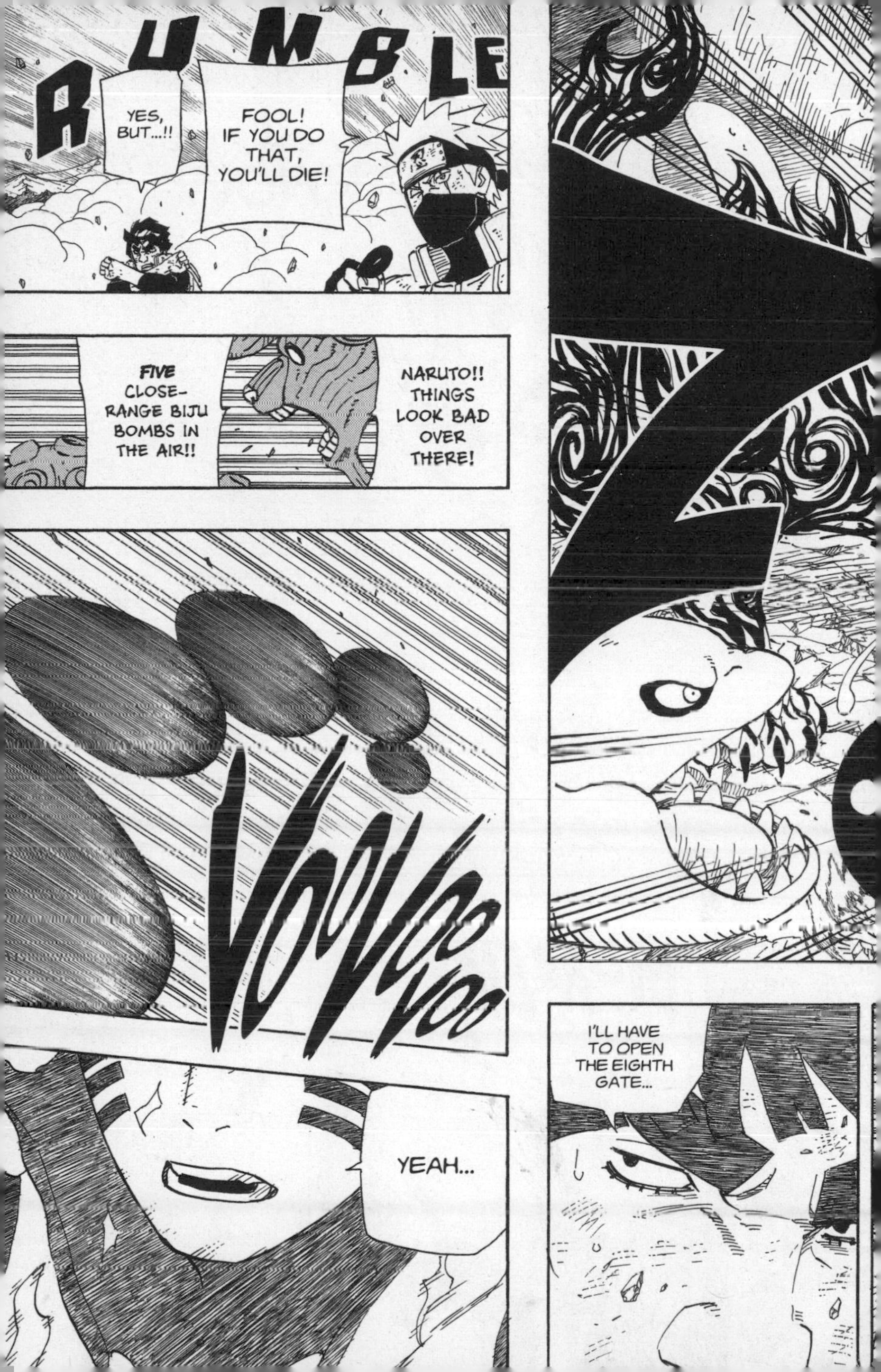
I'LL HAVE TO OPEN THE EIGHTH GATE...
RUMBLE
FOOL! IF YOU DO THAT, YOU'LL DIE!
YES, BUT...!!
NARUTO!! THINGS LOOK BAD OVER THERE!
FIVE CLOSE-RANGE BIJU BOMBS IN THE AIR!!
VOOOOO
YEAH...

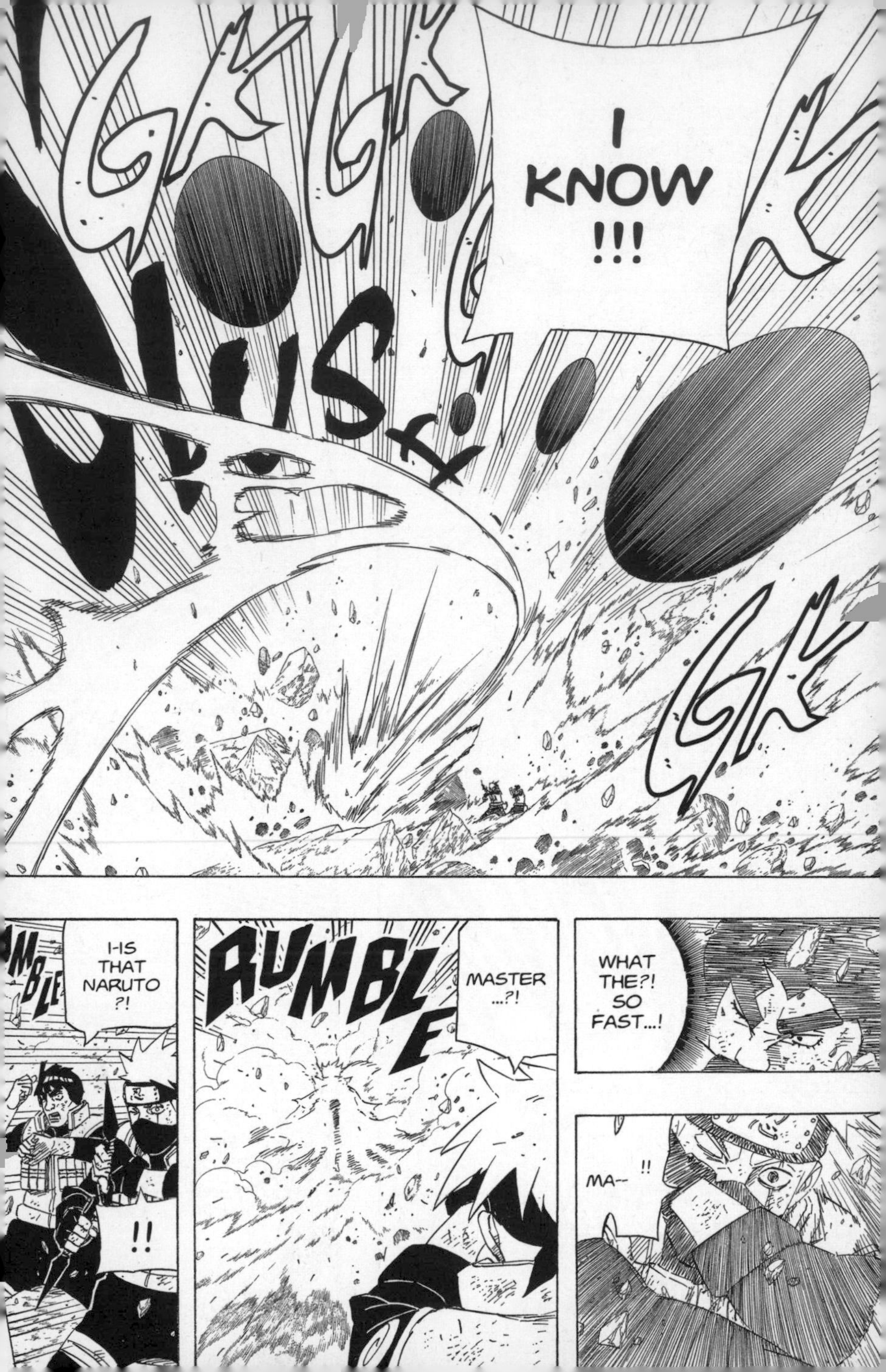
I KNOW !!!
GK
WHAT THE?! SO FAST...!
MA-- !!
MASTER ...?!
RUMBLE
I-IS THAT NARUTO ?!
!!

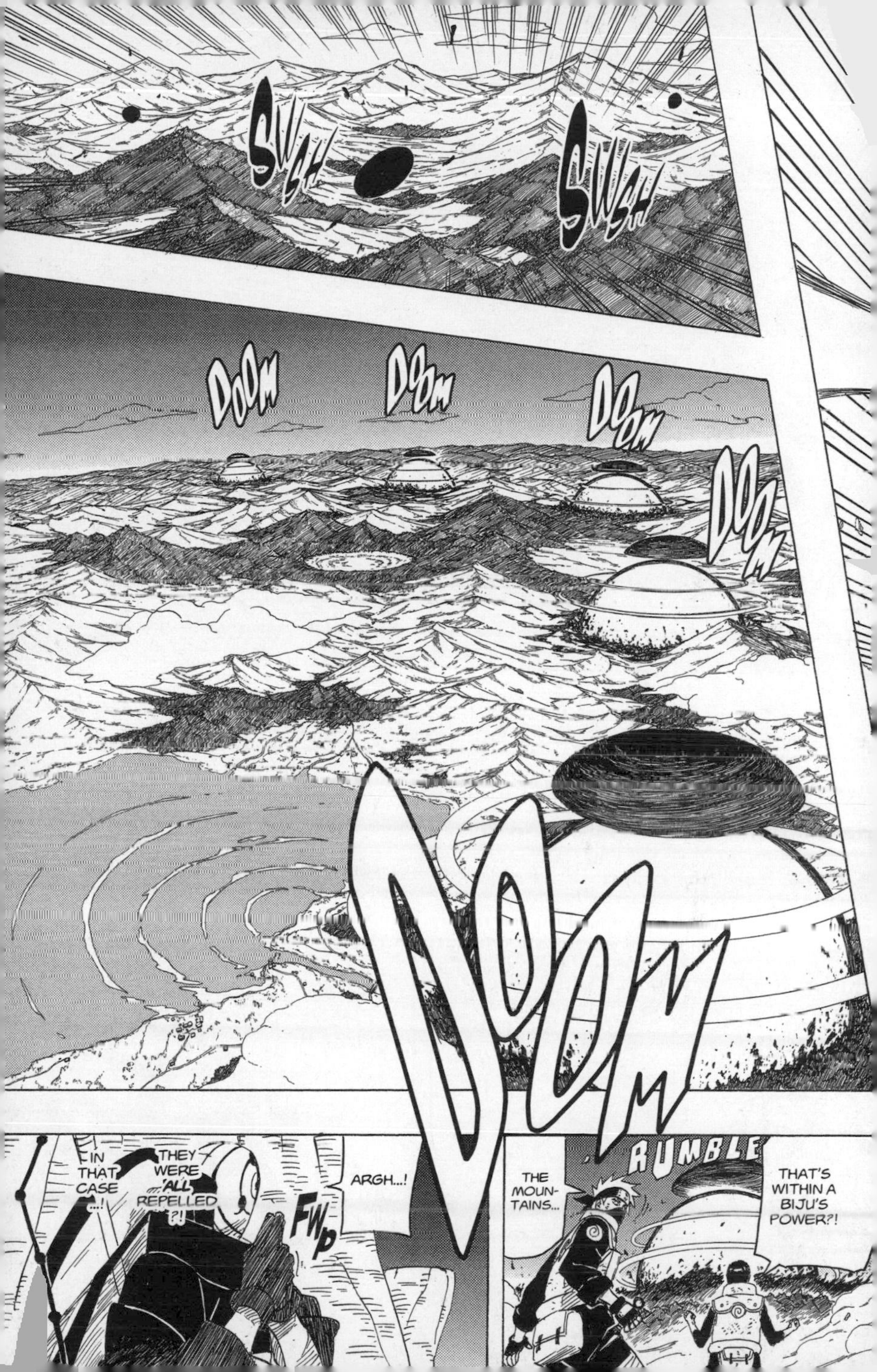
SWISH
SWISH
DOOM
DOOM
DOOM
DOOM
DOOM
DOOM
RUMBLE
THAT'S WITHIN A BIJU'S POWER?!
THE MOUNTAINS...
ARGH...!
FWP
THEY WERE ALL REPELLED?!
IN THAT CASE...!

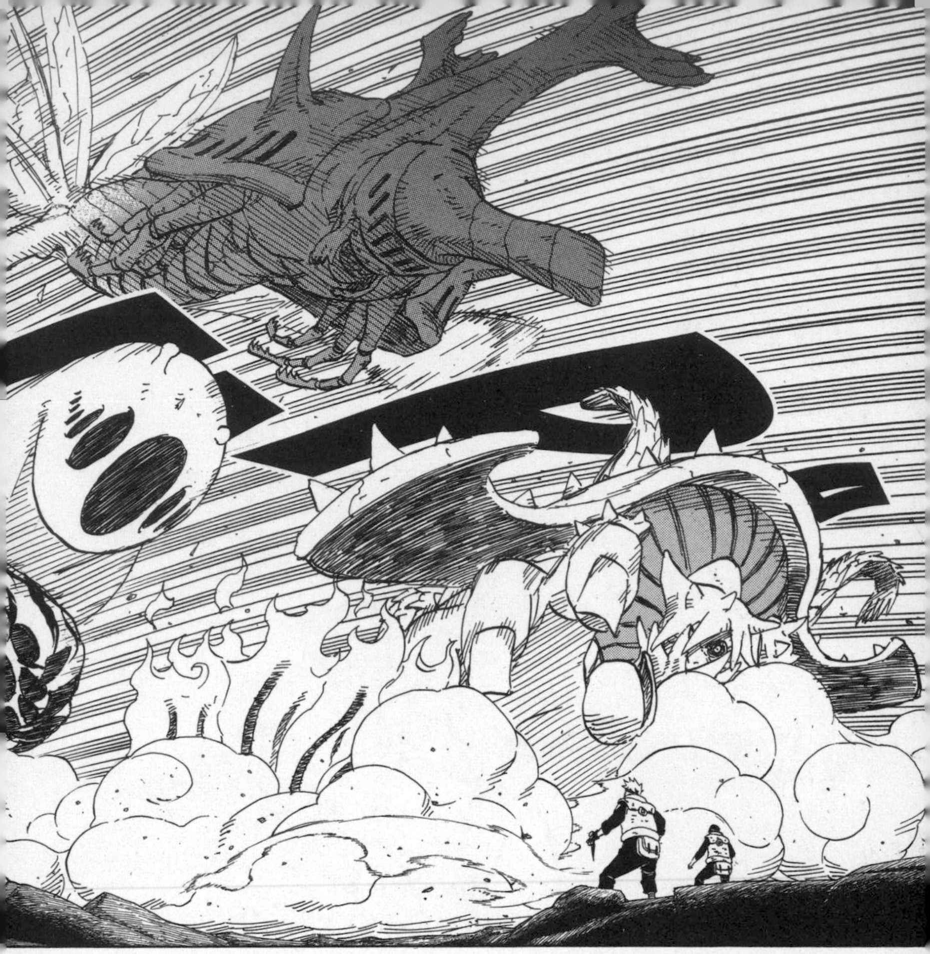

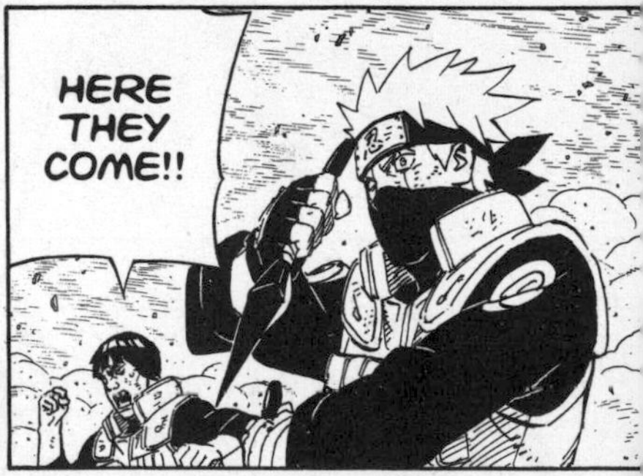
HERE THEY COME!!

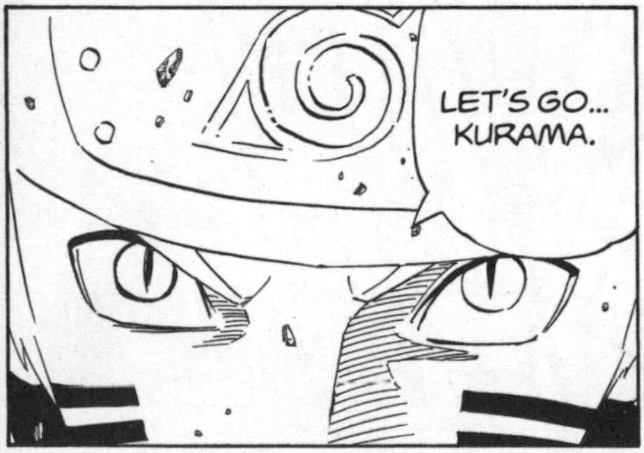
LET'S GO... KURAMA.

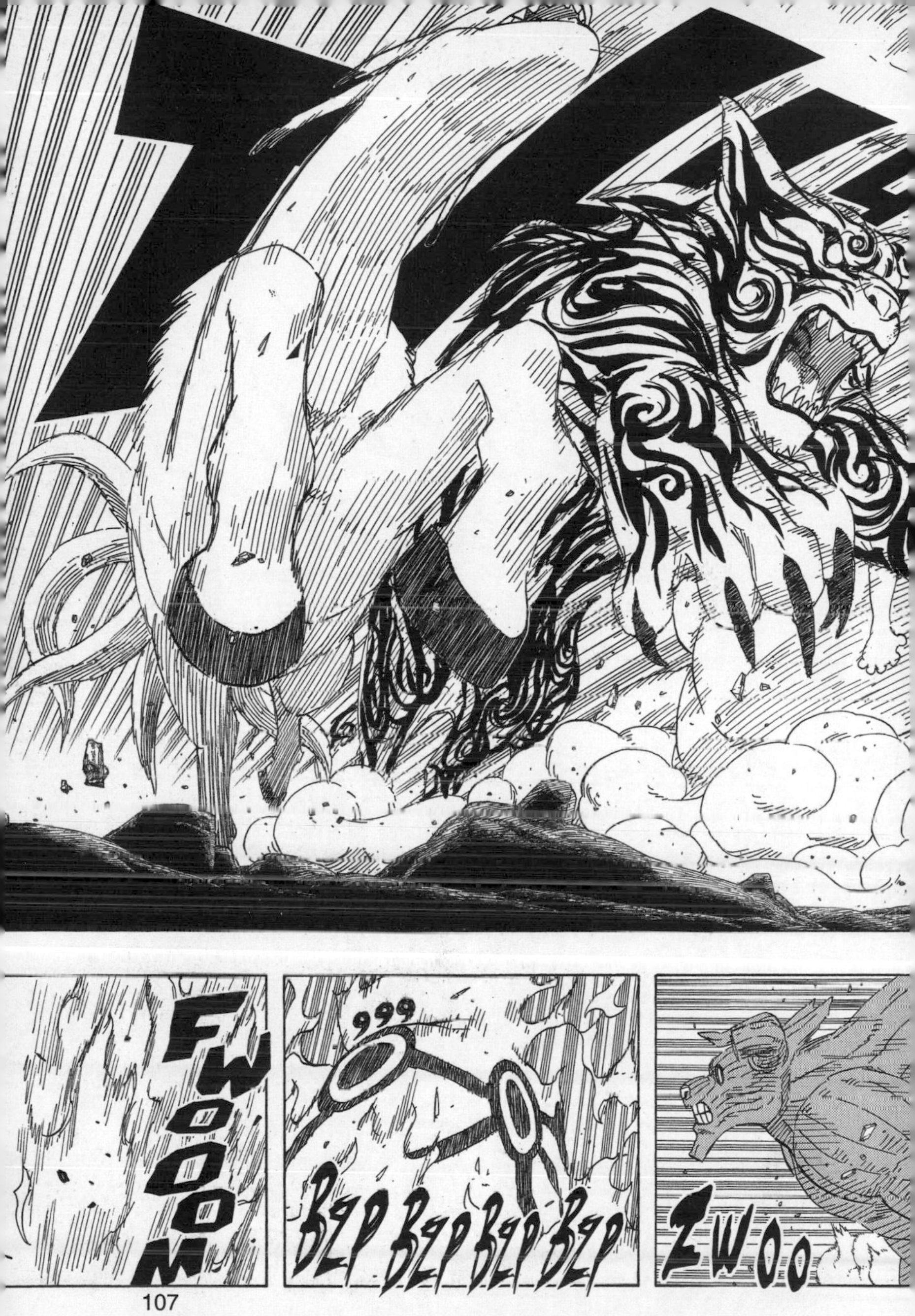
ZWOO
BZP BZP BZP BZP
FWOOOM

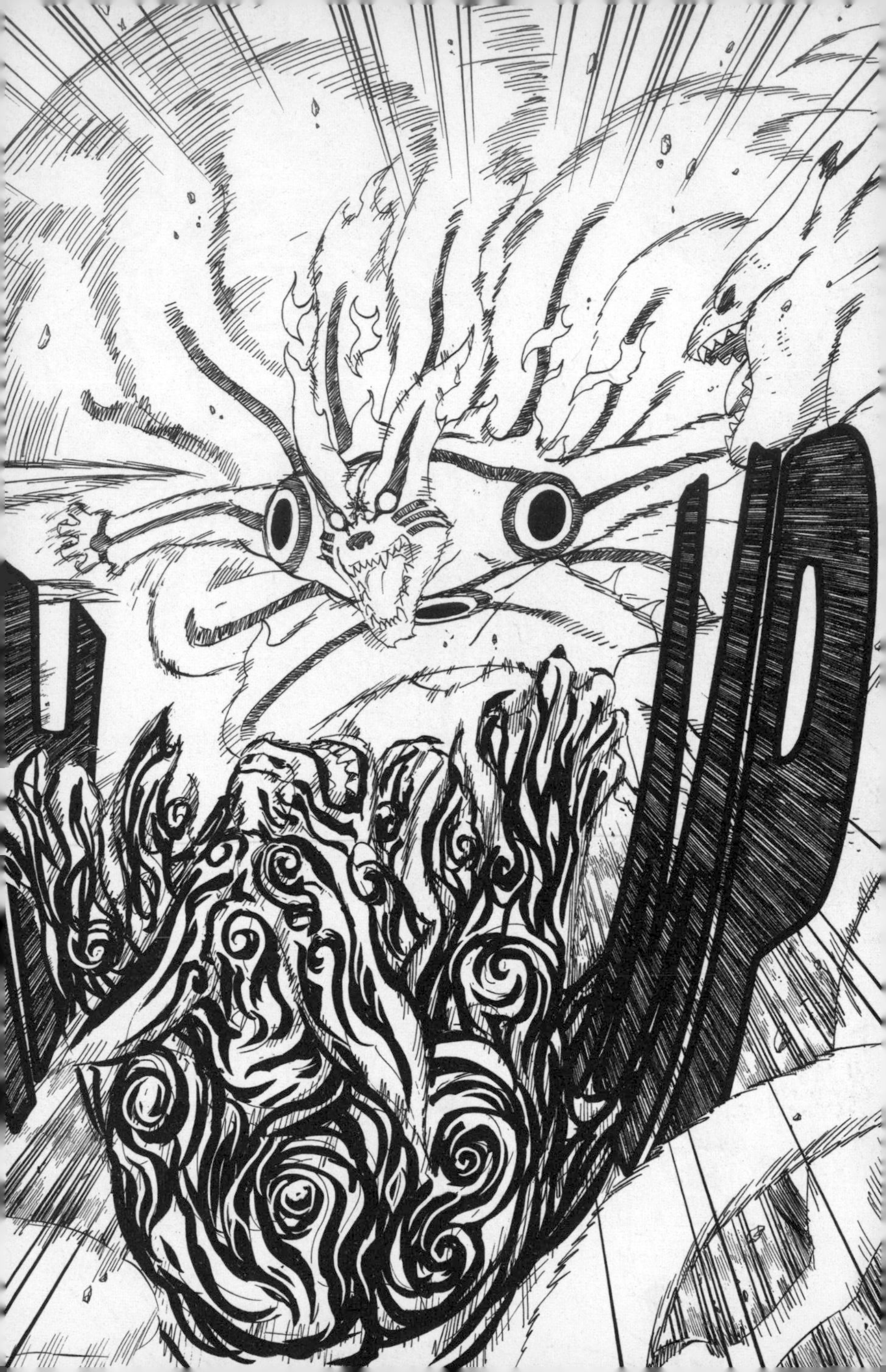

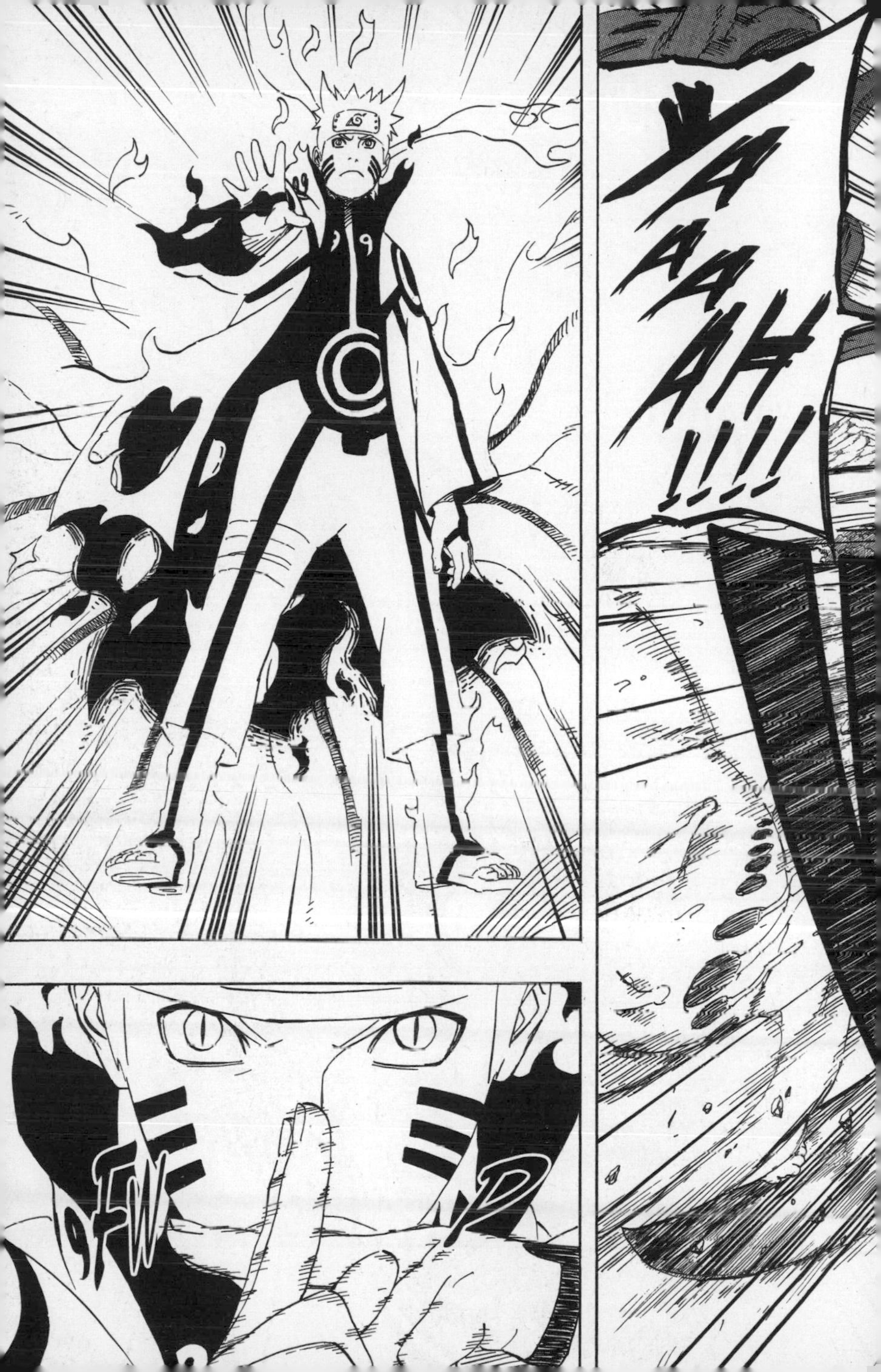
YAAAAH!!!!
FWD

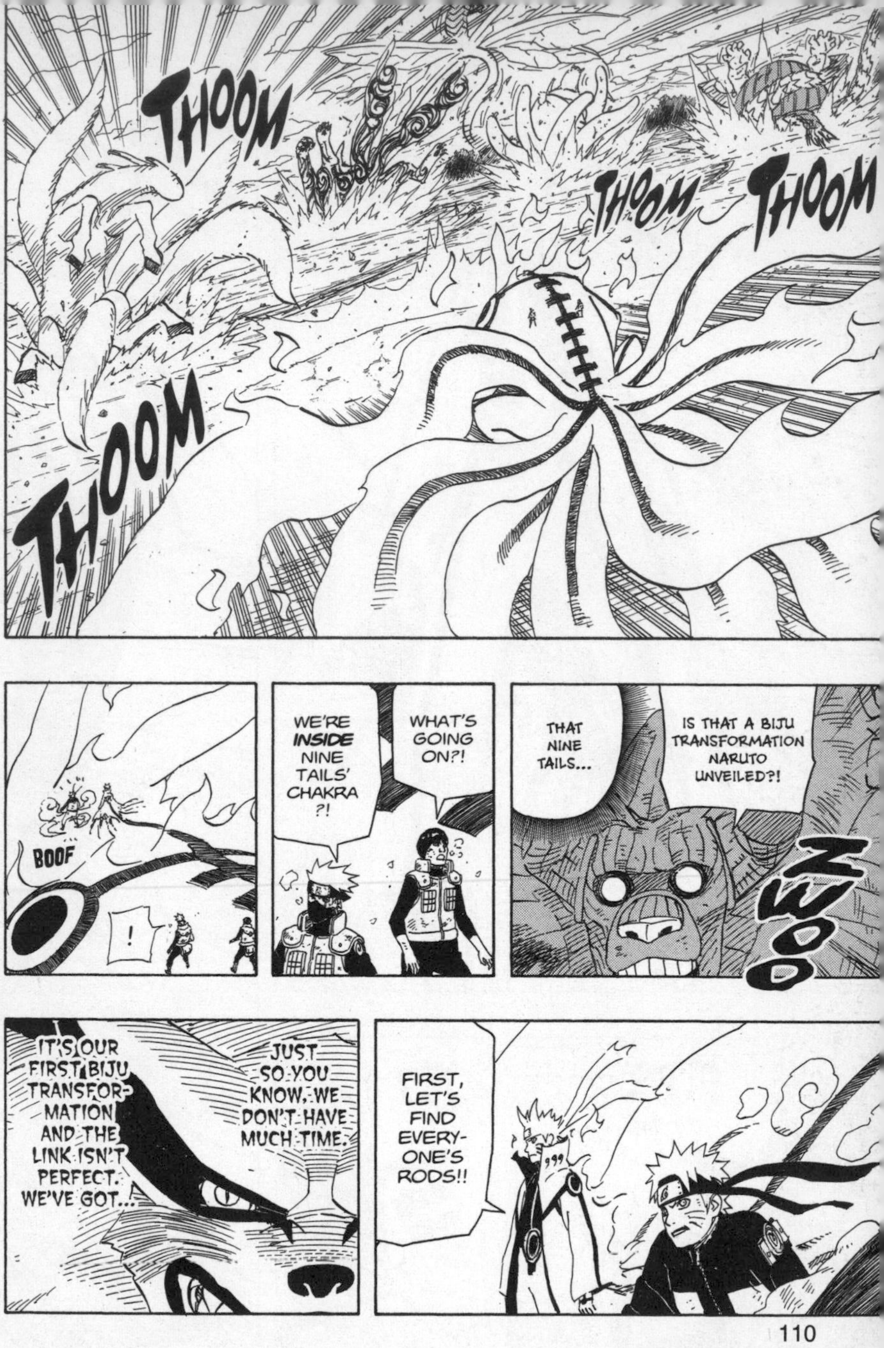
THOOM
THOOM
THOOM
THOOM
THOOM
IS THAT A BIJU TRANSFORMATION NARUTO UNVEILED?!
THAT NINE TAILS...
ZWOO
WHAT'S GOING ON?!
WE'RE **INSIDE** NINE TAILS' CHAKRA?!
BOOF
!
FIRST, LET'S FIND EVERYONE'S RODS!!
JUST SO YOU KNOW, WE DON'T HAVE MUCH TIME.
IT'S OUR FIRST BIJU TRANSFORMATION AND THE LINK ISN'T PERFECT. WE'VE GOT...

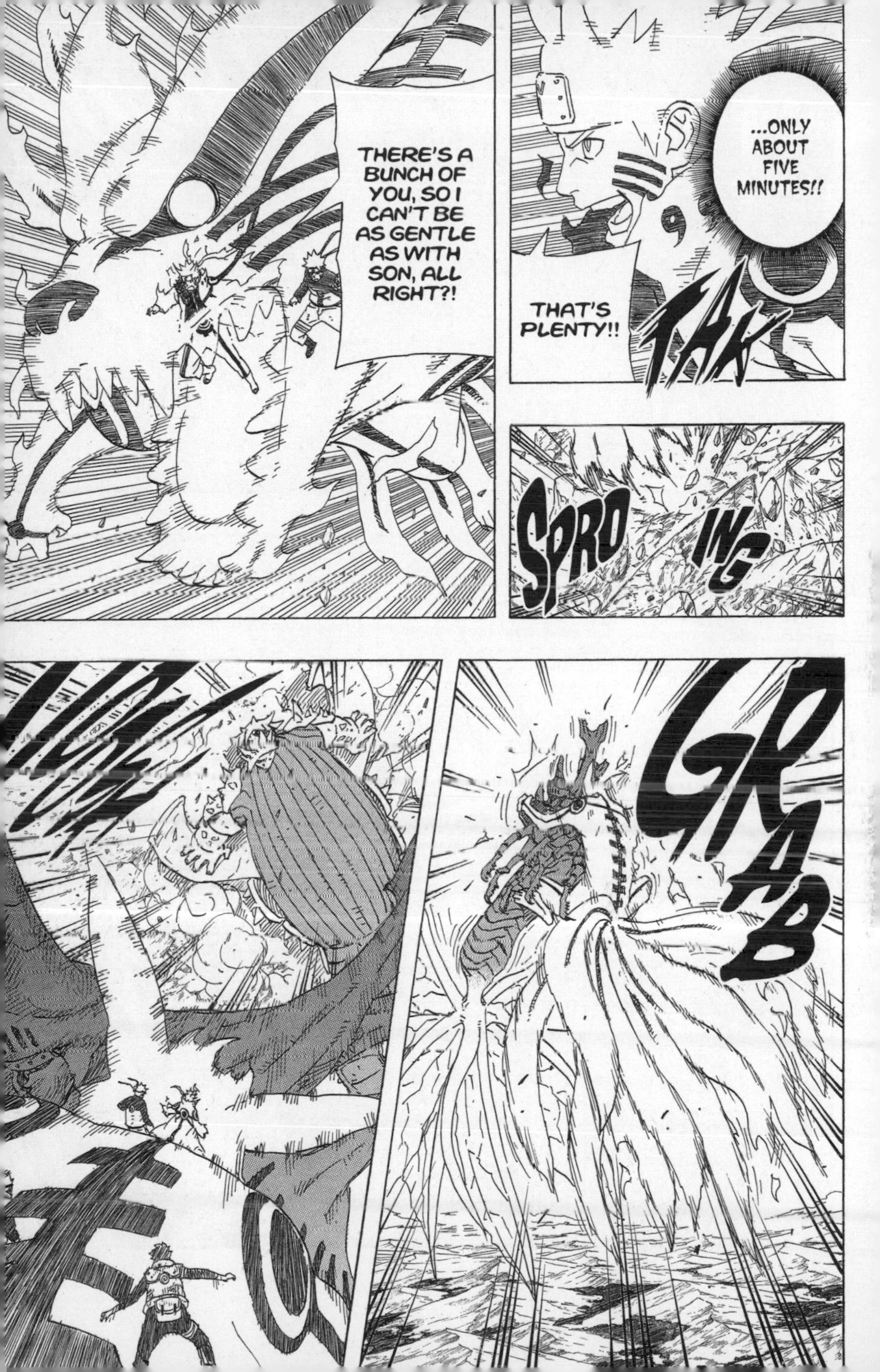
...ONLY ABOUT FIVE MINUTES!!
THAT'S PLENTY!!
TAK
SPROING
THERE'S A BUNCH OF YOU, SO I CAN'T BE AS GENTLE AS WITH SON, ALL RIGHT?!
GRAB

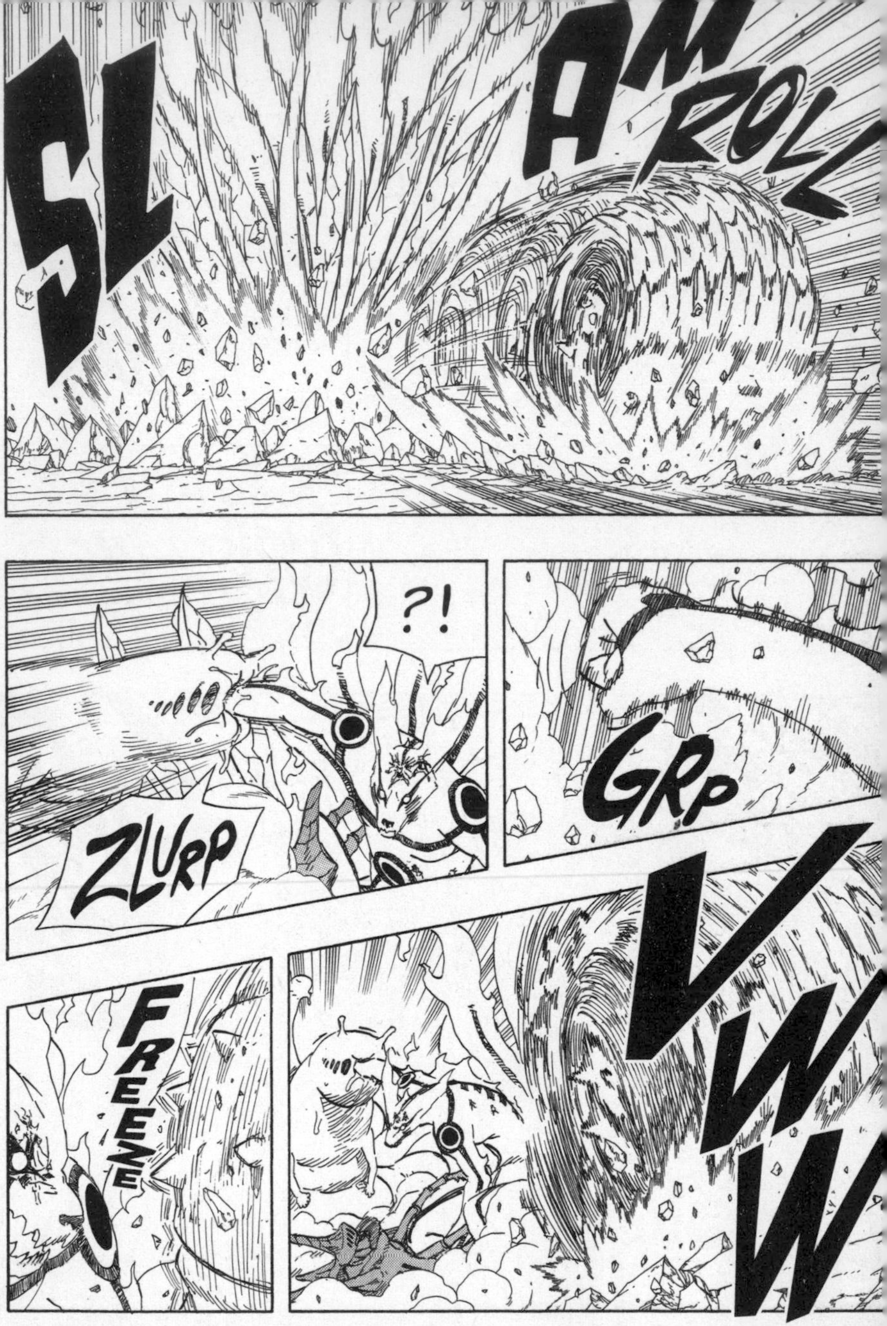
ROLL
SLAM
GRP
?!
ZLURP
VWW
FREEZE

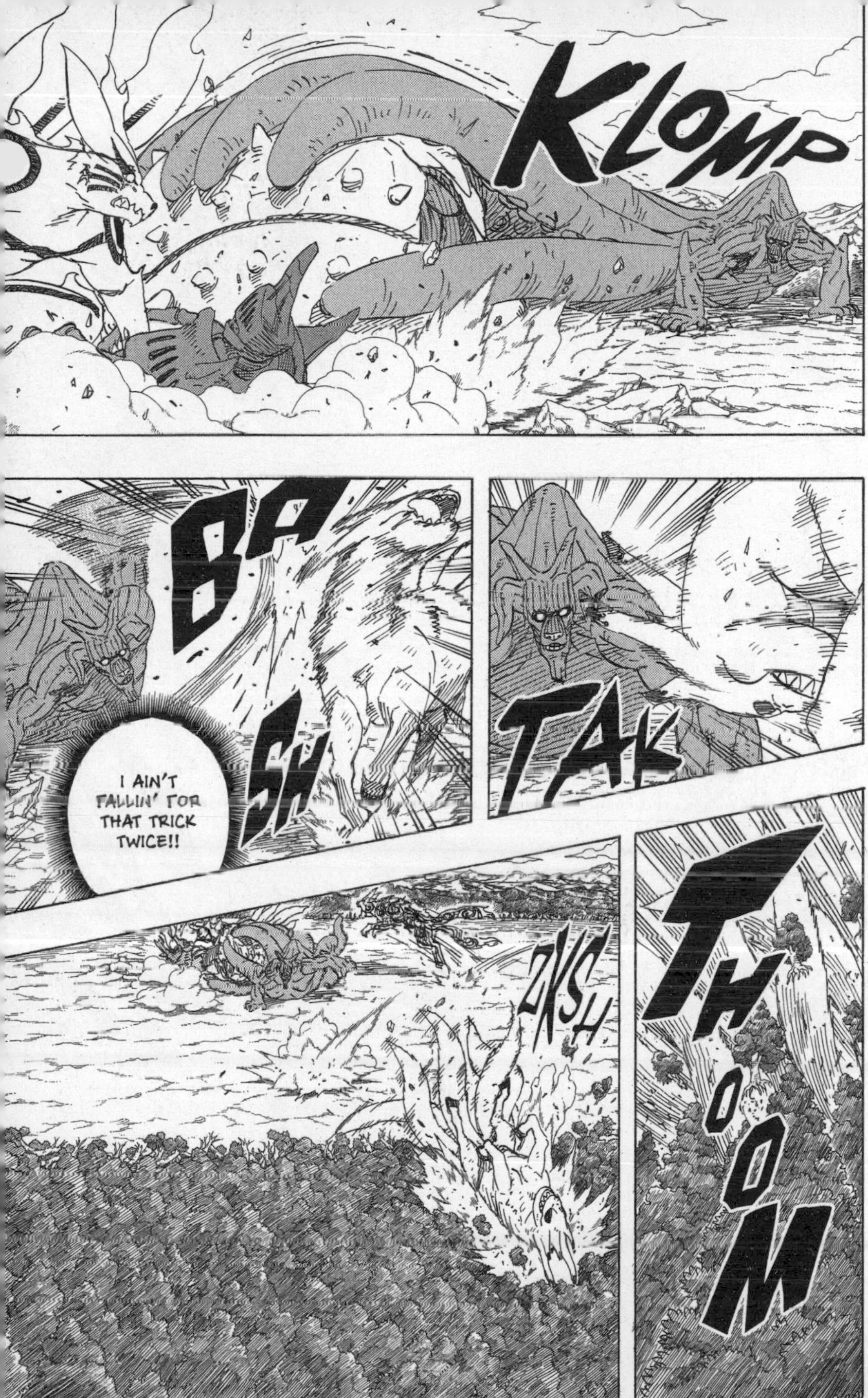
KLOMP
TAK
BASH
I AIN'T FALLIN' FOR THAT TRICK TWICE!!
THOOM
ZKSH

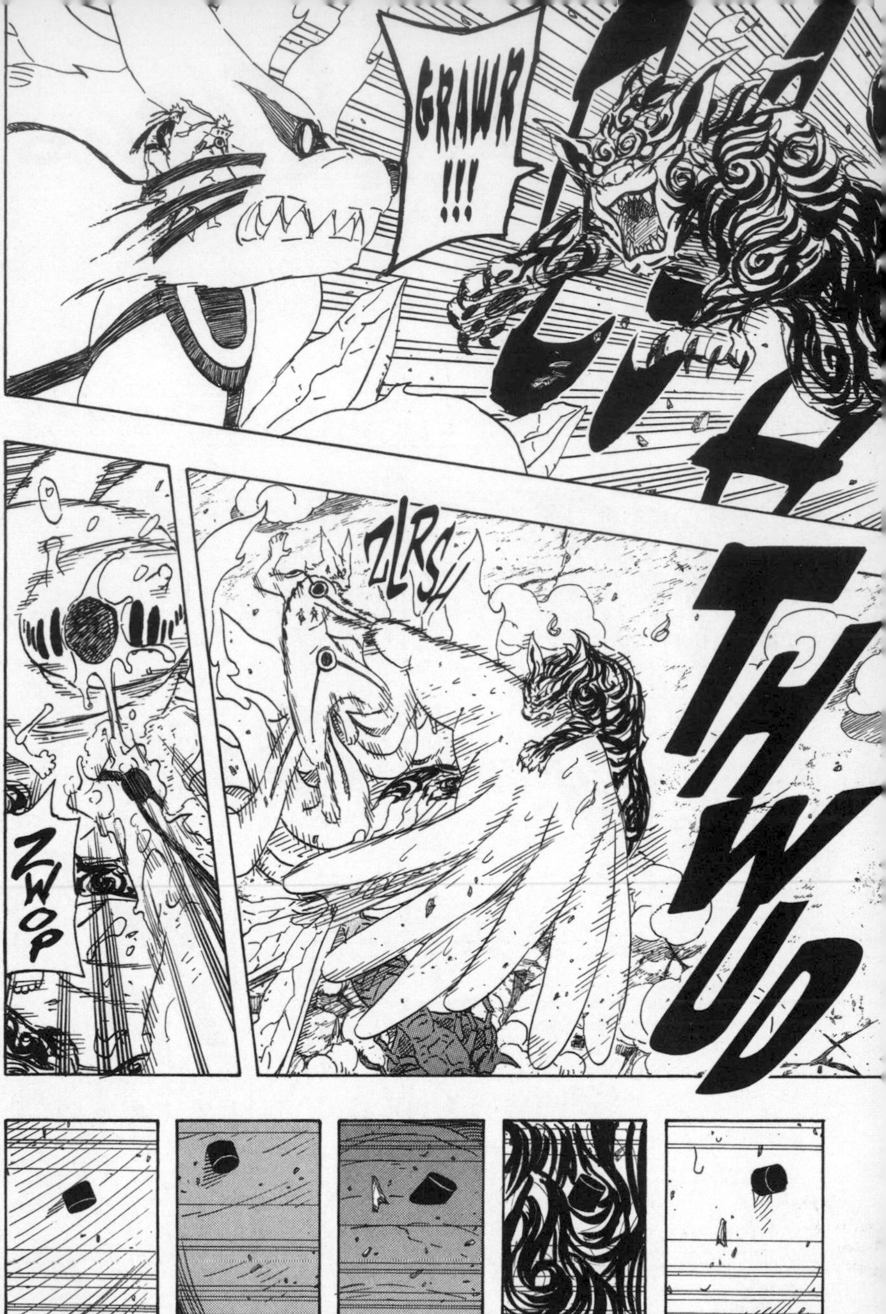
GRAWR!!!
ZLRSH
THWUD
ZWOP

READ THIS WAY

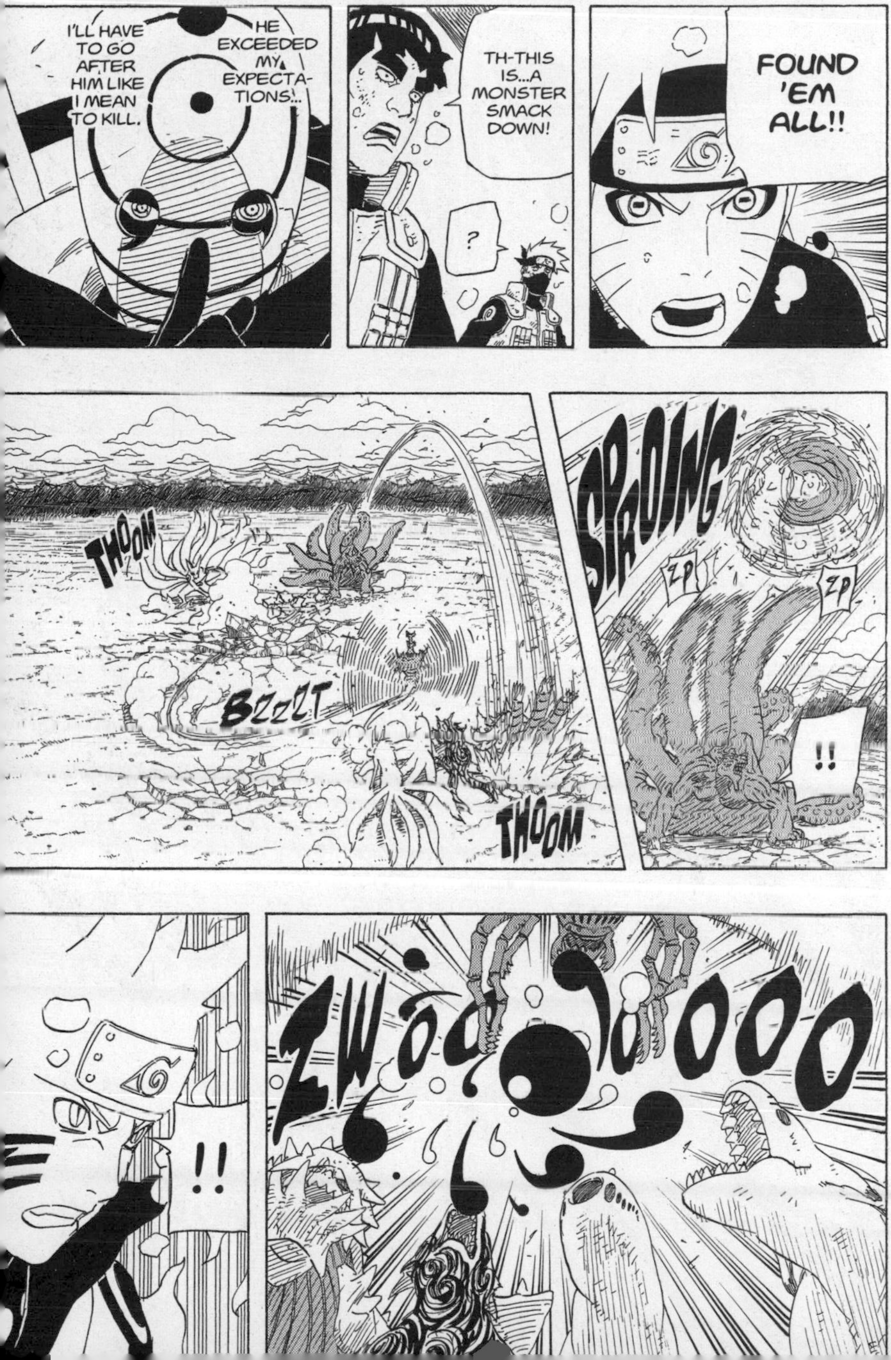
FOUND 'EM ALL!!
TH-THIS IS...A MONSTER SMACK DOWN!
?
HE EXCEEDED MY EXPECTATIONS...
I'LL HAVE TO GO AFTER HIM LIKE I MEAN TO KILL.
SPROING
ZP
ZP
!!
THOOM
BZZZT
THOOM
ZWOOOOOOOOO
!!

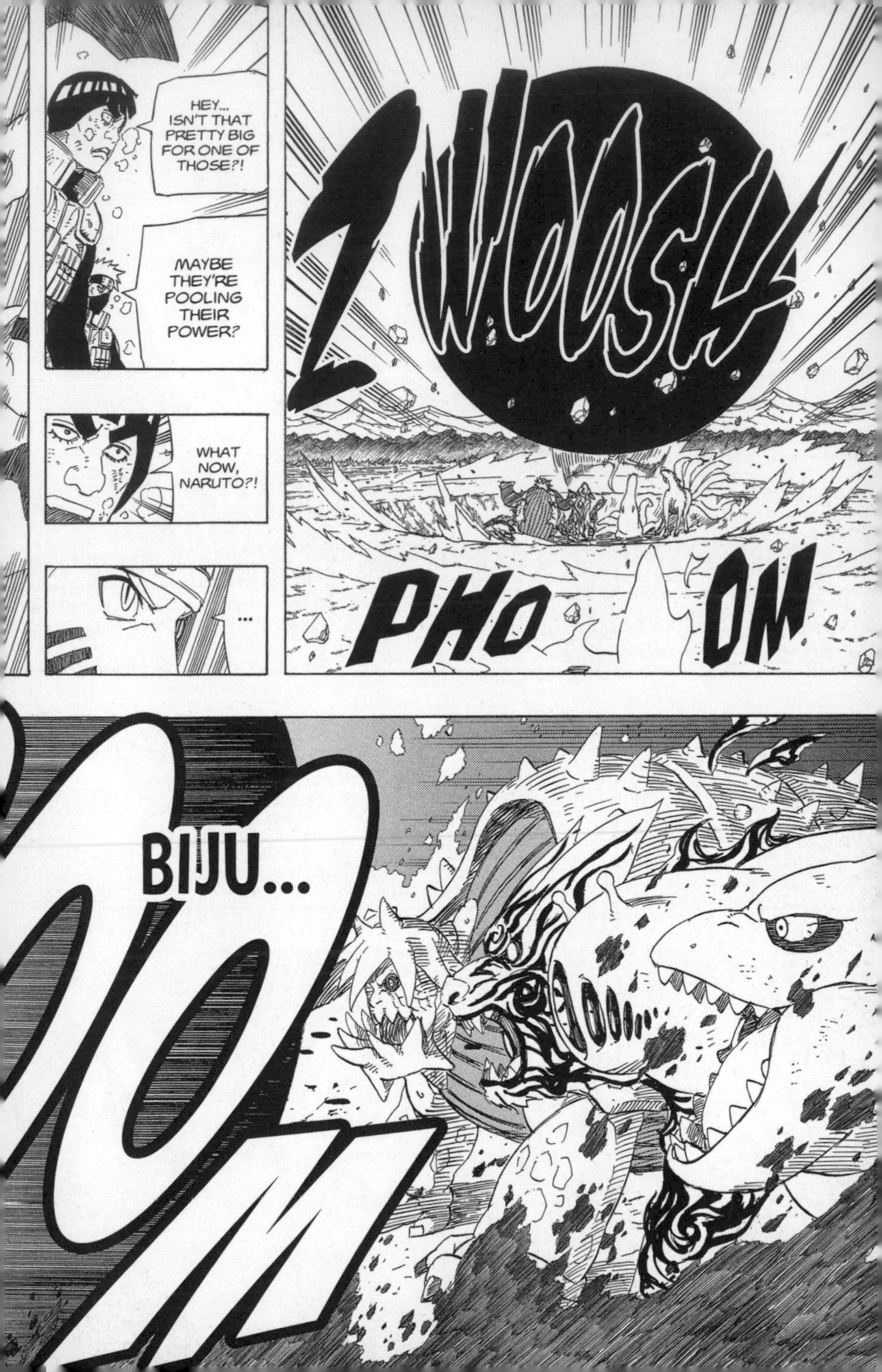
ZWOOSH
PHO OM
HEY... ISN'T THAT PRETTY BIG FOR ONE OF THOSE?!
MAYBE THEY'RE POOLING THEIR POWER?
WHAT NOW, NARUTO?!
...
BIJU...

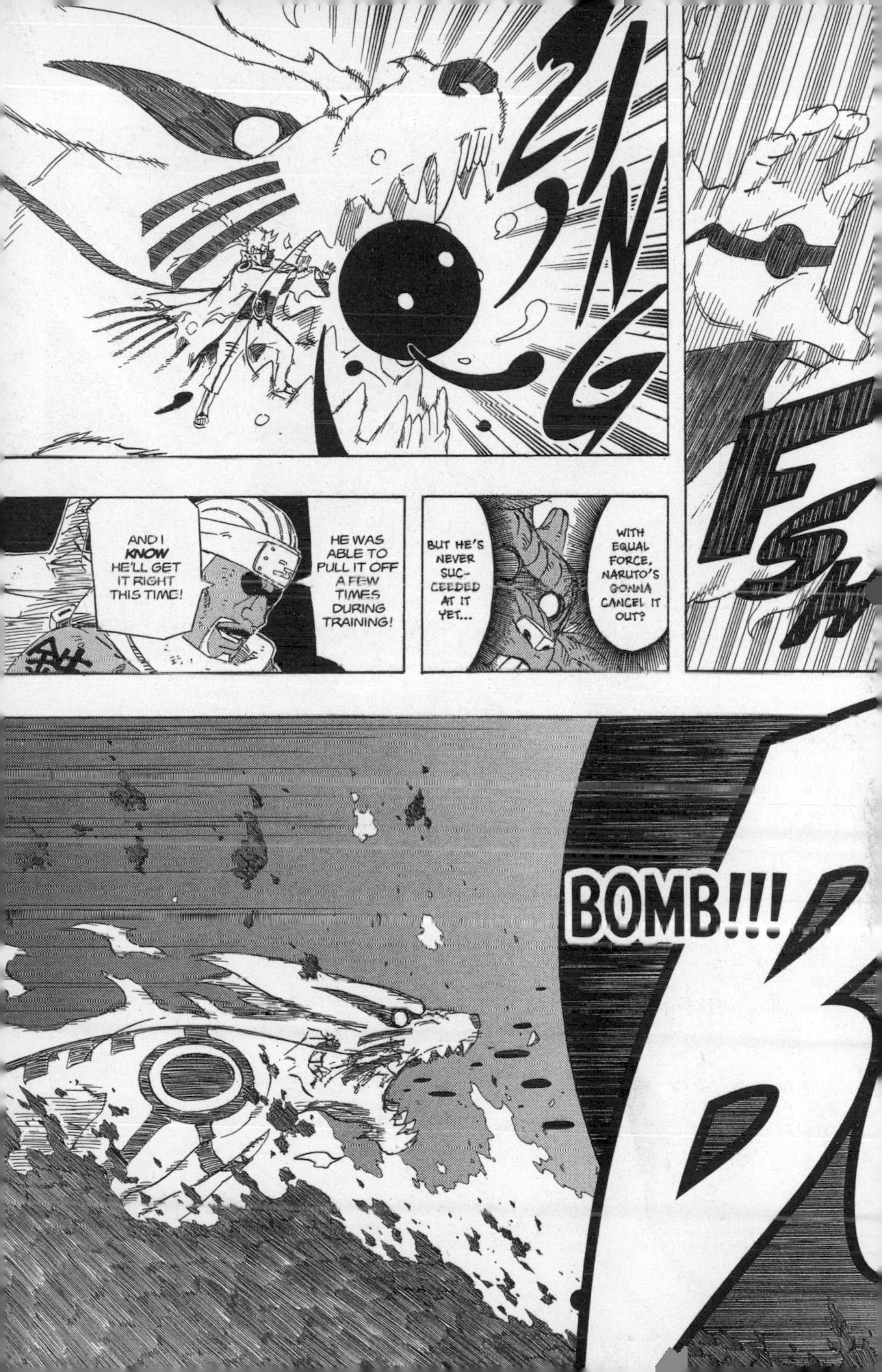
FSH
ZING
WITH EQUAL FORCE, NARUTO'S GONNA CANCEL IT OUT?
BUT HE'S NEVER SUC-CEEDED AT IT YET...
HE WAS ABLE TO PULL IT OFF A FEW TIMES DURING TRAINING!
AND I **KNOW** HE'LL GET IT RIGHT THIS TIME!
BOMB!!!

Illustration to Commemorate Reaching Volume 60 [7]

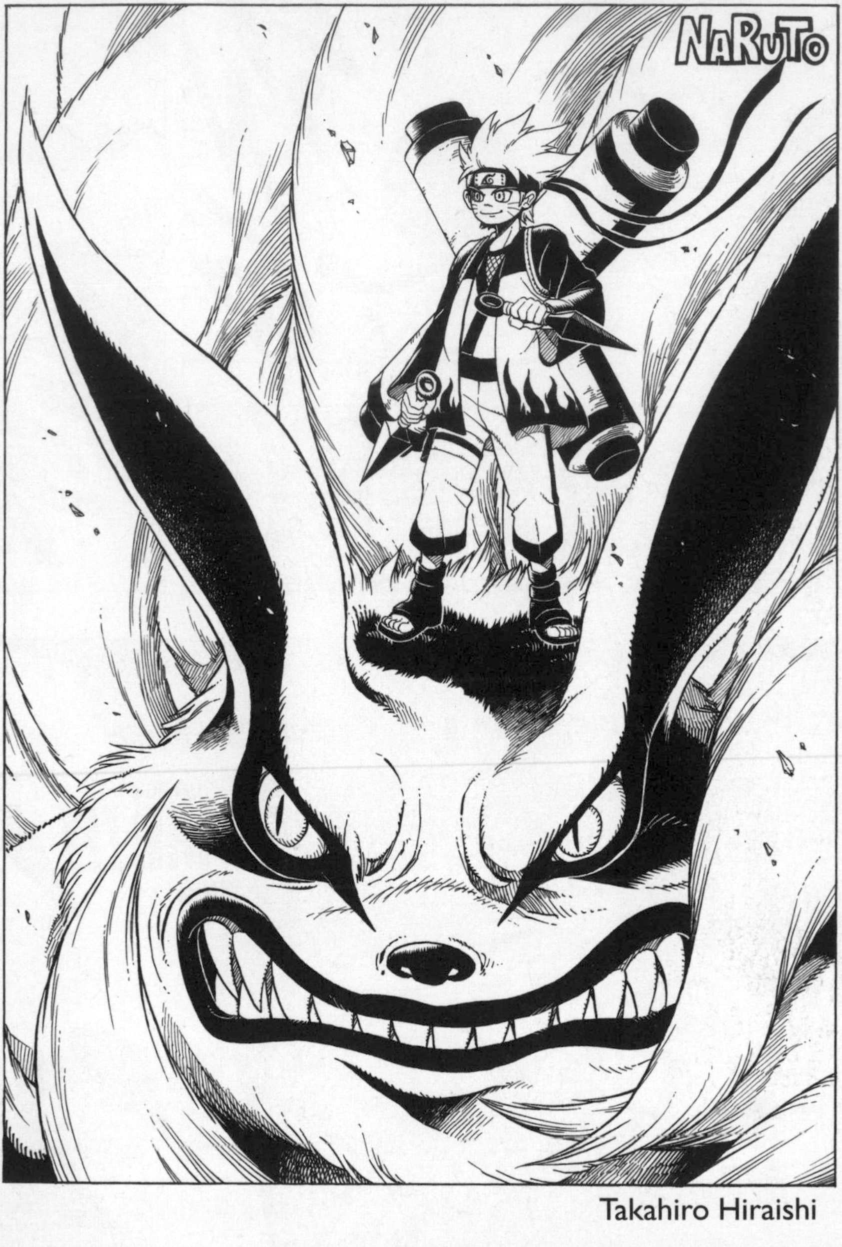
NARUTO

Takahiro Hiraishi

Number 572: Nine Names

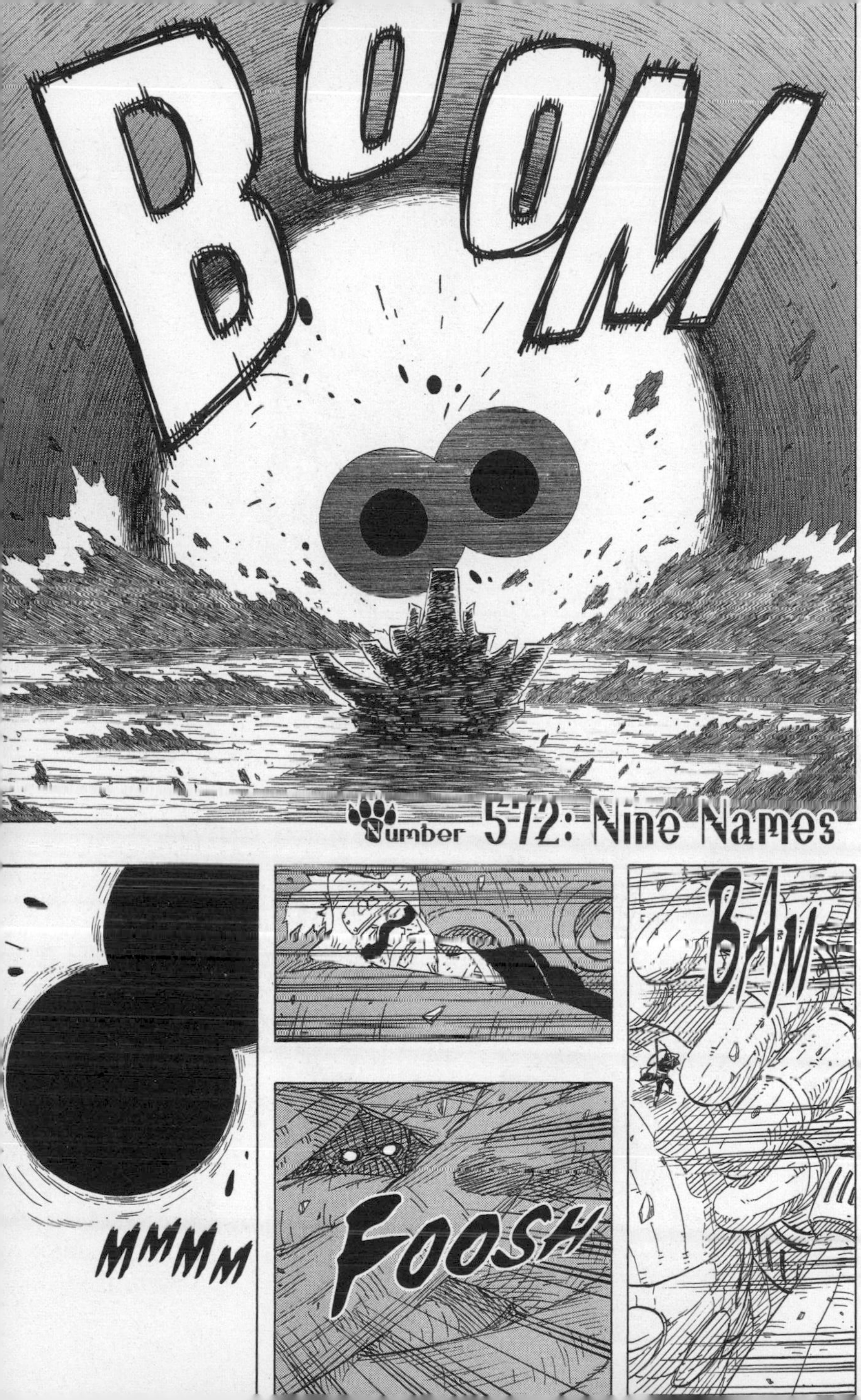
BOOM
Number 572: Nine Names
BAM
FOOSH
MMMM

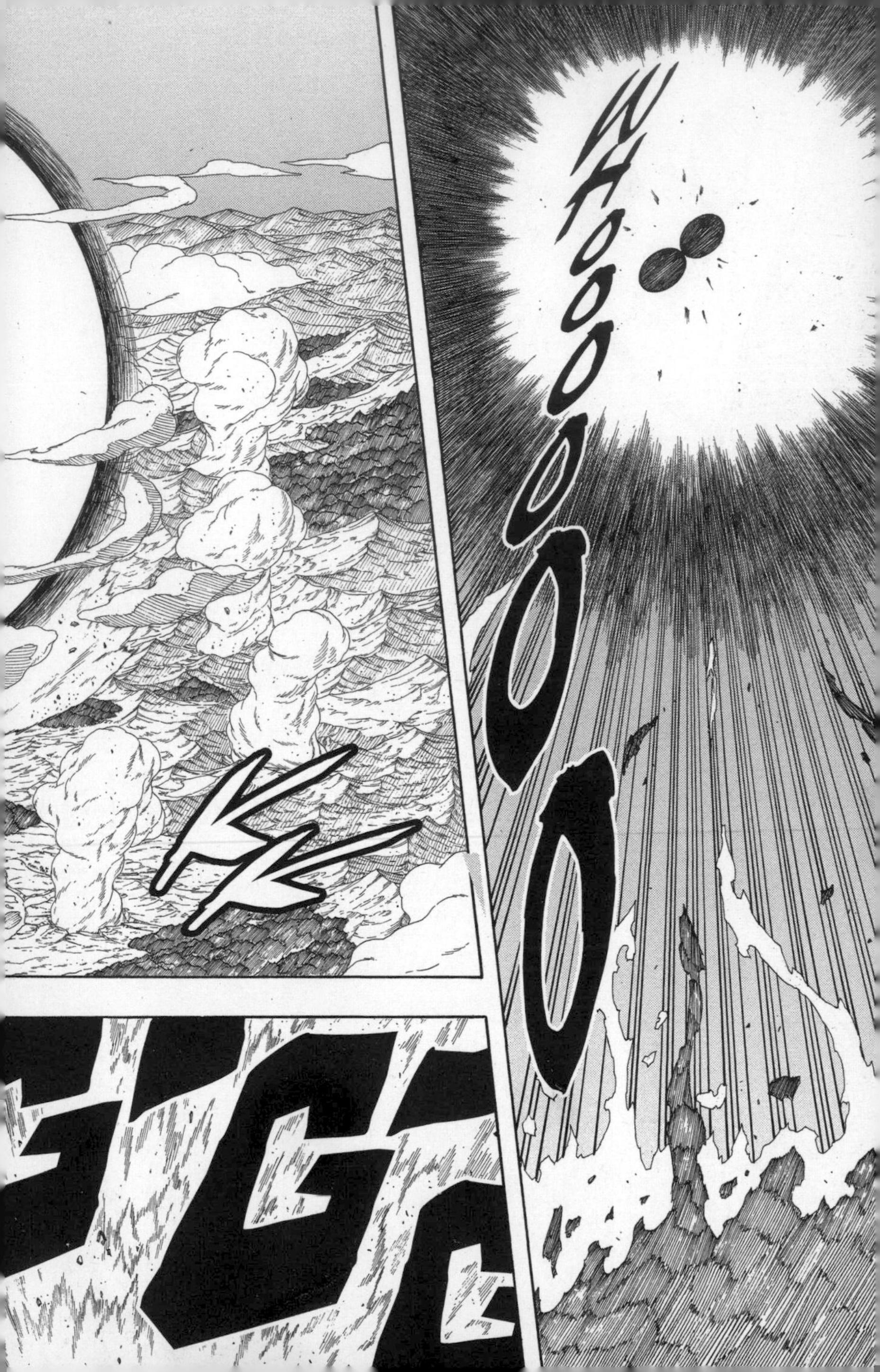
WHOOOOOOO

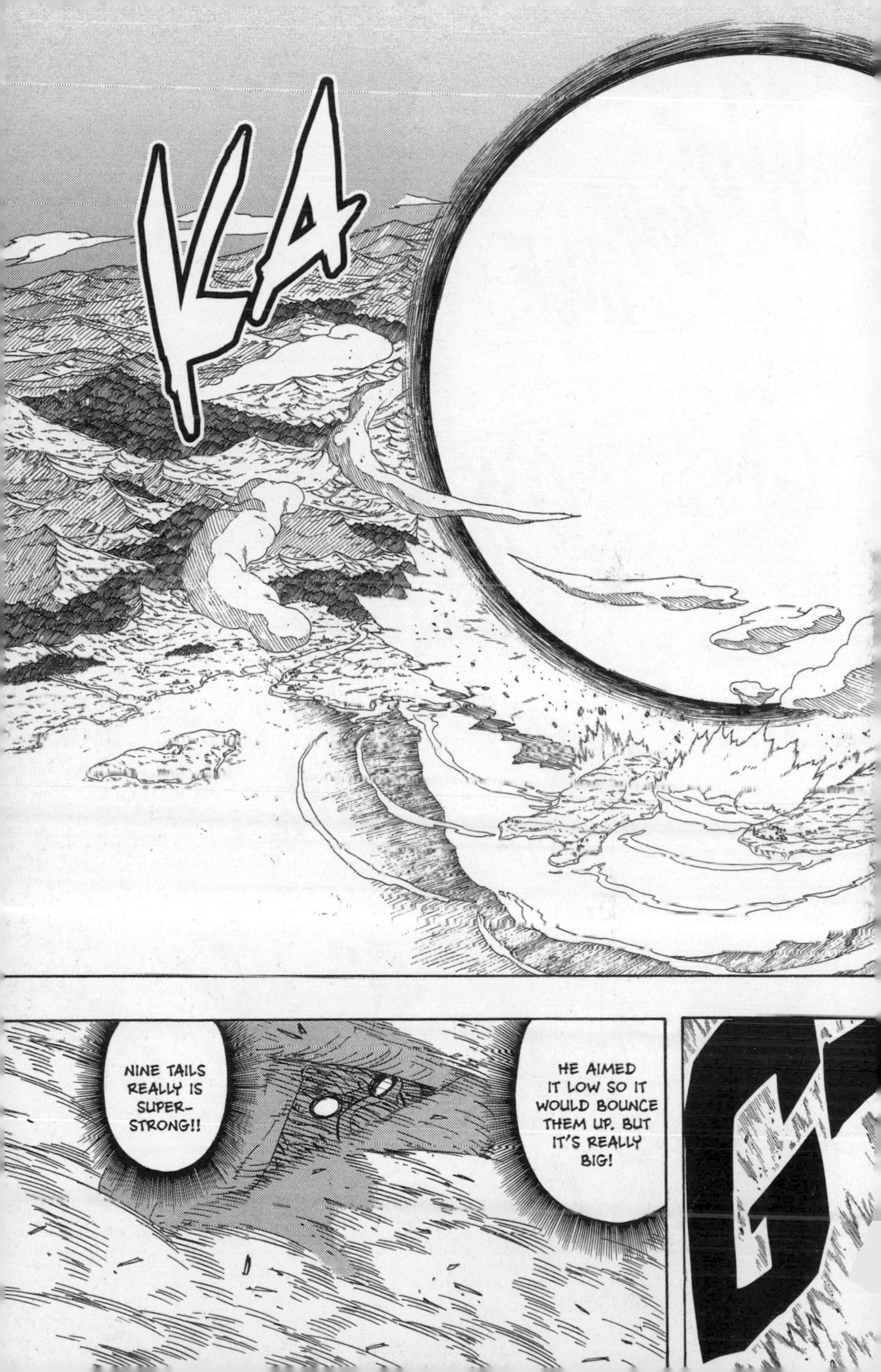
VA
HE AIMED IT LOW SO IT WOULD BOUNCE THEM UP. BUT IT'S REALLY BIG!
NINE TAILS REALLY IS SUPER-STRONG!!

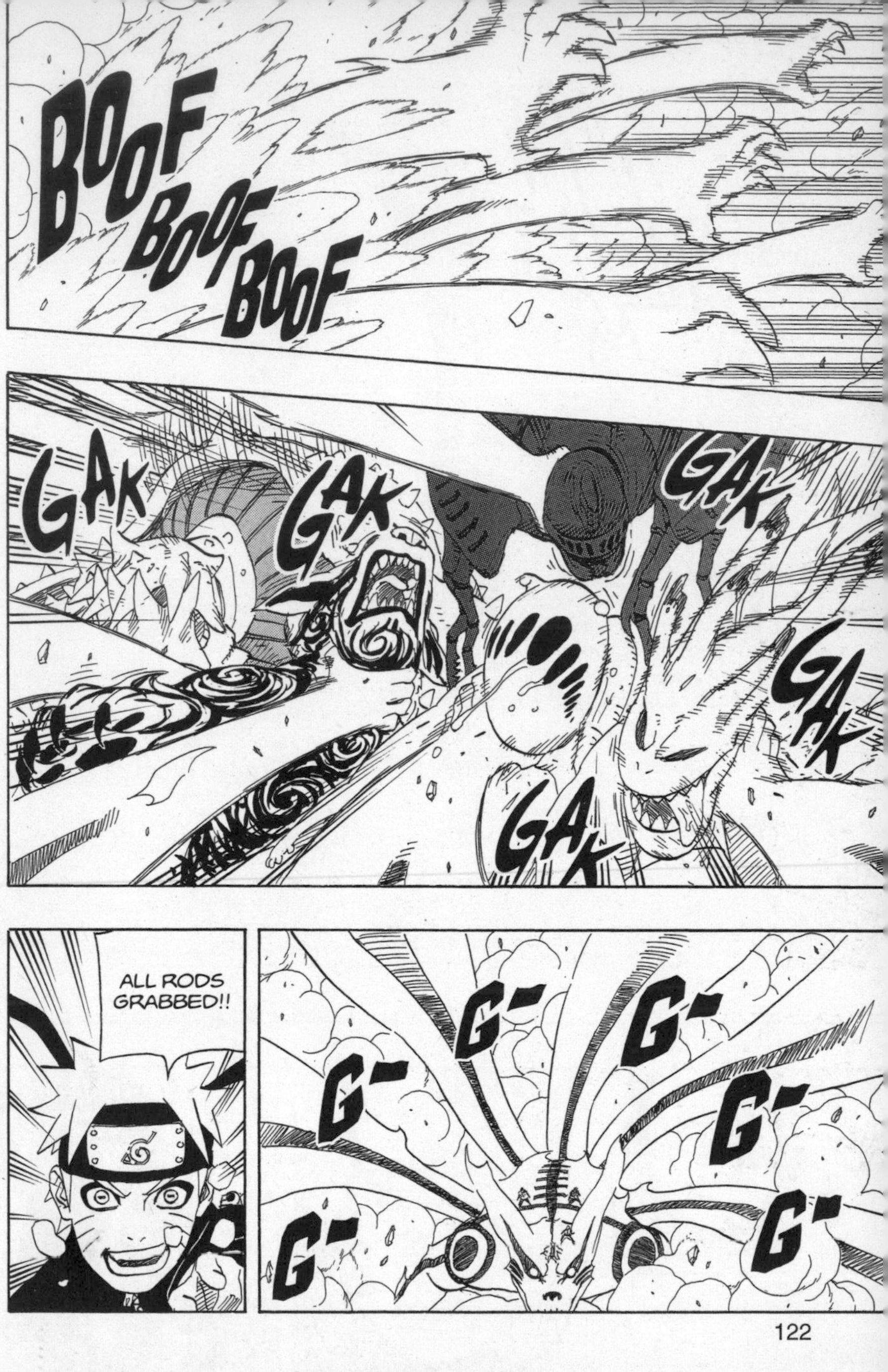
BOOF BOOF BOOF
GAK
GAK
GAK
GAK
GAK
G-
G-
G-
G-
G-
G-
G-
ALL RODS GRABBED!!

READ THIS WAY

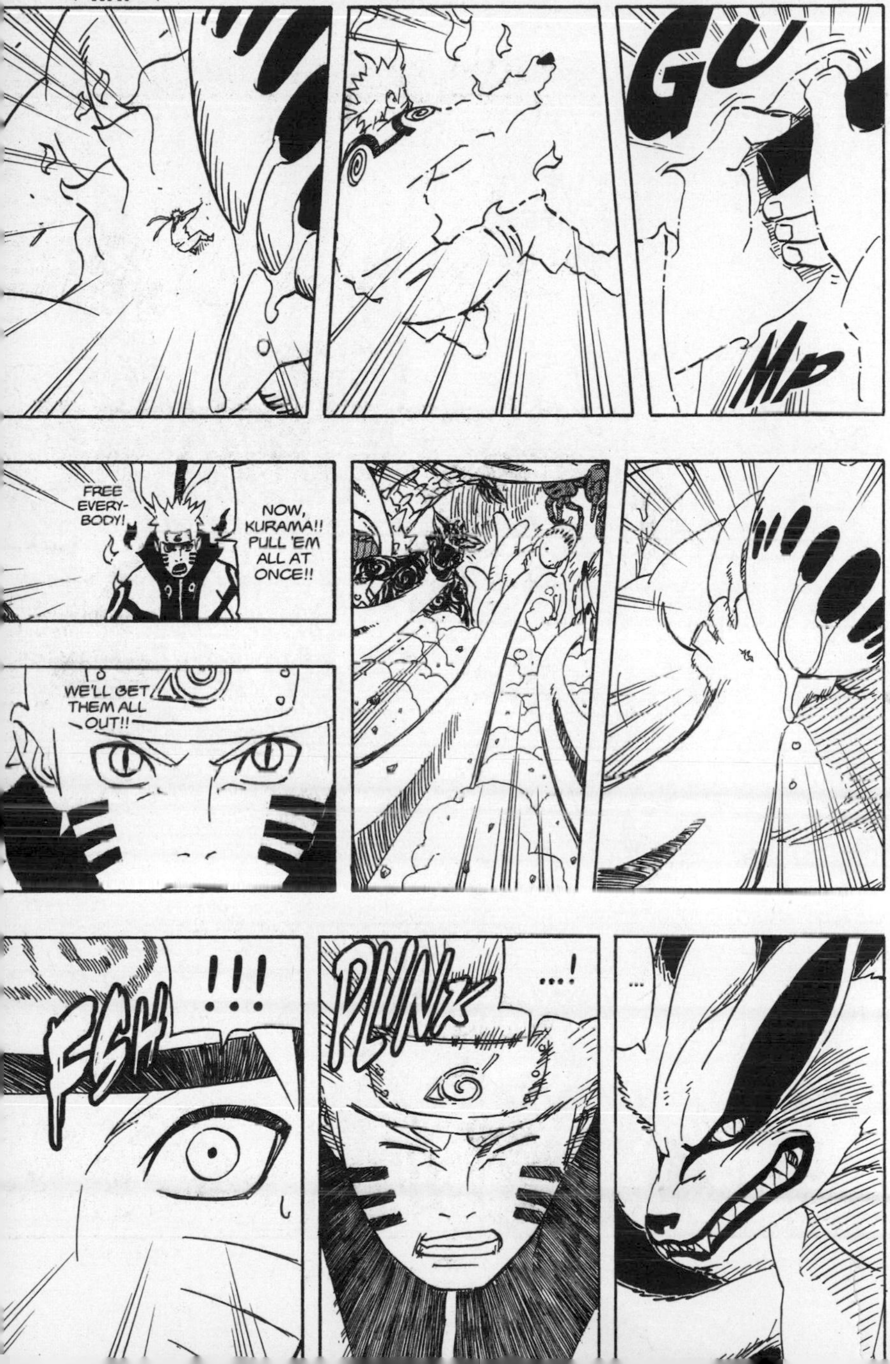
GU
MP
NOW, KURAMA!! PULL 'EM ALL AT ONCE!!
FREE EVERY-BODY!
WE'LL GET THEM ALL OUT!!
...
...!
PLINK
!!!
FSH

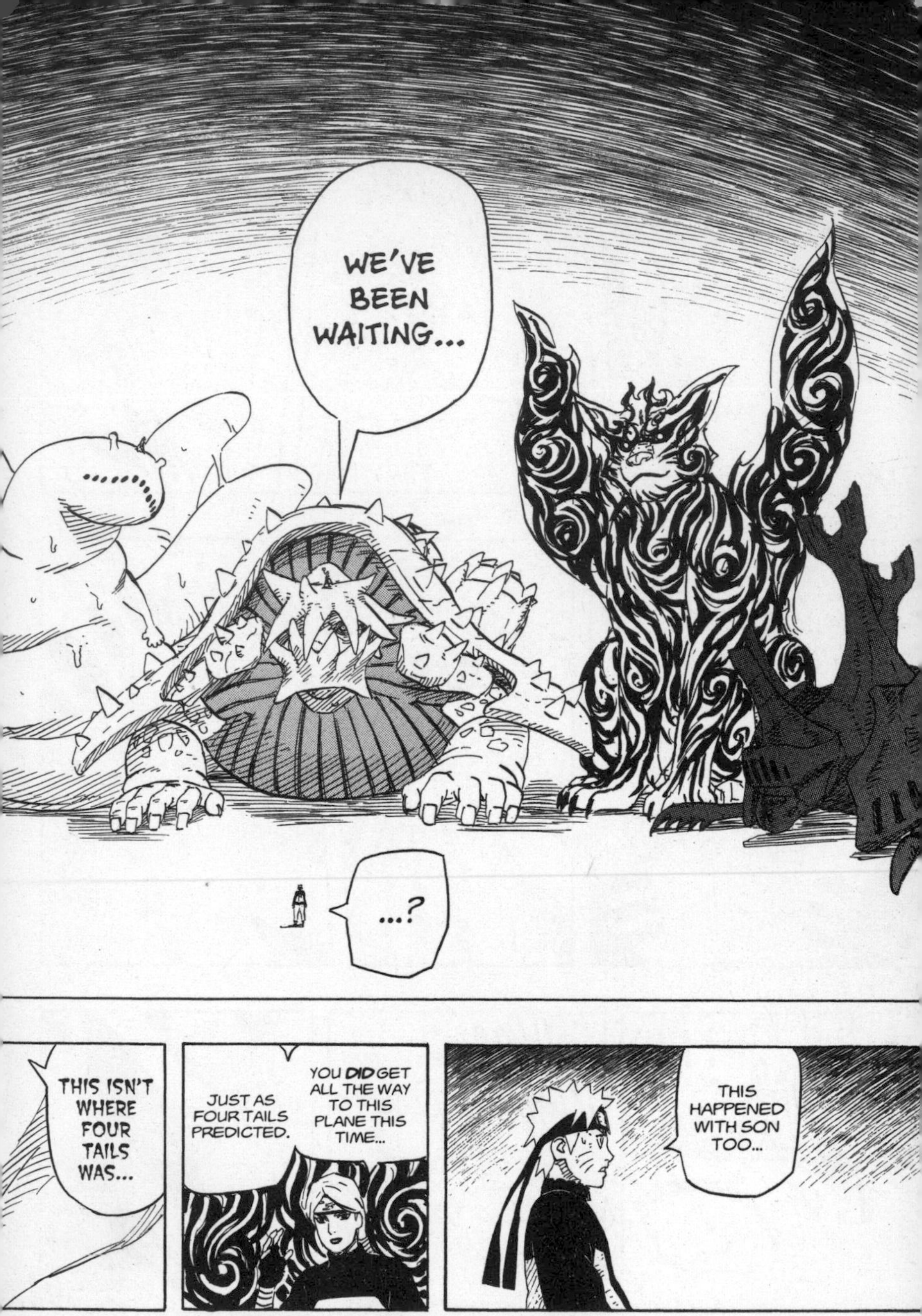
WE'VE BEEN WAITING...
......
...?
THIS HAPPENED WITH SON TOO...
YOU **DID** GET ALL THE WAY TO THIS PLANE THIS TIME...
JUST AS FOUR TAILS PREDICTED.
THIS ISN'T WHERE FOUR TAILS WAS...

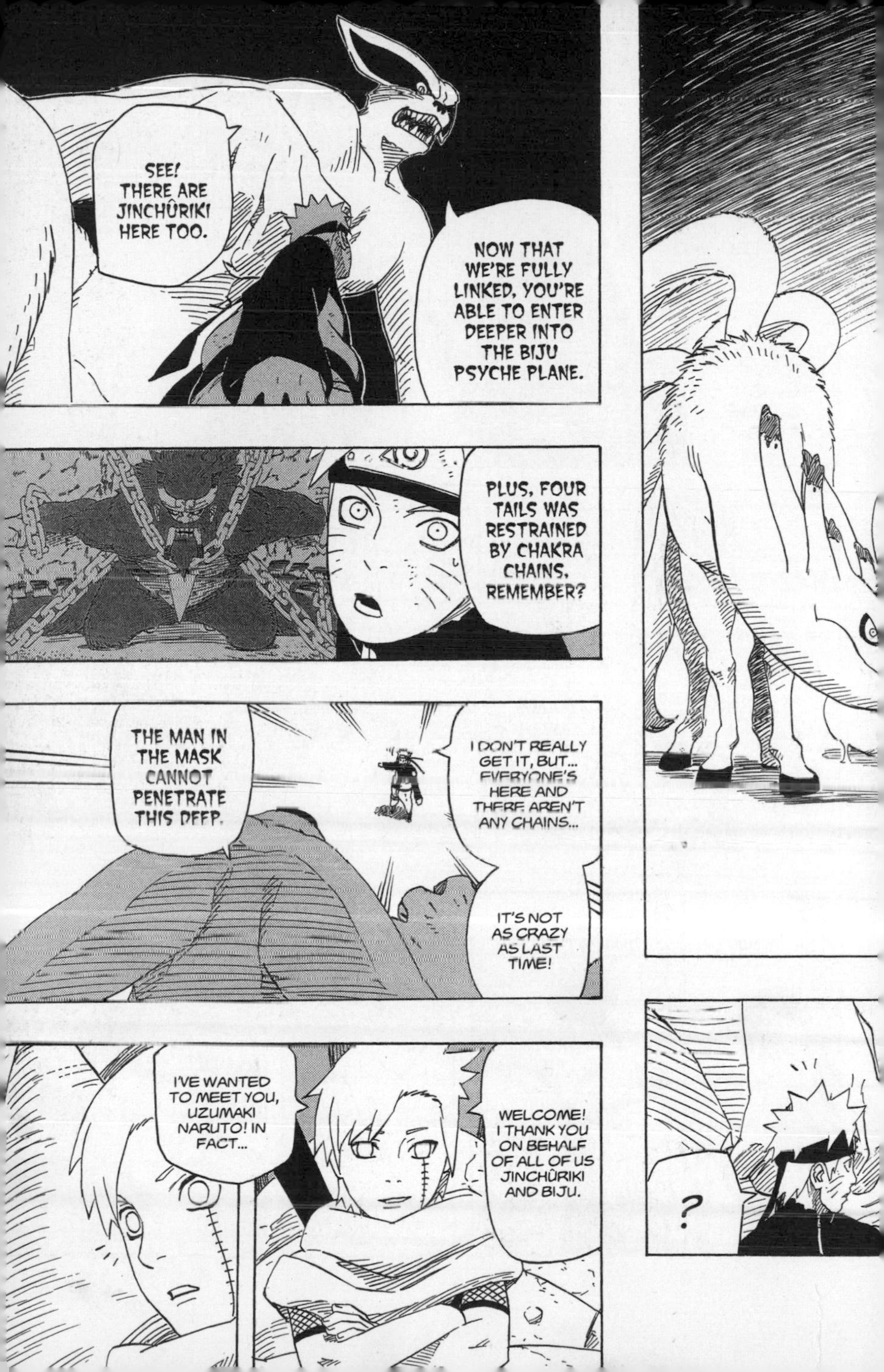
NOW THAT WE'RE FULLY LINKED, YOU'RE ABLE TO ENTER DEEPER INTO THE BIJU PSYCHE PLANE.
SEE! THERE ARE JINCHÛRIKI HERE TOO.
PLUS, FOUR TAILS WAS RESTRAINED BY CHAKRA CHAINS, REMEMBER?
I DON'T REALLY GET IT, BUT... EVERYONE'S HERE AND THERE AREN'T ANY CHAINS...
IT'S NOT AS CRAZY AS LAST TIME!
THE MAN IN THE MASK CANNOT PENETRATE THIS DEEP.
?
WELCOME! I THANK YOU ON BEHALF OF ALL OF US JINCHÛRIKI AND BIJU.
I'VE WANTED TO MEET YOU, UZUMAKI NARUTO! IN FACT...

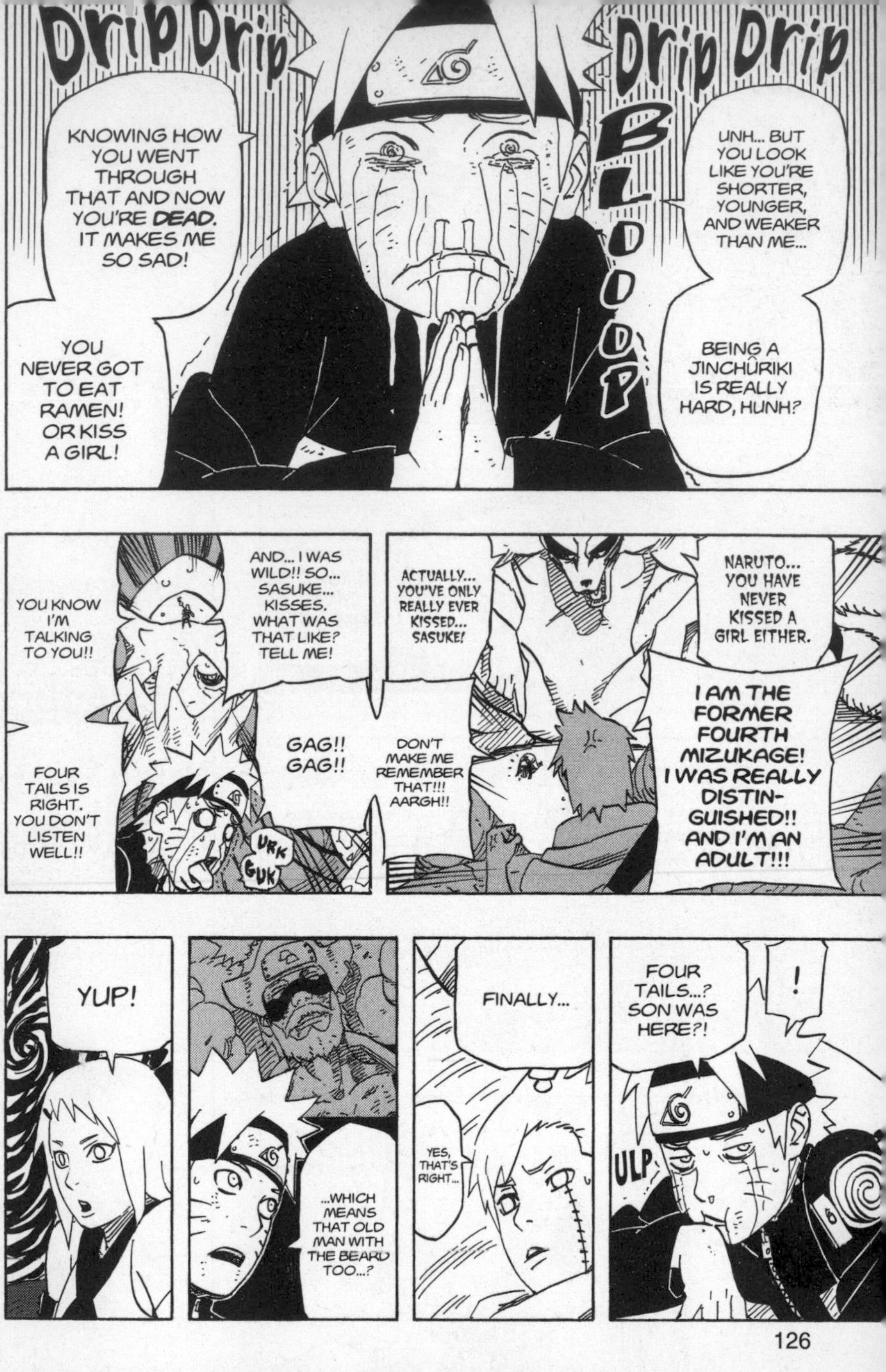
Drip Drip
UNH... BUT YOU LOOK LIKE YOU'RE SHORTER, YOUNGER, AND WEAKER THAN ME...
BEING A JINCHÛRIKI IS REALLY HARD, HUNH?
Drip Drip
KNOWING HOW YOU WENT THROUGH THAT AND NOW YOU'RE **DEAD**. IT MAKES ME SO SAD!
YOU NEVER GOT TO EAT RAMEN! OR KISS A GIRL!
NARUTO... YOU HAVE NEVER KISSED A GIRL EITHER.
I AM THE FORMER FOURTH MIZUKAGE! I WAS REALLY DISTIN-GUISHED!! AND I'M AN ADULT!!!
ACTUALLY... YOU'VE ONLY REALLY EVER KISSED... SASUKE!
DON'T MAKE ME REMEMBER THAT!!! AARGH!!
AND... I WAS WILD!! SO... SASUKE... KISSES. WHAT WAS THAT LIKE? TELL ME!
YOU KNOW I'M TALKING TO YOU!!
GAG!! GAG!!
URK
GUK
FOUR TAILS IS RIGHT. YOU DON'T LISTEN WELL!!
!
FOUR TAILS...? SON WAS HERE?!
ULP
FINALLY...
YES, THAT'S RIGHT...
...WHICH MEANS THAT OLD MAN WITH THE BEARD TOO...?
YUP!

READ THIS WAY

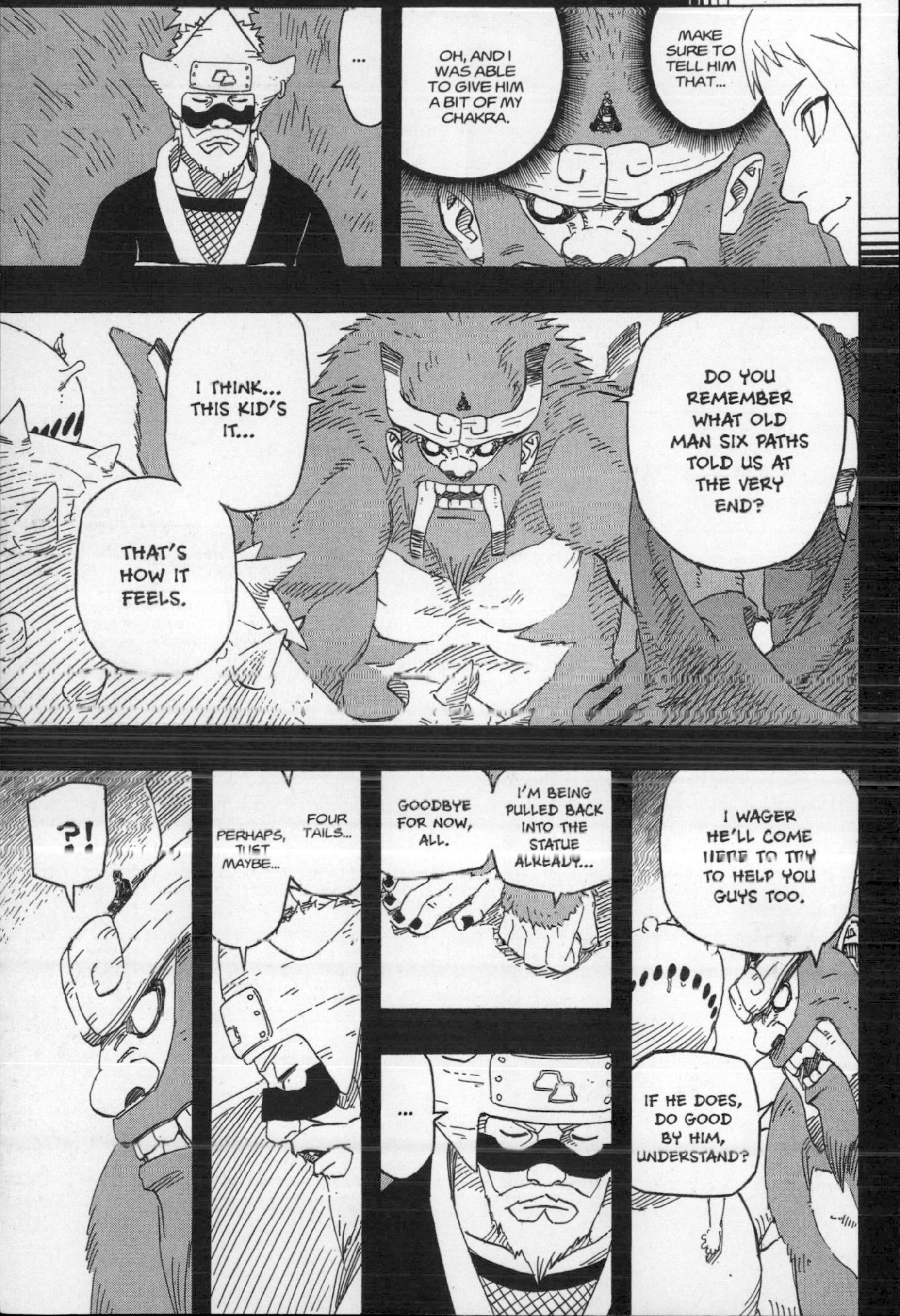
MAKE SURE TO TELL HIM THAT...
OH, AND I WAS ABLE TO GIVE HIM A BIT OF MY CHAKRA.
...
DO YOU REMEMBER WHAT OLD MAN SIX PATHS TOLD US AT THE VERY END?
I THINK... THIS KID'S IT...
THAT'S HOW IT FEELS.
I WAGER HE'LL COME HERE TO TRY TO HELP YOU GUYS TOO.
IF HE DOES, DO GOOD BY HIM, UNDERSTAND?
I'M BEING PULLED BACK INTO THE STATUE ALREADY...
GOODBYE FOR NOW, ALL.
...
FOUR TAILS...
PERHAPS, JUST MAYBE...
?!

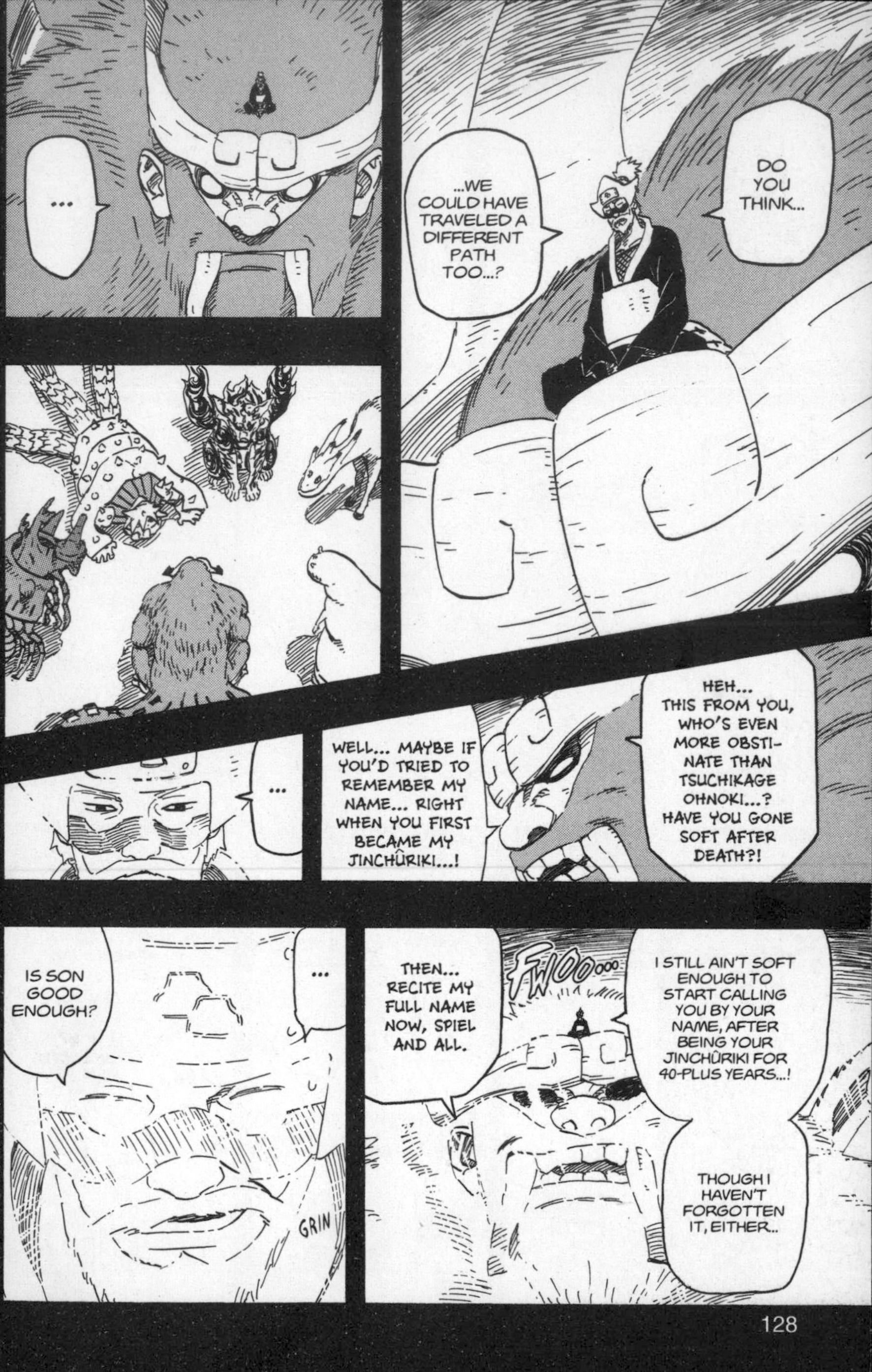
DO YOU THINK...
...WE COULD HAVE TRAVELED A DIFFERENT PATH TOO...?
...
HEH... THIS FROM YOU, WHO'S EVEN MORE OBSTI-NATE THAN TSUCHIKAGE OHNOKI...? HAVE YOU GONE SOFT AFTER DEATH?!
WELL... MAYBE IF YOU'D TRIED TO REMEMBER MY NAME... RIGHT WHEN YOU FIRST BECAME MY JINCHÛRIKI...!
...
I STILL AIN'T SOFT ENOUGH TO START CALLING YOU BY YOUR NAME, AFTER BEING YOUR JINCHÛRIKI FOR 40-PLUS YEARS...!
THOUGH I HAVEN'T FORGOTTEN IT, EITHER..
FWOOooo
THEN... RECITE MY FULL NAME NOW, SPIEL AND ALL.
...
IS SON GOOD ENOUGH?
GRIN

READ THIS WAY

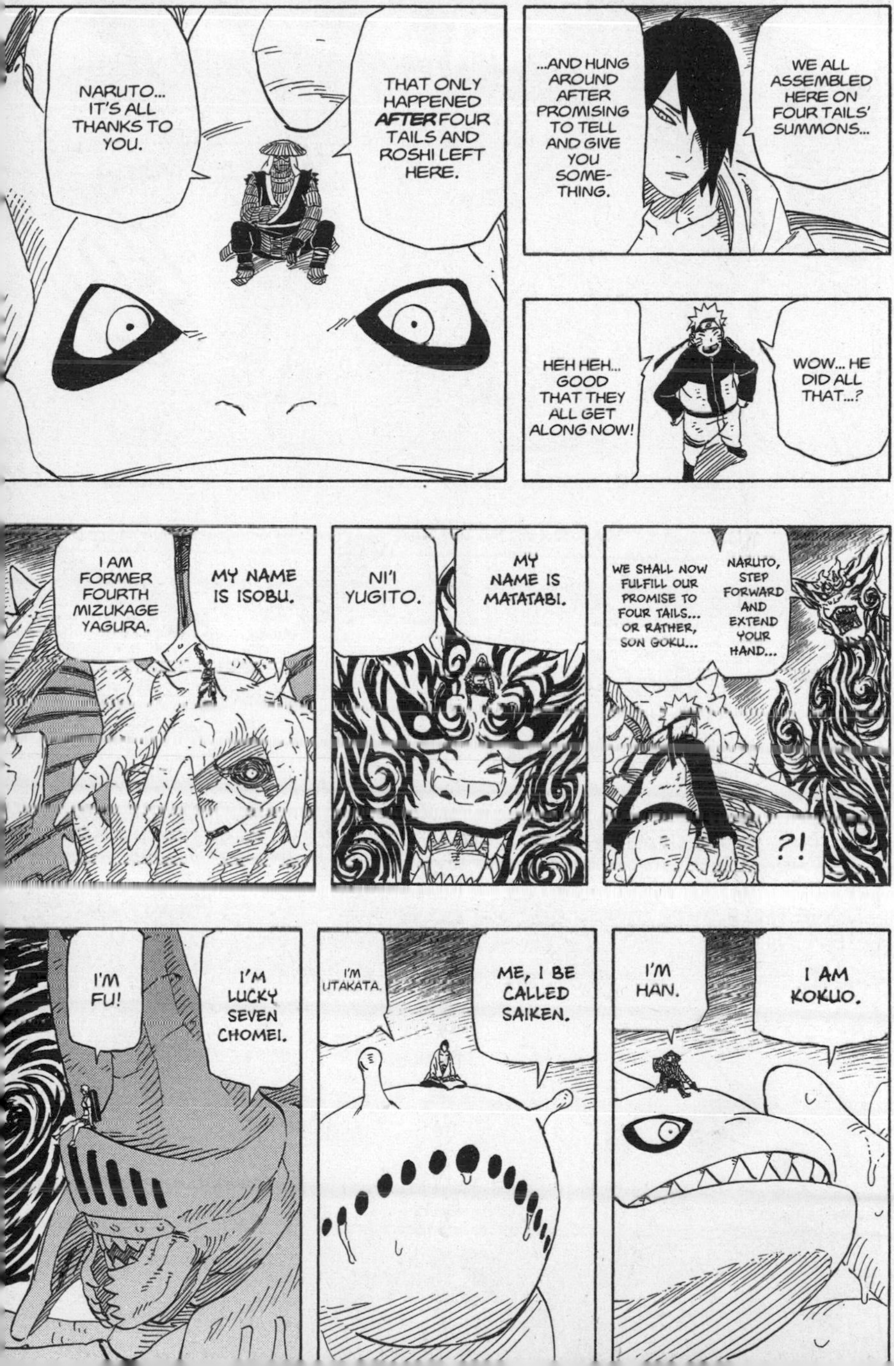
WE ALL ASSEMBLED HERE ON FOUR TAILS' SUMMONS...
...AND HUNG AROUND AFTER PROMISING TO TELL AND GIVE YOU SOME-THING.
WOW... HE DID ALL THAT...?
HEH HEH... GOOD THAT THEY ALL GET ALONG NOW!
THAT ONLY HAPPENED **AFTER** FOUR TAILS AND ROSHI LEFT HERE.
NARUTO... IT'S ALL THANKS TO YOU.
NARUTO, STEP FORWARD AND EXTEND YOUR HAND...
WE SHALL NOW FULFILL OUR PROMISE TO FOUR TAILS... OR RATHER, SON GOKU...
?!
MY NAME IS MATATABI.
NI'I YUGITO.
MY NAME IS ISOBU.
I AM FORMER FOURTH MIZUKAGE YAGURA.
I AM KOKUO.
I'M HAN.
ME, I BE CALLED SAIKEN.
I'M UTAKATA.
I'M LUCKY SEVEN CHOMEI.
I'M FU!

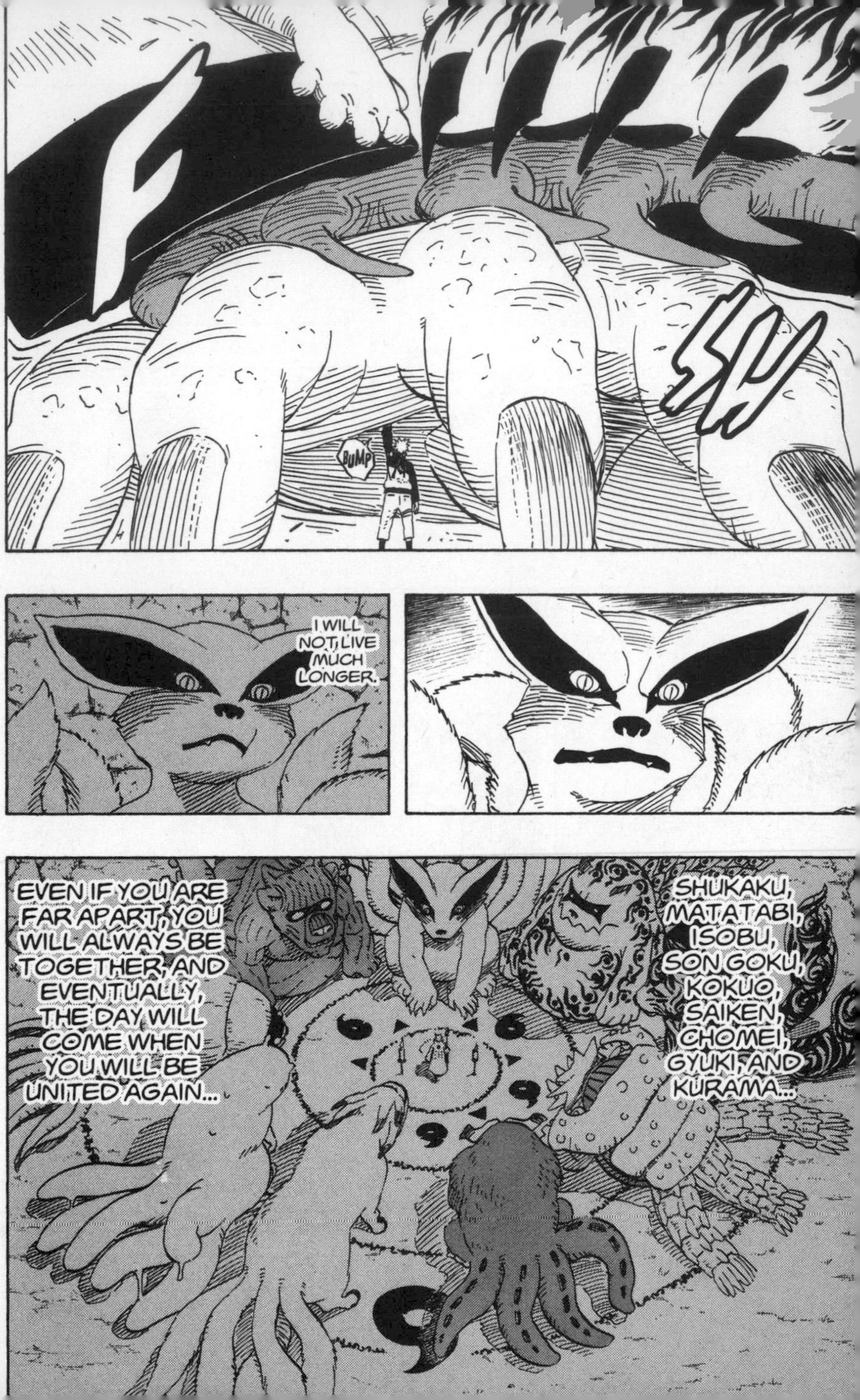
BUMP
I WILL NOT LIVE MUCH LONGER.
SHUKAKU, MATATABI, ISOBU, SON GOKU, KOKUO, SAIKEN, CHOMEI, GYUKI, AND KURAMA...
EVEN IF YOU ARE FAR APART, YOU WILL ALWAYS BE TOGETHER, AND EVENTUALLY, THE DAY WILL COME WHEN YOU WILL BE UNITED AGAIN...

READ THIS WAY

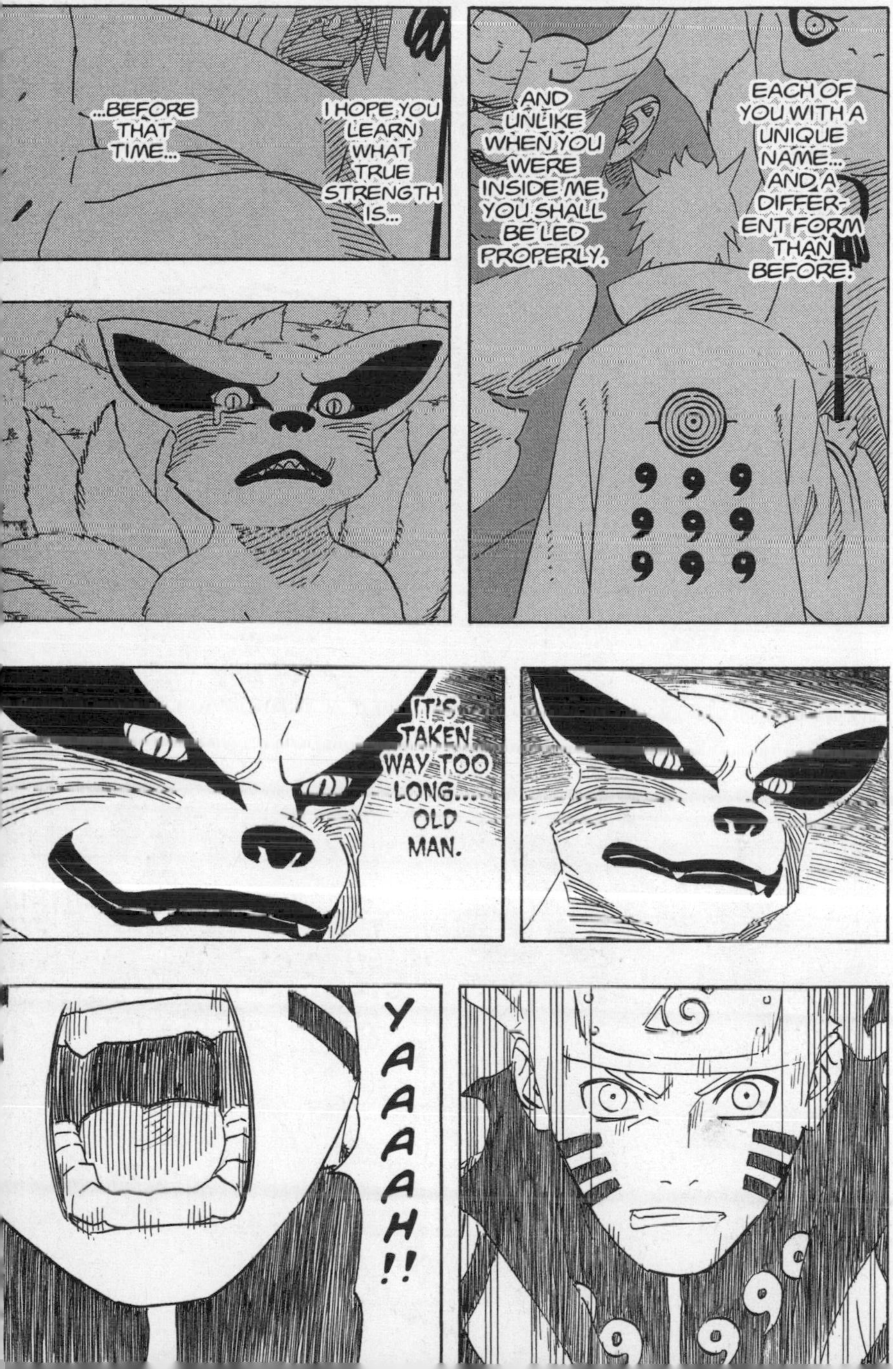
EACH OF YOU WITH A UNIQUE NAME... AND A DIFFER-ENT FORM THAN BEFORE.
AND UNLIKE WHEN YOU WERE INSIDE ME, YOU SHALL BE LED PROPERLY.
I HOPE YOU LEARN WHAT TRUE STRENGTH IS...
...BEFORE THAT TIME...
IT'S TAKEN WAY TOO LONG... OLD MAN.
YAAAAAH!!

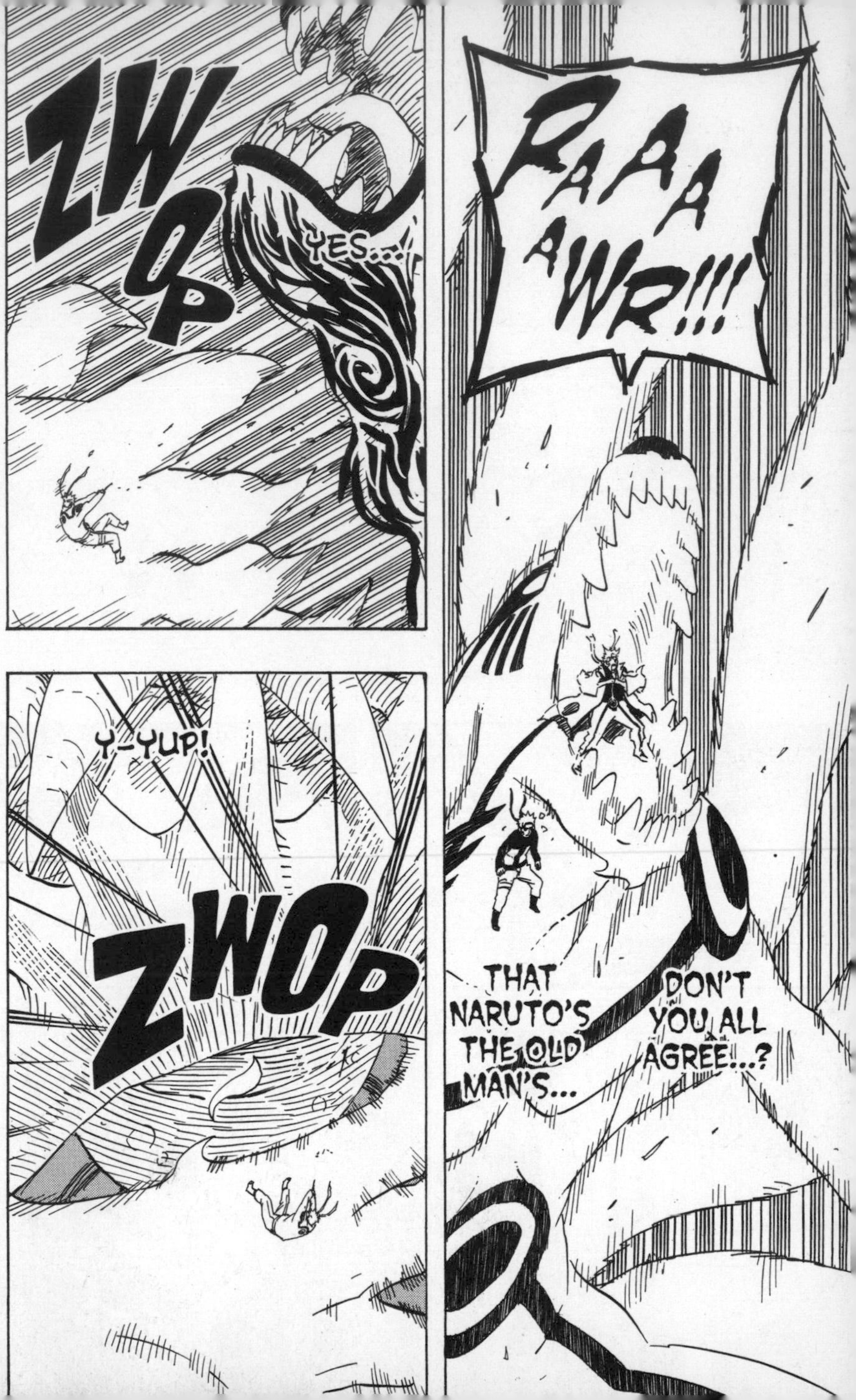
PAAAAWR!!!
DON'T YOU ALL AGREE...?
THAT NARUTO'S THE OLD MAN'S...
ZWOP
YES...
Y-YUP!
ZWOP

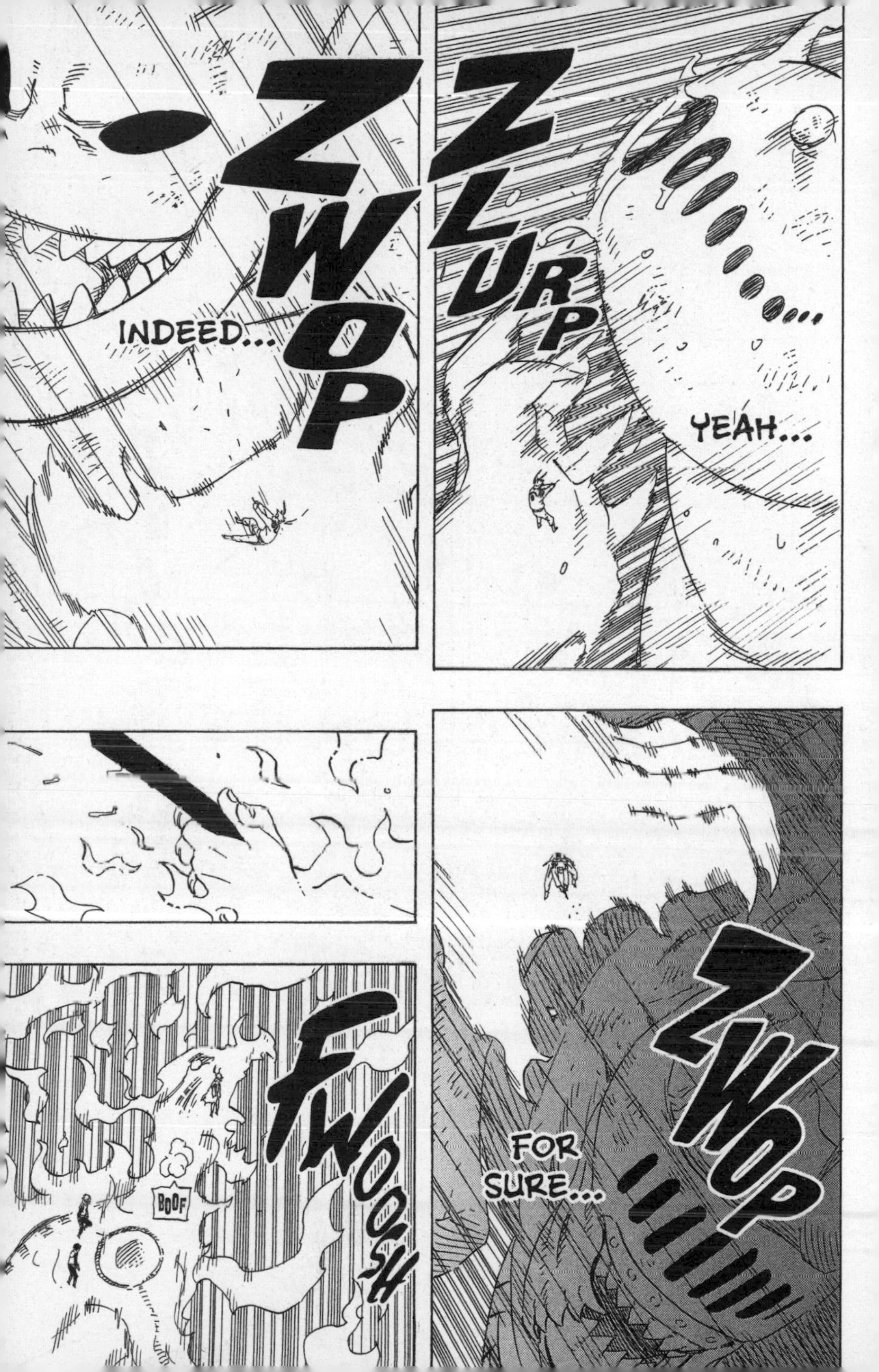
ZLURP
YEAH...
ZWOP
INDEED...
ZWOP
FOR SURE...
FWOOSH
BOOF

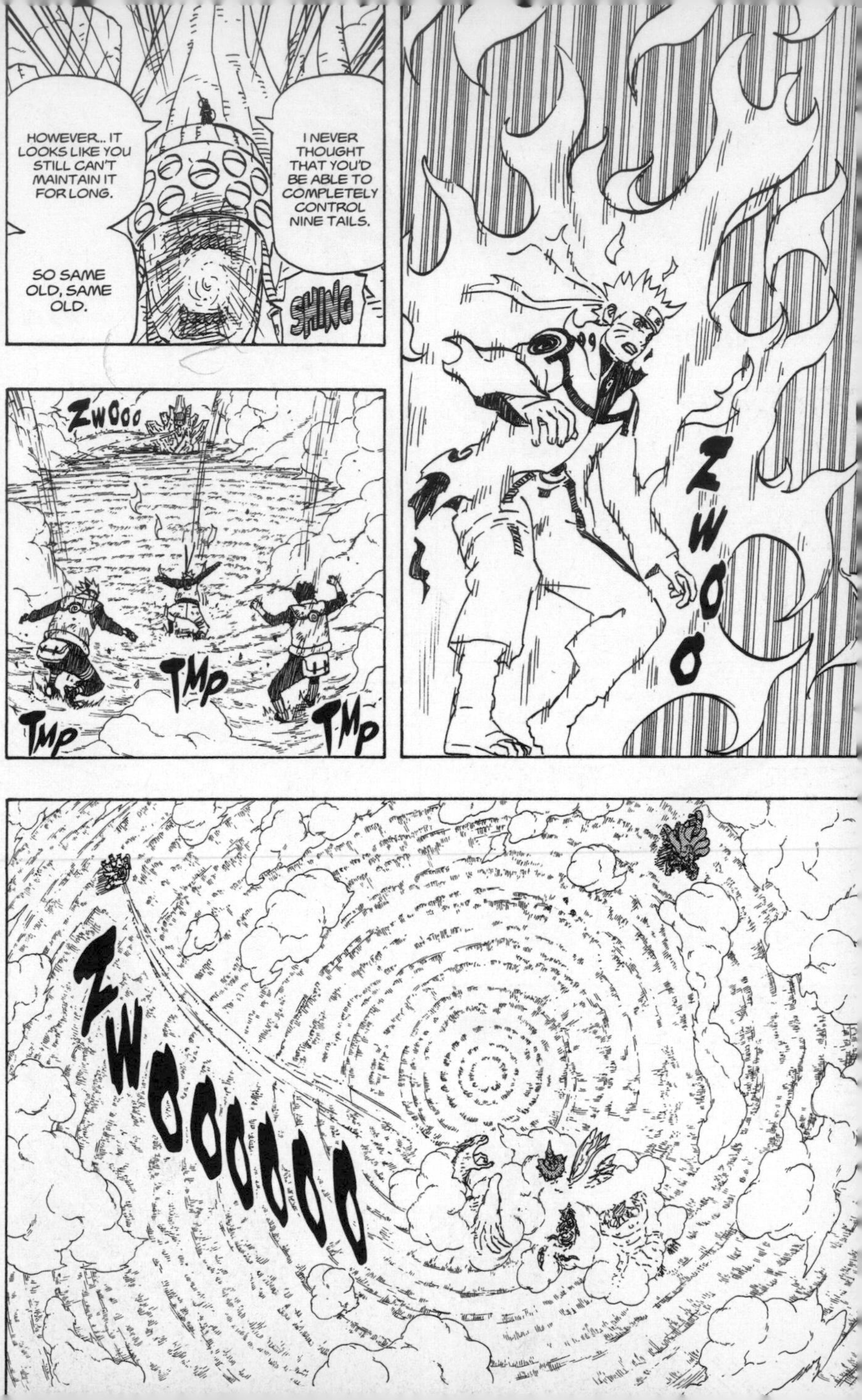
ZWOOO
I NEVER THOUGHT THAT YOU'D BE ABLE TO COMPLETELY CONTROL NINE TAILS.
HOWEVER... IT LOOKS LIKE YOU STILL CAN'T MAINTAIN IT FOR LONG.
SO SAME OLD, SAME OLD.
SHING
ZWOOO
TMP
TMP
TMP
ZWOOOOOOO

READ THIS WAY

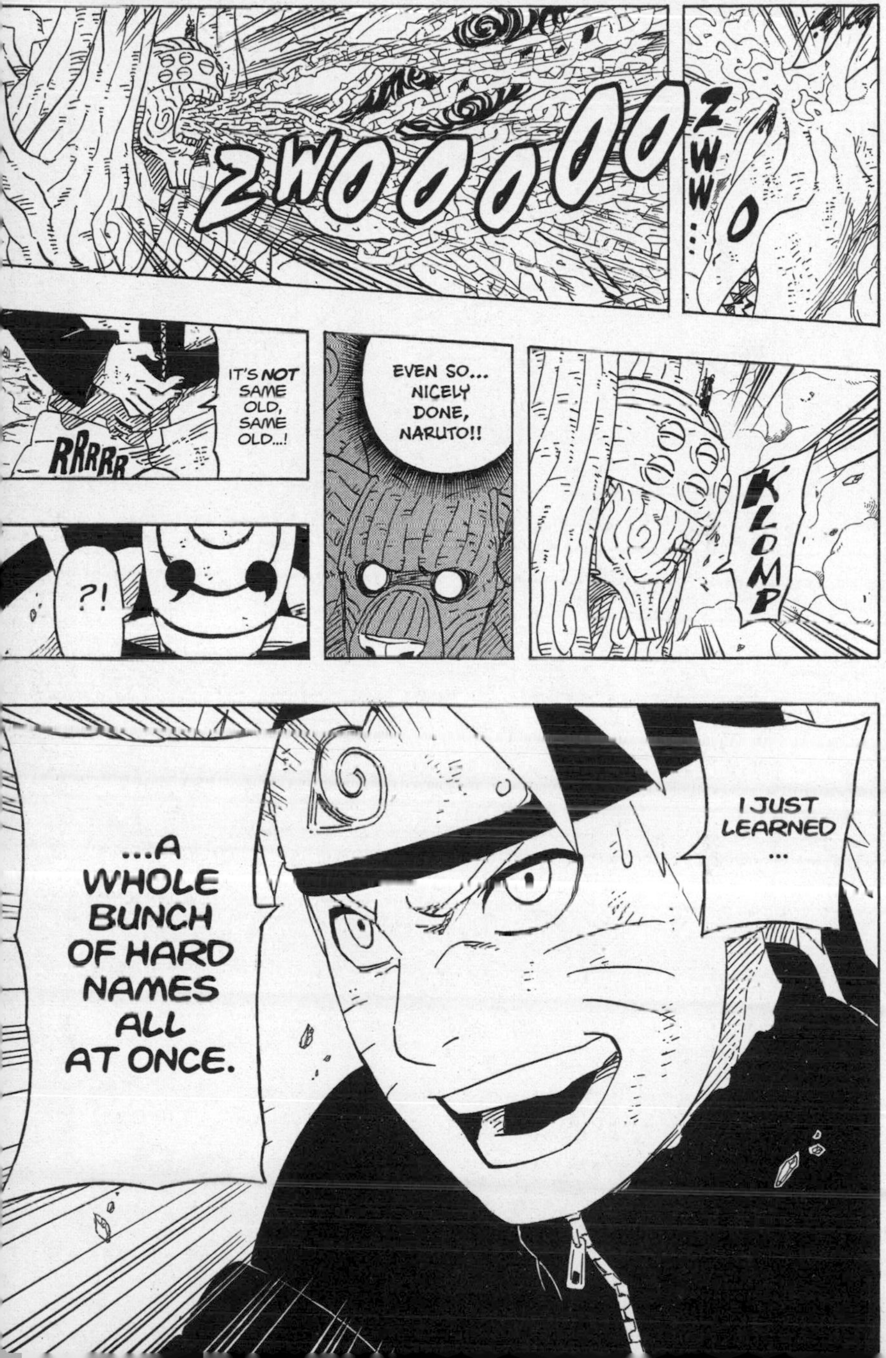
ZWWW...O
ZWOOOOOO
KLOMP
EVEN SO... NICELY DONE, NARUTO!!
IT'S NOT SAME OLD, SAME OLD...!
RRRRR
?!
I JUST LEARNED ...
...A WHOLE BUNCH OF HARD NAMES ALL AT ONCE.

Illustration to Commemorate Reaching Volume 60 [8]

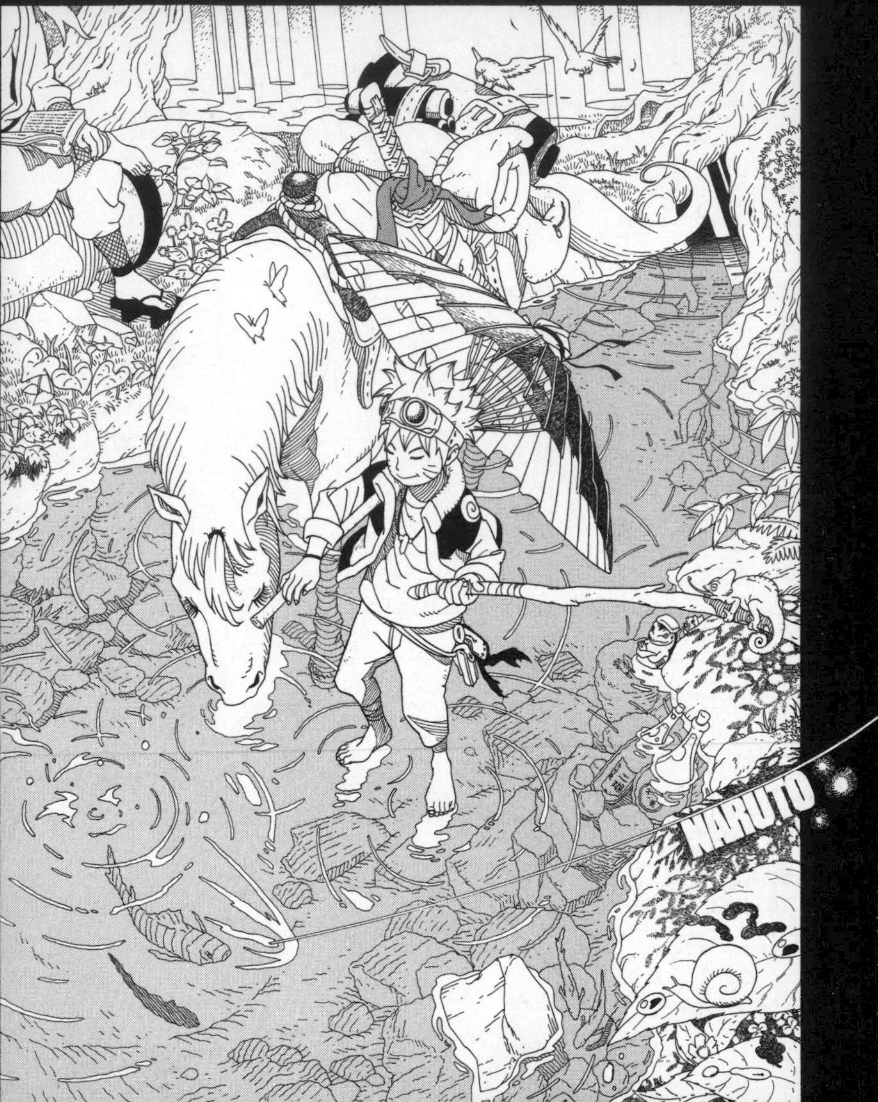
NARUTO

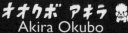

オオクボ アキラ
Akira Okubo

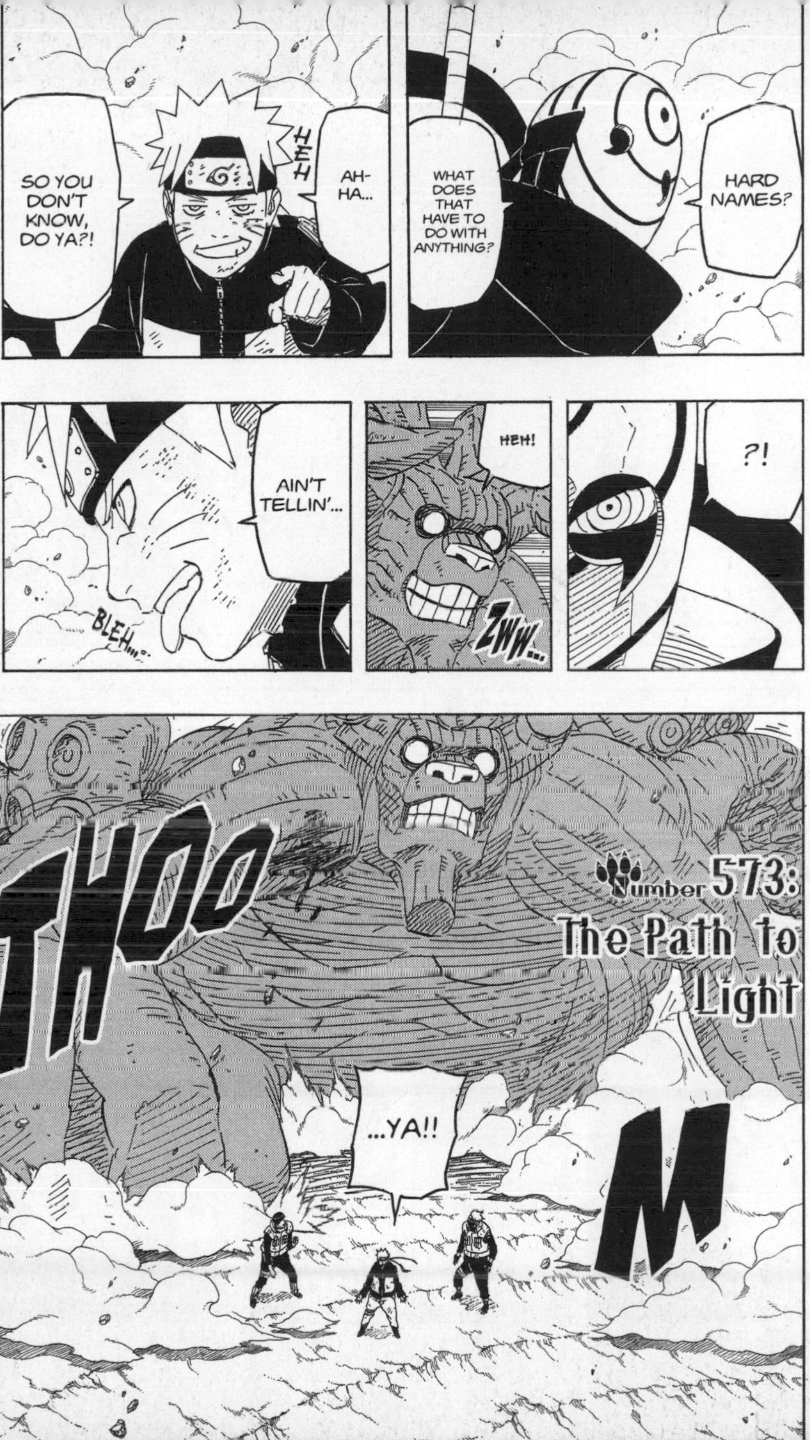
HARD NAMES?
WHAT DOES THAT HAVE TO DO WITH ANYTHING?
HEH
AH-HA...
SO YOU DON'T KNOW, DO YA?!
?!
HEH!
ZWW...
AIN'T TELLIN'...
BLEH...
Number 573: The Path to Light
THOOM
...YA!!

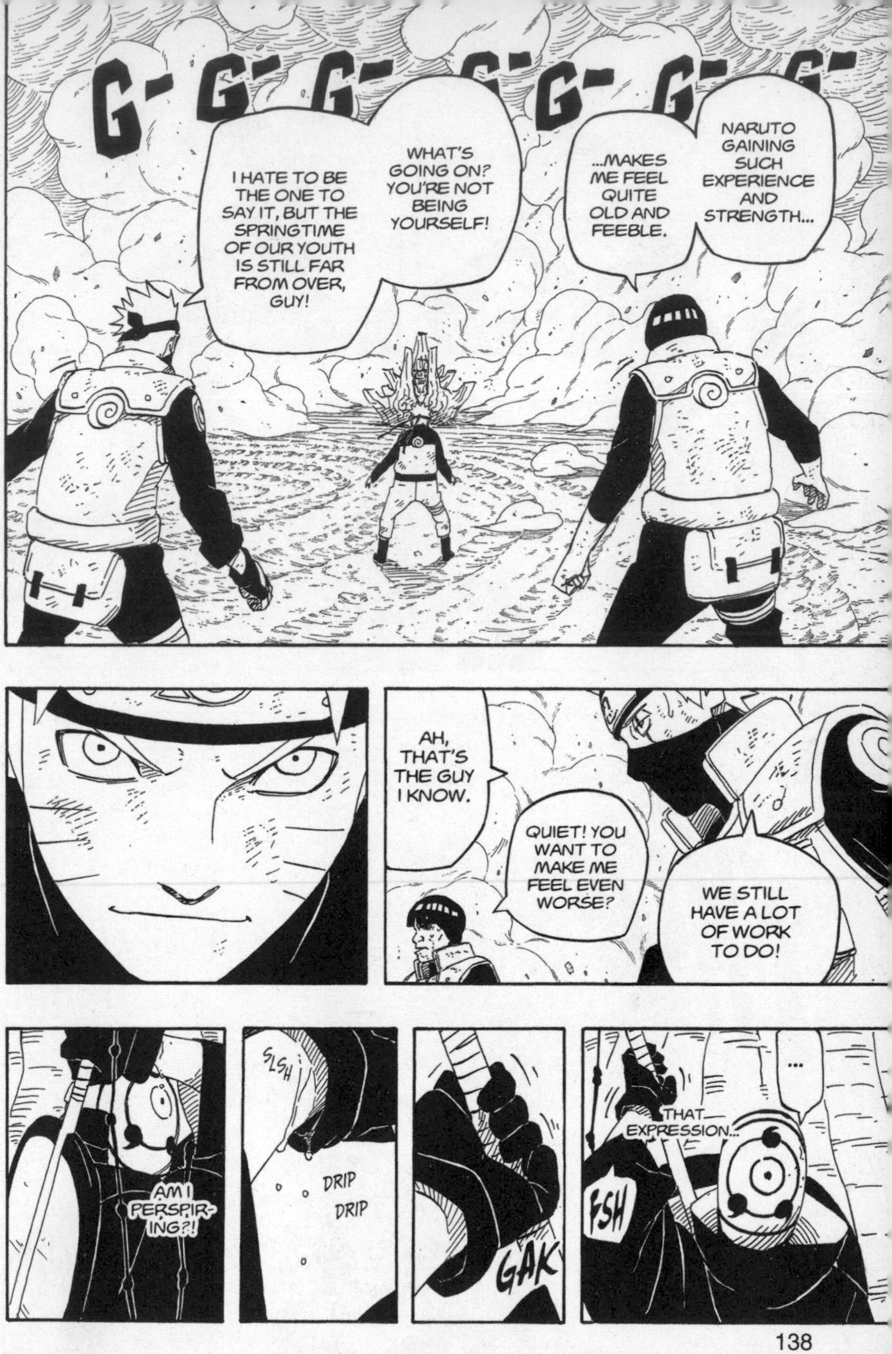
G- G- G- G- G- G- G-
NARUTO GAINING SUCH EXPERIENCE AND STRENGTH...
...MAKES ME FEEL QUITE OLD AND FEEBLE.
WHAT'S GOING ON? YOU'RE NOT BEING YOURSELF!
I HATE TO BE THE ONE TO SAY IT, BUT THE SPRINGTIME OF OUR YOUTH IS STILL FAR FROM OVER, GUY!
AH, THAT'S THE GUY I KNOW.
QUIET! YOU WANT TO MAKE ME FEEL EVEN WORSE?
WE STILL HAVE A LOT OF WORK TO DO!
...
THAT EXPRESSION...
FSH
GAK
SLSH
DRIP
DRIP
AM I PERSPIRING?!

READ THIS WAY

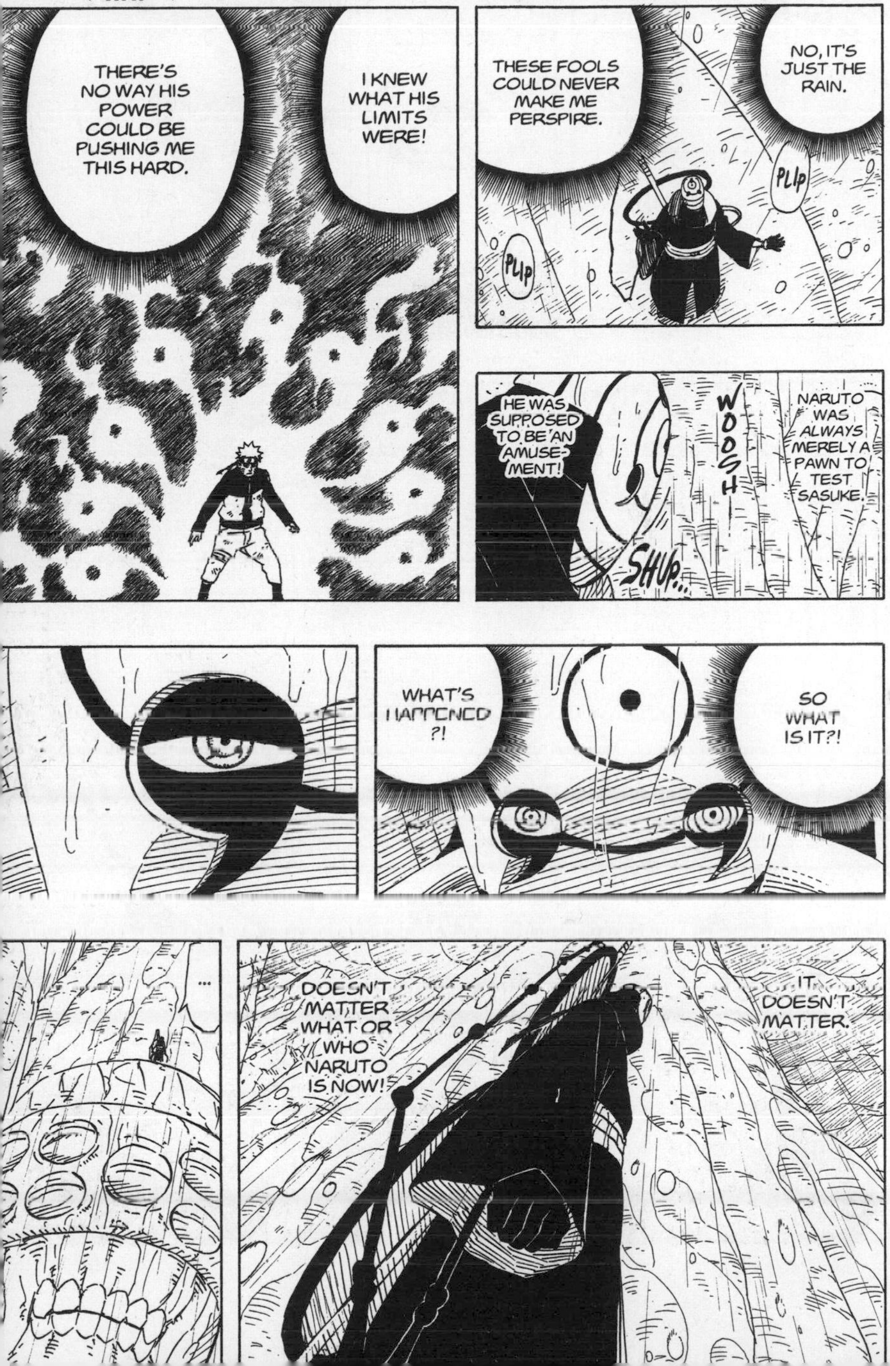
NO, IT'S JUST THE RAIN.
THESE FOOLS COULD NEVER MAKE ME PERSPIRE.
PLIP
PLIP
NARUTO WAS ALWAYS MERELY A PAWN TO TEST SASUKE.
WOOSH
HE WAS SUPPOSED TO BE AN AMUSEMENT!
SHUP...
I KNEW WHAT HIS LIMITS WERE!
THERE'S NO WAY HIS POWER COULD BE PUSHING ME THIS HARD.
SO WHAT IS IT?!
WHAT'S HAPPENED ?!
IT DOESN'T MATTER.
DOESN'T MATTER WHAT OR WHO NARUTO IS NOW!
...

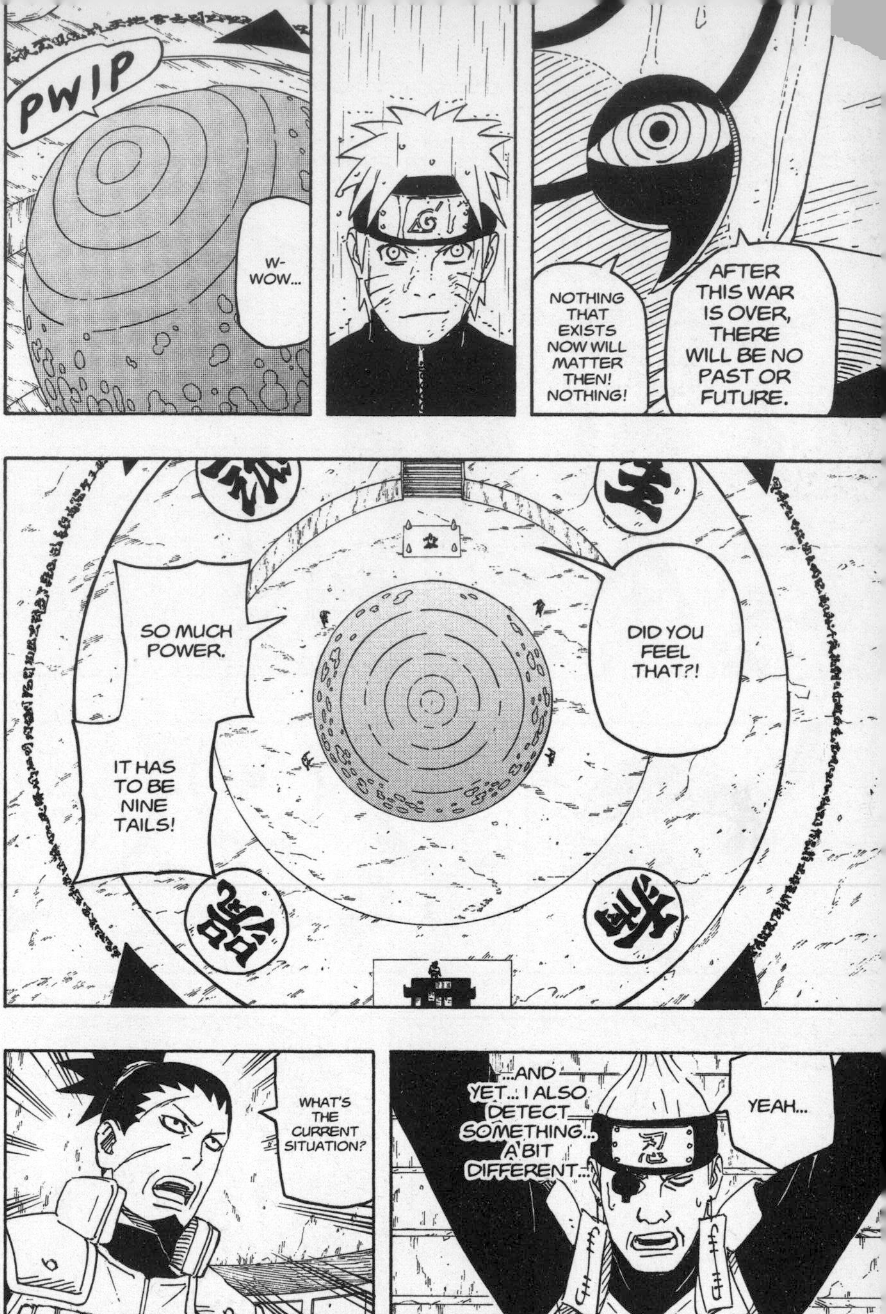
AFTER THIS WAR IS OVER, THERE WILL BE NO PAST OR FUTURE.
NOTHING THAT EXISTS NOW WILL MATTER THEN! NOTHING!
PWIP
W-WOW...
DID YOU FEEL THAT?!
SO MUCH POWER.
IT HAS TO BE NINE TAILS!
YEAH...
...AND YET... I ALSO DETECT SOMETHING... A BIT DIFFERENT...
WHAT'S THE CURRENT SITUATION?

READ THIS WAY

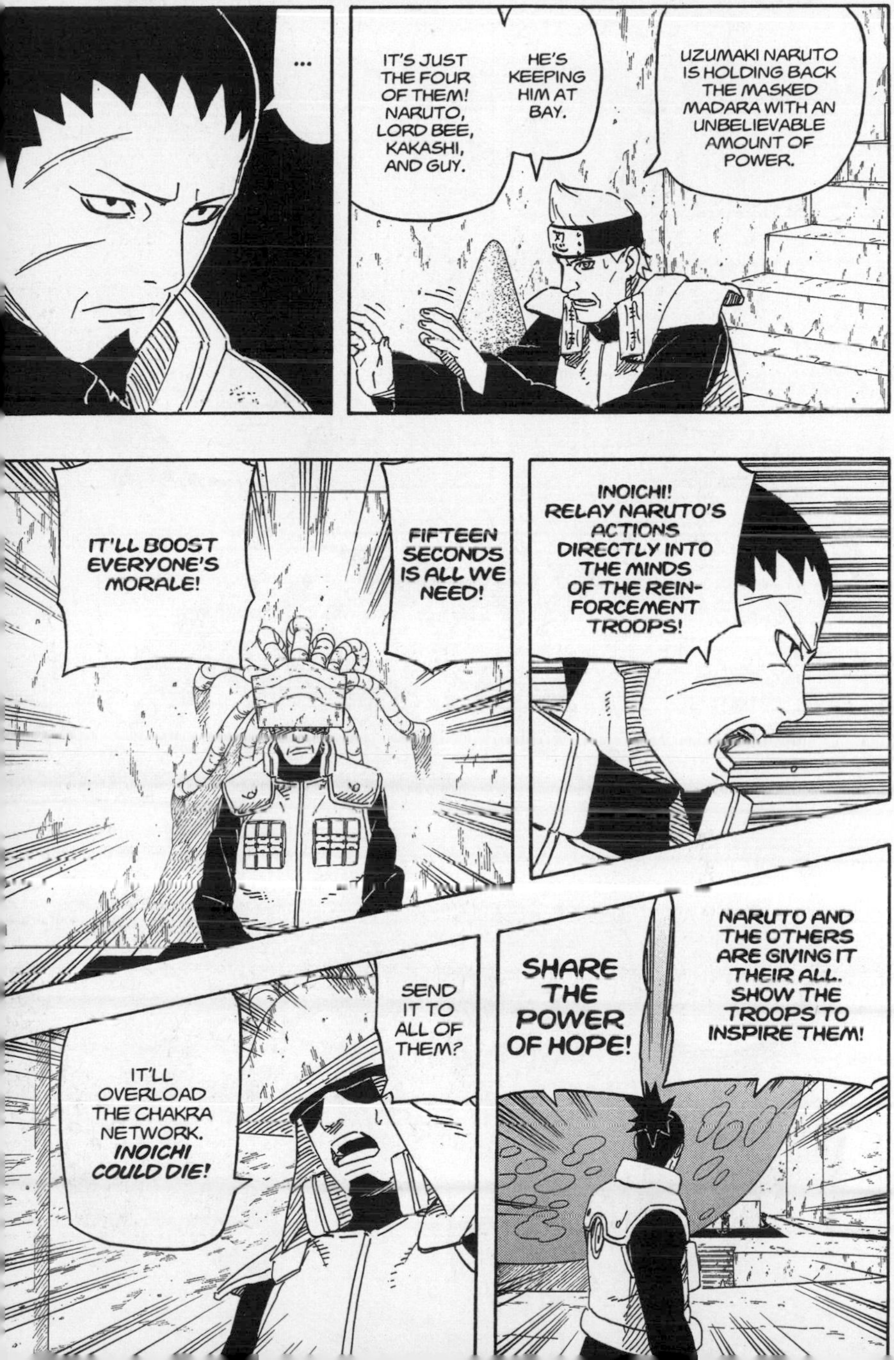

UZUMAKI NARUTO IS HOLDING BACK THE MASKED MADARA WITH AN UNBELIEVABLE AMOUNT OF POWER.
HE'S KEEPING HIM AT BAY.
IT'S JUST THE FOUR OF THEM! NARUTO, LORD BEE, KAKASHI, AND GUY.
...
INOICHI! RELAY NARUTO'S ACTIONS DIRECTLY INTO THE MINDS OF THE REIN-FORCEMENT TROOPS!
FIFTEEN SECONDS IS ALL WE NEED!
IT'LL BOOST EVERYONE'S MORALE!
NARUTO AND THE OTHERS ARE GIVING IT THEIR ALL. SHOW THE TROOPS TO INSPIRE THEM!
SHARE THE POWER OF HOPE!
SEND IT TO ALL OF THEM?
IT'LL OVERLOAD THE CHAKRA NETWORK. INOICHI COULD DIE!

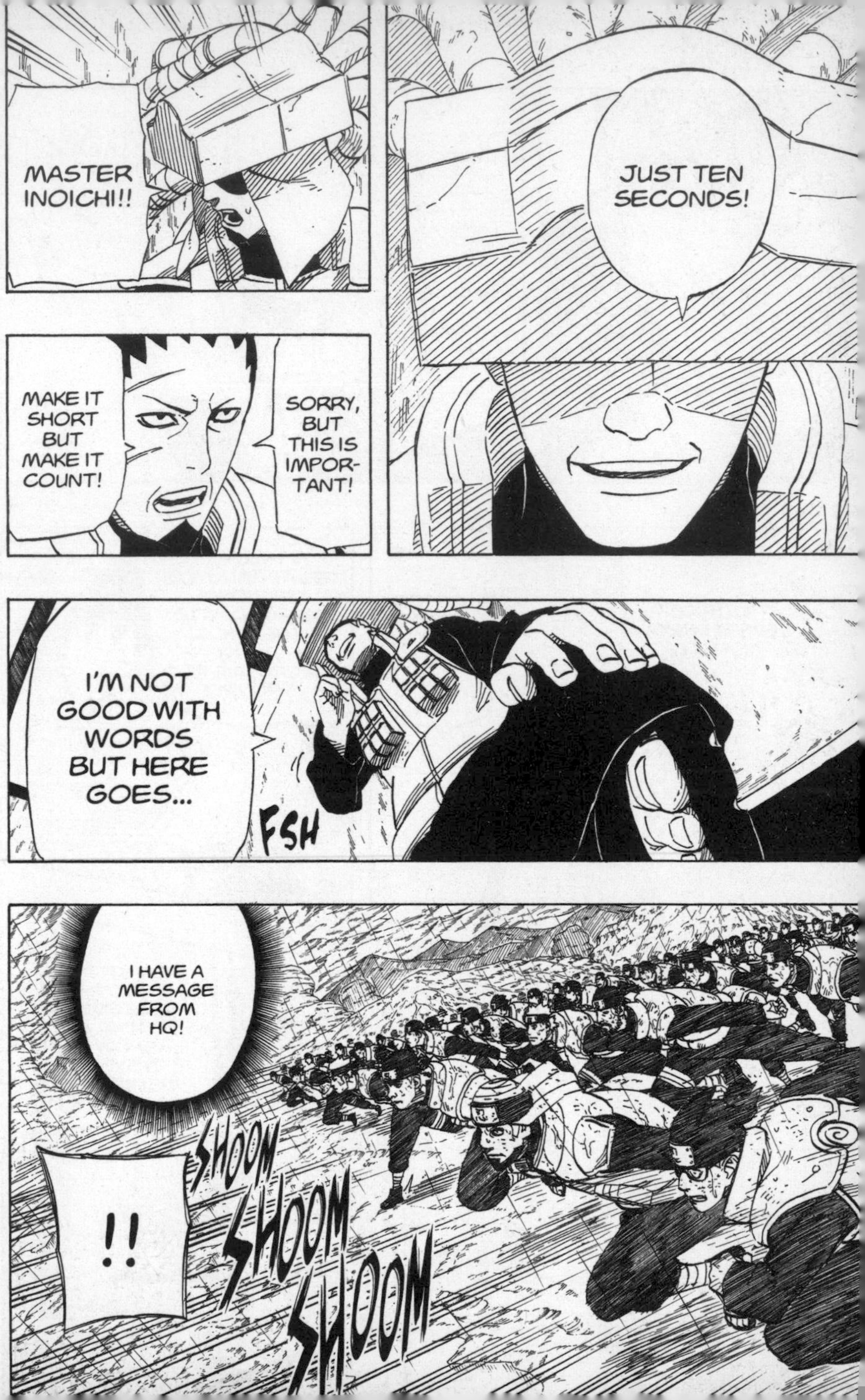
JUST TEN SECONDS!
MASTER INOICHI!!
SORRY, BUT THIS IS IMPOR-TANT!
MAKE IT SHORT BUT MAKE IT COUNT!
I'M NOT GOOD WITH WORDS BUT HERE GOES...
FSH
I HAVE A MESSAGE FROM HQ!
SHOOM SHOOM SHOOM
!!

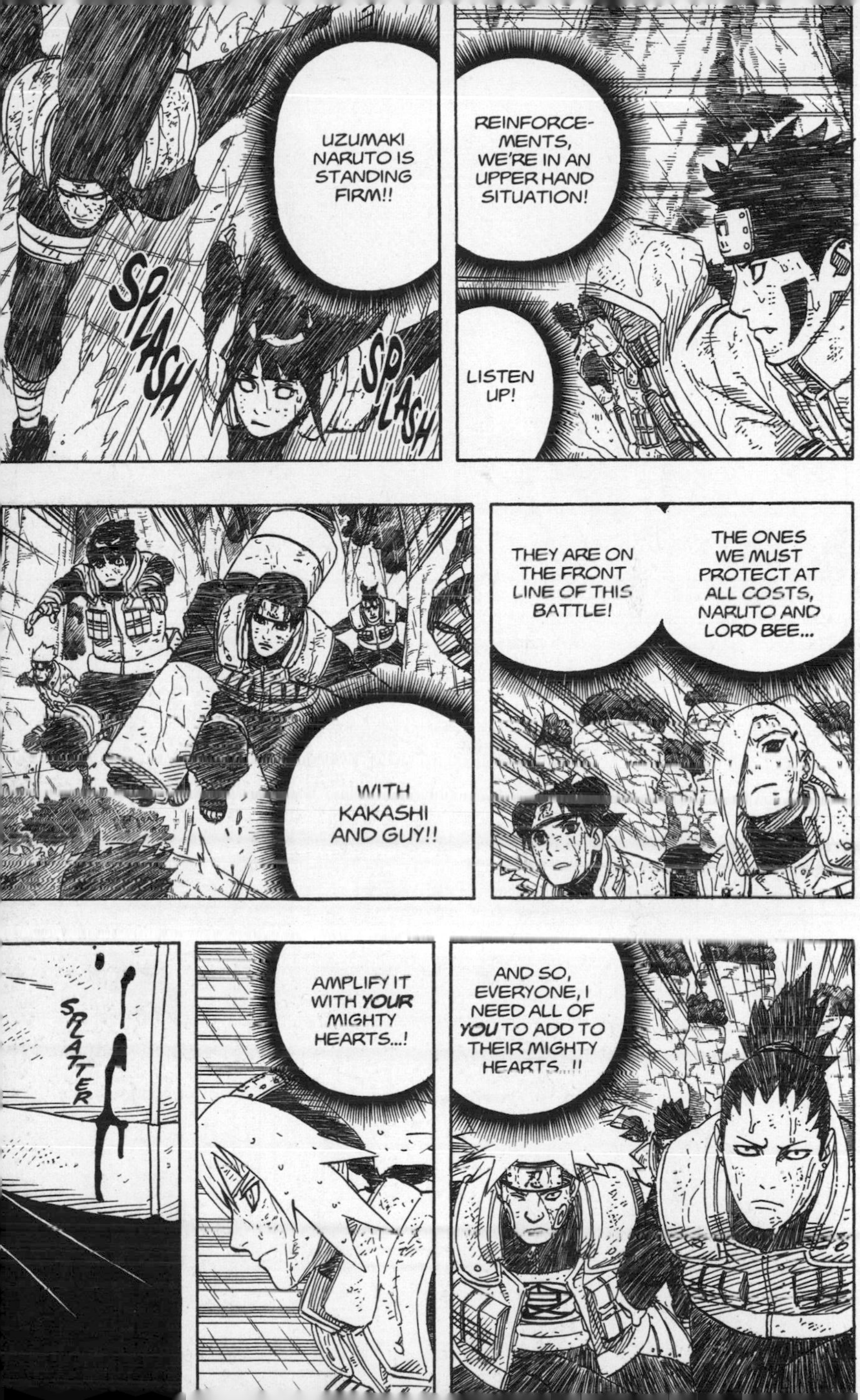

REINFORCEMENTS, WE'RE IN AN UPPER HAND SITUATION!
LISTEN UP!
UZUMAKI NARUTO IS STANDING FIRM!!
SPLASH
SPLASH
THE ONES WE MUST PROTECT AT ALL COSTS, NARUTO AND LORD BEE...
THEY ARE ON THE FRONT LINE OF THIS BATTLE!
WITH KAKASHI AND GUY!!
AND SO, EVERYONE, I NEED ALL OF *YOU* TO ADD TO THEIR MIGHTY HEARTS...!!
AMPLIFY IT WITH *YOUR* MIGHTY HEARTS...!
SPLATTER

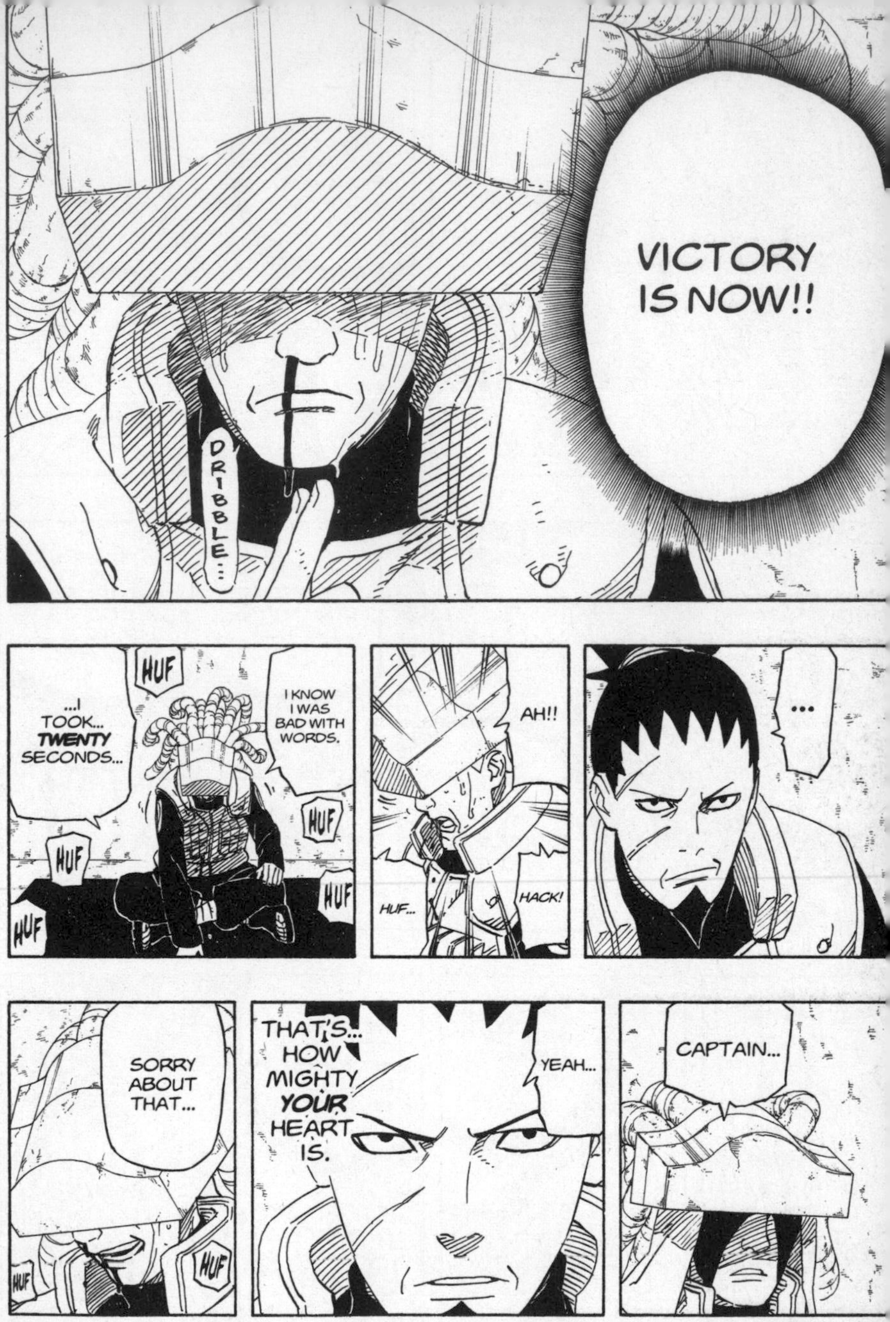
VICTORY IS NOW!!
DRIBBLE...
...
AH!!
HACK!
HUF...
I KNOW I WAS BAD WITH WORDS.
HUF
...I TOOK... **TWENTY** SECONDS...
HUF
HUF
HUF
HUF
CAPTAIN...
YEAH...
THAT'S... HOW MIGHTY **YOUR** HEART IS.
SORRY ABOUT THAT...
HUF
HUF

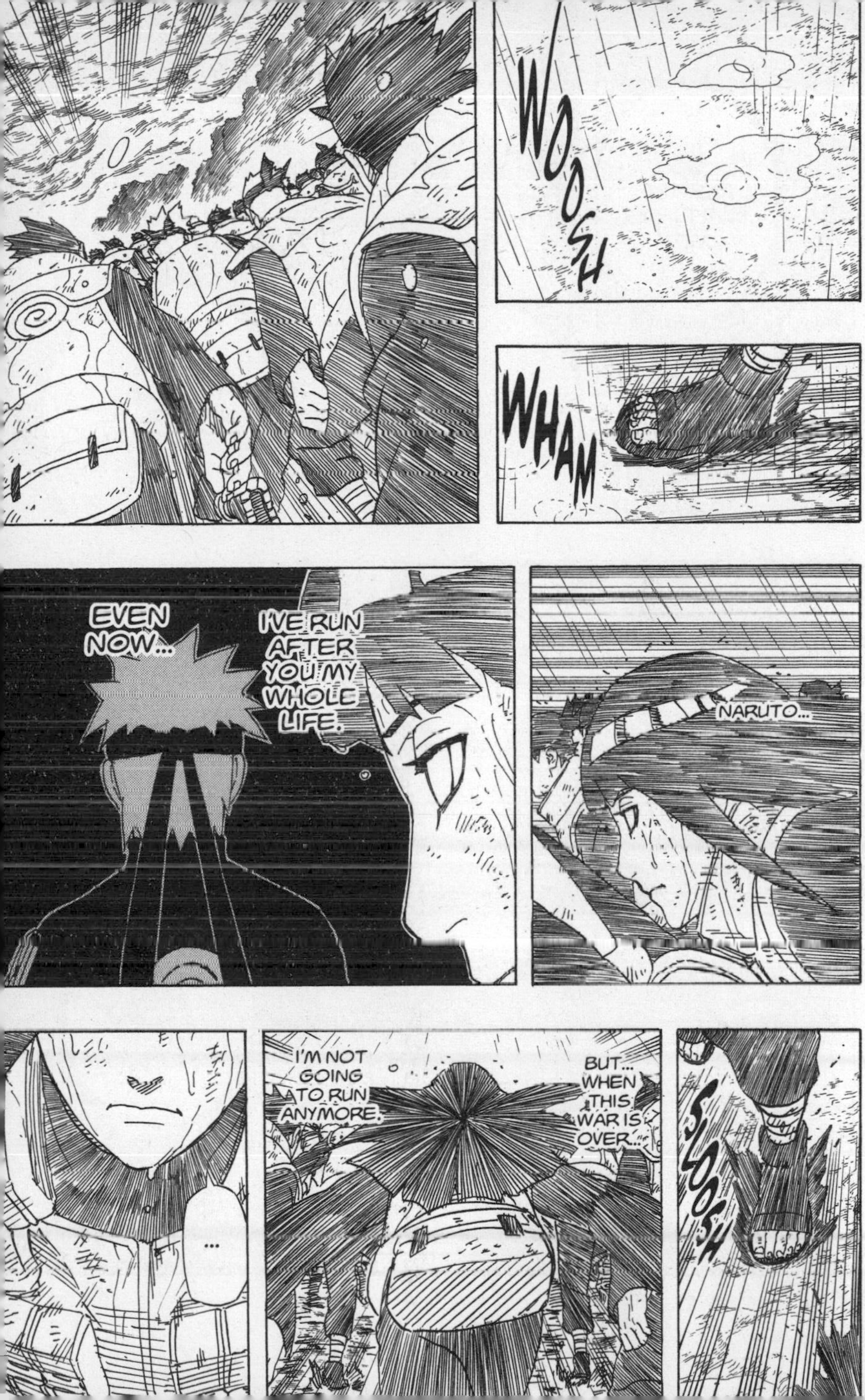
WOOSH
WHAM
NARUTO...
I'VE RUN AFTER YOU MY WHOLE LIFE.
EVEN NOW...
SLOOSH
BUT... WHEN THIS WAR IS OVER...
I'M NOT GOING TO RUN ANYMORE.
...

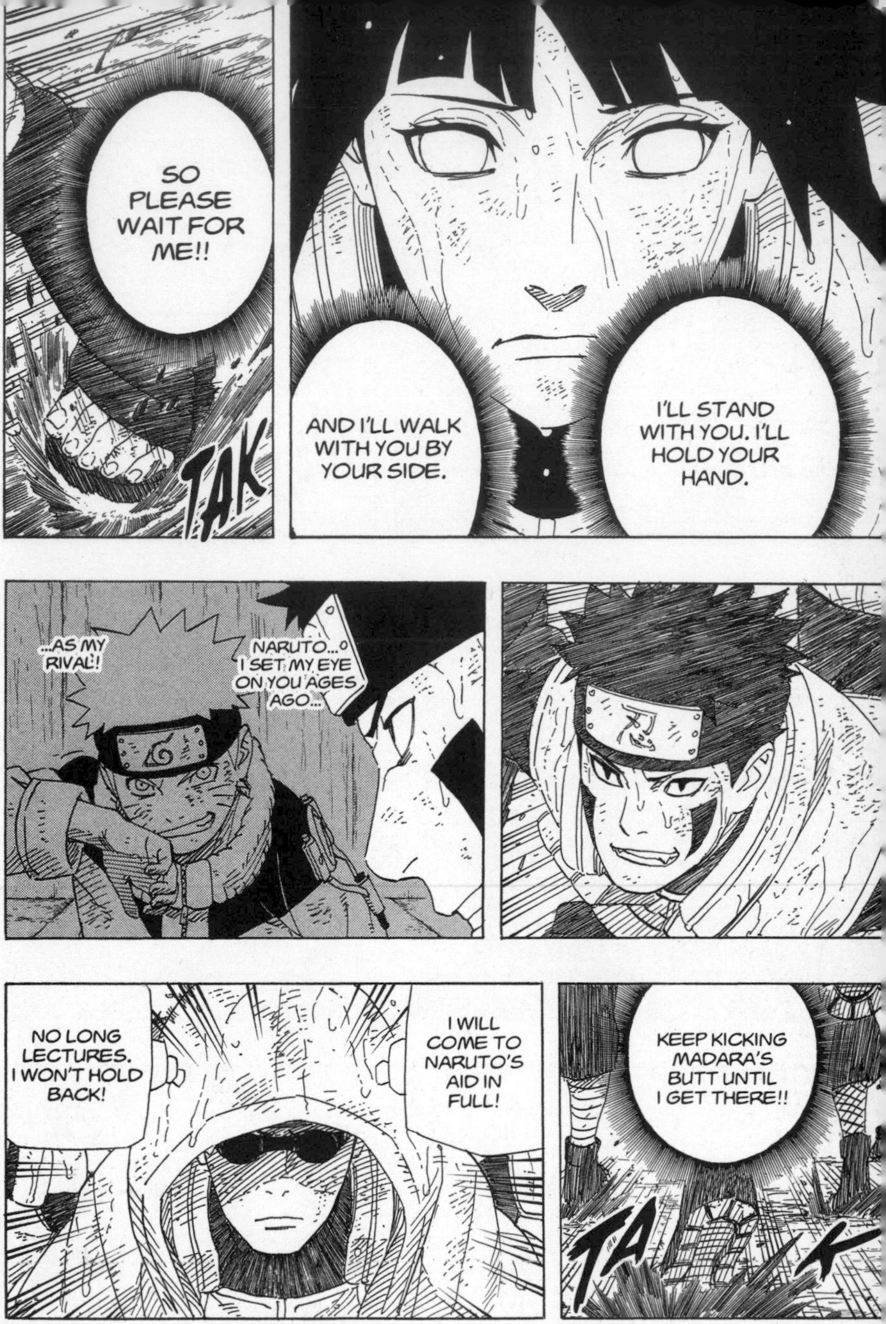
I'LL STAND WITH YOU. I'LL HOLD YOUR HAND.
AND I'LL WALK WITH YOU BY YOUR SIDE.
SO PLEASE WAIT FOR ME!!
TAK
NARUTO... I SET MY EYE ON YOU AGES AGO...
...AS MY RIVAL!
KEEP KICKING MADARA'S BUTT UNTIL I GET THERE!!
TAK
I WILL COME TO NARUTO'S AID IN FULL!
NO LONG LECTURES. I WON'T HOLD BACK!

READ THIS WAY

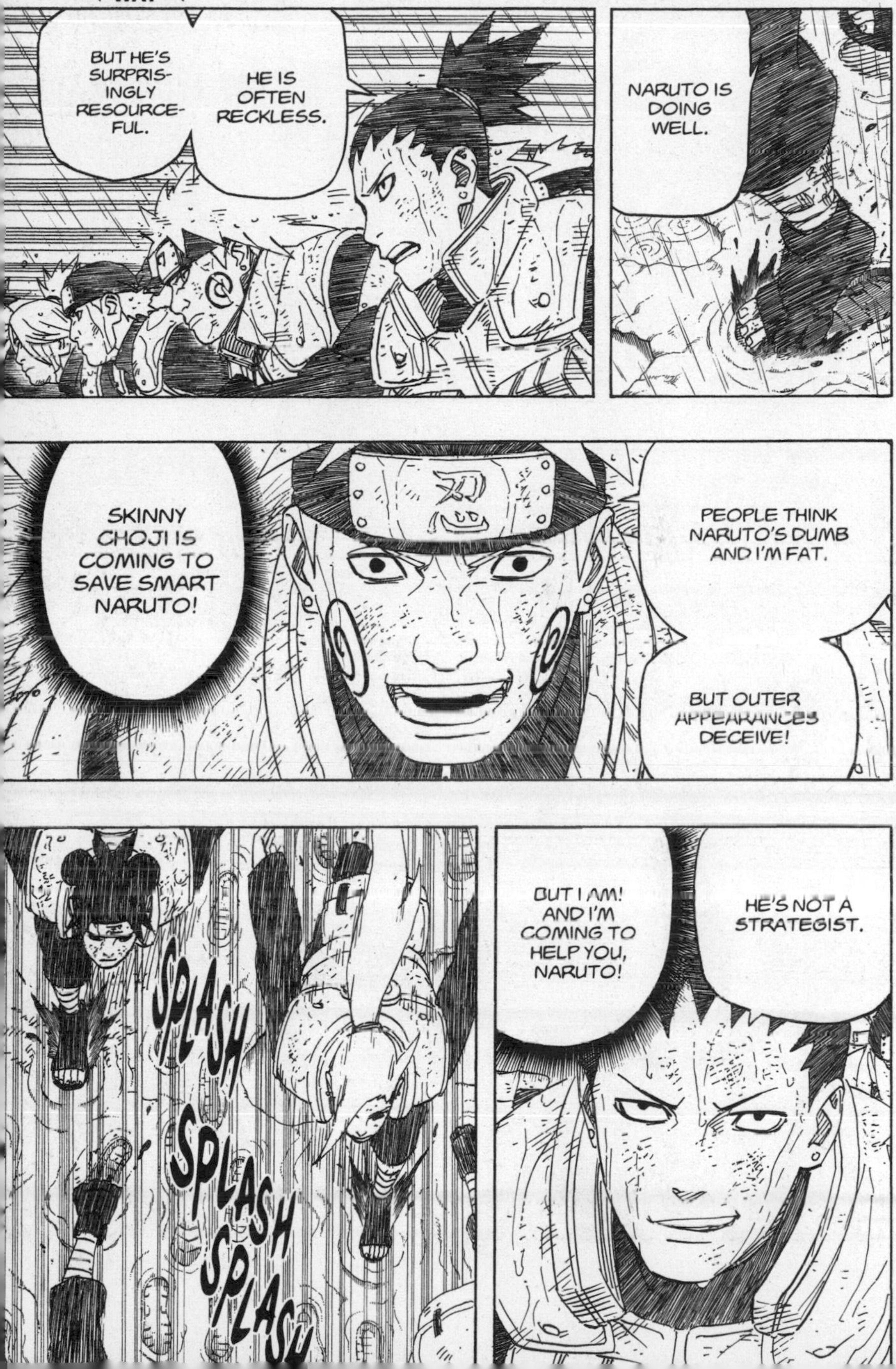
NARUTO IS DOING WELL.
HE IS OFTEN RECKLESS.
BUT HE'S SURPRISINGLY RESOURCEFUL.
PEOPLE THINK NARUTO'S DUMB AND I'M FAT.
BUT OUTER APPEARANCES DECEIVE!
SKINNY CHOJI IS COMING TO SAVE SMART NARUTO!
HE'S NOT A STRATEGIST.
BUT I AM! AND I'M COMING TO HELP YOU, NARUTO!
SPLASH
SPLASH
SPLASH
SPLASH

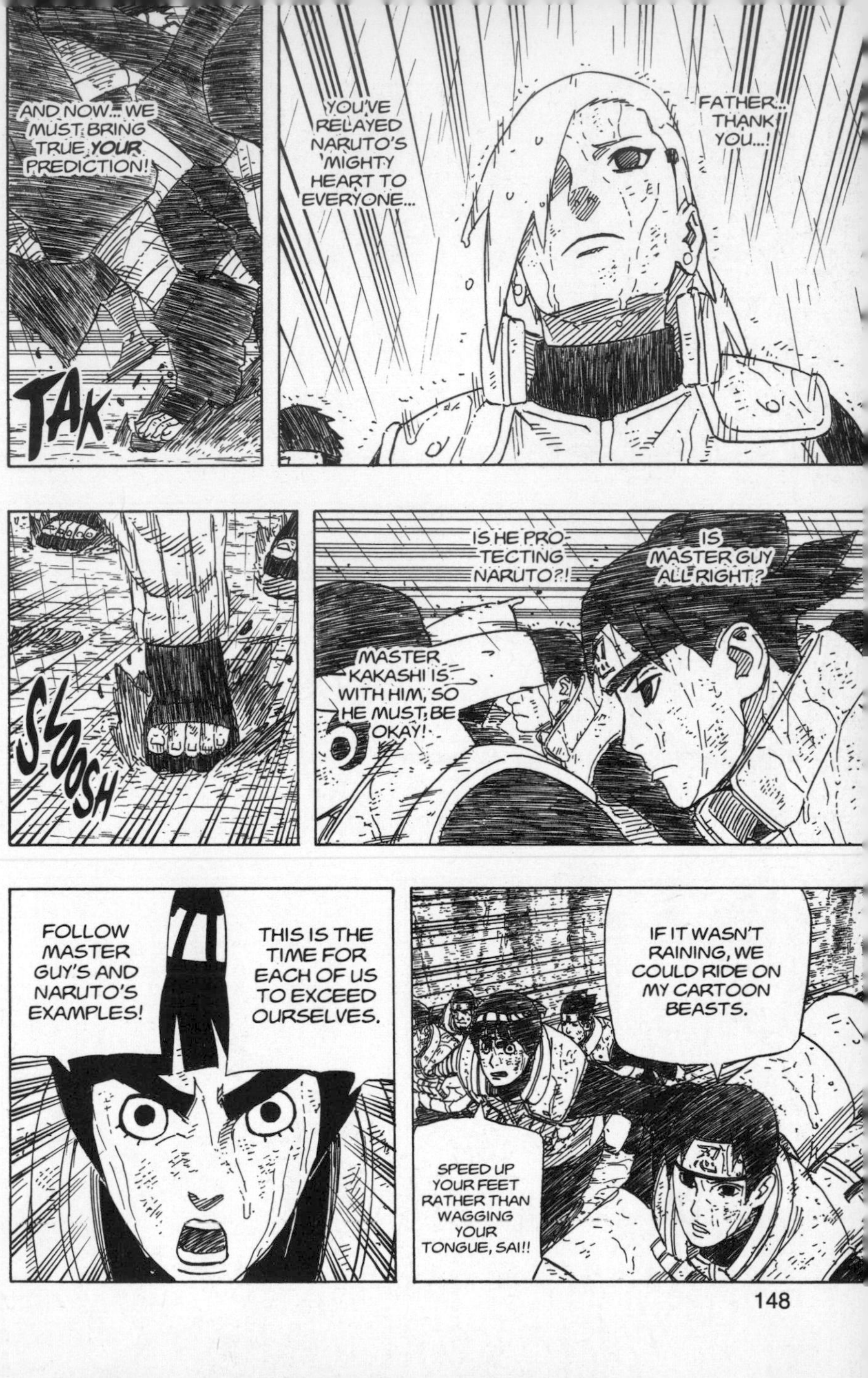
FATHER... THANK YOU...!
YOU'VE RELAYED NARUTO'S MIGHTY HEART TO EVERYONE...
AND NOW... WE MUST BRING TRUE **YOUR** PREDICTION!
TAK
IS MASTER GUY ALL RIGHT?
IS HE PRO-TECTING NARUTO?!
MASTER KAKASHI IS WITH HIM, SO HE MUST BE OKAY!
SLOOSH
IF IT WASN'T RAINING, WE COULD RIDE ON MY CARTOON BEASTS.
SPEED UP YOUR FEET RATHER THAN WAGGING YOUR TONGUE, SAI!!
THIS IS THE TIME FOR EACH OF US TO EXCEED OURSELVES.
FOLLOW MASTER GUY'S AND NARUTO'S EXAMPLES!

READ THIS WAY

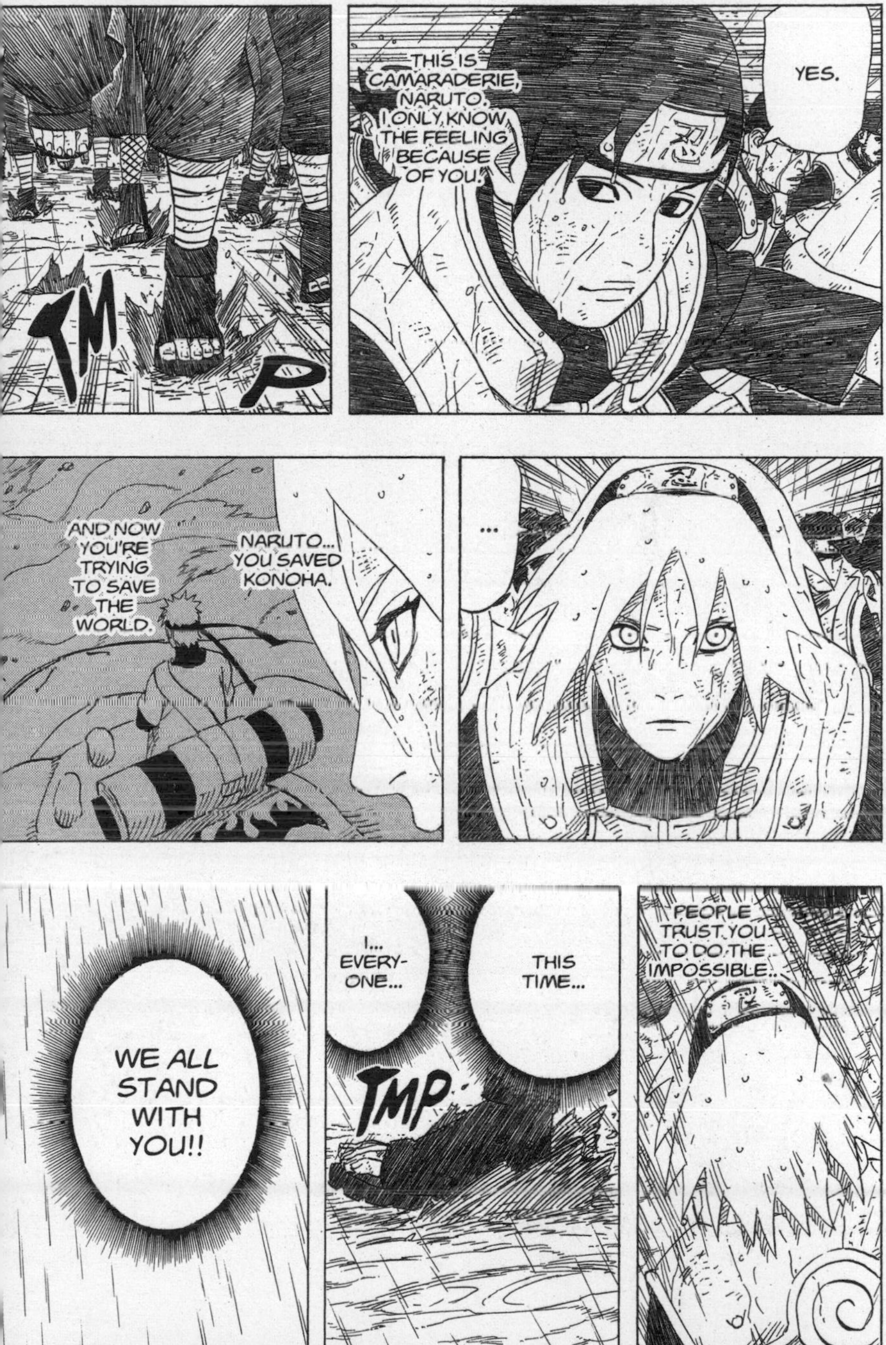
YES.
THIS IS CAMARADERIE, NARUTO. I ONLY KNOW THE FEELING BECAUSE OF YOU.
TMP
...
NARUTO... YOU SAVED KONOHA.
AND NOW YOU'RE TRYING TO SAVE THE WORLD.
PEOPLE TRUST YOU TO DO THE IMPOSSIBLE...
THIS TIME...
I... EVERY-ONE...
TMP
WE ALL STAND WITH YOU!!

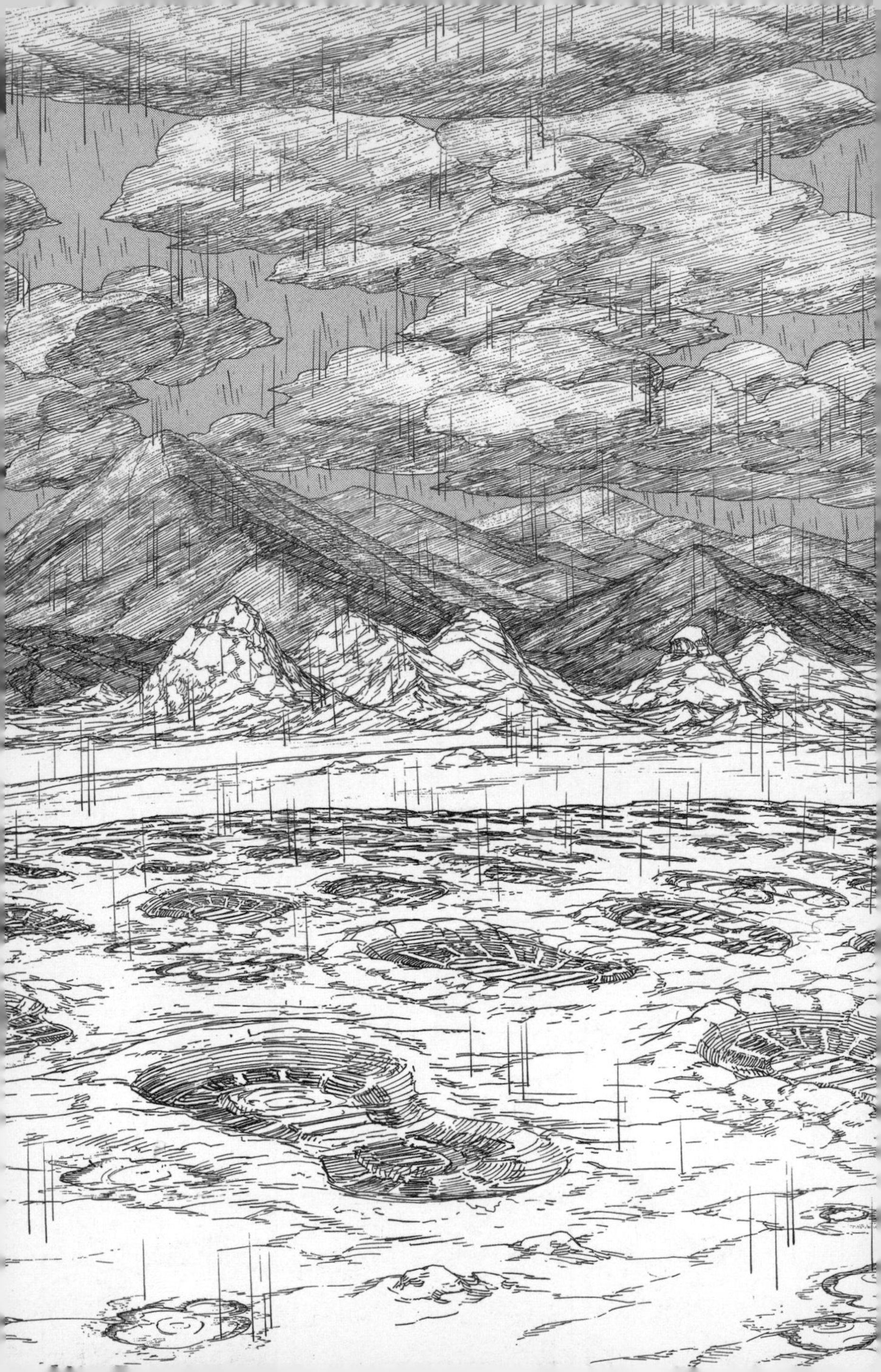

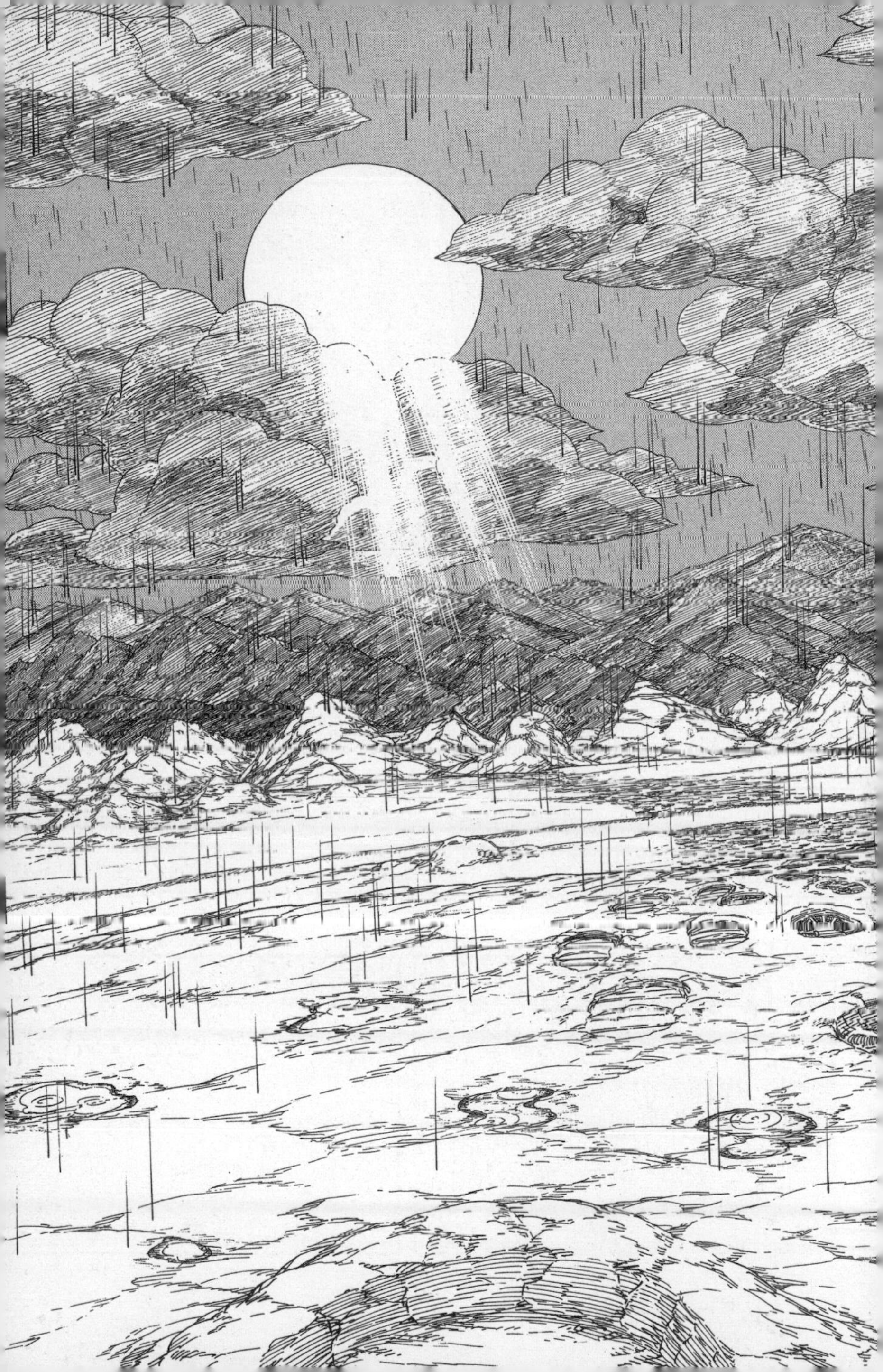

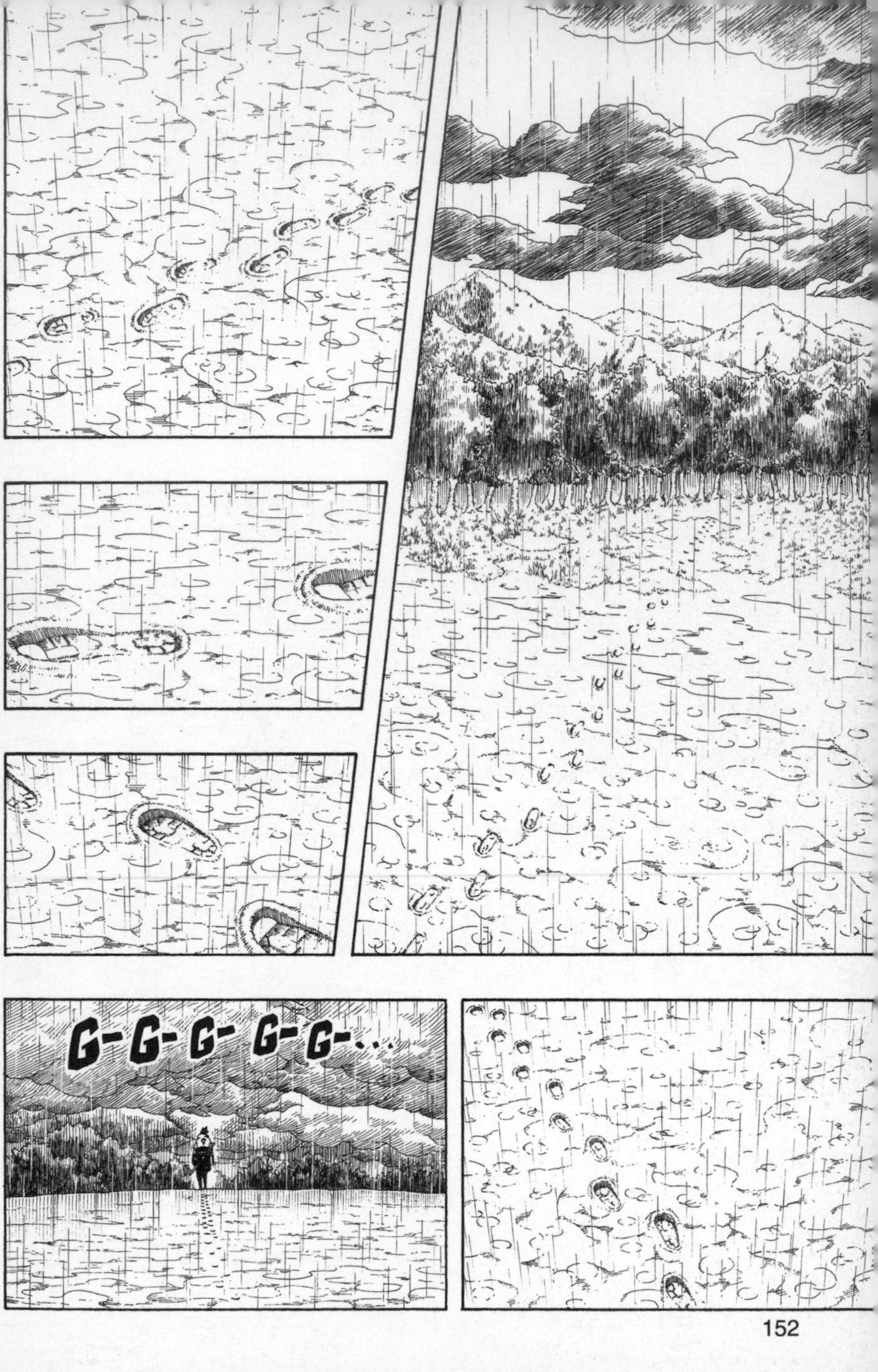
G-G-G-G-G-...

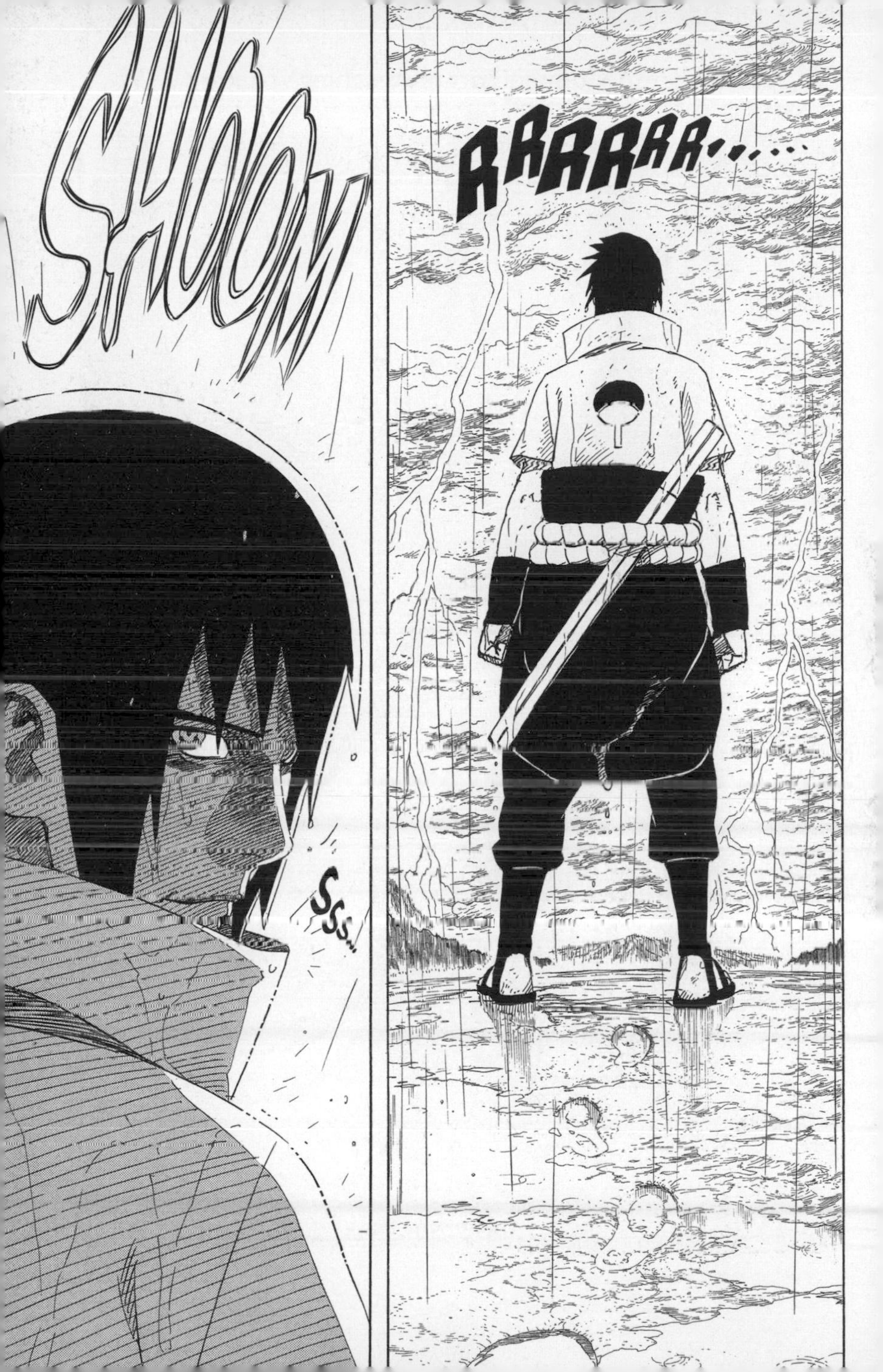
RRRRRR......
SHOOM
SSS...

Illustration to Commemorate Reaching Volume 60 [9]

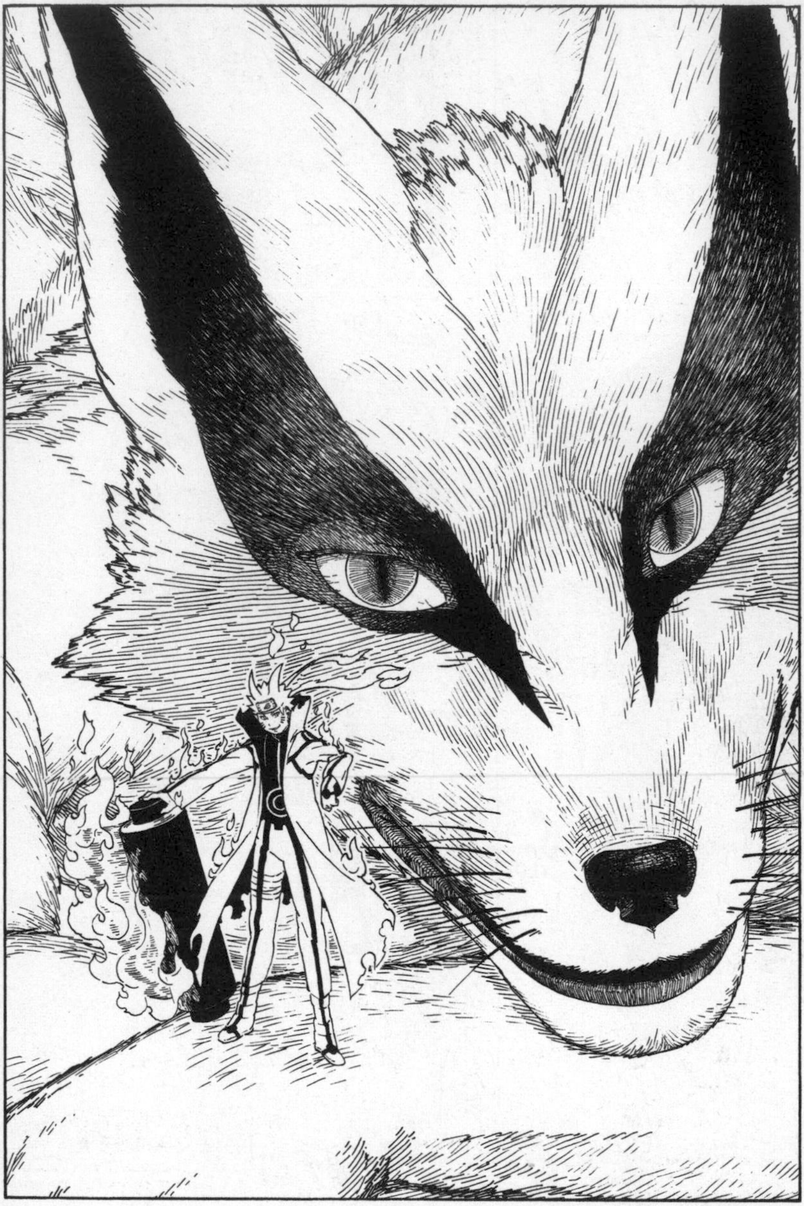

Koichi Nishiya

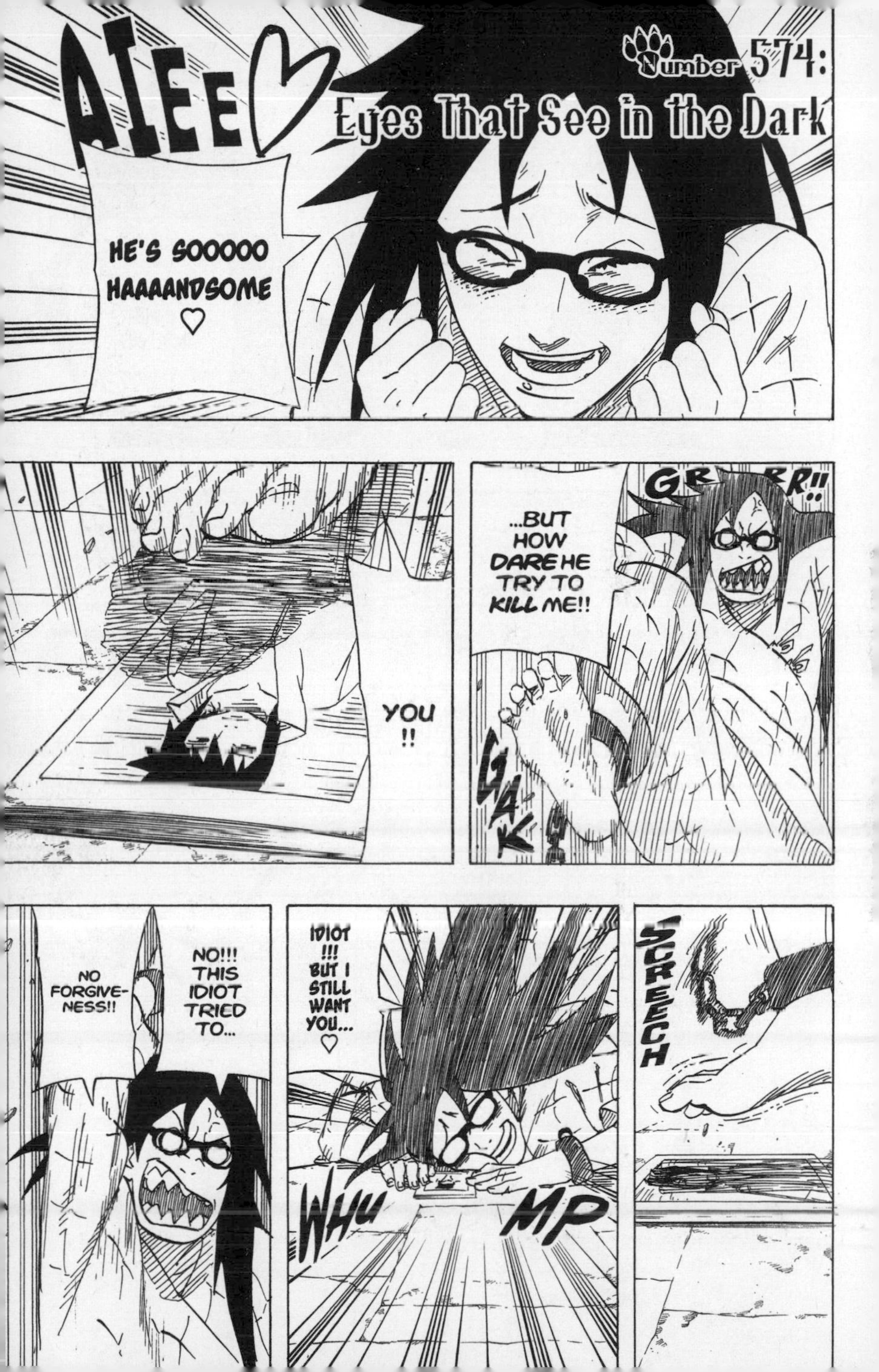
Number 574: Eyes That See in the Dark
AIEE ♡
HE'S SOOOOO HAAAANDSOME ♡
GR RR!!
...BUT HOW DARE HE TRY TO KILL ME!!
GAK
YOU !!
SCREECH
IDIOT !!! BUT I STILL WANT YOU... ♡
WHU MP
NO!!! THIS IDIOT TRIED TO...
NO FORGIVE-NESS!!

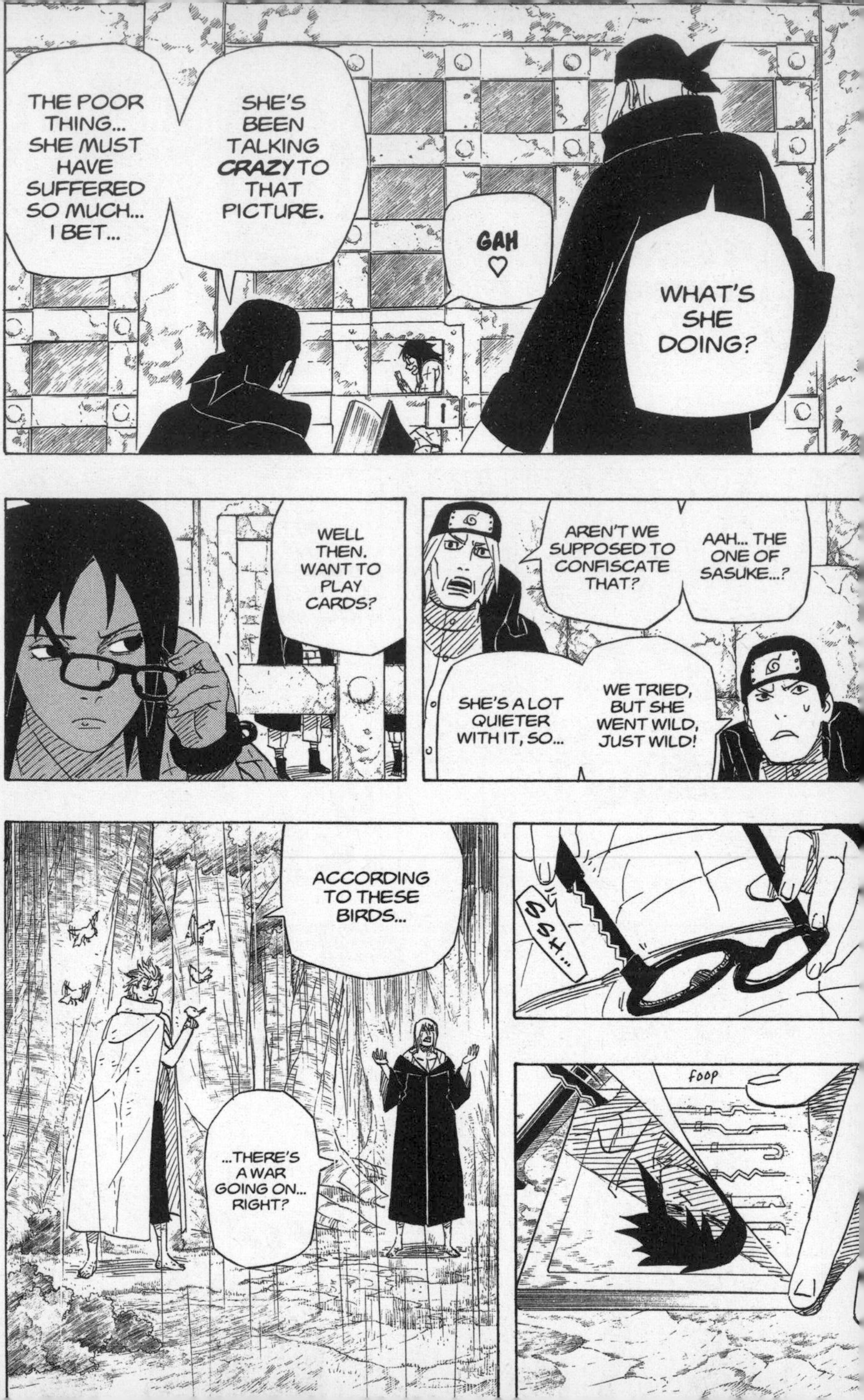
WHAT'S SHE DOING?
GAH ♡
SHE'S BEEN TALKING CRAZY TO THAT PICTURE.
THE POOR THING... SHE MUST HAVE SUFFERED SO MUCH... I BET...
AAH... THE ONE OF SASUKE...?
AREN'T WE SUPPOSED TO CONFISCATE THAT?
WE TRIED, BUT SHE WENT WILD, JUST WILD!
SHE'S A LOT QUIETER WITH IT, SO...
WELL THEN. WANT TO PLAY CARDS?
SSH...
foop
ACCORDING TO THESE BIRDS...
...THERE'S A WAR GOING ON... RIGHT?

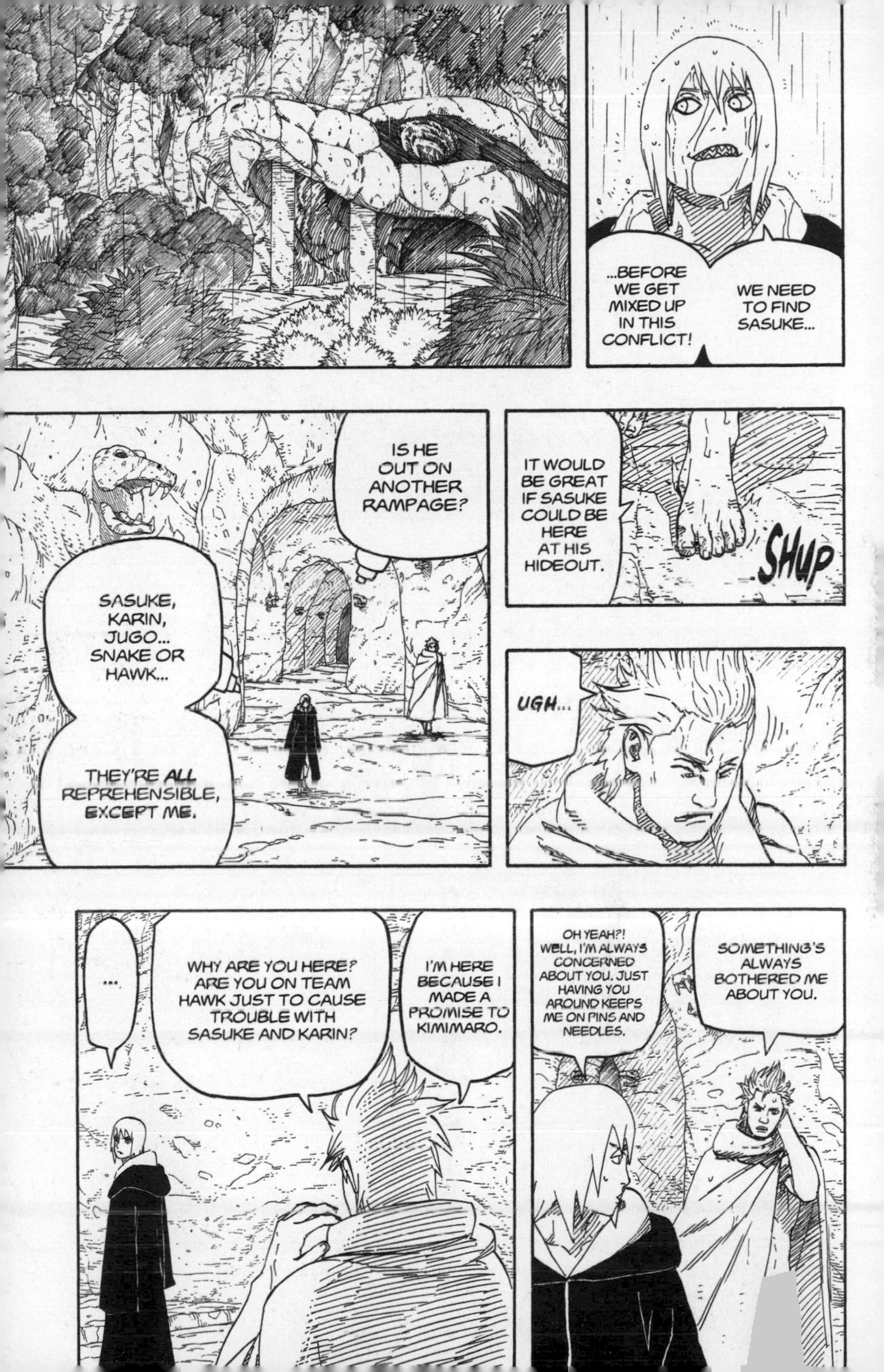
WE NEED TO FIND SASUKE...
...BEFORE WE GET MIXED UP IN THIS CONFLICT!
SHUP
IT WOULD BE GREAT IF SASUKE COULD BE HERE AT HIS HIDEOUT.
IS HE OUT ON ANOTHER RAMPAGE?
SASUKE, KARIN, JUGO... SNAKE OR HAWK...
THEY'RE ALL REPREHENSIBLE, EXCEPT ME.
UGH...
SOMETHING'S ALWAYS BOTHERED ME ABOUT YOU.
OH YEAH?! WELL, I'M ALWAYS CONCERNED ABOUT YOU. JUST HAVING YOU AROUND KEEPS ME ON PINS AND NEEDLES.
I'M HERE BECAUSE I MADE A PROMISE TO KIMIMARO.
WHY ARE YOU HERE? ARE YOU ON TEAM HAWK JUST TO CAUSE TROUBLE WITH SASUKE AND KARIN?
...

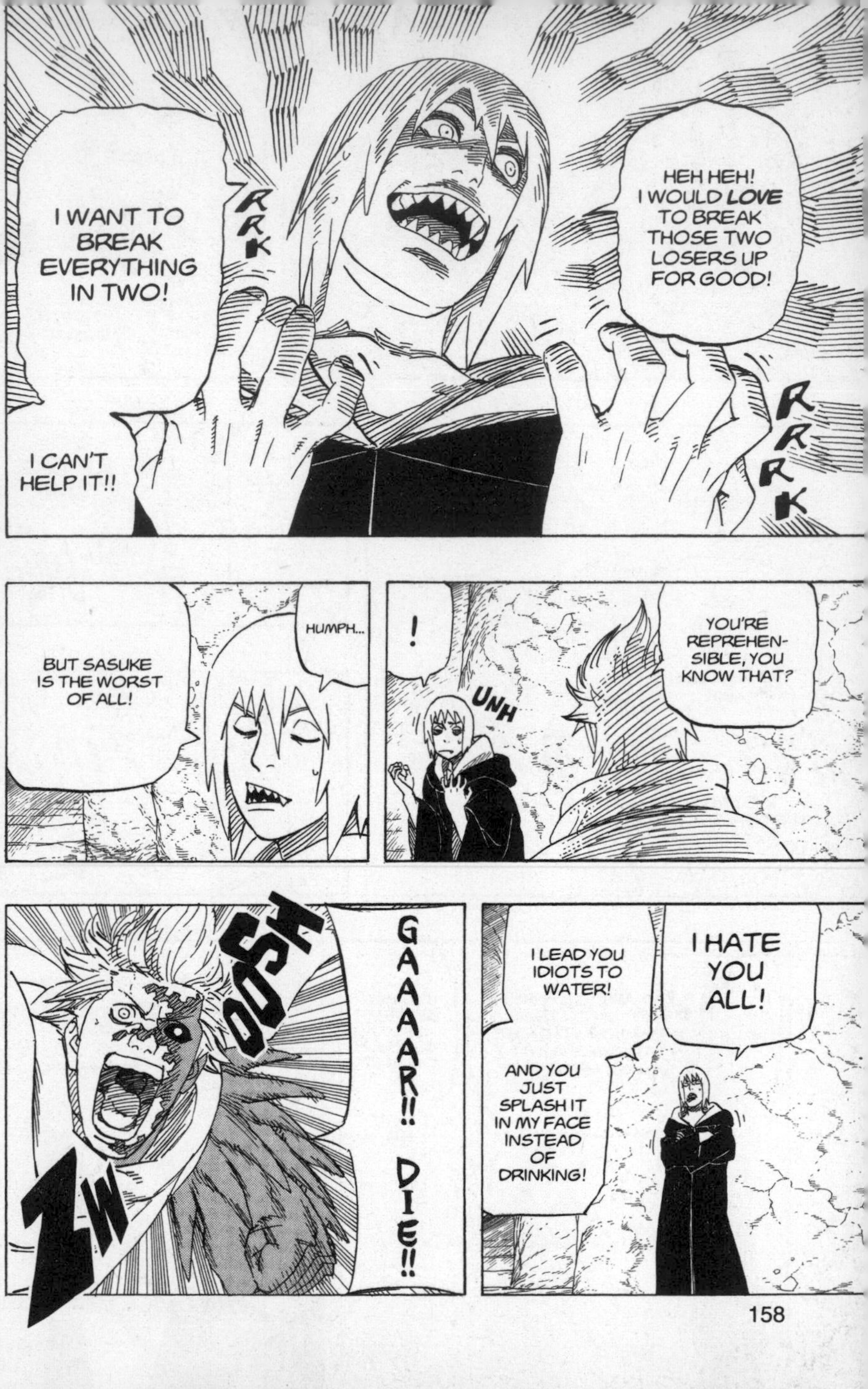
HEH HEH! I WOULD LOVE TO BREAK THOSE TWO LOSERS UP FOR GOOD!
RRRK
I WANT TO BREAK EVERYTHING IN TWO!
RRK
I CAN'T HELP IT!!
YOU'RE REPREHEN-SIBLE, YOU KNOW THAT?
UNH
!
HUMPH...
BUT SASUKE IS THE WORST OF ALL!
I HATE YOU ALL!
I LEAD YOU IDIOTS TO WATER!
AND YOU JUST SPLASH IT IN MY FACE INSTEAD OF DRINKING!
GAAAAR!! DIE!!
ZWOOSH

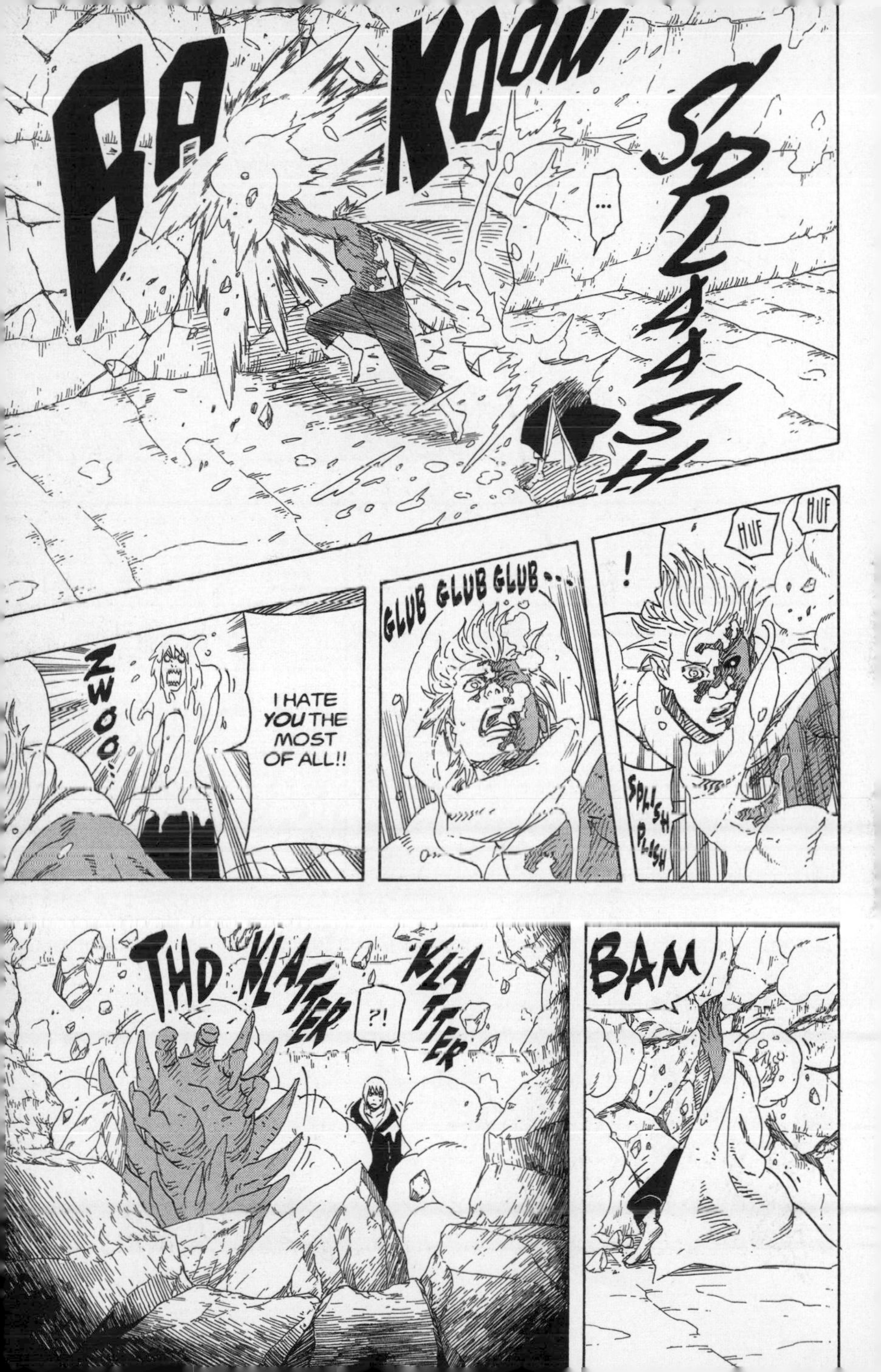
BA-KOOM
SPLAAASH
...
HUF
HUF
!
SPLISH PLISH
GLUB GLUB GLUB...
ZWOO...
I HATE YOU THE MOST OF ALL!!
BAM
KLATTER
?!
KLATTER
THD

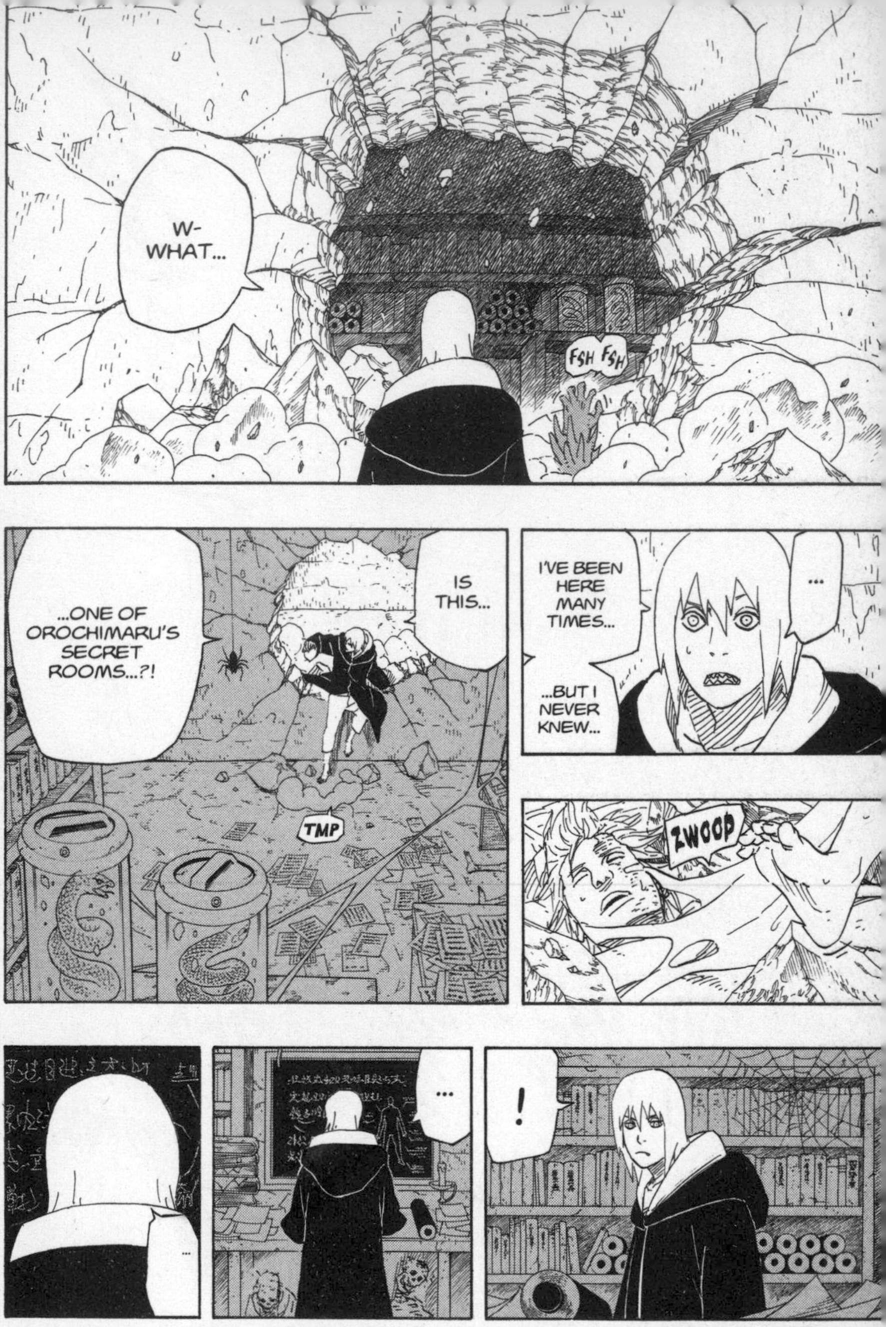
W-
WHAT...
FSH FSH
...
I'VE BEEN HERE MANY TIMES...
...BUT I NEVER KNEW...
ZWOOP
IS THIS...
...ONE OF OROCHIMARU'S SECRET ROOMS...?!
TMP
!
...
...

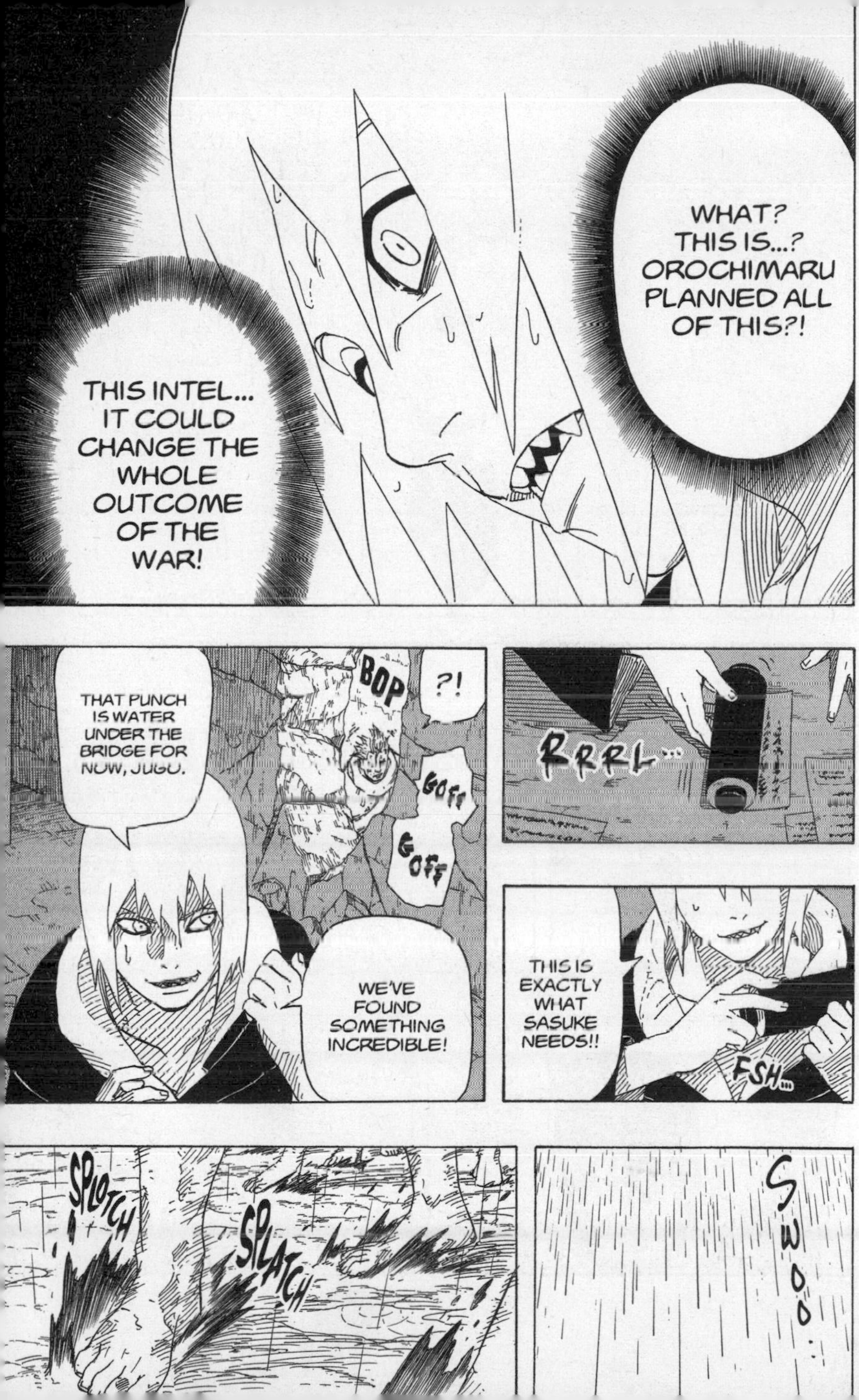
WHAT? THIS IS...? OROCHIMARU PLANNED ALL OF THIS?!
THIS INTEL... IT COULD CHANGE THE WHOLE OUTCOME OF THE WAR!
RRRL...
THIS IS EXACTLY WHAT SASUKE NEEDS!!
FSH...
?!
BOP
THAT PUNCH IS WATER UNDER THE BRIDGE FOR NOW, JUGO.
GOFF
GOFF
WE'VE FOUND SOMETHING INCREDIBLE!
SWOO...
SPLATCH
SPLOTCH

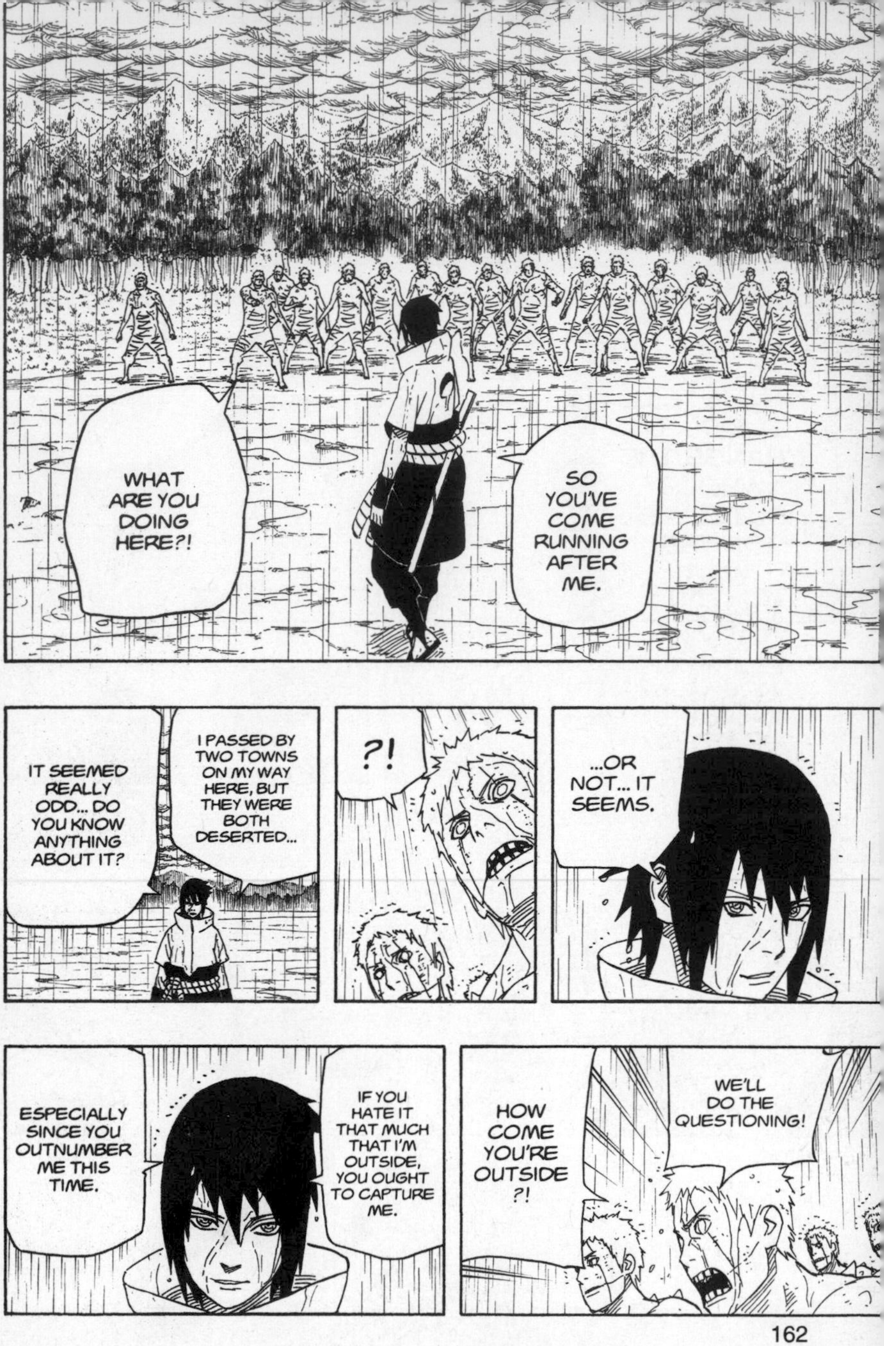
SO YOU'VE COME RUNNING AFTER ME.
WHAT ARE YOU DOING HERE?!
...OR NOT... IT SEEMS.
?!
I PASSED BY TWO TOWNS ON MY WAY HERE, BUT THEY WERE BOTH DESERTED...
IT SEEMED REALLY ODD... DO YOU KNOW ANYTHING ABOUT IT?
WE'LL DO THE QUESTIONING!
HOW COME YOU'RE OUTSIDE?!
IF YOU HATE IT THAT MUCH THAT I'M OUTSIDE, YOU OUGHT TO CAPTURE ME.
ESPECIALLY SINCE YOU OUTNUMBER ME THIS TIME.

READ THIS WAY

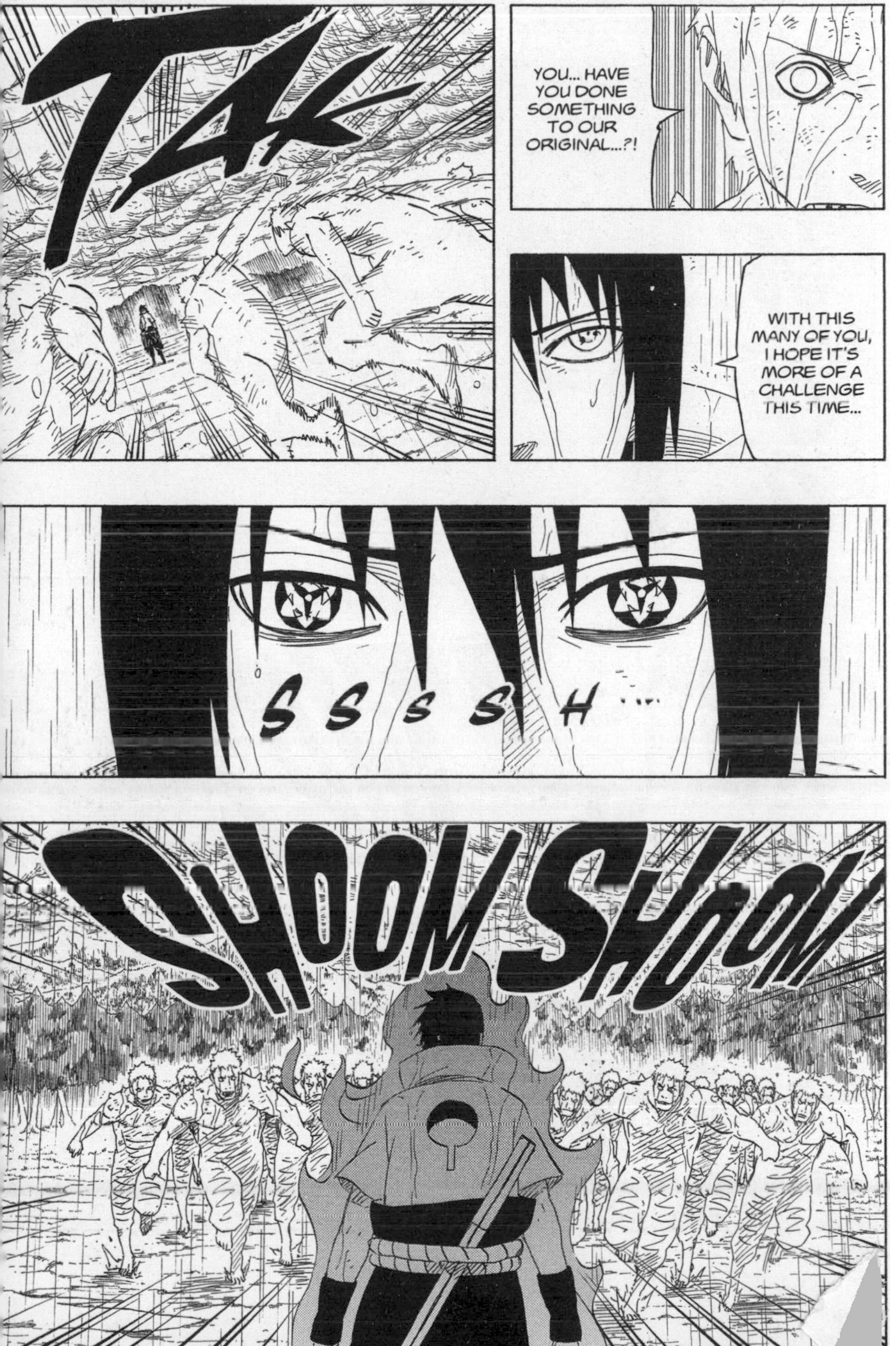
YOU... HAVE YOU DONE SOMETHING TO OUR ORIGINAL...?!
WITH THIS MANY OF YOU, I HOPE IT'S MORE OF A CHALLENGE THIS TIME...
TAK
SSSSH...
SHOOM SHOOM

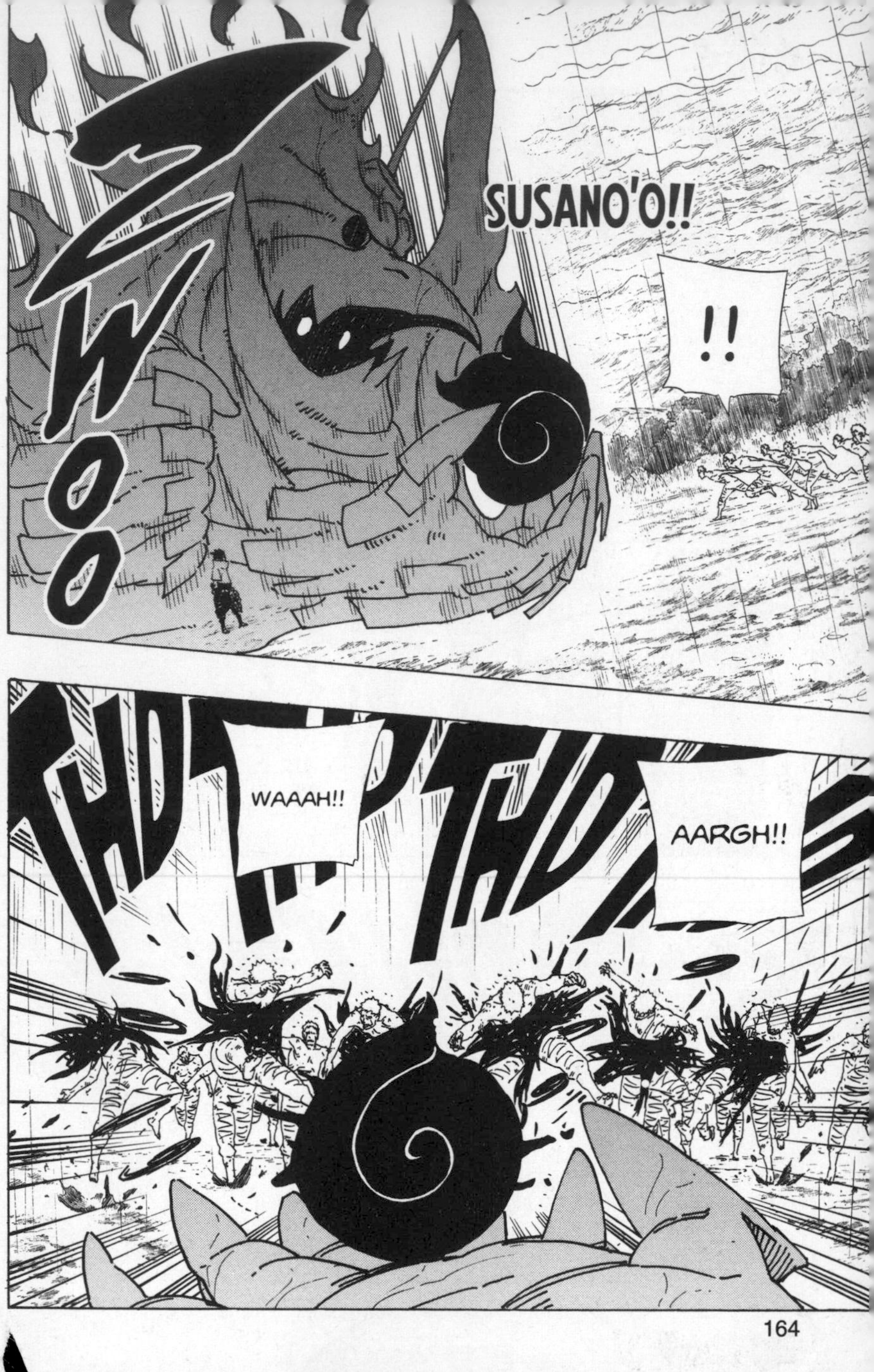
SUSANO'O!!
!!
AARGH!!
WAAAH!!

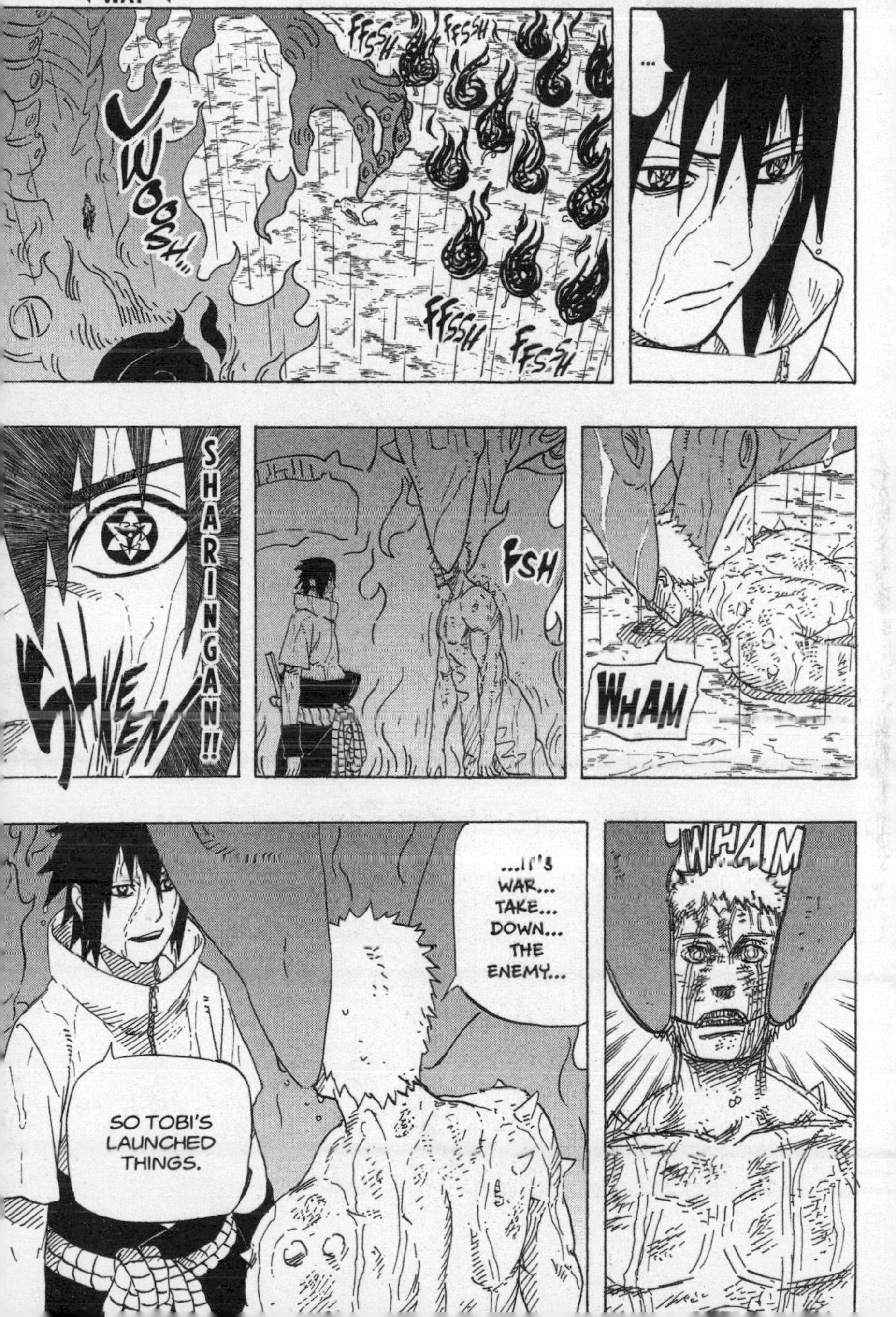
READ THIS WAY
...
FFSSH
FFSSH
FFSSH
FFSSH
VWOOSH...
WHAM
FSH
SHARINGAN!!
SHKEN
WHAM
...IT'S WAR... TAKE... DOWN... THE ENEMY...
SO TOBI'S LAUNCHED THINGS.

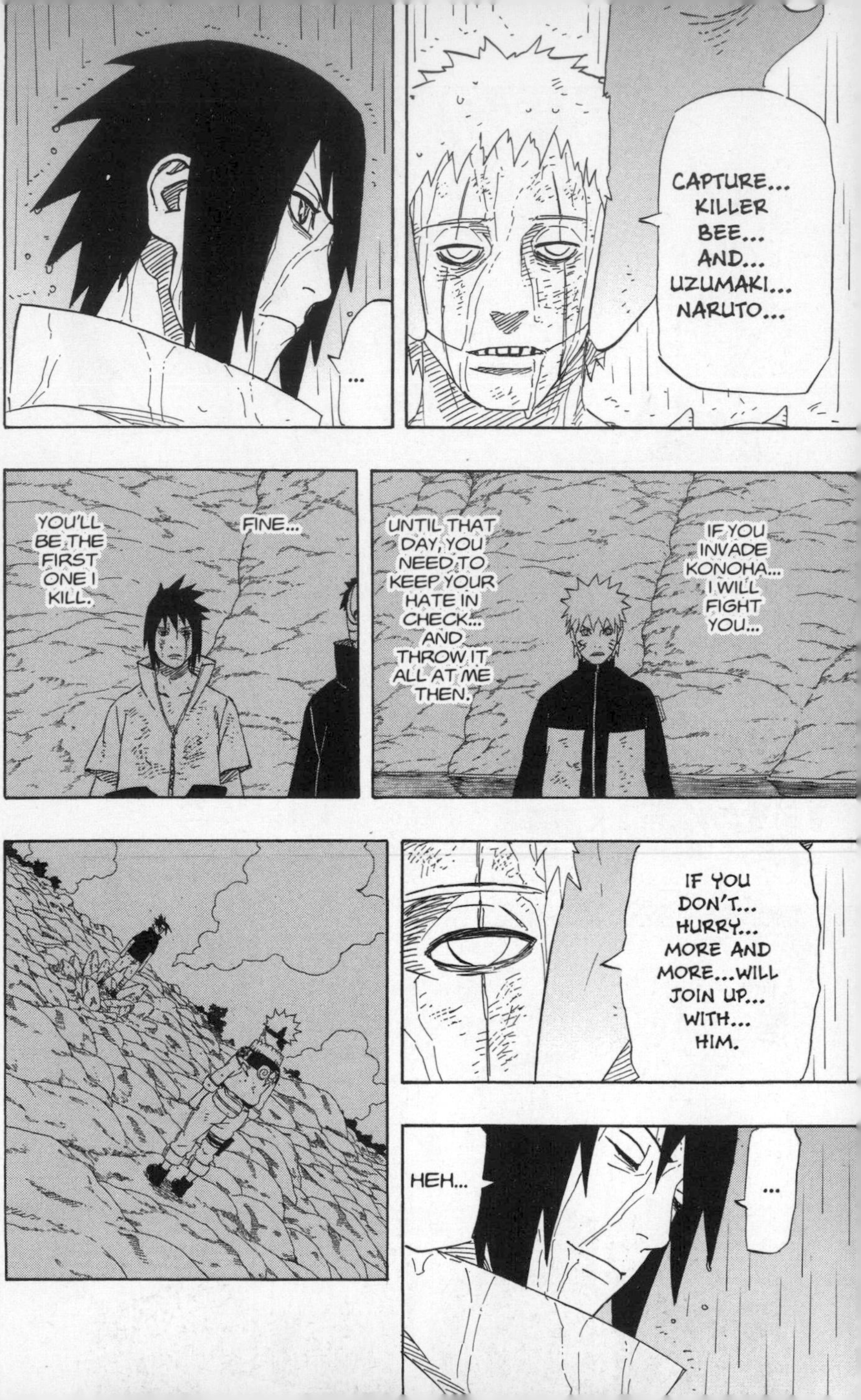
CAPTURE... KILLER BEE... AND... UZUMAKI... NARUTO...
...
IF YOU INVADE KONOHA... I WILL FIGHT YOU...
UNTIL THAT DAY, YOU NEED TO KEEP YOUR HATE IN CHECK... AND THROW IT ALL AT ME THEN.
FINE...
YOU'LL BE THE FIRST ONE I KILL.
IF YOU DON'T... HURRY... MORE AND MORE...WILL JOIN UP... WITH... HIM.
...
HEH...

READ THIS WAY

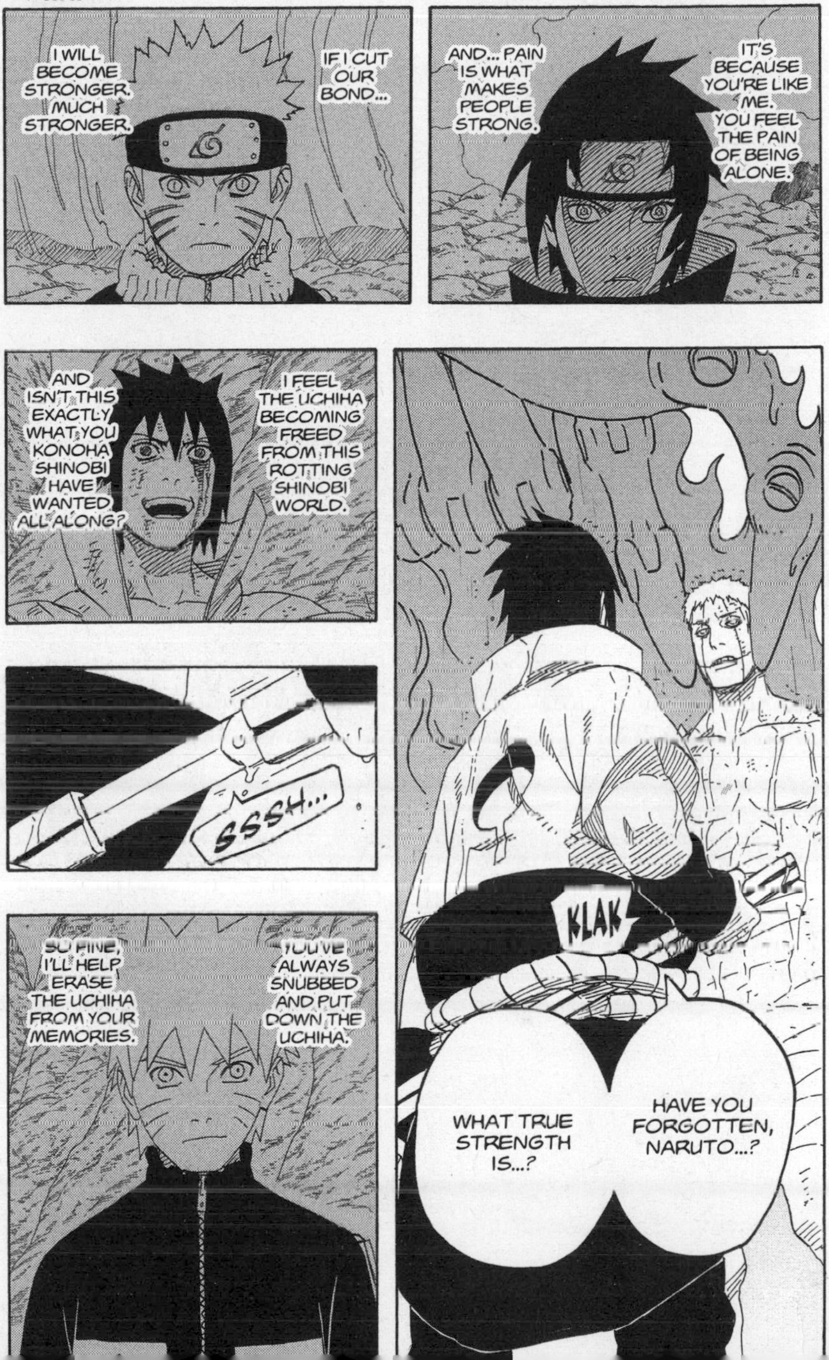
IT'S BECAUSE YOU'RE LIKE ME. YOU FEEL THE PAIN OF BEING ALONE.
AND... PAIN IS WHAT MAKES PEOPLE STRONG.
IF I CUT OUR BOND...
I WILL BECOME STRONGER. MUCH STRONGER.
KLAK
HAVE YOU FORGOTTEN, NARUTO...?
WHAT TRUE STRENGTH IS...?
I FEEL THE UCHIHA BECOMING FREED FROM THIS ROTTING SHINOBI WORLD.
AND ISN'T THIS EXACTLY WHAT YOU KONOHA SHINOBI HAVE WANTED ALL ALONG?
SSSH...
YOU'VE ALWAYS SNUBBED AND PUT DOWN THE UCHIHA.
SO FINE, I'LL HELP ERASE THE UCHIHA FROM YOUR MEMORIES.

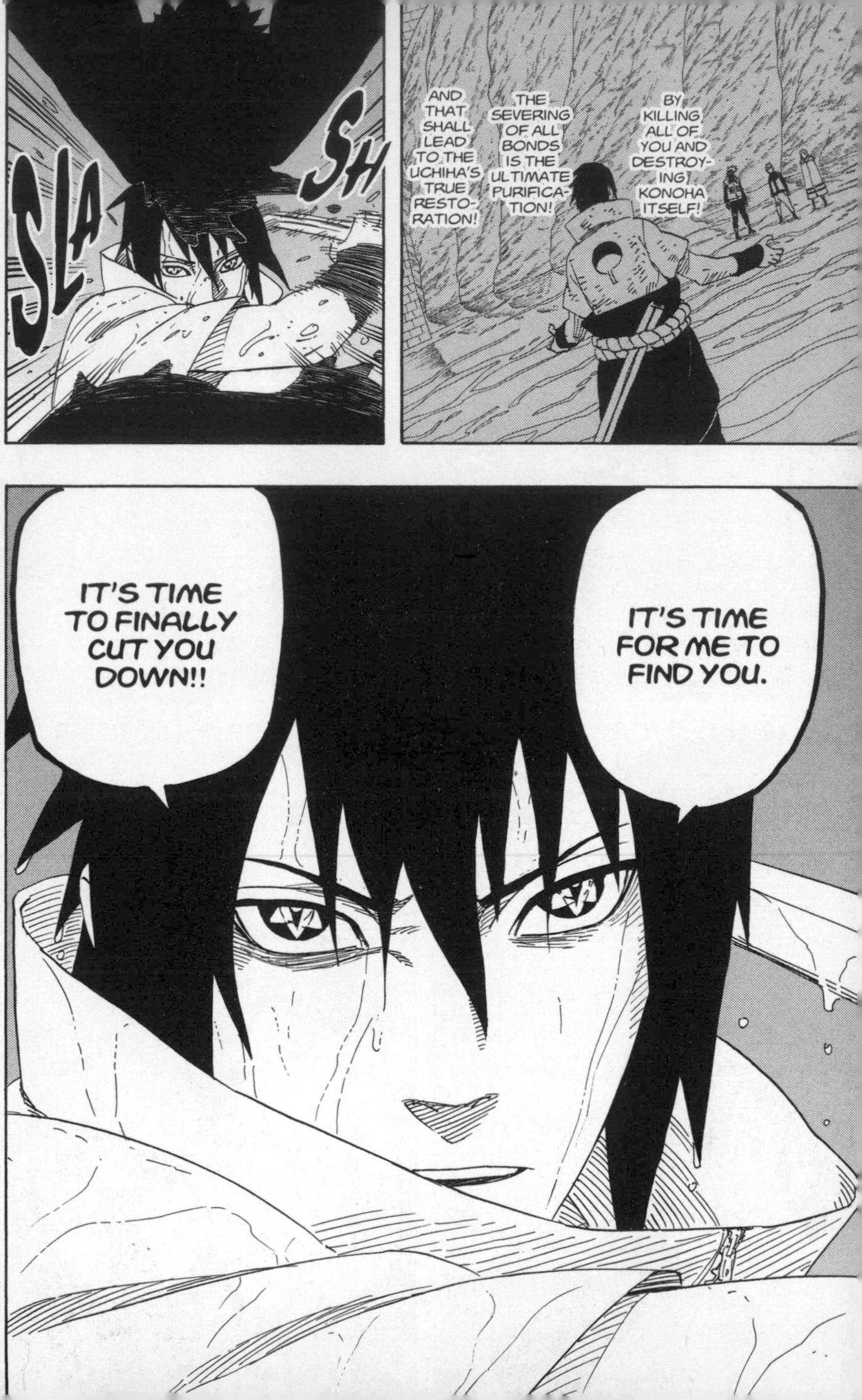
BY KILLING ALL OF YOU AND DESTROYING KONOHA ITSELF!
THE SEVERING OF ALL BONDS IS THE ULTIMATE PURIFICATION!
AND THAT SHALL LEAD TO THE UCHIHA'S TRUE RESTORATION!
SLASH
IT'S TIME FOR ME TO FIND YOU.
IT'S TIME TO FINALLY CUT YOU DOWN!!

READ THIS WAY

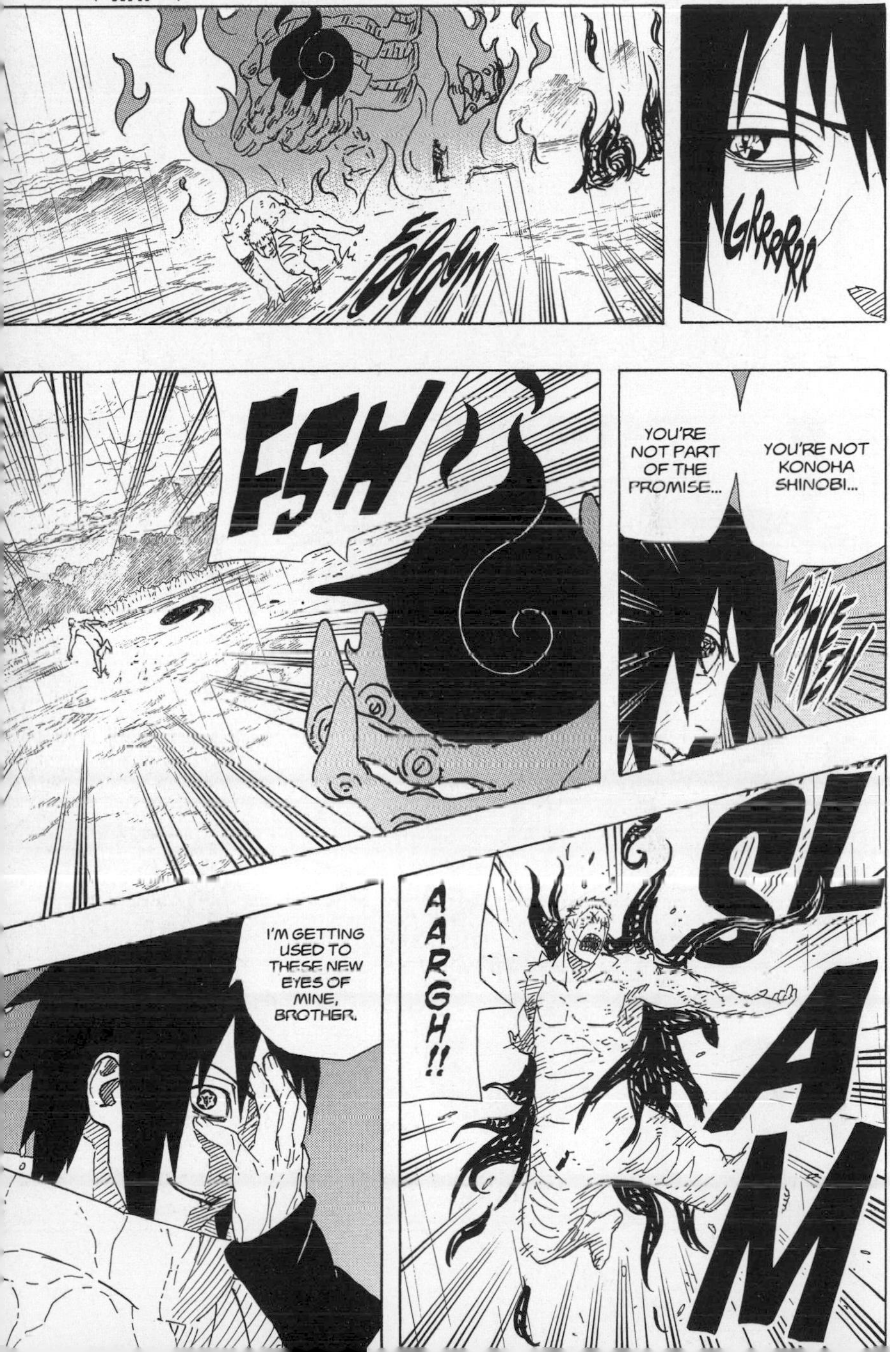
YOU'RE NOT KONOHA SHINOBI...
YOU'RE NOT PART OF THE PROMISE...
FSH
SLAM
AARGH!!
I'M GETTING USED TO THESE NEW EYES OF MINE, BROTHER.

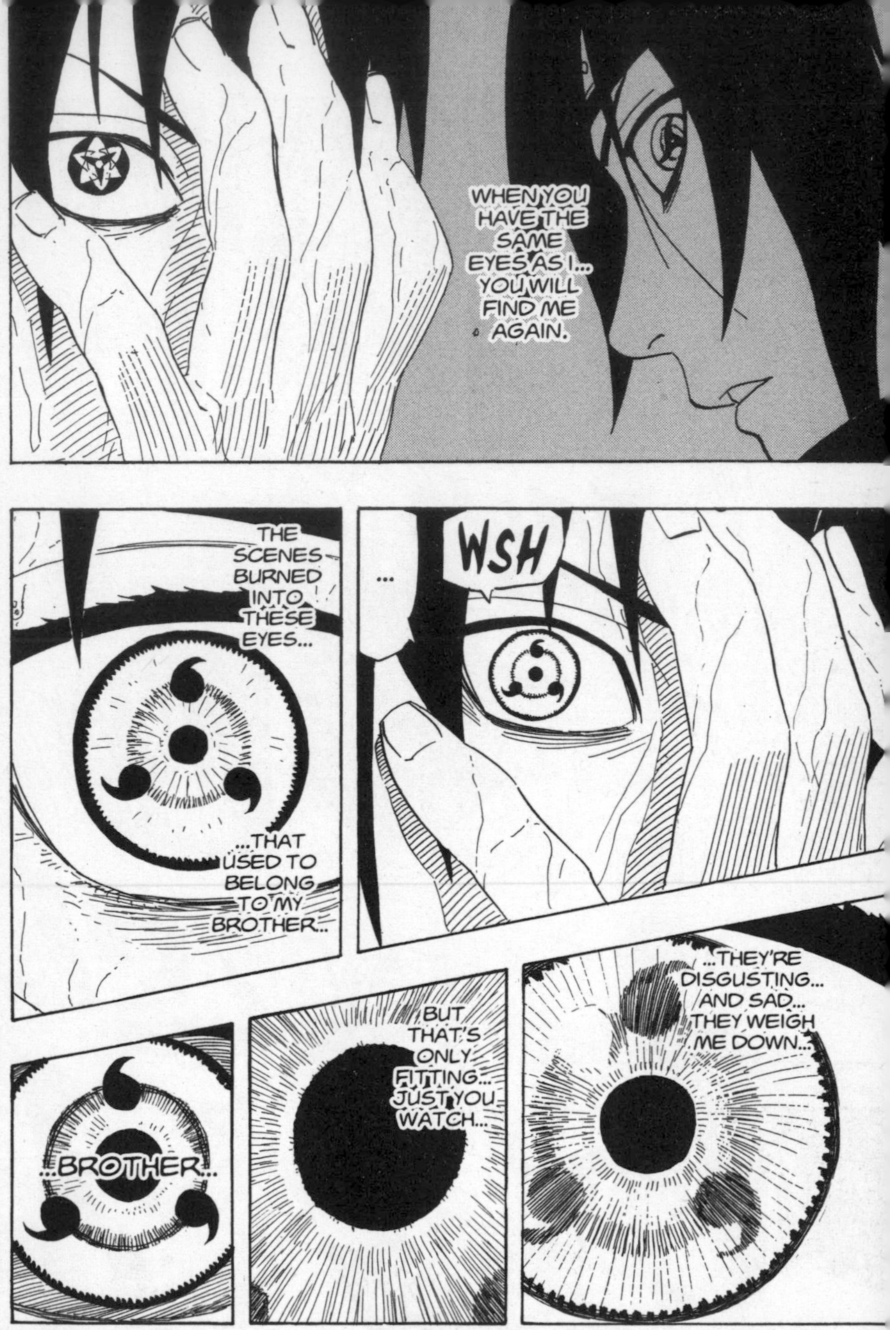
WHEN YOU HAVE THE SAME EYES AS I... YOU WILL FIND ME AGAIN.
WSH
...
THE SCENES BURNED INTO THESE EYES...
...THAT USED TO BELONG TO MY BROTHER...
...THEY'RE DISGUSTING... AND SAD... THEY WEIGH ME DOWN...
BUT THAT'S ONLY FITTING... JUST YOU WATCH...
...BROTHER...

READ THIS WAY

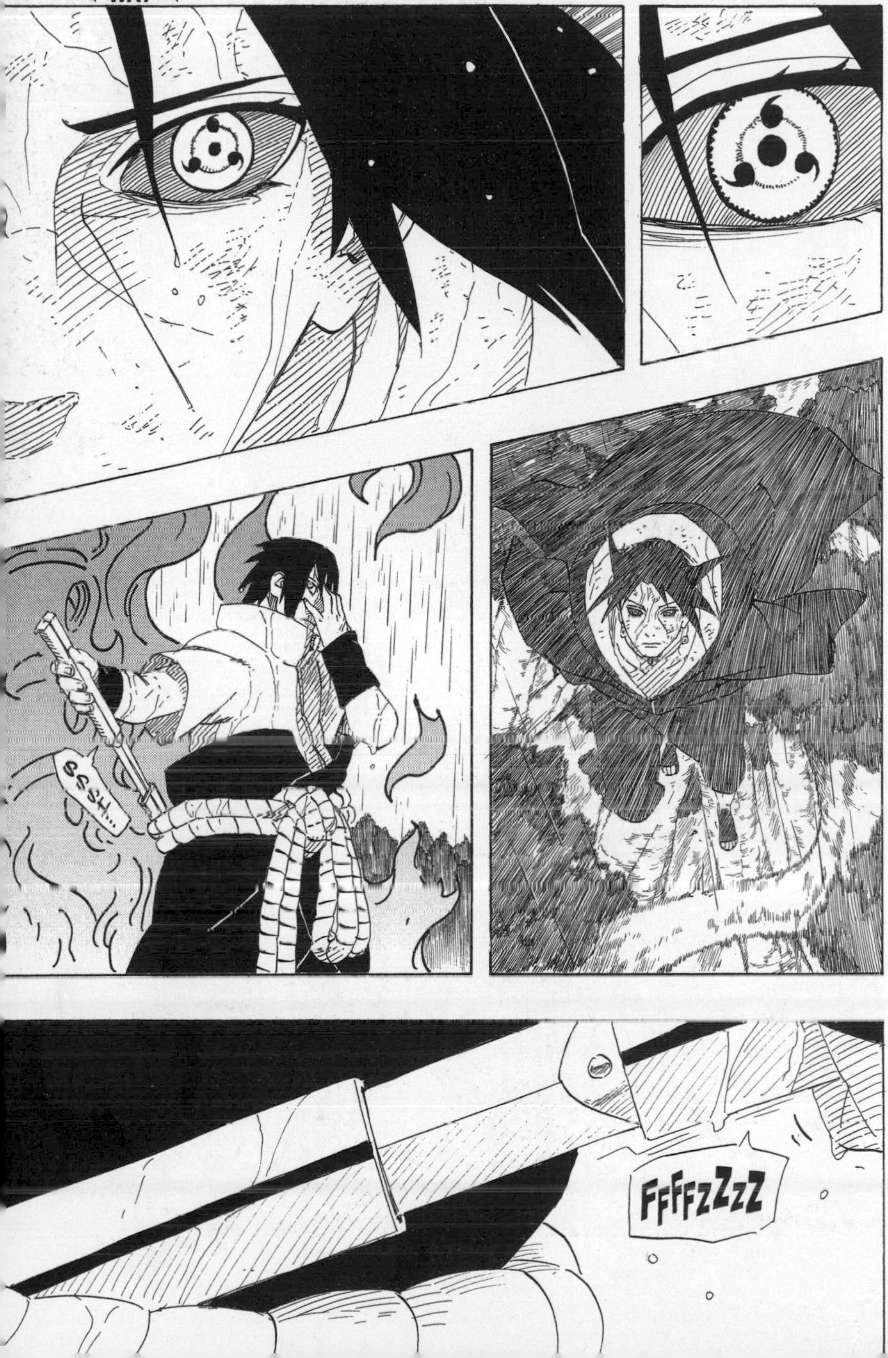
SSSH...
FFFFZZZZ

NARUTO

Number 575: A Will of Stone

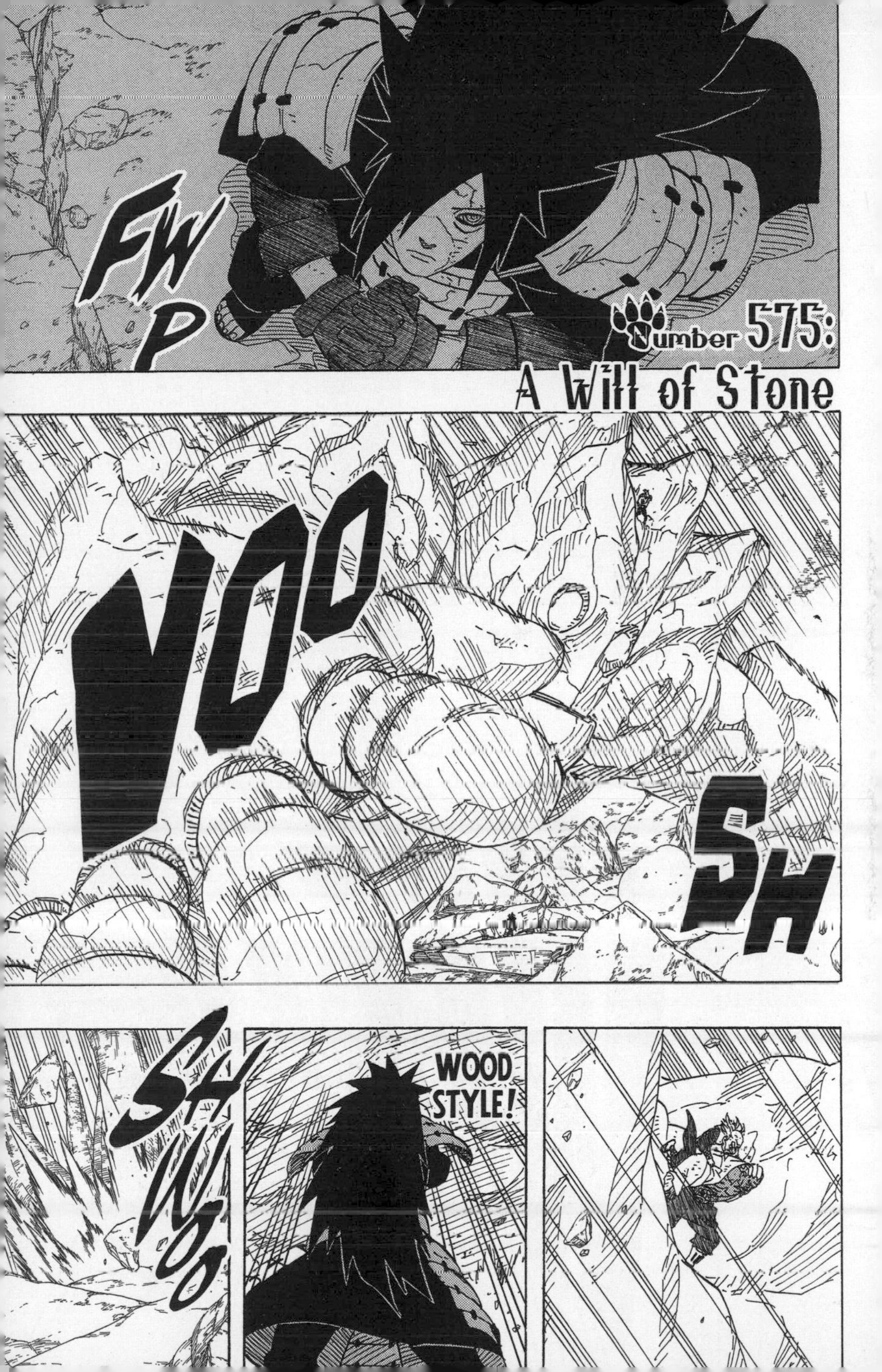
FWP
VOOOSH
WOOD STYLE!
SHWOO

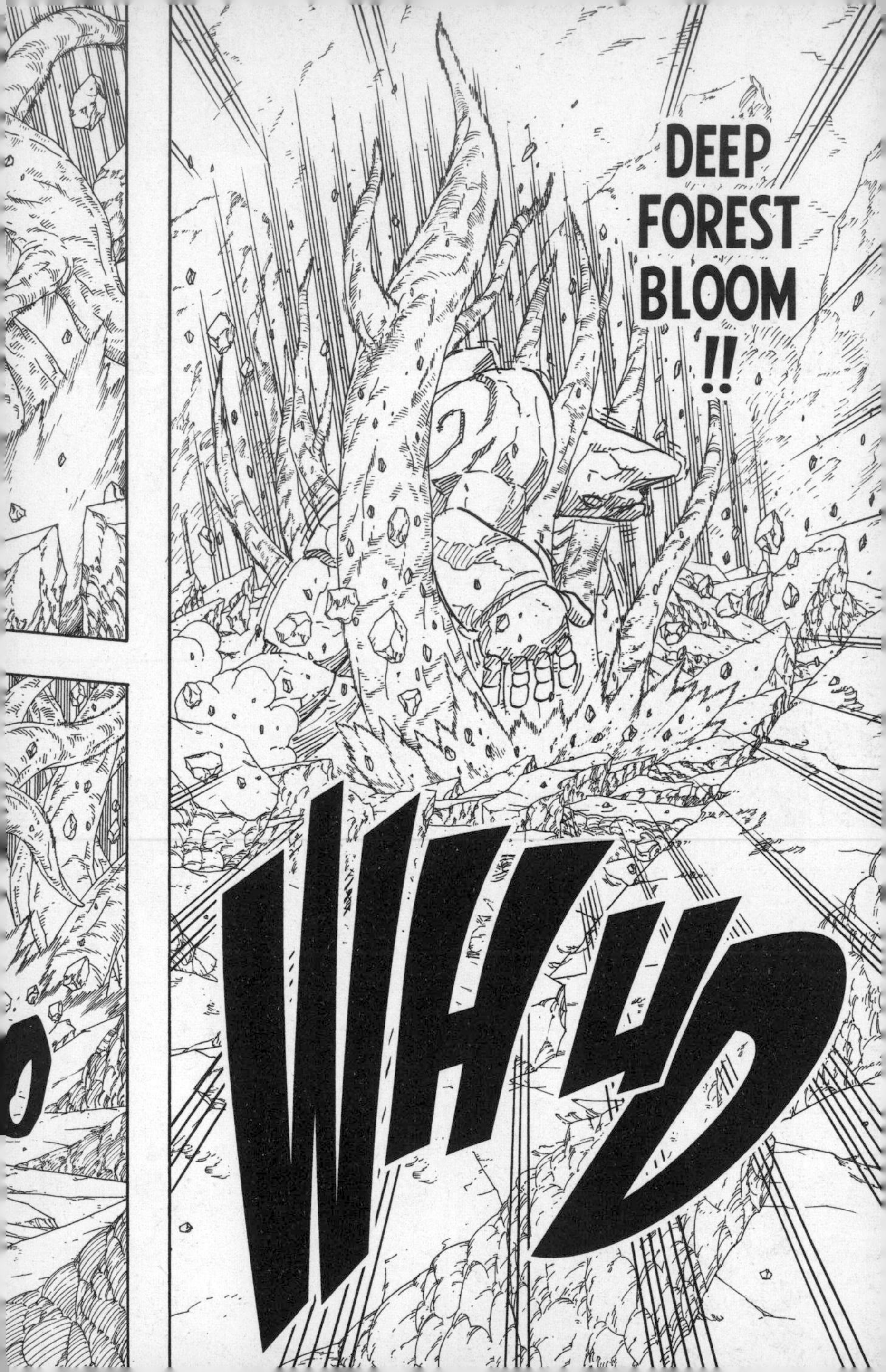
DEEP FOREST BLOOM!!
WHUD

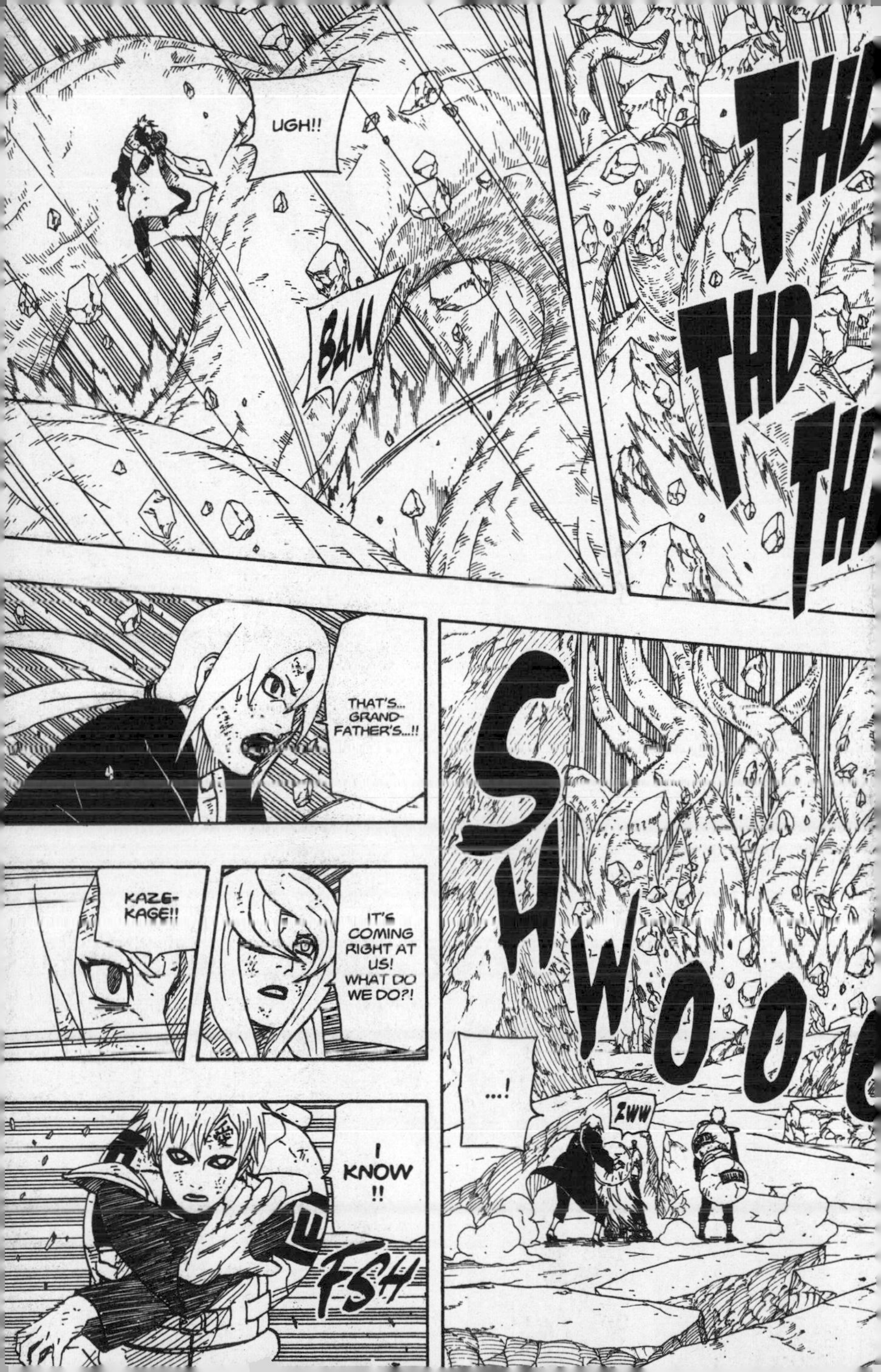
THD
UGH!!
BAM
SHWOOO
...!
ZWW
THAT'S... GRAND-FATHER'S...!!
IT'S COMING RIGHT AT US! WHAT DO WE DO?!
KAZE-KAGE!!
I KNOW!!
FSH

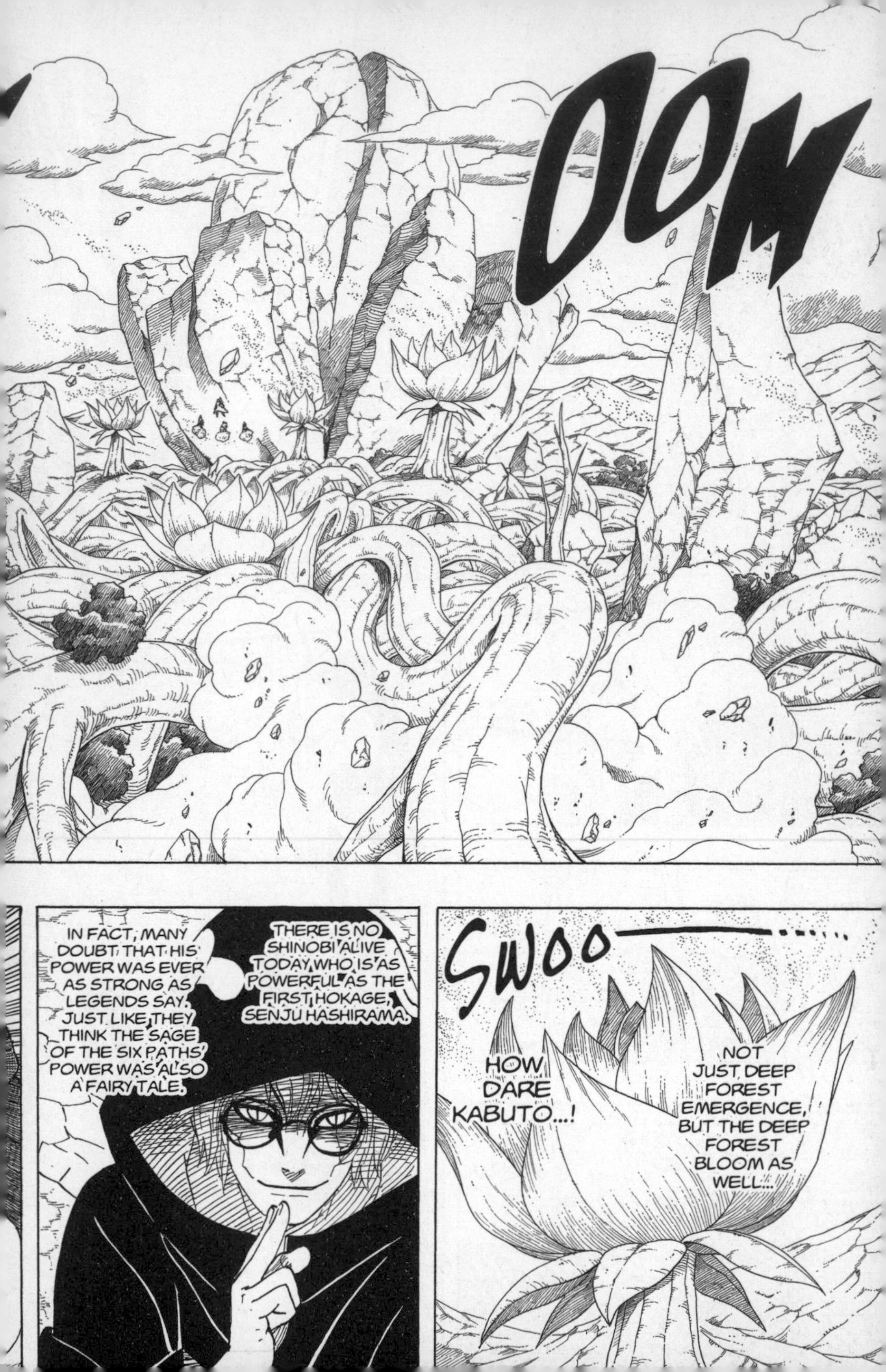
OOM
SWOO
NOT JUST DEEP FOREST EMERGENCE, BUT THE DEEP FOREST BLOOM AS WELL...
HOW DARE KABUTO...!
THERE IS NO SHINOBI ALIVE TODAY WHO IS AS POWERFUL AS THE FIRST HOKAGE, SENJU HASHIRAMA.
IN FACT, MANY DOUBT THAT HIS POWER WAS EVER AS STRONG AS LEGENDS SAY. JUST LIKE THEY THINK THE SAGE OF THE SIX PATHS' POWER WAS ALSO A FAIRY TALE.

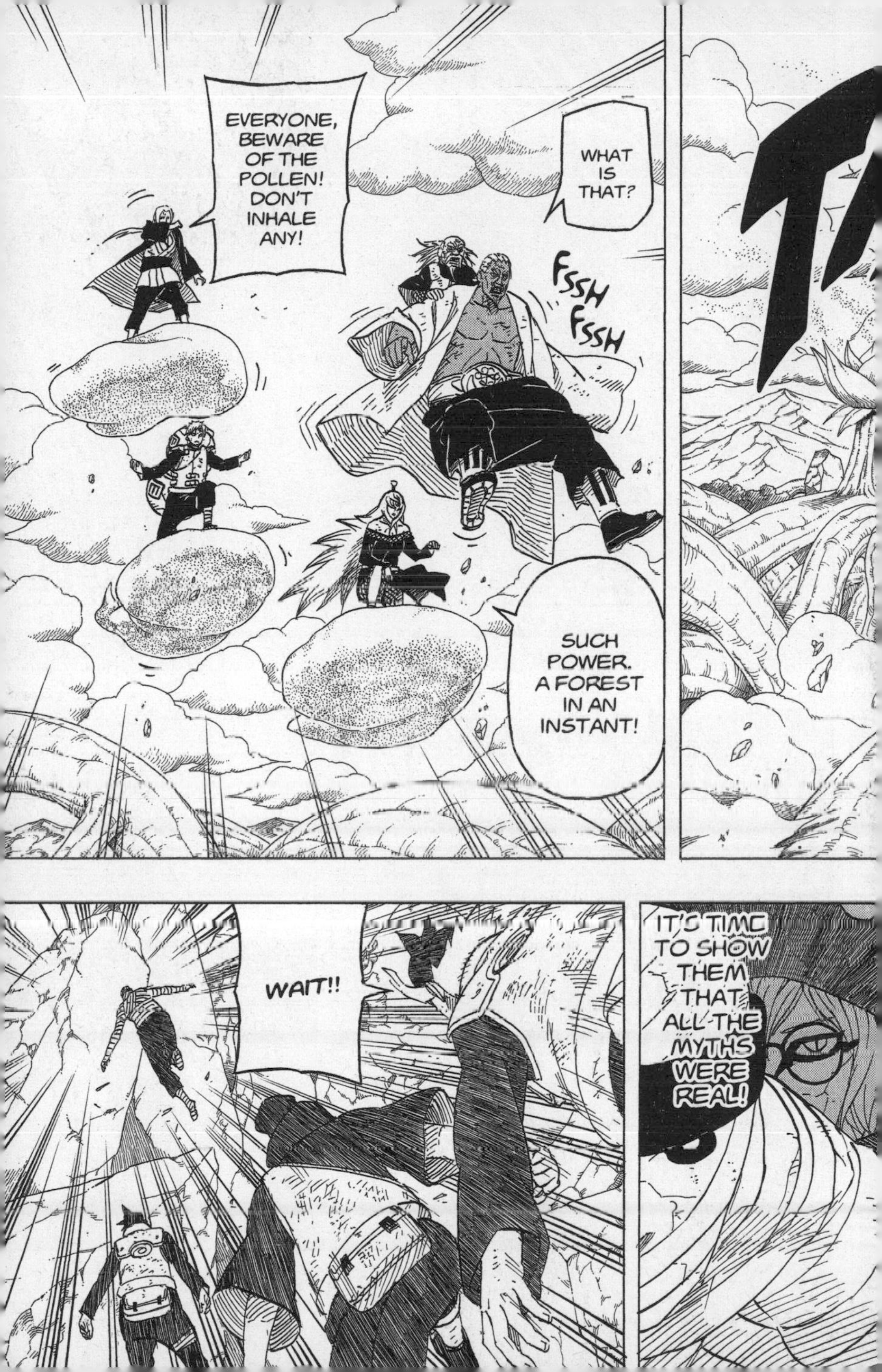
WHAT IS THAT?
EVERYONE, BEWARE OF THE POLLEN! DON'T INHALE ANY!
FSSH FSSH
SUCH POWER. A FOREST IN AN INSTANT!
IT'S TIME TO SHOW THEM THAT ALL THE MYTHS WERE REAL!
WAIT!!

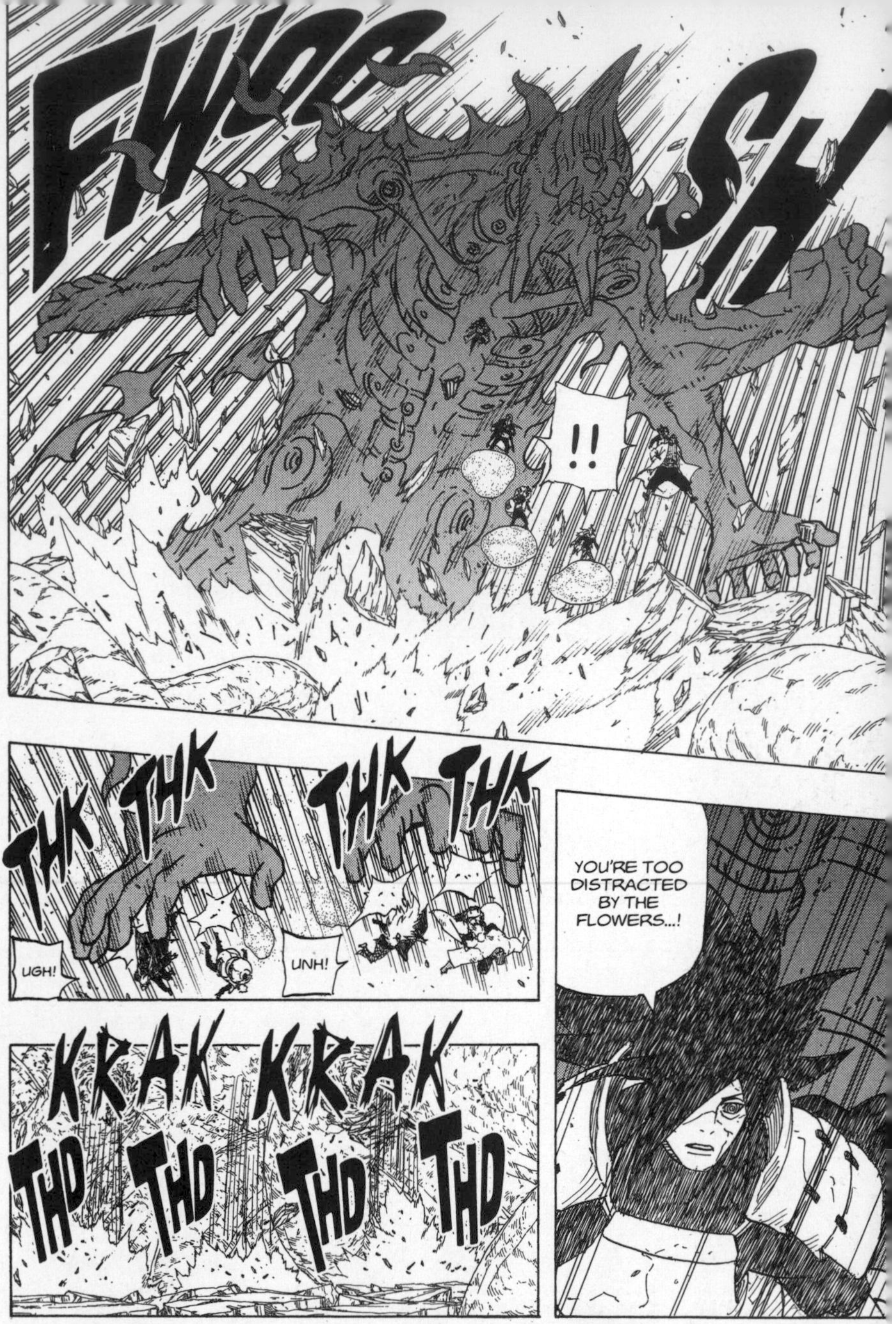
FWOOSH
!!
YOU'RE TOO DISTRACTED BY THE FLOWERS...!
THK THK THK THK
UNH!
UGH!
KRAK KRAK
THD THD THD THD

READ THIS WAY

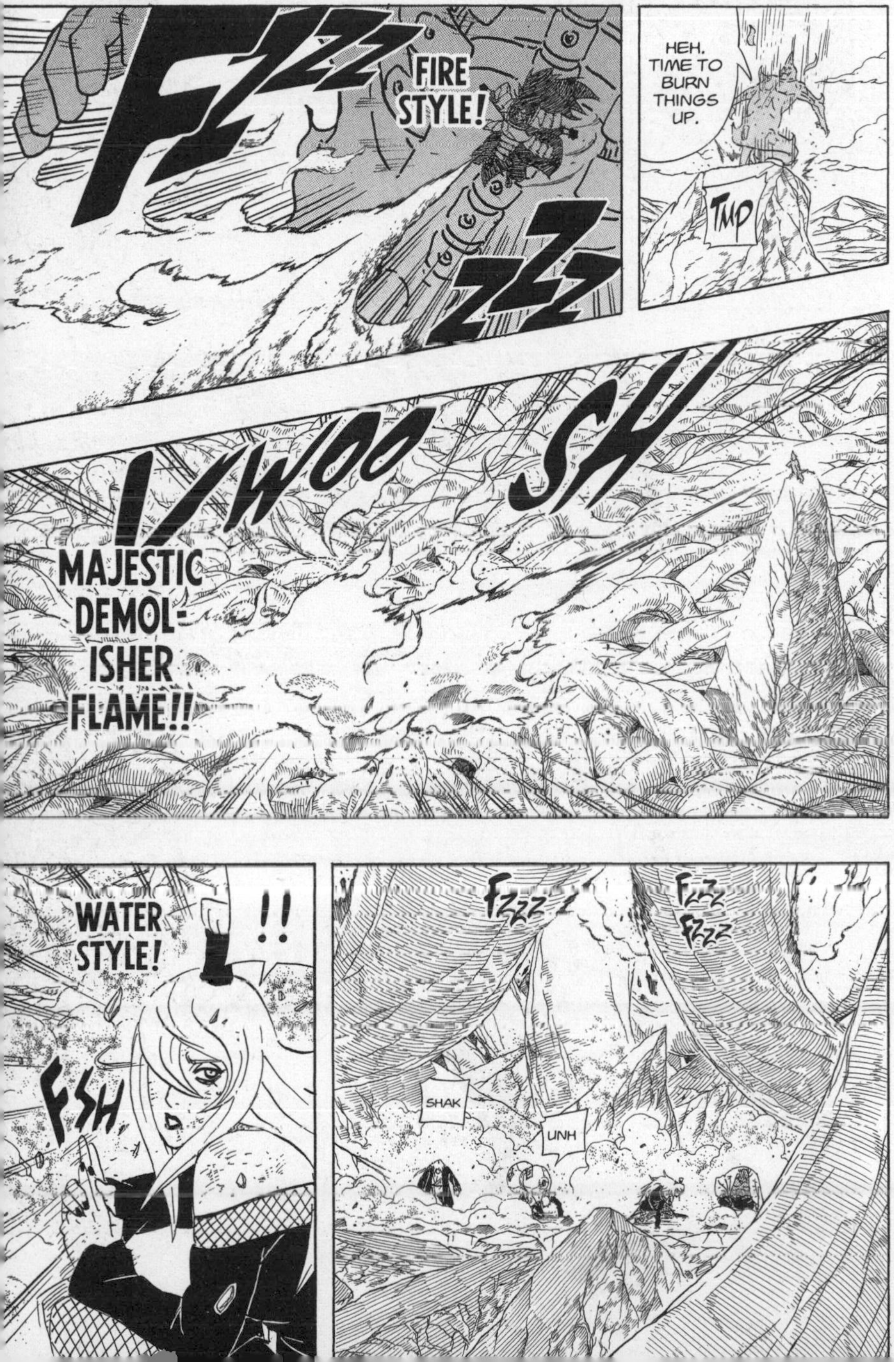
HEH. TIME TO BURN THINGS UP.
TMP
FZZZ
FIRE STYLE!
ZZZ
VWOOSH
MAJESTIC DEMOL-ISHER FLAME!!
FZZZ
FZZZ FZZZ
SHAK
UNH
!!
WATER STYLE!
FSH

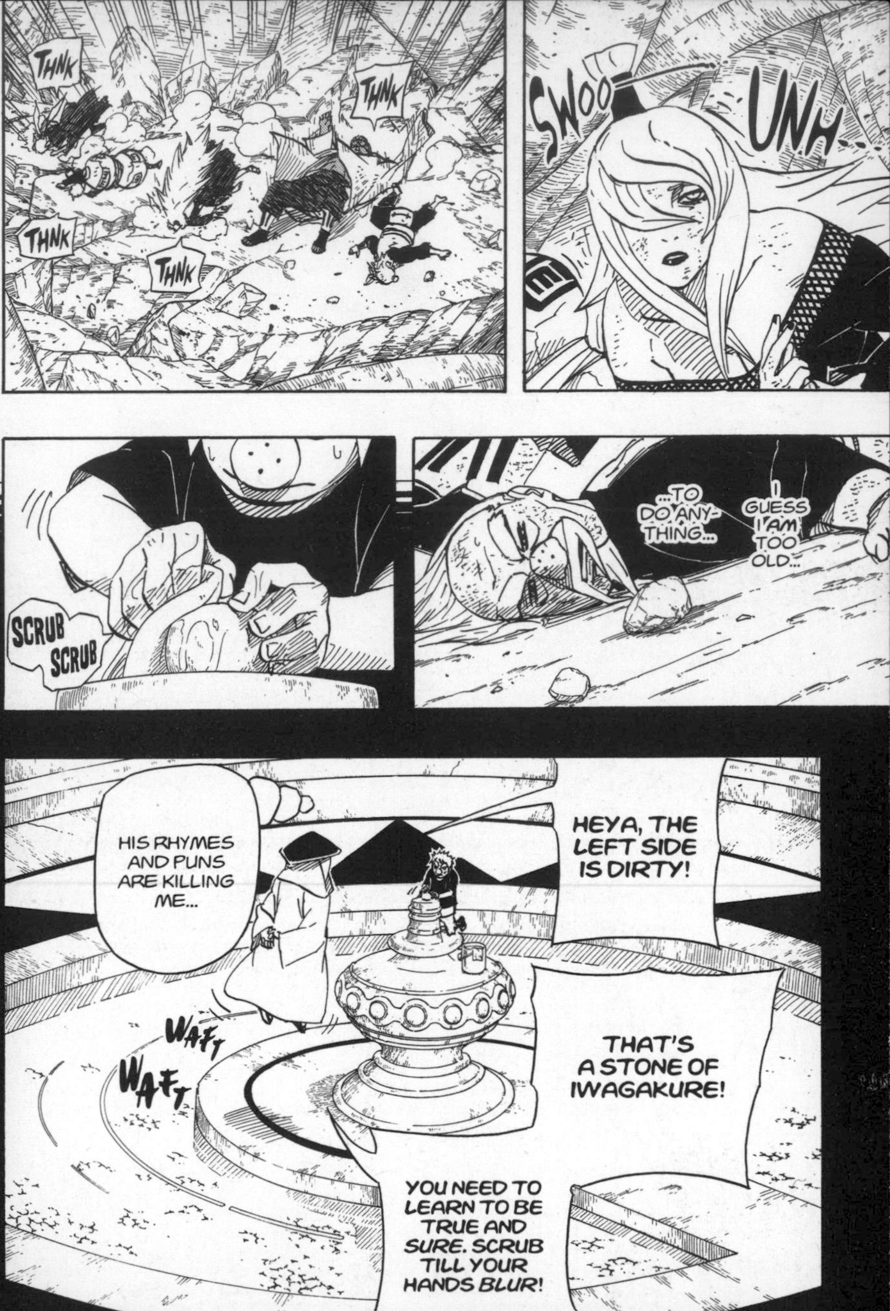
SWOO
UNH
THNK
THNK
THNK
THNK
I GUESS I AM TOO OLD...
...TO DO ANYTHING...
SCRUB SCRUB
HEYA, THE LEFT SIDE IS DIRTY!
THAT'S A STONE OF IWAGAKURE!
YOU NEED TO LEARN TO BE TRUE AND SURE. SCRUB TILL YOUR HANDS BLUR!
HIS RHYMES AND PUNS ARE KILLING ME...
WAFT
WAFT

READ THIS WAY

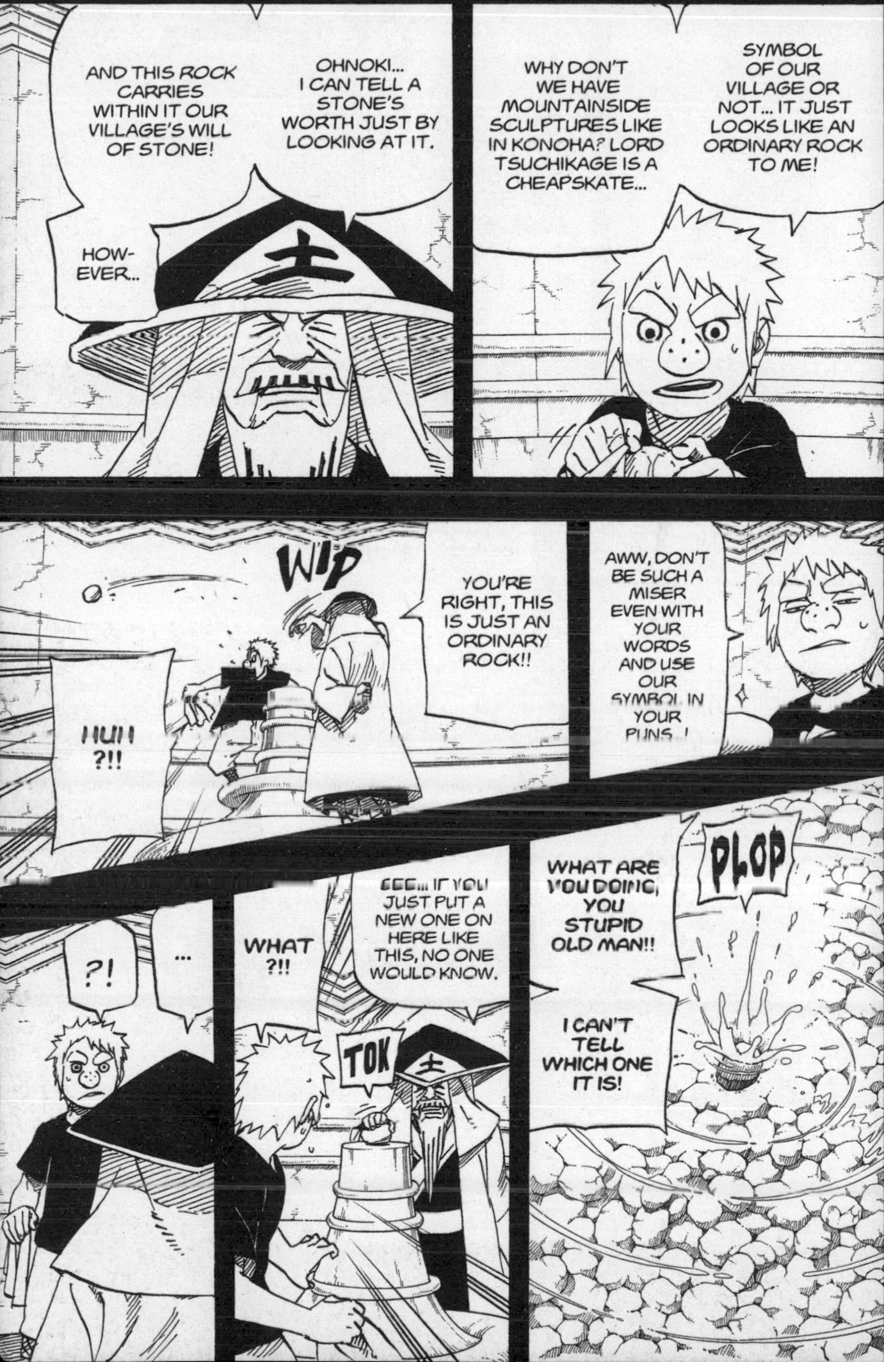
SYMBOL OF OUR VILLAGE OR NOT... IT JUST LOOKS LIKE AN ORDINARY ROCK TO ME!
WHY DON'T WE HAVE MOUNTAINSIDE SCULPTURES LIKE IN KONOHA? LORD TSUCHIKAGE IS A CHEAPSKATE...
OHNOKI... I CAN TELL A STONE'S WORTH JUST BY LOOKING AT IT.
AND THIS ROCK CARRIES WITHIN IT OUR VILLAGE'S WILL OF STONE!
HOW-EVER...
AWW, DON'T BE SUCH A MISER EVEN WITH YOUR WORDS AND USE OUR SYMBOL IN YOUR PUNS..!
YOU'RE RIGHT, THIS IS JUST AN ORDINARY ROCK!!
WIP
HUH?!!
PLOP
WHAT ARE YOU DOING, YOU STUPID OLD MAN!!
I CAN'T TELL WHICH ONE IT IS!
SEE... IF YOU JUST PUT A NEW ONE ON HERE LIKE THIS, NO ONE WOULD KNOW.
WHAT?!!
TOK
...
?!

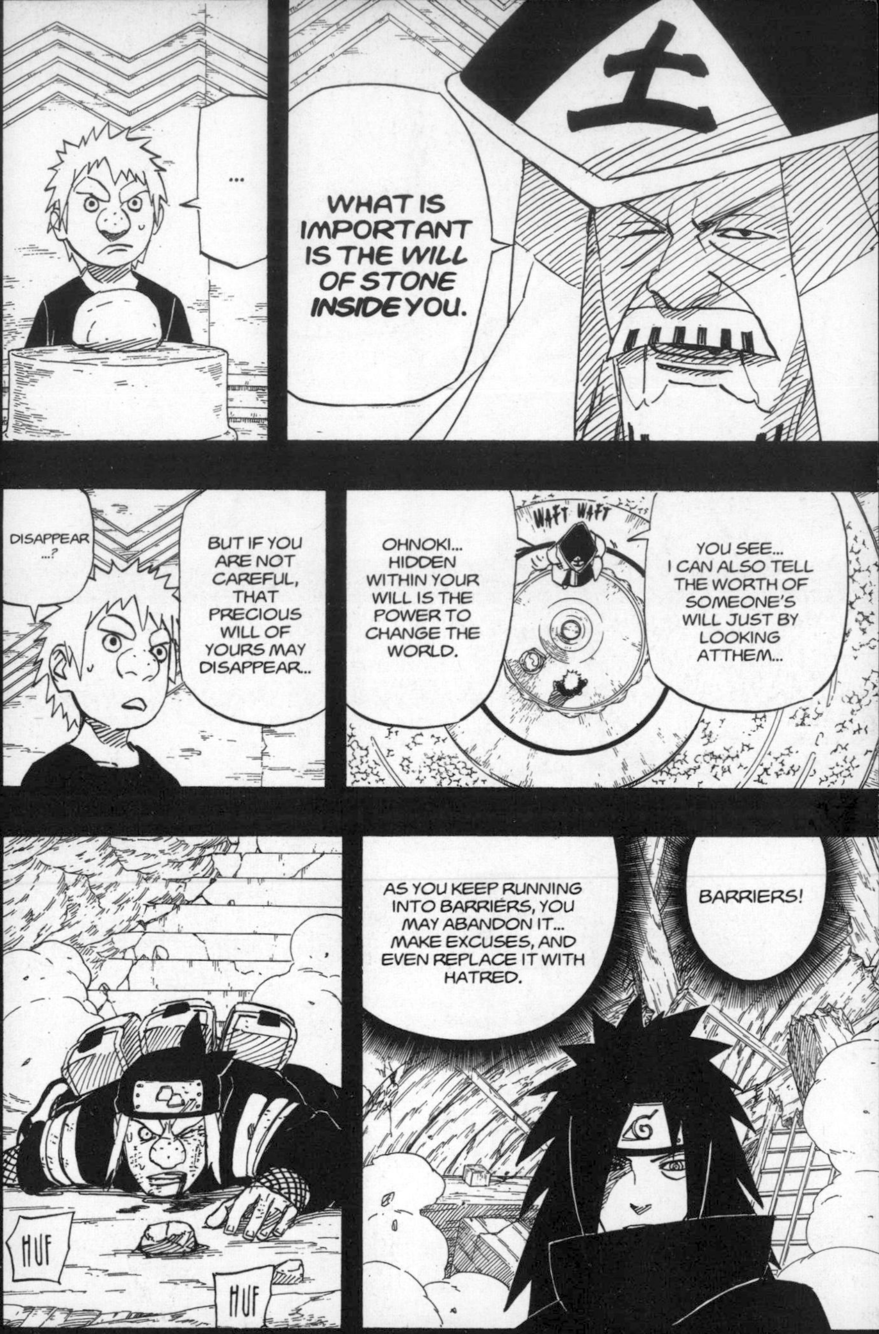
WHAT IS IMPORTANT IS THE WILL OF STONE INSIDE YOU.
...
YOU SEE... I CAN ALSO TELL THE WORTH OF SOMEONE'S WILL JUST BY LOOKING ATTHEM...
WAFT WAFT
OHNOKI... HIDDEN WITHIN YOUR WILL IS THE POWER TO CHANGE THE WORLD.
BUT IF YOU ARE NOT CAREFUL, THAT PRECIOUS WILL OF YOURS MAY DISAPPEAR...
DISAPPEAR ...?
BARRIERS!
AS YOU KEEP RUNNING INTO BARRIERS, YOU MAY ABANDON IT... MAKE EXCUSES, AND EVEN REPLACE IT WITH HATRED.
HUF
HUF

READ THIS WAY

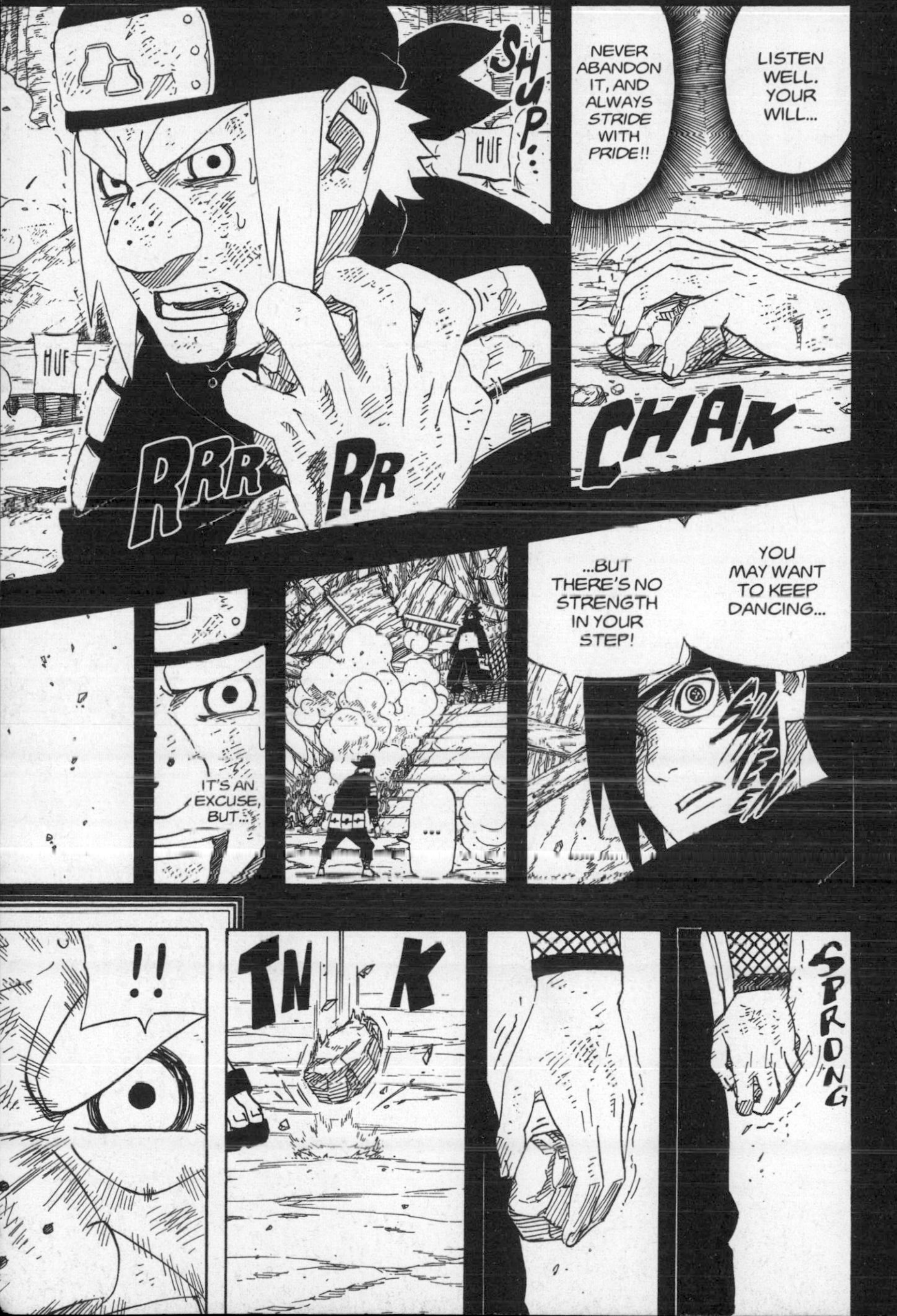
LISTEN WELL. YOUR WILL...
NEVER ABANDON IT, AND ALWAYS STRIDE WITH PRIDE!!
CHAN
SHUP...
HUF
HUF
RRR
RR
YOU MAY WANT TO KEEP DANCING...
...BUT THERE'S NO STRENGTH IN YOUR STEP!
...
IT'S AN EXCUSE, BUT...
SPRONG
TNK
!!

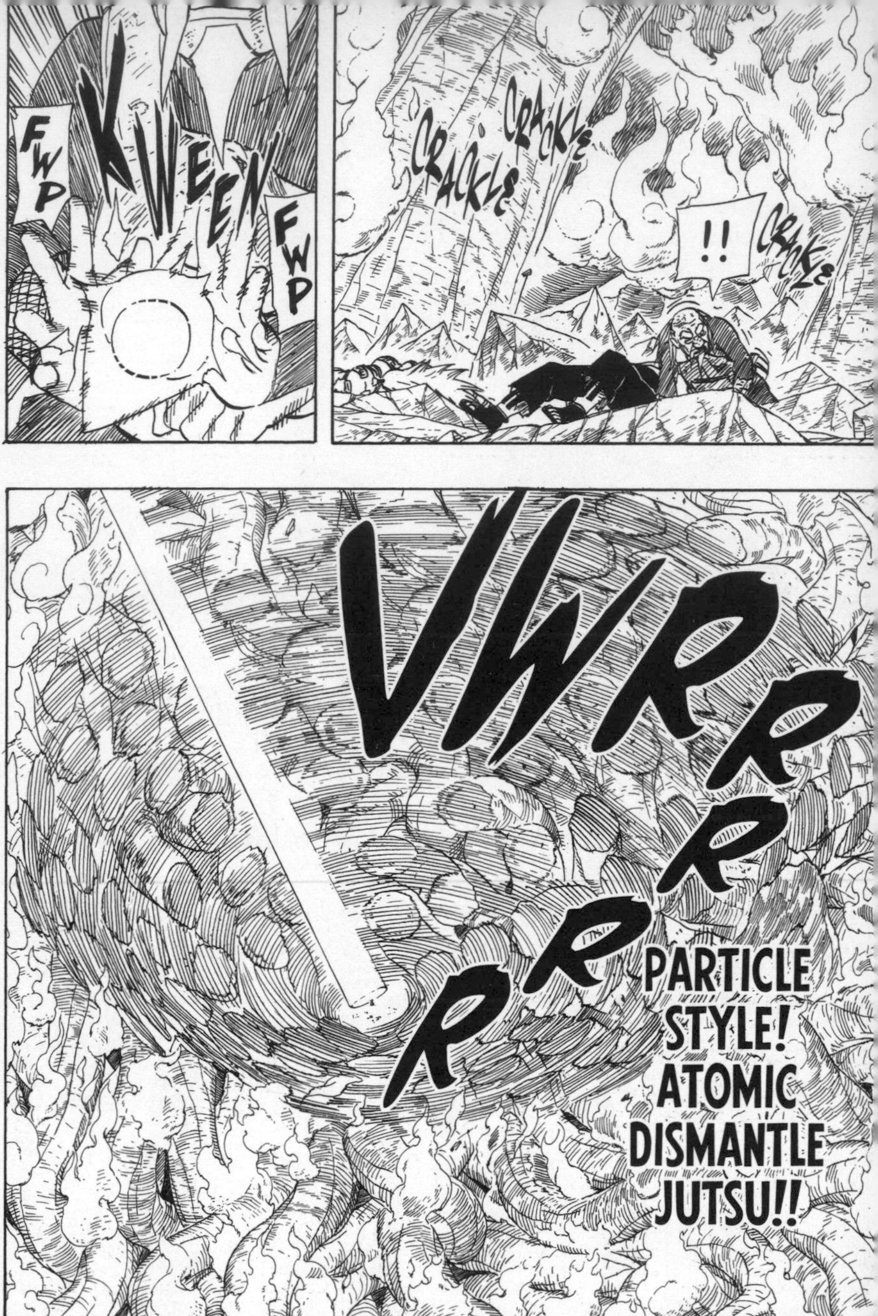
CRACKLE
!!
CRACKLE
CRACKLE
FWP
KWEEN
FWP
VWRRRRR
PARTICLE STYLE! ATOMIC DISMANTLE JUTSU!!

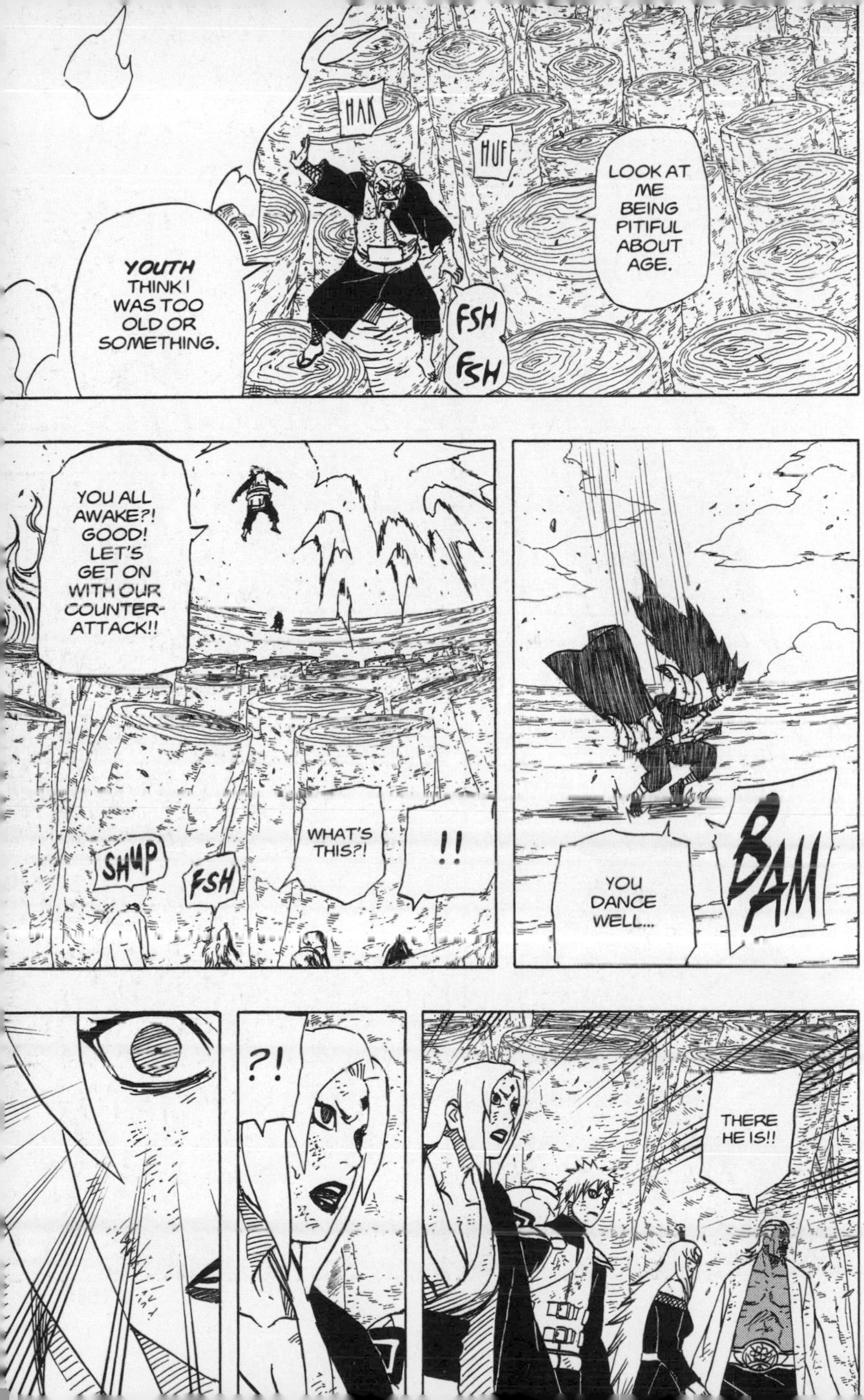

LOOK AT ME BEING PITIFUL ABOUT AGE.
HAK
HUF
YOUTH THINK I WAS TOO OLD OR SOMETHING.
FSH
FSH
BAM
YOU DANCE WELL...
YOU ALL AWAKE?! GOOD! LET'S GET ON WITH OUR COUNTER-ATTACK!!
!!
WHAT'S THIS?!
FSH
SHUP
THERE HE IS!!
?!

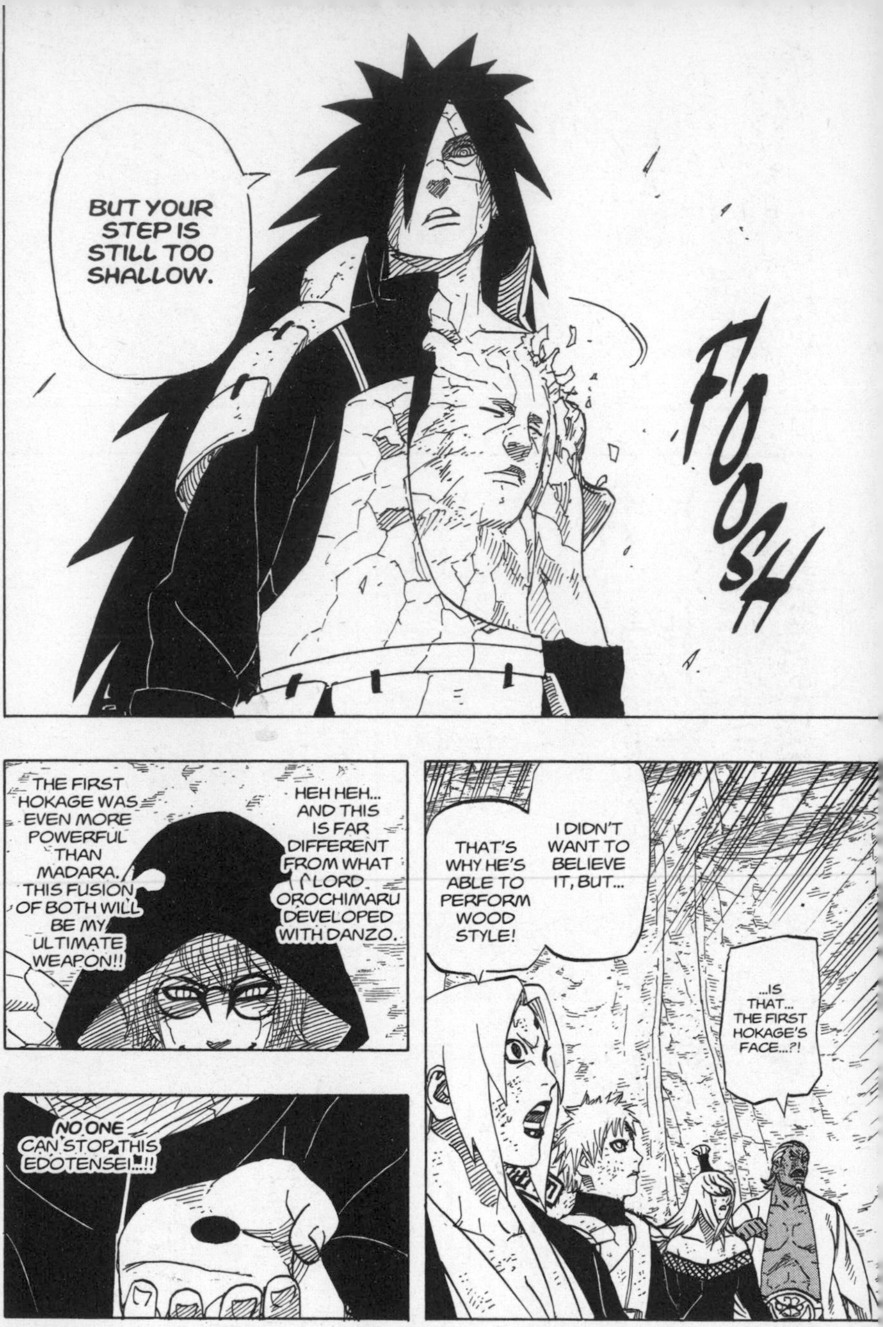
BUT YOUR STEP IS STILL TOO SHALLOW.
FOOSH
...IS THAT... THE FIRST HOKAGE'S FACE...?!
I DIDN'T WANT TO BELIEVE IT, BUT...
THAT'S WHY HE'S ABLE TO PERFORM WOOD STYLE!
HEH HEH... AND THIS IS FAR DIFFERENT FROM WHAT LORD OROCHIMARU DEVELOPED WITH DANZO.
THE FIRST HOKAGE WAS EVEN MORE POWERFUL THAN MADARA. THIS FUSION OF BOTH WILL BE MY ULTIMATE WEAPON!!
NO ONE CAN STOP THIS EDOTENSEI...!!

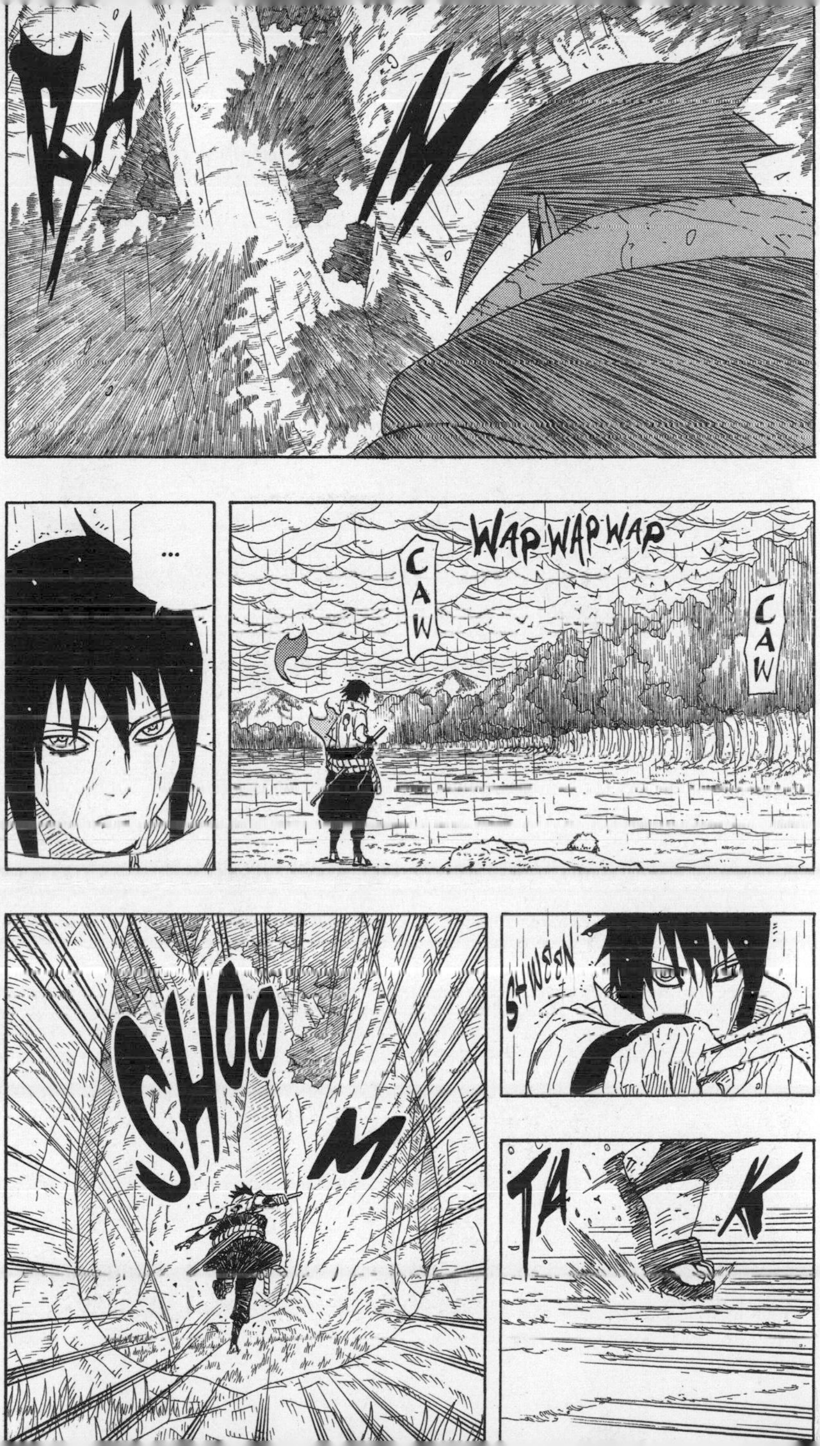
BAM
WAP WAP WAP
CAW
CAW
...
SHWEEN
TA K
SHOO M

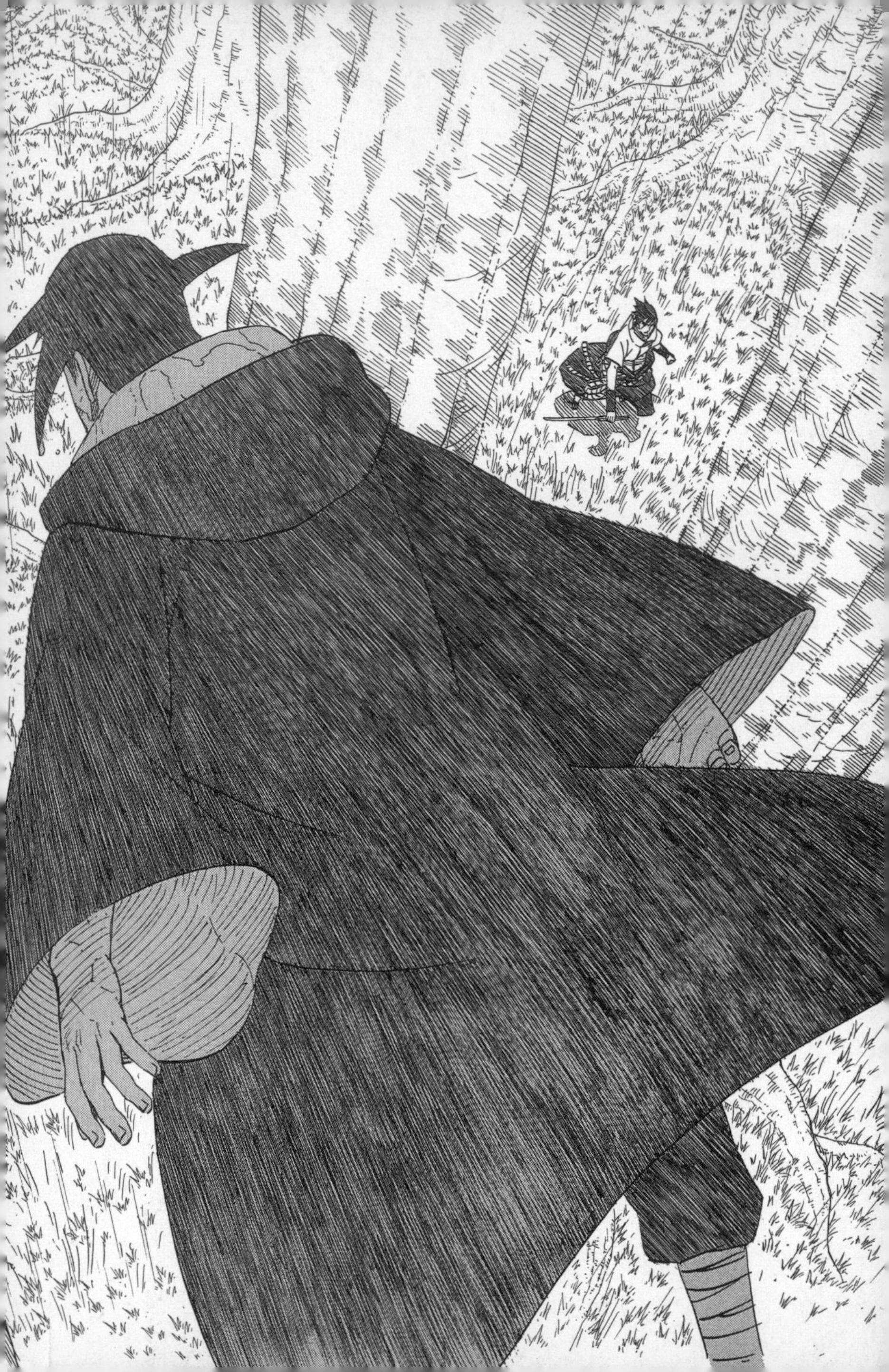

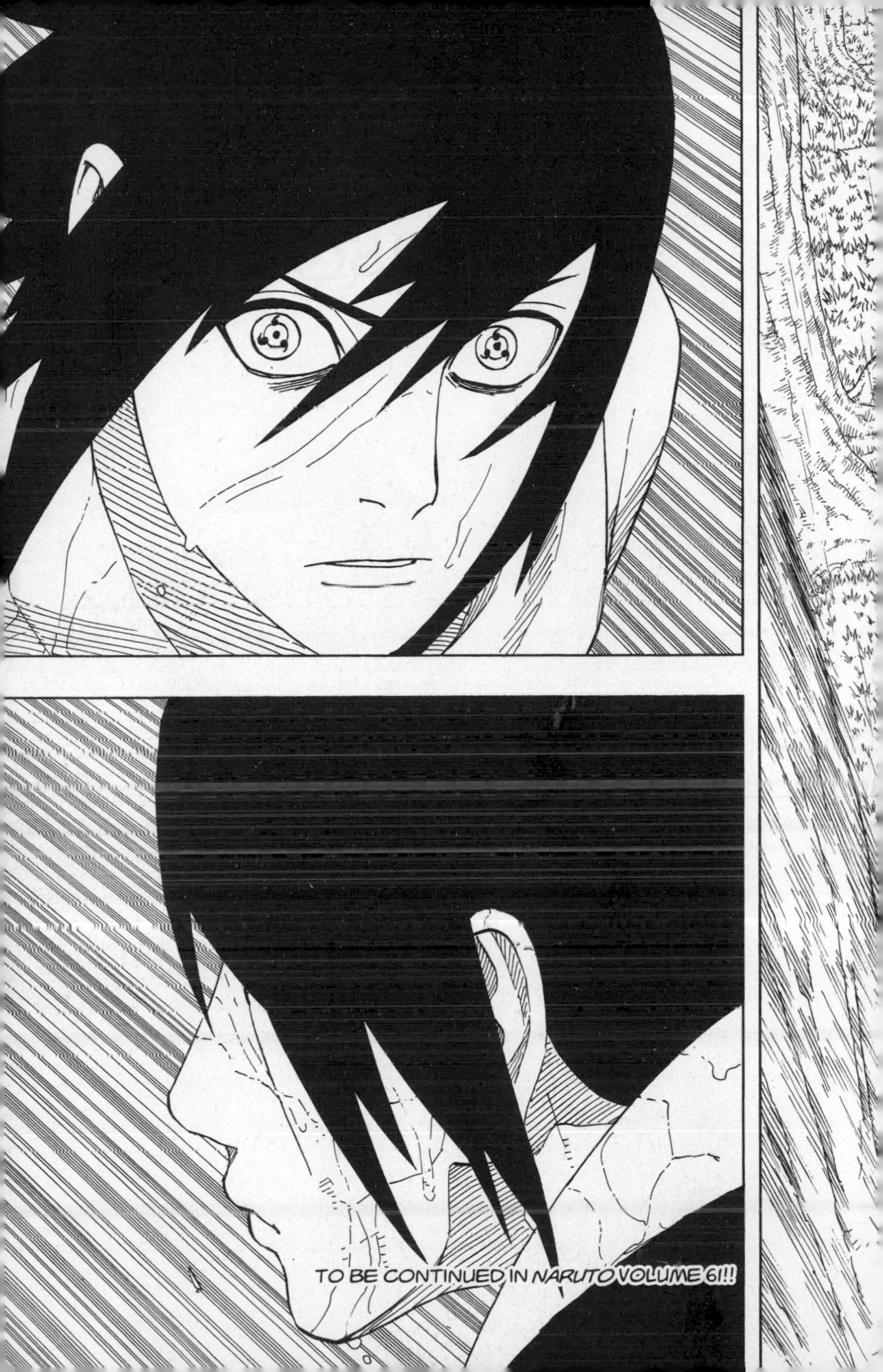
TO BE CONTINUED IN NARUTO VOLUME 61!!

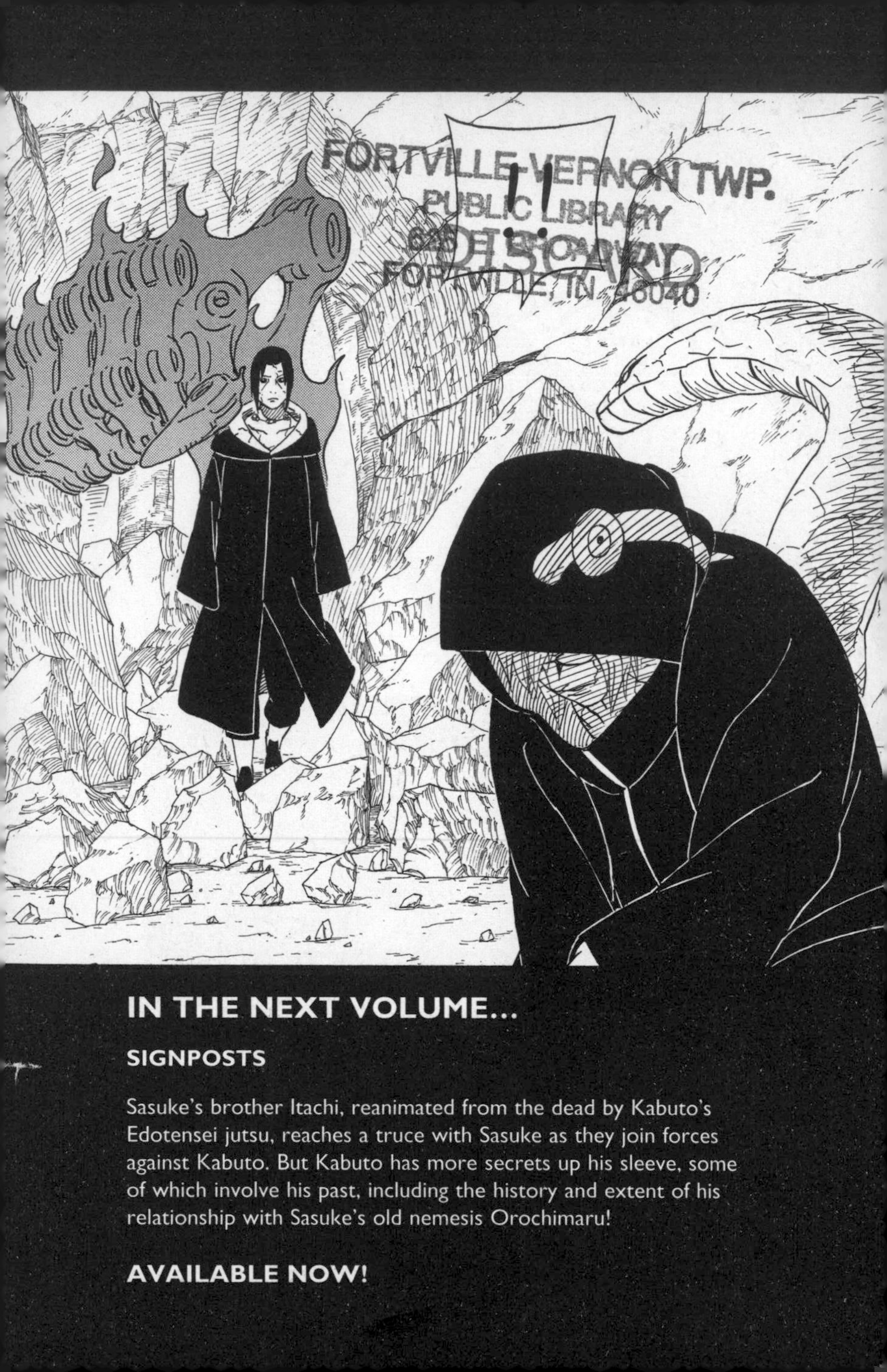

IN THE NEXT VOLUME...

SIGNPOSTS

Sasuke's brother Itachi, reanimated from the dead by Kabuto's Edotensei jutsu, reaches a truce with Sasuke as they join forces against Kabuto. But Kabuto has more secrets up his sleeve, some of which involve his past, including the history and extent of his relationship with Sasuke's old nemesis Orochimaru!

AVAILABLE NOW!